FAMILY TREE DETECTIVE

The family tree detective

A manual for tracing your ancestors in England and Wales

Fourth edition

Colin D. Rogers

Manchester University Press

The right of Colin D. Rogers to be identified as the author of this work has been asserted by him in accordance with the Copyright, Designs and Patents Act 1988.
First edition published 1983 by Manchester University Press, reprinted with corrections 1984
Second edition 1985, reprinted 1986, with corrections 1988, with corrections 1989, 1996
Third edition 1997, reprinted 1999, 2000, 2002 and 2004

This edition published 2008 by Manchester University Press

Oxford Road, Manchester M13 9NR, UK
and Room 400, 175 Fifth Avenue, New York, NY 10010, USA

Distributed in the United States exclusively by
Palgrave Macmillan, 175 Fifth Avenue, New York,
NY 10010, USA

Distributed in Canada exclusively by
UBC Press, University of British Columbia, 2029 West Mall, Vancouver, BC, Canada V6T 1Z2

British Library Cataloguing-in-Publication Data
A catalogue record for this book is available from the British Library

Library of Congress Cataloging-in-Publication Data applied for

ISBN   978 0 7190 7126 3   paperback

This edition first published 2008

17 16 15 14 13 12 11 10 09 08   10 9 8 7 6 5 4 3 2 1

Typeset
by Carnegie Book Production, Lancaster
Printed in Great Britain
by Bell & Bain Ltd, Glasgow

To my parents; to Maureen despite her cats; to Mark, Sue, Luke, Morgan, Jack and Samantha; to Keith, Angela, Jennifer, Katherine, and the memory of Christopher; to Geoffrey, Debora and Emily; to John, Julia, Aidan and Nathan; and to all their descendants.

Contents

List of illustrations   xii

List of abbreviations   xiii

Acknowledgements   xiv

Preface   xv

A note on presentation   xviii

I Introduction   1

Preamble   1
Where to start   3
Getting organised   8
Asking questions   11

II Looking for parents   18

Birth certificates, 1837 to the present day   18
   Obtaining copy certificates from a register office   20
   Obtaining copy certificates from the General Register
     Office   22
   The copy certificate   25
   Failure to find a birth entry in the indexes   31
     Registration in another district   31
     Birth not registered   32
     Birth incorrectly indexed   34
     Birth not in England or Wales   36
     Index entry missed by the searcher   38
     Misleading clues   39
     Child was adopted   44
     Change of name after registration   49
   Finding more than one possible birth   53
   Indexes or certificates not accessible: alternative sources   54
     Marriage and death certificates   56
     Records of the armed forces   56

Records of the mercantile marine 60
Education records 60
Health records 65
Pension and insurance records 67
Affiliation orders 68
Trade union and friendly society records 68
Poor Law Union records and the workhouse 70
Criminal records 70
Miscellaneous records 71
The census, 1801 to the present day 71
Censuses less than 100 years old 72
Censuses 1841–1911 73
Finding addresses in the census 77
Failure to locate individual addresses in the census 85
Failure to locate individuals in the census 87
Censuses 1801–31 91
Church baptism, 1538 to the present day 91
Failure to find an Anglican baptism 101
Baptism in another parish 102
Baptism not recorded 117
Baptism not in England or Wales 121
Entry missed by the searcher 122
Misleading clues 122
Change of name after baptism 129
Late baptism 130
Finding more than one possible baptism 131
Non-Anglican baptism 135
Registers not accessible: alternative sources 138
Bishops' transcripts 140
Other copies of parish registers 142
Manorial records 144
Military records and school registers 146
The poll tax 146
Records of the College of Arms 147
Inquisitions *post mortem* 149
Freemen rolls 149
Apprenticeship records 150
Royalist composition papers 151
The Middle Ages, *c.* 1300–1538 151
General problems 151
Looking for parents 154
Baptism 155

Manorial records 156
Inquisitions *post mortem* 156
Final concords (or 'feet of fines') 157
Education records 158
Patent rolls 158
Close rolls 158
Fine rolls 159
Charter rolls 159
Curia Regis rolls 159
Miscellaneous deeds 159
Probate 160
Guilds and freemen 161
Lay subsidies 161
The poll tax 163
Hundred rolls 163

III Looking for marriages 164

Marriage certificates, 1837 to the present day 164
The copy certificate 168
Failure to find a marriage entry in the indexes 170
Registration in another district 170
Marriage not registered 172
Marriage incorrectly indexed 173
Marriage not in England and Wales 173
Index entry missed by searcher 173
Misleading clues 174
Change of name before or after marriage 175
Finding more than one possible marriage 175
Civil partnerships 180
Indexes or certificates not accessible: alternative sources 181
Records of the armed forces 182
Divorce 182
Marriage in church, 1538 to the present day 185
Failure to find an Anglican marriage 191
Marriage in another parish 191
Marriage not recorded 198
Marriage not in England or Wales 200
Entry missed by the searcher 200
Misleading clues 200
Finding more than one possible marriage 203
Non-Anglican marriage 206

Registers not accessible: alternative sources   207
Finding a marriage before 1538   207

IV Looking for deaths   208

Death certificates, 1837 to the present day   209
    The copy certificate   209
    Failure to find a death entry in the indexes   212
        Death in another district   212
        Death not registered   213
        Death incorrectly indexed   214
        Death not in England and Wales   214
        Index entry missed by the searcher   215
        Misleading clues   215
    Finding more than one possible death   216
    Indexes or certificates not accessible: alternative sources 217
        Local authority burial records, 1827 to the present day 217
        Cremation records, 1884 to the present day   221
        Funeral directors' records   223
        Gravestones, and failure to find them   223
        Monumental masons' records   228
        Obituaries   228
        Probate since 1858   229
        Hospital records   232
        Records of the armed forces   233
        Workhouse records   235
        Trade union and friendly society records   235
        Coroners' records   235
        Professional bodies' records   237
Church burial, 1538 to the present day   237
    Failure to find an Anglican burial   240
        Burial in another parish   240
        Burial not recorded   241
        Burial not in England or Wales: evidence of emigration 245
        Entry missed by searcher   248
        Misleading clues   248
    Finding more than one possible burial   248
    Non-Anglican burial   249
    Registers not accessible: alternative sources   251
        Probate before 11 January 1858   251
        Failure to find a probate record before 1858 253
        Wills proved by another jurisdiction   254

Wills not proved   255
Wills poorly indexed   255
Wills proved late   255
Lost wills   256
Letters of administration   257
Miscellaneous probate records   258
Records of the College of Arms   259
Miscellaneous records   260
Finding a death before 1538   260

V Epilogue   262

Appendices   264

1. Underregistration in the early years of civil registration   264
2. The National Registration Act of 1915   266
3. The National Registration Act of 1939   271
4. Employing professional help   274

References   278

Index   303

Illustrations

1   Change of name during lifetime   *page* 40, 41
2   Change of name following baptism   48
3   Twins with the same name   50, 51
4   Different family trees which may be connected   100
5   An extraordinary 'carry-over' error   124, 125
6   Two children with identical names and baptism dates, reproduced by courtesy of the vicar and PCC of St Thomas, Heaton Norris   132
7   A forename added and occupation changed   176, 177
8   Two birth entries which will not lead to the previous marriage   178, 179
9   When registrars competed for custom   218, 219
10   Poster advertising National Registration Instructions to the Public, August 1915 [D\R\yeo 36/1], courtesy of the Somerset Record Office   267
11   The National Registration Act of 1915 [UDBA acc 3274 census 10], reproduced by permission of the County Archivist, Lancashire Record Office   268
12   Register of previous addresses [D\R\ch 34/4], courtesy of the Somerset Record Office   269
13   Register of forms received from other authorities [D\R\lo 34/4], courtesy of the Somerset Record Office   270

The design of the birth/marriage/death certificates is Crown copyright and is reproduced with the permission of the Controller of HMSO.

Abbreviations

Anc	*Ancestors*
BT	bishops' transcripts
DPR	District Probate Registry
FFHS	Federation of Family History Societies
FHM	*Family History Monthly*
FTM	*Family Tree Magazine*
GM	*Genealogists' Magazine*
GRO	General Register Office
IGI	International Genealogical Index
IHGS	Institute for Heraldic and Genealogical Studies
LDS	Church of Jesus Christ of Latter-Day Saints
LEA	Local Education Authority
MI	monumental inscription(s)
MN	*Marginal Notes* (the registration service's in-house magazine)
MRS	*Magazine of the Registration Service*
NA	The National Archives
NALD	National Archives Leaflet (domestic records series)
NALL	National Archives Leaflet (legal records series)
NALM	National Archives Leaflet (military records series)
NALO	National Archives Leaflet (overseas records series)
NHSCR	National Health Service Central Register
NLW	National Library of Wales
PCC	Prerogative Court of Canterbury
PCY	Prerogative Court of York
PFH	*Practical Family History*
PRO	National Archives (formerly Public Record Office)
RBD	Registrar of Births and Deaths
RON	registration on line
SoG	Society of Genealogists

Acknowledgements

Those without whom the first edition would never have been written (Jeffrey Adams, Registrar of Births and Deaths in the Manchester Register Office, and Eileen Simpson, formerly Senior Assistant Archivist in the Cheshire Record Office and now Archivist for the Grosvenor Estate) continued to guide my efforts to cut a course through the jungle of documents which we all leave behind; others, both official and individual, would be too numerous to name without seriously increasing the length of the book. For this edition, the General Register Office and the Manchester Registration Service have been particularly helpful. And still, behind the minutiae of the text, is the lurking presence of Philip Simpson, who first challenged anyone to write such a book, and who has produced a remarkably well-illustrated life story of his late wife Elizabeth; and the late W. E. Tate, who first breathed the spirit of local history into me over forty years ago.

Preface

Let battle commence!

The first two editions of this book were written in an age of genealogical innocence, when many of our records were freely available but not so easy to access; the third edition (1996) appeared as computing and the Internet were widening our ambitions into an age of genealogical optimism, heralding the horizon of touch-button (not to say couch-potato) ancestral enquiry. Many archivists, indeed, warn of an over-reliance on the computer screen, leading to many useful but undigitised sources being ignored.

This new edition reflects a new century in which, as in so many other aspects of life, even investigating the dead now has its dark side.

Alterations to the recording and archive systems of civil registration had been discussed – abortively – for some decades before the General Register Office (GRO) recently proposed changes so far-reaching that the House of Lords deemed them impractical! We have therefore reached an era in which administrative amendments without the need for legislation are being introduced by a GRO who must be still smarting from the rebuff.

The exploitation of the Internet has transformed the degree to which genealogists can view documents and their indexes, so much so that my earlier apology for even quoting those available only in London for the great majority who never visit the capital, is slowly and surely evaporating. Even if you have no domestic access to the web, there is rarely anything to prevent you from using the facilities of your nearest library which should help you to do so. Indeed, there are extra advantages in doing so even for those with home computers, because the library system can be on line to such sources as the *Dictionary of National Biography*, *The Times* Digital Archive (1785–1985), the *(Manchester) Guardian* 1821–1975 and *The Observer* (1791–1975), or British Parliamentary Papers (*Anc* 64 Dec 07; *FTM* 24.4 Feb 08). Anyone searching for particular sources can look to www.A2A.org. uk which cross refers to those sources in local repositories, especially useful for the holdings of County Record Offices.

The last quarter of the twentieth century saw a slow erosion of the state's library and archive repository institutional ideals of free public service in the face of tightening general fiscal policy. As a result, the genealogist is regarded as less of a nuisance and more of a customer. Whereas, decades ago, County Record Offices had the time to undertake albeit limited searches, many began to provide a list of search agents (for whose work they have no responsibility) instead; now, they will probably offer a paid service themselves. Similarly some councils, freed by recent local government legislation, are now telling Superintendent Registrars to add an administrative charge to the cost of civil registration certificates. A few even target family historians in particular. You can't blame them – we are a gift horse hard to ignore!

This dilemma about how far to make data freely accessible can be seen in individuals as well as institutions. As Hon. General Editor of the Lancashire Parish Register Society for thirty years, I was committed to making registers available to the public through our publications – but we would rapidly have run out of funds to do so had we allowed free access to our publications through the Internet.

On a national scale, the government which strengthened the original data protection legislation also passed the 2000 Freedom of Information Act, both of which have impacted on the way genealogists operate. (For the former, see Lambert, 2000.) These opposing trends can be seen in the tension between librarians and electoral registration officers working for the same council. I'm not the first genealogist to wonder how many of our historical records would not have survived if data protection legislation had been in force when they were created! Add into the mixture political correctness, terrorism, identity theft, the deliberate misinterpretation of the Data Protection Acts in order to impose a self-determined policy of confidentiality, and the ease with which data held in electronic form can be destroyed – and we have a recipe for disaster for the preservation and accessibility of our modern records. (New Zealand has proposed banning access to birth, marriage and death records on the Internet because of fears of identity fraud. Australia and the UK have placed restrictions on access to electoral registration data, and the Council of Europe has recently concluded that, 'It is clear that the electoral system in Great Britain is open to electoral fraud. This vulnerability is mainly the result of the rather arcane system of voter registration without personal identifiers.') The introduction of ID cards could well lead to the abolition of the decennial census, as the former would be cheaper, more efficient, and more up to date. In this regard, and despite the associated independence of the Office for National Statistics from government, I find the transfer of responsibility for the General Register Office from the Office for National Statistics to the Identity and Passport Service on 1 April 2008 disquieting.

As major repositories go into partnership with private, for profit, organisations to market their product (i.e. our records), we can still look on the bright side with David Hey who suggests that it is the very growth of genealogy, through its pressure to pay for access to sources, that has already saved many documents from destruction. In this battle at least, we have numbers on our side!

A *note* on *presentation*

This new edition is still organised around the need to solve problems rather than around sources, the three basic problems in genealogy being how to find the records of parents, of marriage and of death. For example, the section on marriages discusses where to find an entry, the reasons why you may fail to do so, and what you can do to bypass intractable documentary problems. References in the text are to authors, normally with the appropriate year of publication.

The answers to each of these three main questions are arranged in three historical periods, however, reflecting the major changes in the way those sources have developed. Higgs (2004a) has shown how the Victorians began to govern from the centre in ways alien to their predecessors, founding the General Register Office in 1838, the Design Registry in 1839, the Patent Office in 1852, the Principal Probate Registry in 1857, the General Medical Council in 1858, the Land Registry in 1862 (albeit on a voluntary basis at first; see *NALL* 7), and many other similar institutions. Before the Victorian era, central government operated largely through locally based institutions whose records are still locally preserved; before the sixteenth century, no record was made of the birth, marriage and death of most inhabitants. For almost a thousand years, however, there have been two exceptions to this general trend – warfare and taxation, each of which have generated a huge amount of documentation by central governments.

Note that the mouthwatering possibilities of DNA scarcely get a mention in this new edition. That is because the greatest use of this facility for family historians has been in connection with tracing the history of surnames, in order to discover whether, for example, all bearers of a particular surname are genetically connected with each other, having arisen from a single family in the past. See Redmonds (1987) and the work of Prof. Sykes at the University of Oxford. You might also be able to discover from what part of a particular continent you originated, but women seeking more detailed historical analysis of their DNA should use samples from a close male relative (father, full brother etc) though not from their own children. Even when we have a much-needed national DNA database, it will be several generations before it could be used for what we think of as basic genealogy. Advice about its limitations, and firms which supply associated services, are in *FHM* 113 Jan 05.

Publication of this fourth edition has been delayed in order to incorporate significant changes to civil registration systems and other digitisation projects. In particular, the DoVE project covers the quarterly copies of vital events received by the GRO (1837–1934), which has now been transferred to its EAGLE database for use in supplying copies of birth, marriage and death certificates. Later events are part of the MAGPIE project which includes the re-indexing of all events since 1837 and making that index freely available via the GRO website, but that has been delayed because of problems relating to funding. The relevant sections of this book have therefore been written to accommodate DoVE, but can only look forward to MAGPIE.

Throughout, I have used the word 'genealogist' to describe anyone who is tracing a family tree, only occasionally distinguishing amateur from professional. 'Family historian' is normally avoided, as implying wider concerns than the genealogist, as explored in Rogers & Smith (1991). Genealogy has its own intellectual demands and demographic needs, which give it respectability in its own right. The generalities of life on an eighteenth-century Devon farm or in late nineteenth-century Wolverhampton are about as much use to the core of genealogical activity as sociology is to the police trying to prove that an accused is guilty of a particular crime. All 'ologies' correctly warn against what Laslett terms the 'sample of one'; but an individual family tree *is* a sample of one. It is evidence, and the judgement of its credibility, that enable the genealogist to move into family history *only after firm genetic connections have been established*, and you are sure that you have not traced someone else's forebears by mistake!

I *Introduction*

Preamble

One of the great attractions of genealogy is that, no matter how clever you may be at exploiting surviving documents, you can never be certain of discovering the next generation further back. Taking an optimistic view, if a normal English surname is being traced, the mid-seventeenth century seems a reasonable target. Beyond that point life begins to get markedly more difficult, as only half the country's parish registers survive from before the Civil War; but there are some who will fail to find their great-grandparents, and a few for whom even that would be impossible anyway.

There are no strict rules governing the way ancestors must be traced, and there is nothing illegal about inventing a whole family tree, unless there is an intention to defraud. Success comes from a combination of knowing which records exist, how to get access to them at a price you can afford, being able to select from alternative solutions and knowing how to use several documents in combination with each other. There is no single record providing a whole life history for each of our ancestors – the story has to be pieced together from many different sources created for quite different purposes. However, there is a normal way to proceed and often a set of options if the normal way proves fruitless.

A student in my first evening class illustrates one approach which cannot be recommended. She had been attracted to genealogy having been told of a belief that her family was descended from the second Duke of Buckingham. Blissfully unaware of the possibility that it was the name of a pub rather than a person, she had spent a large part of her life tracing the second duke's descendants, the first generation of whom were illegitimate. Needless to say, although she had acquired a lot of information, it was probably the most inefficient and expensive way to establish a family connection because the descendants of all the children of each generation would have had to be traced – and even then the rumour might have been incorrect in the first place. Her surname might have changed over time, or been the result of the Anglicisation of an immigrant's name.

If your tree is not to be a figment of your imagination, you may adopt the opposite extreme and feel you should accept as family connections only those which are nothing less than certain. However, genealogists adhering to this approach had better choose another pastime, for they will not be very successful at this one. Paternity can never be proved, except by using DNA, even when no one has expressed any doubt about it. For an interesting assessment of the rate of illegitimacy within marriage see Swart (1989). Often a connection will have to be accepted because there is no apparent alternative; and sooner or later all genealogists must consciously accept what is only the most probable solution to a problem they are trying to solve. Drs Margaret Jackson and Mary Barton started the human artificial insemination by donor programme in Exeter in 1939, and for the first two or three years, until the practice proved too traumatic, the recipients were told the identity of the donors. (Since 2005, a child conceived by donor insemination has the right, on reaching the age of 18, to know the donor's identity. Donors are unable to opt for anonymity.) Births from donor insemination rose to about 200 a year after the war, and now stand in the thousands, with no indication of the true paternal origin of the children in the civil registration birth entries.

How then can the genealogist build up a family tree which is based on neither absolute truth nor the imagination? In my greener days I tried to find the baptism of one Thomas Rogers in or about 1790 in the parish in north Cheshire where he married. It could not be found in either that or the surrounding parishes; but there was only one local Rogers family which could have given birth to him, and, on the assumption that my unbaptised Thomas was one of their offspring, I happily traced their ancestors back to the 1630s. The bombshell which hit me when I subsequently discovered that Thomas had been born in Lancaster brought mixed emotions. All that work down the drain – but now I had something closer to 'the truth' (on which genealogical subject, see *FTM* 15.10 Aug 99). What I should have done originally was to make sure that all the available evidence had been consulted before deciding what to do and what to believe. I am still poor at taking my own advice when tracing my own family tree and, as we shall see, it is sometimes very difficult, psychologically, to take steps to try to disprove something which you are half convinced is the truth. Meanwhile I have several generations consigned to that awful file, stained with sweat and tears, which Michael Gandy calls 'Ancestors I used to have'!

The beginner should not be surprised if progress comes in fits and starts. The reactions of my students over the years have varied from ecstasy and almost disbelief when an entry they had long been seeking came to light, to terrible frustration when nothing seems to work, or people take months to reply to letters – if they reply at all. Threatening to give up genealogy, however, is no remedy. Once you have the bug, you have it for life, and it is a bug which thrives on frustration. You may discover three or four generations in a single day, or you may take several years to discover one, but, however far back you are, it will always be a source of annoyance that you have not found that next one further back still.

Where to start

One of the many questions asked by the beginner is, 'Which line shall I trace?' The simple answer is, whichever you want. There is no obligation to trace any one line except, perhaps, for members of the Church of Jesus Christ of Latter-Day Saints (the Mormons). They believe in baptism after eight years of age, either in life or after death, so that even previous generations can be given the retrospective benefit of belonging to the Mormon religion. Church members make promises to God in temples, on behalf of their ancestors, who they believe may then choose to accept them. (Not quite as strange as some inhabitants of south China who believe in *marriage* after death, and are occasionally found guilty of grave robbing!) The Mormons have therefore put considerable resources into making genealogical data available to the general public. If you try to trace all your ancestors, it will be a lifetime's commitment because of the very large numbers involved. From the later Middle Ages, by which time most English surnames began to be inherited, we may each have a million ancestors, though the number will decrease whenever relations marry each other. Three of my mother's great-great-grandparents can be traced to a common predecessor some generations earlier.

If all your ancestors are being traced, your problems, costs and the time you need to expend will all double with every generation discovered. Most people start more sensibly, probably with the surname they were born with – married women usually prefer to trace their birth name. ('Maiden name', by the way, is technically the name women first marry under, not necessarily the name on their birth certificate.) If you know your four grandparents already, my advice would be to choose first the family which used to live closest to where you are living now; or, if that line is of no interest to you, the rarest of the four surnames. There is no doubt that it is easier, quicker and cheaper to learn about ancestors who lived in a county which has a record office or a substantial public library within comfortable travelling distance of your own home. Similarly, a rare name is usually easier to trace than a common one, though I am trying to find a family in Cheshire called Greenaker which seems to disappear altogether in the mid-seventeenth century. A surname which is also the name of a township, village or parish is also to be recommended because there is then a greater chance of reaching back to the early Middle Ages – say, to 700 years ago – than if you have any other kind of surname, few of which became hereditary before the middle of the fourteenth century in England, or the sixteenth century in Wales. However, there is still a snag because, where a name originated, it is quite normal for families of that surname to have been more numerous than Smith, Jones or Taylor; and one of the commonest problems in genealogy, as we shall see, is to decide between various possible couples who may have given birth to an ancestor you have already traced, so the fewer the candidates the better. Rimmer, for example, is concentrated in the south-west of Lancashire, a name surely more suited to the accent of the actor Craig Charles in the cult sci-fi series *Red Dwarf* than the name he was given – Lister – which is much more common in the West Riding. Despite popular belief, place names tended to give rise to surnames near their actual location rather than far away from it – so, sooner or later, a family called Ashton will be traced to one of the eleven places called Ashton in this country. With Hemingway, Wolstencroft or Dearnaley, however, there is only one possible place of origin, and some of them, like Sladen, disappeared as inhabited places perhaps centuries ago (see Beresford, 1954). McKinley (1990) provides a well-researched introduction to the development of British surnames, and Rogers (1995) describes how to trace their geographical distribution over several centuries. You can also access surname lists and interest groups via such websites as www.genuki.org.uk:8080/Societies/, www.CyndisList.com, and www.one-name.org.

Forenames, incidentally, have a very different story to tell. Before the sixteenth century they were very few in number, and even the increase during the seventeenth and eighteenth centuries could still leave numbers of people with the same name in the same village. The expanding population during the industrial revolution saw more parents giving their children two or more first names, but even then the number being used was very limited. Only after the world wars do we get a large ramification, greatly boosted by varied and often inventive immigrants.

However, the surname is only one of many factors which will affect the time and cost of tracing your family tree. Others are: how far away the records are; how quickly you learn to manipulate them to best advantage; whether there are serious gaps in the main series of records, especially the church registers, in 'your' parish; how mobile your ancestors were; and what their social status or profession was. On the whole, because they leave more records, the rich are easier to trace than the poor, and those who had a profession for which they had been trained are easier than those who did not. Criminals who are caught are easier to find than the honest, as are (and therefore will one day be) those receiving an Anti Social Behaviour Order. ('Bartholomewe Wightman presented [to the bishop] to be an often swearer, a dronkarde, a ribalde, contentyouse, and uncharitable person, a common slanderer of his neighbours, a railor and sower of discord.' Borthwick Texts and Calendars, p. 76.) On the other hand, those so poor that they had to depend on the welfare state (or its predecessors) left behind sometimes lavish records in compensation, as descendants of workhouse inmates can testify. It should not be assumed that the most successful genealogists are those who have had rich, professional criminals in their families, but it certainly helps! According to Emily Brontë, 'Any relic of the dead is precious, if they were valued living,' but to the genealogist all ancestors arouse curiosity and some affection, no matter how they were regarded in their own lifetime.

Fortunate are those who find that their ancestors left clues through naming patterns – often, an unusual first name. Marmaduke for example, or even Hugh, can run down through several generations, and some parts of the country, and religious groups (for example, Jews) encouraged parents to name their children in sequence after specified relatives.

The quickest way to acquire a long family tree through your own efforts is to trace one of the easier lines first until you get stuck; then, instead of waiting weeks or years for the mud to clear, you should transfer to the female line of the earliest marriage you have already traced, and follow that one. If you can exploit someone else's efforts, it may be even quicker. Another student in my first class was told by an uncle to look in the back of the case of an old grandfather clock in his attic – inside was a list of his ancestors since 1740. More recently, an elderly student who had very little time to trace her family tree made little or no progress during the twenty-week course. On the final evening a keen young beaver who had obviously done a lot of work long before the class started brought in the fruits of her researches. It was one of those magnificent wallpaper charts, the reverse side of wallpaper being commonly used by those who acquire vast acreages of information and feel the urge to display it on a single sheet of paper.

The first lady looked at this in awe, then admiration, then disbelief, for there at the foot of the chart was one of her own relations!

The Internet provides a useful means of contacting others who may be researching the same family, as well as asking advice on the detailed availability of, and access to, records. Those fortunate enough to be connected can join a variety of groups whose members communicate with each other, and I have been able to put members of the same family in touch by this means. You are, of course, dependent on the right persons being connected up to the system, but the number is growing at a rate which will soon mean that a serious reader could spend all day reading the messages of others from all over the world. *FTM* 13.2 Dec 96 has a helpful introduction to the use genealogists are now making of the Internet – the magazine started the admirable feature of concluding articles with relevant websites from October 2003. Major sources of British genealogy, and societies you can join, both national and local, are found at www.genuki.org.uk, and help with searching distant records may be available through www. raogk.com. The former site has links, surname lists, research interest groups, and lists of family history societies, as well as great detail on genealogical sources in the UK and Ireland.

Also recommended, especially for those of you living a distance away from the area where your ancestors lived, is the placing of a suitable enquiry letter in a local newspaper. This can produce useful information from people who are not necessarily connected to you genetically.

Genealogy could be quite a lonely activity if it were not so absorbing, and there are many who welcome the chance to share their interests with others. Activities of a typical family history society include lectures, consultations with experienced genealogists, visits, a directory of members' interests, periodicals, and the transcription and indexing of local records such as monumental inscriptions or the census. It can provide contacts with others who are tracing the same surnames as yourself and one-way or reciprocal research arrangements with members of other societies. There are also commercial firms which specialise in tracing surname origins (e.g. www.nameswell.info) and many wider interest sites like that of the Federation of Family History Societies (FFHS), www.familyhistoryonline.net, or www.rootsweb.com which have surname sections.

Societies available to genealogists are numerous, and are of several kinds. Some are national, the most famous being the Society of Genealogists (SOG), 14 Charterhouse Buildings, Goswell Road, London EC1M 7BA (see www.britishorigins.com. Their website, www.sog.org. uk, includes a list of their many explanatory leaflets, and the library catalogue is at www.sog.org.uk/sogcat/index.html. The Society also runs a helpline on 020 7490 8911; see the website for details. A large list of surnames in their collection can be seen by clicking on 'Surnames and Families'. There are outline descriptions of the library in *Anc* 38 Oct 05 and *FHM* 133 Aug 06); others are of a more specialised nature. Most, however, are societies which are based on a locality, designed to help those whose ancestors came from that area, and genealogists who now live there. There is at least one, and often there are more, in each county, and several with strong British interests in other countries, especially Australasia, North America and South Africa.

The FFHS, embracing some 200 genealogical and related societies, is a registered charity with a role which facilitates exchange of information and ideas (see *FTM* 21.3 Jan 05 for a brief history). Only bodies (not individuals) can join the Federation itself. The *News and Digest*, published until recently, included an up-to-date list of secretaries of each member society, news of changes in record systems, news of individual societies, the Federation's education newsletter for teachers of the subject (which includes notices of future courses) and over 400 abstracts of articles from family history society journals. The Federation organises conferences, makes representations through and to official bodies concerning changes which might affect genealogists (for example, the Record Users' Group, the British Association for Local History, the Society of Antiquaries, the British Records Association and the British Records Society), promotes courses and lectures, and co-ordinates some national projects such as the National Burial Index. The Federation produces a very comprehensive free information leaflet, which is also available to download via their website, www.ffhs.org.uk, where you can subscribe to their free bimonthly electronic newsletter. The Federation's publication programme, however, has recently been consolidated and publications are now being produced in partnership with a number of other publishers, e.g. the FHP.

A full list of member societies, with links to their websites, is available at www.ffhs.org.uk, via www.genuki.org.uk, or email info@ffhs.org.uk. For more information contact the FFHS Joint Administrator, PO Box 2425, Coventry CV5 6YX, or the Federation's headquarters, the Benson Room, Birmingham and Midland Institute, Margaret Street, Birmingham, West Midlands B3 3BS (please enclose three international reply coupons if writing from abroad).

You might also enquire whether any local organisation, or even a Family History Society itself, runs evening classes in the subject, as many individuals and not a few societies have been launched on their genealogical way through this route.

For those who do not wish to join a society, there are evening courses, books, regular magazines, and even a website (www.parostutors.com) offering tuition. The market is buoyant enough to support several magazines in bookshops which are informative in many different ways – I make no apology for referring to their articles in the pages that follow. The best known is *Family Tree Magazine* (*FTM*). (On their website, www.family-tree.co.uk, there is an index to previous past copies, leading to page images.) From the same stable is the more recent *Practical Family History* (*PFH*) which issues indexes to back numbers every quarter. More recent is *Family History Monthly* (*FHM*), also full of up-to-date information about changes affecting genealogists as well as lots of useful advertising. Also on the shelves is *Ancestors* (*Anc*), published by the National Archives. All these publications are packed with articles written from the point of view of the genealogist or family historian. They also have adverts for many useful payview sites for genealogists (e.g. www.ancestry.co.uk or www.originsuk.com), forthcoming events such as exhibitions, professional research services and so on.

Stuart Raymond has a good introduction to the National Archives (basically the old Public Record Office) in *Anc* 62 Oct 07. The National Archives itself has an excellent series of leaflets, available for downloading, on a wide variety of subjects, arranged in separate series – those for domestic, legal, military and overseas records being particularly useful for our purposes – see www.catalogue.nationalarchives.gov.uk/researchguidesindex.asp. We can also use this organisation to locate quite detailed lists of sources in local repositories through www.nationalarchives.gov.uk/archon. Their medium-term digitisation programme to get many of the national's main historical documents on line is available at www.nationalarchives.gov.uk/documents/digitisation-programme2005–2011.pdf.

Getting organised

Setting out the information can indeed be quite a problem – or rather, it is two problems. Firstly, most books advise the beginner to write notes in a logical order so that the information is both presentable and easily accessible. This advice ignores the fact that most readers will have already accumulated large files full of undifferentiated data before they realise that they need to seek advice on how to organise it properly – by which time it is often too late, for the genealogist is already buried under tons of paper. Correspondence, scraps of notes on old envelopes scribbled during a quick half-hour in the library, the odd birth certificate, all become boxed in a great jumble, and the whole lot has to be searched every time you need to see who married great-great-great-grandfather. Secondly, there really has to be an answer better than wallpaper for the presentation of the final product, even though it never will be final. Gerald Hamilton-Edwards and Alexander Sandison compared genealogy to a jigsaw puzzle which has no boundary edges. It also has an unpredictable number of missing parts! See Matthews (1982), McLaughlin (1989), *PFH* 74 Feb 04, the SoG's leaflet *Family records and their layout*, and Herber (2005, chapter 3) for suggestions on how to lay out your family tree.

Several writers have offered solutions to these problems, but in the end the answer must be whatever suits the individual best, so long as it is methodical and consistent. The manual method which I use, a combination of various others, is as follows. A loose-leaf folder for pedigree charts, arranged in reverse chronological order and with each chart having a connecting reference to earlier or later ones, allows me to search rapidly through all the direct male and female lines over as many generations as have already been traced. Uncertain or unproved connections are entered in pencil until confirmed, and no earlier research goes into those lines until they are firmly established. These blank charts are obtainable from a variety of sources, and many societies affiliated to the Federation of Family History Societies produce their own at a few pence each.

Associated with the chart folder, I use a loose-leaf file in which there are sheets for each individual ancestor, in alphabetical order, recording birth, marriage, children, occupation, wealth, death and miscellaneous matters. If the data on any one person become too numerous, I put them on separate sheets immediately following, together with any copies of certificates, wills and other documentary remains of mortal existence. It can save a lot of unnecessary searching later if you record where you found all the data, and what you have already searched fruitlessly, including the archive reference numbers in case you want to refer to them again later.

Finally, but by no means of least importance, I include a sheet devoted to each of those ancestors whose birth, baptismal record or marriage has not yet been discovered and is presenting difficulties. After a statement of the problem, I write a list of the direct and circumstantial evidence already accumulated, and a list of possible ways by which the birth or marriage might be discovered. It is most important not to treat this as a once-and-for-all compilation made in a few minutes; rather, it is the result of thinking about the problem over a long time, and I note down possible ways to solve it as they occur to me – on the train, in the bath or wherever. I once thought of a quite beautiful way of getting round one problem while cleaning out my poultry house, but did not make a note of it at the time and then could never recall what it was. Finally, it is useful to note down on this sheet all the searches which have already been undertaken without success – otherwise it is quite possible to find yourself going over the same ground twice, wasting valuable time, effort and perhaps money.

I keep this dual filing system up to date on a regular basis and consult it whenever it becomes possible to visit a library, record office or other likely repository of the information I am seeking. A glance through the pedigree charts quickly shows which are the next problems to be solved. The alphabetical file will then show what I have already done to solve them and what ideas I have had for where to look next.

My system did not evolve slowly. It was a radical response to a situation which was rapidly getting out of hand, with my old notes in a chaotic state as more and more information came in. Although it took a little time to go through them all to make the rearrangements, it has repaid the effort many times since, saving time, frustration and loss of data. I can find anyone recorded in it faster than the time it takes my PC to boot up!

Had I started two decades later, I would have had the option of entering information, as it was acquired, using a genealogical program on a computer, one of the principal developments since the first edition of this book in 1983. So fascinating are the various modern electronic systems of recording and manipulating genealogical data that whole societies, magazines and a lucrative software industry are now devoted to them, but it is not by oversight that they have no central place in this edition. David Hawgood, doyen of writers on the subject, wrote (1994a, p. 5) that 'the essence of family history is storing, processing and communicating information about people, their families, and events in their lives'. To me, however, it is the discovery of those data which is central to genealogy, and no matter how useful programs may be in helping to organise, and reorganise, our material, they cannot discover it in the first place. Furthermore, I don't want to have to boot up every time I want some details from my ancestry.

Nevertheless, the advantages of using computer programs for storing, manipulating, copying, retrieving and presenting genealogical data are very substantial, and programs are regularly reviewed in the genealogical journals. GEDCOM enables data to be transferred in a standard format without having to reinput. There is a free website for entering your family at www.Geni.com. For an introduction see the works of Bloore (1989) and Hawgood (1994, 1996) in the references.

Asking questions

Frustration is experienced not only by those who are in danger of being overwhelmed by a mountain of miscellaneous pieces of paper. It is also common among beginners, who in addition have to cope with the fear that they are going to be among the unlucky ones whose grandfather, for example, had no birth certificate or whose parent was a foundling or adopted. My student who was or was not descended from the Duke of Buckingham had at least done the correct thing to start with – she had gone to her most elderly relatives and asked a series of questions. Responses are usually helpful and valuable information may be gleaned in that way. 'Well, I remember my mother telling me …' spoken by a lady in her eighties will even now be carrying the budding genealogist back into the nineteenth century, though it is not always the oldest who remember most, or who are necessarily the most willing to reveal it to you. A not uncommon response is, 'What do you want to know that for? Nothing interesting has ever happened in our family.' Roughly translated, this normally means 'There are skeletons in our cupboard, and I'm not going to help you youngsters to uncover them.' Many writers have issued good advice about this process – see, for example, Burns (1962), Cole & Titford (2003), Currer-Briggs & Gambier (1981), Drake & Finnegan (1994, vol. 4, chapter 7), *FTM* 5.9 Jul 89, Gardner & Smith (1956, I), McLaughlin (1989), and Pelling & Litton (1991).

It should perhaps be said that in all families there will be found, sooner or later, criminality, insanity and/or illegitimacy. One of my correspondents moans that he should have had danger money for researching his wife's family! About one in 400 was a certified lunatic 100 years ago, most of their individual records having been destroyed (see *NALD* 104; Faithfull, 2002; *FTM* 20.4 Feb 04; *FHM* 139 Jan 07; *Anc* 57 May 07; *FTM* 23.9 Jul 07; *PFH* 120 Dec 07). An instance of criminality probably creates more hostility among surviving relatives, and places more barriers in the way of innocent questions from those trying to trace the family tree, than anything else. If a crime has been committed in the recent past, there is no doubt that its subsequent discovery would be embarrassing to all concerned, not least to the genealogist who uncovered it. However, crimes which were committed over about fifty years ago are slowly becoming transmuted into a prime cause of historical, or perhaps antiquarian, interest. Once crimes are over a century old, the criminal becomes an object of pity or occasionally mirth and even admiration – my wife actually boasts because she has an outlaw in her family tree in 1372, even though it was in Rochdale. For records of criminality see Hawking (1992), and *FHM* 108 Sep 04 for records of medieval outlaws in the National Archives.

Of the three skeletons above, illegitimacy is by far the commonest, and the one you are most likely to find hidden when you begin to unravel the secrets of your family's past.

Those of us who trace family trees become quickly obsessed by what we are doing. There is an apocryphal (and therefore truthful) story of a lady who, having sat enraptured through a talk on the Civil War, told the lecturer that she had discovered an ancestor who had fought at the battle of Marston Moor. 'Which side was he on?' asked the naturally curious speaker. She replied, 'My mother's.'

Another sensitive area to try to avoid is illustrated in the reaction, 'There's no money left, you know.' We forget that normal people have no interest in genealogy themselves and that, because they cannot understand what the interest is for others, they may simply put a base interpretation on our motives. There is no doubt that, as we shall see, the rules governing access to records are so illogical that we are encouraged to ask nosy questions. You can, for example, see a dead neighbour's recently proved will, or learn your living neighbours' first names, but you cannot see your own birth entry because of the Registrar General's directive that the public shall have no right of access to any register book except those currently in use, or those required during litigation.

Incidentally, records of dormant funds held in Chancery are published until the 1920s only in the *London Gazette*, but are available upon application thereafter; see *NALL* 21. However, it is very unlikely that the thrill of this particular chase will reward you with better odds than the National Lottery, and any prize at the end will have considerably less value; see Moore (2004). Many families have rumours about 'their' money being lodged in Chancery, but few are correct, and fewer still have sums of any significance. See www.courtservice/gov. uk/cfo/dormant.htm, and *Anc* 48 Aug 06 for a number of articles on Chancery records.

Please ignore all attempts to deter you from tracing your family tree. The greater the difficulties, the more that is hidden from you, the greater the pleasure in making the discoveries. I do not wish to be offered my family tree, complete, back to the Middle Ages – I want the interest and excitement of finding it for myself.

There is a useful and methodical way to proceed when older relatives are being questioned, without which much information may be lost. I can illustrate this by describing what happened when my wife once tried to find a gravestone. She was puzzled to find that although two uncles described the spot where their father had been buried she still could not find the stone after visiting Heywood cemetery twice. Eventually an aunt let slip the fact that the family could not afford a stone. When our looks elicited a defence from the uncles, they simply said, 'You didn't ask us if there was a stone.' *You didn't ask us.* Remember those words, and that other people are sometimes not reticent and secretive because of malice or forgetfulness, but only because they do not realise which pieces of information are important to you. You should not lead them into using words you hope to hear; but neither should you persist in questioning if it is clearly unwelcome. (Try to discover who *does* talk to those relatives, and see if you can find out the information you want through them!) Try taking a bottle of sherry with you to loosen tongues – a useful tip using a useful tipple. A personal visit, if possible, is always more rewarding that a letter.

Ideally, you should seek the date and place of birth of the parent of the oldest living relative along the line you wish to trace. For example, if your father is alive but your grandfather is dead, you require the information about the latter. Date and place of birth, however, are not discovered easily, so you normally need to ask a variety of other questions which will help with the search for your grandfather. These should cover:

Full names and nicknames.
Date and place of marriage.
Wife's maiden name.
Birthday. Women often remember days in the year when people celebrated their birthday.
Religion.
Schools attended, and any professional qualifications.
Date and place of death, burial and cremation, and whether there is a gravestone.
Spouse's death details.
Addresses and house names.
Dates and places where distant relatives lived. Try looking at old letters and envelopes.
Any family heirlooms (valuable or not) – notebooks, diaries,

certificates, old savings books, grave ownership papers, funeral
or memorial cards, records of military service, including
medals and cap badges, and newspaper cuttings.

Bibles. The credibility of entries on the flyleaf of a Bible may be
roughly assessed by noting the date of publication relative to
the date of the entries concerned. Some are available at www.
biblerecords.com. (Mrs R. King of 16 Upper Shott, Cheshunt,
Herts EN7 6DR organises an index to entries in family Bibles;
please enclose a stamped, addressed envelope if you contact
her. See *GM* 25.1.)

Birthday and anniversary notebooks.

Any family rumours – but beware of exaggeration, especially in
social status.

Occupation.

Brothers and sisters and whether the youngest, eldest, and so on.

Other living relatives who may remember more about him – in
particular, people he liked talking to.

Connections with other parts of the country, and whether any
member of the family is known to have emigrated.

(If exact dates are not available, try to approximate in relation
to other family or national events.)

Try taking old photographs along with you, or information you can
acquire about previous neighbours from such sources as the electoral
registers (see below, p. 78) in order to jog memories in a pleasurable
way. For the interpretation of old photographs see Steel & Taylor
(1984), Linkman (2000) and *PFH* 120 Dec 07. Visit the places
concerned before the interview, if possible, so you can talk about them
and what they are like now. Getting relatives together in pairs is a good
technique, because they talk, argue, spark off each other's memories.

At the same time, ask about other branches of the family. One day
you will want to trace them, so you may as well have the information
while it is still available. Using a questionnaire ensures that most of
the important pieces of evidence are sought, and creates a purposeful
impression. It cannot be overemphasised, however, that replies from
elderly people (i.e. anyone over the age of about twenty) should not
be completely trusted, especially when you are expecting them to
remember events which happened generations ago. A useful device
is to pay a second or even a third visit and ask some of the same
questions, but feeding in information you have acquired since the last
one. My father, then about seventy, could not remember the name of
his own grandfather, so I had to buy the birth certificate of one of his

children, which gave the name I wanted. Next time I saw my father, I told him that his grandfather had been called William. 'Oh yes, now I remember. He married Alice Millington.' Now, it is quite probable that no one had mentioned Alice Millington for half a century – she died in 1920 – but it was hearing the extra information which triggered off the name in my father's memory.

Putting these questions to relatives who may remember events and places years ago saves time and money. It is also a way of collecting all those trivia which make our more recent ancestors more colourful than those in remoter times, most of whom will be little more than a name and a note of baptism, marriage, work, children and death, though a lot more if the advice of Macfarlane (1977, chapter 4) is followed. The fortunate beginner will be blessed with an aged relative who, even though their recall of the intervening years may be clouded, still retains a clarity about childhood and the events of a couple of generations ago.

My wife's grandmother was born a Washington, which seemed an admirable line to follow, since we had a famous bearer of the name and a place name to boot. She could remember her own grandfather, Joshua Washington, a farmer in North Wales, selling his produce at Corwen market, living at a place beginning with the letter G between Bala and Corwen and talking Welsh. So, to save time and money, we decided to miss out her own father, John Webb Washington, and try to discover more about Joshua.

Using a holiday in Barmouth as an excuse for the journey, we tramped round both graveyards at Glan yr Afon, the only place beginning with G between Bala and Corwen, without success; we searched the local directories for a farmer called Washington, and found none. We left an enquiry at the local county record office which elicited the response that the only Washington in the area had been an Irish navvy who lived in a shed at Bettwys Gwerfil Goch. This unpromising situation was clarified by another relative who thought that Joshua might have lived in the next valley, which was in the next county, and that the place began with Ll, which would sound like G to an English child. Off to Llangollen, and more unproductive graveyards – there are always at least two in Welsh villages (for the study of the specific problems of tracing ancestors in Wales see Rowlands et al., 1993). So eventually we did what we should have done in the first place – followed the standard procedure and sent for John Webb Washington's birth certificate. Back it came after several frustrating weeks, showing that John Webb was the son not of Joshua but of George Washington, a plumber in Chester!

Moral – never believe what older relatives tell you. Note it down; check it; but do not be surprised if it is wrong. In the above case, the old lady had clearly confused one branch of the family with another (a relative said of her, 'She doesn't tell lies, but she does romance a bit.'). Others will fail to remember dates or occupations and will give any answer rather than admit loss of memory or appear to be unhelpful. This type of confusion casts some doubt, incidentally, on the genre of historical writing called oral history, based on old people's reminiscences; see Taylor (1984). In the end the genealogist must rely on documentary evidence, though even that is not necessarily foolproof. The most important guideline is to seek all the available evidence, and only then judge what to believe and decide what your next course of action should be.

This is not to say, of course, that you should ignore other people's efforts, though you should always check their results whenever feasible. Genealogy has been a popular hobby for over a century, and it is surprising how many beginners are told that 'old uncle so-and-so tried to do that once'. Some family tree records have been kept by individual families; many others have been deposited in libraries and record offices, and a very large number have been published. Lists of family histories in date order can be obtained in Barrow (1977), Marshall (1903/1967), Thomson (1976) and Whitmore (1953), and these should be consulted over the years on a regular basis as progress is made back to earlier centuries on parts of your tree whose surnames are as yet quite unknown to you.

Contact with others tracing the same surname can sometimes be made through the 'members' interests' lists of individual societies, and regularly published research directories – see Caley (annual), K. & T. Park (1992–93), Johnson & Sainty (annual; also available on CD-ROM, and cross-references surnames to one-name study groups) and lists in the monthly *FTM*. The consolidated 'Big R', published by the Federation of Family History Societies, has now effectively replaced some of the earlier lists of researchers and the names they are studying, and there are several 'county surname interest' lists on the Internet, in addition to the main sites for discussion groups.

The register of the Guild of One-name Studies should be checked for appropriate surnames – it can be reached at www.one-name.org. And, of course, there is www.genesreunited.com. The guild, one of the member societies of the FFHS, is an association of individuals, groups and societies each of whom is studying the history and development of a single surname with its commonly accepted variants. Through the guild, therefore, you can be put in touch with others researching the same surnames as yourself. The guild publishes a journal, maintains a register of members involved in one-name studies, and gives advice on the formation of new groups.

General correspondence should be addressed to the Guild of One-name Studies, Box G, Charterhouse Buildings, Goswell Road, London, EC1M 7BA. Please enclose three international reply coupons if appropriate. The list of almost 6,000 names currently registered with the guild is now too large to be included here, but is available on the Internet at www.one-name.org.

You may find that, in investigating the more recent history of your family, there are residents in the area where your ancestors lived who have information about them; one overseas correspondent had success by leaving a note by a graveside. Writing a letter to a local newspaper has been known to yield marvellous results, though some papers now make a charge because they are inundated with such letters. In the case of a rare surname you could even write to many with the same name, obtaining their addresses from telephone directories. A student in one of my classes wrote to one such entry, chosen at random with a pin, and received in return several sheets on which her family tree was written, back to 1728, and with herself included at the foot!

II *Looking for parents*

It has been said that the history of population is all about sex and death; well, genealogy is all about parents and how to find them. It is true, of course, that sooner or later anyone tracing a family tree will be interested in marriages, gravestones, tax returns and a host of documents which supply evidence about named individuals; but in the end, when human beings have learnt how to avoid death and have outgrown marriage as a social institution, the genealogist's basic task will remain the same – to discover parents. It is a genetic quest – few people would prefer to trace foster or adoptive parents rather than their real ones. Thus, early registers which record baptism without naming the parents of the children will probably mark an end to the search for that particular branch of the family. Until those registers are reached, possibly 400 years back, there are several basic sources of information about parents, and it is quite possible to trace a family tree by using only the main ones – the state birth certificates, the census and church baptismal registers.

A great deal has been written about these sources. The following discussion therefore goes into their history only where doing so will help the genealogist to exploit the documents fully, at the least cost and trouble, and where it can help users to overcome problems which can sometimes occur with sources of this kind.

Birth certificates, 1837 to the present day

Everyone born in England or Wales on or since 1 July 1837 should have had their birth registered by the state, which keeps a record of the event in the form of a registration entry. This shows information which an informant, normally the mother or her legal husband, provides to the Registrar of Births and Deaths (RBD) within six weeks of the birth. (There are provisions for late registration, but that incurs a penalty, and any over twelve months have to be processed by the Registrar General.) Bilingual birth and reregistration entries, in Wales and Monmouthshire only, have been permitted since 1 April 1969. Until 2006, registrars sent the Registrar General a copy of each entry at the end of each quarter year, and one great advantage of computerisation from the point of view of an RBD is the death of the 'yellow peril', a dreaded notification from GRO that the RBD had made a mistake.

Twenty-eight days after the registrar's current record book is full, it is handed over to the local Superintendent Registrar, who keeps it permanently. Nowadays, forms are completed, and data are transmitted, electronically through the system known internally (and affectionately?) as 'RON' – registration on line; indeed, parents registering a birth may be surprised to find that the information is already on the screen before they set foot in the office, so close is the relationship between NHS and GRO.

Thus, there should be in existence two birth entries for each person born in England and Wales back to 1 July 1837 – the original with the Superintendent Registrar of the district where the birth took place, and a copy with the Registrar General. *Until the recent introduction of computerised systems, the Superintendent Registrar and Registrar General had their own separate indexing systems, and reference numbers are not interchangeable.*

By a decision of the Registrar General, rather than by statute, the general public has no right of access to the entry books themselves (except those which are still in use by the registrars) which were specifically excluded from the provisions of the 1958 Public Records Act. The only exception to this is an application for a copy of a very recent entry in a book not yet passed across to the Superintendent Registrar – the copy is £3.50, and you are allowed to see the entry. Despite computerisation, these recent entries are still available in hard copy form.

When civil registration started in 1837 the cost of a copy certificate was 2s. 6d. (or 12½p), 1s. of which went to the registrar; it rose next in 1952 – to 3s. 9d.! Now, following the 1968 Public Expenditure and Receipts Act, this aspect of the service has to pay for itself. For the early history of the service see Nissell (1987) and *MRS 8*. The *Efficiency Scrutiny Report* on the registration service (1985) is a useful guide to how the system then operated.

Genealogists tend to forget that civil registration is not run for their benefit; indeed, only one type of record referred to in this book was written basically for a genealogical purpose. Nor is the registration service adequately staffed to cater for all our needs, and there is no statutory requirement to provide a postal service. Paying the price, therefore, seems inevitable until it is recognised that these records should be classed as public documents under the 1958 Public Records Act and made available to the public after, say, 100 years. Unfortunately, the cost of opening them to the public in this way would be substantial, and the change would require legislation time which seems as elusive as the political will to do it. Furthermore, it is clear that, even if such a change were to be approved, the housing of civil register books in the present library system would be very problematic.

Obtaining copy certificates from a register office

There is normally one Superintendent Registrar in each major city and there are several in each county, the number having fallen from 615 in 1837 to 412 in 1996. (Oddly, though most have been promoted from the ranks of RBDs they are not allowed to register any events themselves, unless they are also deputy registrars.) Please note that the registers are housed in 'register' offices, *not* the 'registry' offices so beloved by dramatists and, I fear, even one or two writers on genealogy. This error, described by one GRO inspector as 'infamous', was first recorded in 1911, so it has a long pedigree – but the term 'register office' was used as far back as 1836 in, and by, the General Register Office, and is found in Cap. 86 of the Act setting them up – 'the guardians [of the Poor] shall provide ... a Register Office for securing the registers when deposited therein.'

There were some major boundary changes between districts in 1853 and again in April 1974 at the same time as local government reorganisation. The office of each Superintendent Registrar has lists and addresses of all the other offices in England and Wales, together with an incomplete list of the whereabouts of the records for those districts which have been changed since 1929. You will find registrars' addresses and telephone numbers in the normal phone books, usually available in public libraries, or at www.yell.com for the whole of the United Kingdom, listed under 'Registration of births, deaths and marriages'. (Hull, incidentally, has a private telephone system. This might sound an archaic point, but it is giving their subscribers a headache concerning access to broadband!) A national list may be found on the Internet via GENUKI, or individually at www.gro.gov.uk. Use a search engine to see if the office you want is on the Internet – many will accept on line applications. Maps showing historical registration districts and parish boundaries can be obtained from the Institute of Heraldic and Genealogical Studies: IHGS, Northgate, Canterbury, Kent CT1 1BA.

Indexes in local register offices are normally by district and by year, arranged alphabetically by initial letter of surname, but not necessarily by the whole name, and include a reference number. Until modern times they were not compiled for uniform lengths of time. (The GRO does not seem to have issued instructions on how the local service should index its registers.) The general public has the right to search the district indexes, for a specified, dated event, free of charge, so long as they search within a five-year period, or exceptionally up to ten years if the Superintendent Registrar deems it justifiable. Should you wish to search more than five years' indexes for one entry or more, you (or two people researching the same family) are allowed a 'general search' of six continuous hours for which a fee of £18.00 may be charged. The fee might include up to eight verifications, each further one costing £2.50, but legislation does not provide for such a service so it may be refused. For general searches you do not have to state which entries you are looking for, or why. Searches must be conducted in person – registrars themselves are not allowed to undertake them – but if you can provide the details, registrars will find specific entries in the register books.

Birmingham was the first to reindex its birth registers back to 1837, and it microfilmed the new indexes, an admirable lead which has been followed by some other districts. The most modern entries are completed on computer anyway. In some areas, indexes from adjoining areas are now being combined, most easily identified and accessed through www.ukbmd.org.uk, from which copy certificates can be ordered. Not all districts are in this scheme, which needs GRO approval by the way.

Searches in the local indexes can be in person or by post, provided you give the approximate year of birth, allow the Superintendent a week or two to reply, and supply the reference number from the index if you have already found it yourself. Postal application to a Superintendent Registrar should include the fee, made payable to 'The ... Council'; he can refuse to undertake the search if your information is deemed insufficient. (The advantage of not naming a specific council on the cheque is that the registrar can then forward it to an adjoining district if it is felt that a search there may prove more successful.) Do not go into long, rambling details about your family history – just send the basic question, with as much relevant detail about the event as possible, and the source of your information about the entry you are seeking.

Pressure of work in register offices varies from time to time, partly on staffing levels, but largely on whether genealogy is getting well advertised by, for example, television programmes. When that happens, our applications are likely to be accorded a low priority compared with those applying for their own certificates, and can take weeks rather than days to be sent.

The present location of all registers since 1837, with changes, amalgamations, and so on, can be found at www.fhsc.org.uk/genuki/reg.

Enclose a stamped, addressed envelope, and your phone number in case of queries. I would always recommend asking for a certificate photocopied from the original rather than one newly made out by hand, because then you will have the original signatures of the informants which may be useful for identification as well as being interesting in themselves. There should be no charge for an application simply to know whether a specified event has been registered, but we are not entitled to any data from the entry which we do not already know. If you are applying for more than one certificate, send a cheque for each one, unless you are absolutely sure that the entries will be found. Blank application forms are available in any register office.

Since 1 April 2003, the cost of a certificate by post or by personal application to a Superintendent Registrar is £7.00 (£3.50 if it is a copy of a very modern entry from a book which is still being completed by the RBD). A short certificate costs only a little less (£5.50), and I can think of only one instance in which it is preferable to buy the latter. Some register offices (e.g. Leeds, Salford) put on a surcharge for administration if you apply by phone or on line using a credit card; others (e.g. Durham, South Shields) do not. Some councils go further, adding an extra charge above that laid down by statute. If you find this practice as objectionable as I do, simply order on line from the GRO instead.

Obtaining copy certificates from the General Register Office

The national (as most local) indexes appear sparse, as they comprise only the name and a reference number to the district of the original entry and the page number within the General Register Office's copy entry books. The General Register Office is part of the Identity and Passport Service (IPS) (until 1 April 2008 it was under the Office for National Statistics) and the large, hard-copy indexes, which used to be in Somerset House, then St Catherine's House, and most recently the Family Records Centre, are now in storage in Christchurch (incidentally, and amazingly, at least two of the original handwritten index volumes found their way on to the second-hand book market some years ago!). This is the first time there has been no national, dedicated GRO search room since the start of the system, and you will be asked to use the indexes on microfiche at Kew, or on the Internet. The old indexes cover the whole of England and Wales, and are arranged in alphabetical order within each quarter-year (annual from 1984). They comprise the name of the child, the registration district and a reference number. (They old indexes are very heavy, the earliest weighing over 20 lb, and could be very awkward to use when the search room was crowded.

For physical detail of the old search room system from the inside see
MRS 4.) Until the end of 1865 they were handwritten, then printed
until 1910, typescript to 1962 and finally produced in the form of a
computer printout. The mother's maiden name, which is sometimes
the only information you actually need from the certificate in the first
place, appears in the national indexes from 1 July 1911, but in the
local indexes only from 1969 unless you are lucky.

GRO indexes have been made available in microform to outside
purchasers, so you may find it convenient to approach your local
library or record office which houses them. They are in great demand,
and a user-booking system is normal, though the Internet has now
reduced the pressure to use microfiche. A list of those known to have
been purchased by UK institutions is given in Gibson (1987). They
are available on line on various payview sites, and certificates can be
ordered from the GRO website. Access to the Internet also allows a
search at www.freebmd.org.uk (which includes a facility to search by
forename). The GRO now offers the same facility, including mother's
maiden name, from 1837, having been re-indexed from the quarterly
copies.

Once the MAGPIE system is in place, these indexes will be available
(on line only) showing the mother's maiden name from 1837. (See
A note on presentation, p. xxiii above.) It should include a search
facility to enable, for example, other children of the same parents to
be identified far more quickly than at present.

Use of the indexes is for the most part straightforward, though Mc,
Mac and O' have changed their relative position over the years. Since
1969, Mac and Mc have been brought together sequentially (see *FTM*
14. 10 Aug 98). Hyphenated surnames should be indexed using both
names.

There are significant differences in access and costs between a local
register office and the General Register Office. We have seen that a
general search in the Superintendent Registrar's office costs £18.00,
but you can search the indexes of the Registrar General, which contain
more information than the local indexes, free of charge, and without a
time limit. (In the nineteenth century there was a charge of £1.00 for
a general search in the General Register Office.)

Since mid-1991 all postal applications for normal copy certificates of
birth, marriage or death have been dealt with at the General Register
Office, Smedley Hydro, PO Box 2, Southport, Merseyside PR8 2JD.
Application forms for the GRO are normally available in local register
offices. A copy certificate issued after application by post, phone or
fax costs £8.50 if the GRO reference number is known, otherwise it is

£11.50. (There is also a twenty-four-hour 'priority' application service, at a fee of £24.50 per certificate, or £27.50 if the reference number is not provided.) Cheques should be made payable to 'GRO' until their website suggests otherwise.

Certificates can also be ordered on line, using a credit card, from the General Register Office, via www.gro.gov.uk, which will update you on any fee changes since this was written. The cost is the standard £7.00 if you know the GRO reference number in advance, otherwise £10. Note that there appears to be no extra charge for payment by credit card, unlike some register offices. The GRO offers a reference checking service, by which the applicant can supply additional data in order to confirm that the copy certificate is more likely to be the correct one. There is a charge of £4.50 if the reference supplied does not lead the search staff to the entry requested. The GRO advises on line applicants as to the likely date of copied certificates being posted out.

The GRO will also supply a certificate by post for the basic £7.00 in cases where the Superintendent Registrar's copy has been damaged – some were destroyed during the Second World War, for example. Only if it is needed for a 'statutory purpose' can a certificate be obtained more cheaply. Certificates from the General Register Office are copies from microfilm, often partly illegible – you should ask for a legible copy from the manuscript entry if you cannot read it.

The General Register Office is not as assiduous as most genealogists hope in ensuring that minor variations in spelling should not prevent the correct identification of an entry. See the advice on the back of the application form.

Thus the majority of genealogists, who live beyond easy reach of London, are doubly penalised compared with those in the capital if they do not have Internet access. (For a summary of those trying to trace London ancestors, see *FTM* 23.12, Oct 07.) They must pay dearly for their local general searches, and pay extra (and wait longer) for their postal requests to the General Register Office. This advantage enjoyed by those in the Home Counties explains the concerted effort a few years ago to prevent the Registrar General moving the national indexes to the provinces (*GM* 18.2 and *Local Population Studies* 14.)

So far, so good. We know that there are two sources from which to obtain a copy birth certificate. Which method you use will depend on how much information you already have about the birth. If you know where the person was born, and the approximate date, it is quicker and (for those without the Internet) cheaper to apply to the relevant Superintendent Registrar, and there are examples in which it is easier to locate an entry in the local rather than in the national indexes (Gardner & Smith, 1956, I, pp. 63–5). If the place of birth is not known, you will need to use the national indexes. The General Register Office will also supply 'special occasion' certificates, for which you should apply to the Commemorative Certificates Section of the General Register Office, PO Box 2, Southport, Merseyside PR8 2JD, giving a fortnight's notice.

Always apply to the Superintendent Registrar of the district where the event was registered and let them know if you require a copy showing the original signature of the informant.

The copy certificate

It is worth stressing that a birth or death entry is a record *not* of birth or death but of what a registrar believed an informant said on a specific date.

A certified copy of a birth registered before 1 April 1969 provides the date and place of birth, the forename(s) of the child, its sex, the name and occupation of the father, the name and maiden name of the mother (which can lead you to the parents' marriage), the place of birth, the informant's signature, name and address, and the date of registration. Since 1 April 1969, the format of the birth certificate has changed, so that the child's surname, and the place of birth of each parent (if in the United Kingdom – only the country if outside) and their usual address, all now appear, additionally.

Since 1904, the Registrar General has issued a directive concerning births (and deaths) in certain institutions (especially prisons, mental institutions and workhouses) that the name of such an institution should not appear on the entry, only its recognised address. Any address unfamiliar to you in the family's history could be in this category, and should be checked in a local directory – see p. 80.

The new system was only two days old when the Registrar General issued a short-lived direction to record the *time* of birth. Normally, however, if time of birth is given in the entry, a multiple birth can normally be inferred, except in the first year or two of civil registration, another consequence of the need to establish primogeniture more efficiently than relying on baptismal registers. However, if one of a pair of twins was stillborn, the time should not have been included on the birth entry of either, a rule which must be borne in mind by anyone looking for evidence of twinning in the family (for an article on the registration of twins see *GM* 16.5). Twins are not identified as such in the indexes, but a check through the remainder of the entries of the same surname in the same quarter should give the same or adjoining reference number. (This is not an infallible guide to identifying twins, however, as there were five entries per page in the pre-1969 entry books in the General Register Office. Quite often, cousins were registered together, and the surname may be common in the area anyway.)

The surname of the child, which can be any name under which the informant says the child will be brought up, has been entered only since 1 April 1969. Before that date it has to be inferred from the parents' name.

The sex of the child may seem superfluous, though in a few cases it is not obvious from the forename, and it establishes which sex you are allowed to marry in the United Kingdom unless you acquire a full Gender Recognition Certificate under the Act of 2004. Even then, the original birth entry remains unaltered, because it is a correct statement of events on that date. Changing sex in this way involves a similar process to adoption, with a confidential Gender Recognition Register kept by the Registrar General in a system presumably modelled on the adoption register (see www.grp.gov.uk). Incidentally, I have never understood why most forenames are associated with one sex rather than the other, but it is a good thing for the genealogist that the practice exists!

A mother who has been married twice should show as 'Mary Jones, late Smith, formerly Brown', but only if the registrar was informed of the situation. 'Formerly' always refers to her maiden name (*defined as the name in which she was first married*), not to any previous married name. The maiden surname of a mother who herself was illegitimate is normally the name in which she was brought up. If a married mother has died, the word 'afterwards' will follow her maiden name.

In the case of an illegitimate child, only the mother's name is normally given after 1874. If the father's name does appear, the mother of an illegitimate child will probably be called, for example, 'Elizabeth Smith' instead of 'Elizabeth Jones, formerly Smith', although, of course, a married woman can have an illegitimate child and still provide her maiden and married names in this way. 'Elizabeth Jones "otherwise" Smith' implies an alias. Official use of the word 'illegitimate' was forbidden by the 1987 Family Law Reform Act, by the way, and only relatively recently have RBDs been allowed, and required, to ask if the parents are married to each other.

Until 1969 the surnames of both mother and father were indexed if they appear on the entry, but only in the case of an illegitimate child (inside or outside marriage) are both natural parents allowed to sign as informants, a facility not encouraged by thoughts of future custody cases. All previous names used by the mother should have been included.

Before 1875 the mother was allowed to name any man as the father – he was not required to acknowledge paternity. (The name of the father of an illegitimate child might also appear on the child's later marriage entry.) An illegitimate child registered before 1 April 1969 can be issued with a short birth certificate which gives him or her the surname of either the father or the mother, but the father's name could appear on the entry only if an affiliation order had been issued, or if he signed the entry, or if he acknowledged paternity through a statutory declaration. In 2000, 60 per cent of children were born to married parents, 25 per cent to cohabiting parents (i.e. those living as a family unit), and the remainder split between single parents or those giving the same address.

Interesting cases have gone through the courts, even to the Court of Appeal, with conflicting outcomes, brought by husbands who did not wish their biological offspring to be given surnames different from their own by wives who had since remarried. (See MRS 39.) In 1996, 8 per cent of all birth registrations did not contain the name of the father of the child, but the government has recently announced its intention to make the insertion of the father's name compulsory on all birth entries in order to facilitate subsequent paternal support.

If the father of the child was already dead when the birth was registered, the word 'deceased' should appear after his name or in his occupation column, but does not always do so. Occasionally the registrar would incorrectly omit the father's name altogether if he was dead, or provide both his name and occupation as if he were alive. There are also cases of this column containing the word 'illegitimate', or even 'had no father'! As always, the registrars are dependent on the information supplied by the informant, and some might not know whether he was still alive. Although the question is asked by RBDs nowadays, I don't know if the practice started in 1837.

The gainful occupation of the mother could be entered from 1986, with a designated space being provided for it from 1995. However, after 1978 it may be found on Anglican baptism entries and it is also in health authority records – see below, p. 65.

It is worth paying close attention to the entry in the 'informant' column, where the name and qualification are given. Priority to be an informant is given equally to the mother or to her husband if he is the father of the child, secondly to a person present at the birth, thirdly to a person in charge of the child, and fourthly to the occupier of the house in which the birth occurred. Only in certain specified circumstances can the father of an illegitimate child be the informant. Addresses can be useful additions to that given in the 'place of birth' column, though in the last century they were often the same. Normally only one parent signs, unless the child is illegitimate and the father accompanies the mother and makes the request to be entered. Informants can be minors, so long as they appear to be 'of credible age'.

Until modern times, when some of the larger offices send photocopies of the original entries quarterly, the informant's signature can be seen only on the Superintendent Registrar's copy. (As we shall see, it is sometimes important to be able to see original signatures, but it appears to be in the discretion of Superintendent Registrars to provide, for the normal £7.00 fee, a photocopy of an entry instead of the normal certified copy.)

Column 10 of the certificate, normally blank, records any change of forename up to twelve months after the original registration based on information on a baptismal or naming certificate; see p. 91. Such an addition can be entered, via the Registrar General, at any time afterwards – over a century later in at least one case!

Marginal notes (which give their name to the Registration Service's in-house magazine) are deemed to be part of the official record, and should therefore be on any copy certificate issued. Such notes include later alterations to the entry, or the fact that the child was adopted or has had a sex change. They were introduced in 1875, enabling a registration officer to correct an error of fact which came to light later. (Clerical errors by the registrar, however, had to be referred to the GRO.)

Between the wars, there was continued concern about the size of the population, as a result of which in 1938 registrars began to collect other information from informants of births and, more recently, stillbirths – nowadays, the number of children already in the family (anachronistically collected from only married women!), the date of birth of each parent, whether the mother has been married before, how many live and stillbirths she has had before, how many of her children have died, and occupational background. Unfortunately for the genealogist this information is sent to the Registrar General for statistical purposes only and is then destroyed. The main statistical purposes can be seen listed in MN 36 Autumn 07. (It is this position of being able to collect 'other information' which leads me to fear that the service might be abused by an erratic local government council, now that registrars are local government employees following the Statistics and Registration Service Act of 2007. They remain statutory officers, but only for that part of the service relating to civil registration. They are forbidden to strike, for example.)

The 'short' birth certificate was introduced in December 1947 for those who might not wish their parents to be entered. It is slightly cheaper to buy (£5.50) than a full certificate, but with one exception it is of no genealogical value, and shows, incidentally, only the name in column 10 (space 17 since 1969) if that has been completed. Earlier, apparently short, certificates, in different colours, were issued in relation to various pieces of legislation, in particular the need to prove age when leaving school and starting work, and these have often survived in family archives rather than the full-copy certificates. They contain little *direct* genealogical information.

Since 1927 a registrar can supply (and since 1953 must reregister) a new birth certificate for a child, even for one born long before 1927, making it seem to have been legitimate, upon the subsequent marriage of the parents. Such a certificate would give a misleading clue to finding the marriage. (Jabez Mann, born in 1867, was reregistered in 1929!) The births of such children are therefore entered three times in the GRO indexes: the original index entry remains, but the new name is added in the same quarter, together with a second new entry at the time of reregistration. The Act authorised the Registrar General to reregister if there had been no legal impediment to the parents' being married at the time of the birth, a restriction removed in 1953; since 1997, RBDs themselves have been allowed to reregister. It is not a simple process, as it requires detailed evidence in order to avoid fraud, and such cases may be referred to the GRO for investigation. The new certificate should contain the phrase 'on the authority of the Registrar General', and copies of the original entry should contain a marginal note 'reregistered on ...' with the date. There is no separate index of reregistrations, and a copy of the original entry, which should contain an appropriate marginal note, can be issued if requested. However, the original National Health Service number of the child is retained, a direct reference to the first entry, and since 1969 the original date of birth is shown in the indexes. Hence no fewer than fourteen children, born between 1948 and 1965, could apparently be registered to the same parents in Shepway in the March quarter of 1978. By 1970 some 13,000 cases per annum were being reregistered. On the rather complicated rules governing legitimation see *MRS* 7 on the issue of reregistration following illegitimacy within a former marriage. See also *MN* 8 Summer 89 and 22 Autumn 97.

A further reform (the Parental Order Register) was introduced by the Human Fertilisation and Embryology Act of 1990, which provides for the reregistration, by the commissioning parents, of children born to surrogate mothers. The original entry is annotated, and the child can obtain a copy (showing the birth mother) once reaching the age of eighteen and following counselling. (Section 28(6) of this Act gave rise to an extraordinary situation, corrected only ten years later, in which children born as a result of donor insemination but conceived posthumously were barred from having a legal father!)

Recently, DNA has enabled courts to issue a Declaration of Parentage, at the request of either the mother or the Child Support Agency. In that case, the birth can be reregistered without the father's consent, showing him to be the father of the child, though the child's surname remains as originally registered. At the time of writing, a new Human Fertilisation and Embryology Bill is going through Parliament, due to become law in 2009. One of its proposals is that the civil registration birth entry would allow a same-sex partner to be listed as the second legal parent on a child's birth certificate, if that is what the mother chooses, when the child has been conceived by IVF by donor. Let us hope that Parliament recognises that until the true genetic origins of babies are faithfully recorded on a birth entry, the state is conniving in telling lies.

Until 1977 foundlings were registered by boards of guardians or social services departments, and are indexed in the usual way under the name given by those agencies, and the age assessed by medical examination. When named, they are given 'Foundling' as the mother's maiden name – see, for example, William Gray, registered at Westminster in the September quarter of 1941. In the present phone book is E. G. Ignotus, the grandson of a baby found floating in a basket during a Leeds flood in the last century. They are normally included in the 'Unknown' section of the indexes after the Zs. Following the Children Act of 1975, foundlings now form the bulk of entries in the General Register Office's Register of Abandoned Children, and should no longer be registered by RBDs. Astonishingly few – about half a dozen a year – have been entered so far, perhaps because the requirement is not well enough known. In the same register are older abandoned children who may already have had their birth registered in the normal way. Entries in this register contain no more information than that found on a short certificate, and all are included in the main series of birth indexes, distinguished by an unusual reference number. Only a short-copy certificate can be issued from this register.

The records of Dr Barnardo's begin in 1871 and are complete from 1885. They are now deposited with the University of Liverpool, but only those over 100 years old are available for research. Enquiries should be addressed to The After-Care Department, Barnardo's, Tanner's Lane, Barkingside, Ilford, Essex IG6 1QG (*not* to Liverpool). See also p. 99 for the Coram Foundling Hospital.

Once a birth certificate has been obtained, the next step is to seek the marriage certificate of the parents (see p. 164). For the majority of families, this will be straightforward. The only problems so far will have been the practical ones of access to the indexes. For a large number, however, one of a series of difficulties will have already occurred. The following sections explain why they arise, and what you can do about them.

Failure to find a birth entry in the indexes

This often happens and there are many reasons why. In my experience, such difficulties will occur in up to a third of all attempts to locate an entry in the indexes. The solution depends on the cause, which you may not recognise until you have tried several solutions. Suffice it to say that the cause might be in yourself, or, too often, in the system by which the records were created in the first place. Michael Foster's two books (1998 and 2002) are frightening in their descriptions of our less than perfect, while indispensable, system of civil registration.

Registration in another district

Births are registered in the district or sub-district in which they happen, and until fairly modern times are normally indexed accordingly. This district need not necessarily cover the home address of the parents. I once tried to illustrate to some students how a registrar finds a particular entry among the thousands or even millions in his or her keeping by trying to discover the record of my wife's birth. Much to their amusement, it could not be found. The entry was eventually discovered in a nearby district, recording the birth in a hospital a few miles from her parents' home. The indexes to several or all sub-districts in the Superintendent Registrar's area should therefore be consulted if necessary; after that, those of the GRO. Registration districts are so separate that it was only in 1911 that each was given statistical information about its residents' children born in other districts. From 1837, boundaries were those of the newly created Poor Law Unions, but they had not been uniformly created by 1 July 1837. Note that these can cross the old county boundaries, based as they were on the Poor Law Union boundaries. (Mottram, in Cheshire, was in the registration district of Ashton under Lyne, Lancashire; most of Prestwich was not in the Prestwich registration district!)

Equally, there might be more than one place with the same name in the county concerned, and I've never noticed a census return trying to distinguish between them. If, therefore, you are searching for a birth on the basis of a later census, you might be looking for the wrong registration district.

For a history of the financing of the system see *MRS* 10. Until 1929 registrars were paid on commission, encouraging registration in the wrong district, and some had very little work to do, as sub-districts varied considerably in size by a factor of about 20. They were designed to have about 5,000 inhabitants, creating some 300 events each year, but the information on which boundaries were based was inadequate, and some 71 temporary Superintendent Districts had to be created in the early years. Boundaries were crossed, and at least one register series, North Derwent, in Cumberland, 1837–42, seems to be missing for that reason (see Nissell, 1987).

Those using the GRO indexes should be prepared to find registration districts with unfamiliar names, as well as boundaries, but officials will be able to advise on their location, and the Institute of Heraldic and Genealogical Studies in Canterbury publishes maps for the main periods of boundary stability, 1837–51 and 1852–1946. To illustrate the confusion in some areas, places as Mancunian as Cheetham, Clayton and Newton Heath were in registration districts *outside* the city.

Birth not registered
In some parts of the country as many as 15 per cent of all births were not registered during the first decades after 1837. Cullen (1975) suggests an overall 10 per cent, but higher in towns, and up to 25 per cent in London. Research suggests that the problem was worst in Surrey, Sussex, Middlesex, Essex, Shropshire and Wales, and in the period before 1860; it fell to almost nothing by the 1870s, though that has not prevented Charlie Chaplin's birth entry, supposedly 16 April 1889, having never been found. The Registrar General admitted in 1877 that birth registers were 'not quite complete'. Until the end of the Second World War, a few births went unregistered for religious reasons, lack of public transport, the death of the parents, and simple forgetfulness (see *MN* 16 Summer 93). The number has diminished further because of the administration of the National Health Service.

The extent of unregistered births immediately after 1837 is a controversial issue, as it is not straightforward to discover how many were born after 1 July but not registered – and virtually impossible if they were not baptised either. David Annal has suggested (*Anc* 39 Nov 05) that the figure was nearer 5 per cent than 30 per cent, pointing out that there was no significant increase in numbers of births registered after 1874. See Appendix 1 for some research in Lancashire parishes.

As a result of a Lords' amendment to the original legislation, there was no penalty on parents for failing to register a birth until the Births and Deaths Registration Act of 1874, when a £2 fine was introduced, and parents often wanted to hide the true age of a child in order to send it out to work as early as possible. (From 1833 a series of Acts of Parliament made it illegal to employ children under certain ages in industrial occupations.) The 7s. 6d. penalty for late registration after the permitted six-week interval following a birth did not encourage the stragglers to come forward, and registration was not permitted after six months anyway. Until 1875, as a result of another amendment in the Lords to the 1836 Bill, the onus to register fell on the registrar (who often had to visit the homes concerned with all the difficulties that entailed) rather than on the parents, a fact which helped to determine the original size of the districts. Parents were bound by law to answer the registrar's questions, but not to report the birth in the first place; the public notice stated simply that parents 'may have the Births of their children, born after June, 1837, registered *without any payment being required*, at any time within Six Weeks after the Birth'. The Registrar General's explanation of the change in the law was published in *GM* 7, and copied in Steel (1968, I, p. 146).

Many believed that registration was not necessary if the child was baptised. In 1844 the Registrar General reported that 'I am well aware that many thousands of births annually escape registration'. The efficient recording of the birth of illegitimate children began only a year later, according to Laslett (1980); they do seem to be particularly prone to underregistration in the earliest years, though they may have been baptised. Another common period for underregistration followed 1853 as parents tried to avoid compulsory vaccination of children at three months, introduced in that year. Sometimes a false address was given, and when such cases were discovered the entry was struck through by the General Register Office and copies may not be provided.

The number of *genealogical* complaints about births being unregistered drops significantly after 1875, but they do not disappear altogether, and there seem to be cases well enough authenticated to convince the General Register Office that an omission had indeed occurred. Nevertheless, I recommend assuming that all were registered, and that more ingenuity is needed in order to overcome the *impasse*.

The easiest way to overcome this problem in the nineteenth century is to use registers of baptism (pp. 91–135), the census (pp. 71–91) and wills (pp. 229–32). It may also be possible to trace the parents from a known brother or sister, gleaned from the census, whose birth *was* registered. Failure to find siblings registered would be another indication that the parents had omitted to have your ancestor recorded. Other alternative sources are discussed below, on pages 54–71.

Birth incorrectly indexed

Early in November 1977 I stood in a Superintendent Registrar's office next to a very upset and worried lady named Edith Williamson, who had searched through all the nearby districts for her own birth certificate. She knew that it was there, because she had once had a copy; yet it had not, apparently, been indexed. Eventually, almost by accident, she found it – indexed under Wilkinson.

The causes of poor indexing are not far to seek. Until modern times, certificates were handwritten and subsequently indexed by a different registrar, so that simple misreading of the original writing is quite possible. Confusion over the capital letters T, F, J and I, or small t and l, is common, as is the adding or dropping of a capital H or silent W. H, W and M can easily be mistaken for each other, as can a handwritten u and n. For example, Hood and Flood are easily confused when handwritten, and there are several surnames starting with either F or V, which can cause confusion. Every time the records are copied errors can creep in, so that the GRO indexes contain more mistakes than the local ones, especially before 1911, when carbon paper was first used. Those which have had to be typed up from the original handwritten indexes have further errors (see *New Zealand Genealogist* 22.229). Abbott (1971, p.30) quotes a case of an ancestor registered locally but not appearing in the GRO indexes. About half of such errors are the result of poor copying in the quarterly copies. The original entry was copied by hand; the copy was indexed by hand and in many cases the original indexes are now so worn through use that they have been recopied, again by hand. During this process, particularly in the 1840s, entries were given the wrong district in the index, so may never now be found.

Occasionally, a name will be out of its proper alphabetical place in the index – in the GRO index for March 1838, for example, Kershaw appears after Kerslake.

One way to prevent further deterioration was to have the indexes microfilmed, starting with the years for which there were a large number of applications relating to pensions, and a number of repositories have now bought copies; see Gibson (1987). The price the public has to pay is the much longer time it takes to look up each entry, but since 1985 microfilming has made the national indexes more widely available. The GRO staff use the microfilms for their first attempt to trace an enquiry but revert to the original indexes if the application presents difficulties (*MRS* 14). Indexes are also available on microfiche, and are much easier to use in that form, and of course they are available on line (though still on pay per view at the time of writing).

An index entry can also be wrong if the original certificate was incorrectly completed (see p. 39), but indexes are not always altered following a correction to the original. Normally nowadays every effort is made to ensure that the informant can check what is written on the certificate. We do not know how thoroughly this was done in the last century, but illiteracy was widespread, so that such checking was in many cases impossible. One obvious source of 'error' comes as a result of indexing exactly as the name appears in the entry, so names starting with 'Mac' and 'Mc' are indexed quite separately. If the informant was not the brightest of sparks, the problem might be compounded. One mother of an illegitimate child, asked by the registrar to name the father, looked puzzled, and asked, 'Will the social services know?' Names were written either as common sense suggested or as pronunciation dictated. Some of these errors will cause few problems. Most people with my own surname have to suffer the indignity of seeing it spelled Rodgers and will look under both spellings almost automatically. Hibberts, however, may not look under Ibbert, or Owen under Howin, and the most difficult cases are those where the registrar has misheard the name or had no idea how to spell it. The birth of Elizabeth Hallett on 5 January 1878 was registered by a neighbour and recorded as 'Allot'. Again, the name may well have been misheard if the informant had a bad cold at the time. Lettice Barlow, who died in Stockport in 1837, is indexed as 'Pettice' even in the original handwritten form.

You can get round the problem of poor indexing in exactly the same way as you can overcome the problem of an unregistered birth, but at first it is worth using a bit of imagination and ingenuity to consider various possible spellings under which the name might be indexed. The spelling of forenames can vary – Elizabeth may be indexed as Elisabeth. Some Taylors spell the name Tailor, Tayler, or Tailer. For an account of some indexing errors see *MRS* 14, and *FTM* 7.6 Apr 91 for an example of a second forename indexed as a surname. Foster (1998 and 2002) has done more than anyone to highlight defects in the present system.

Birth not in England or Wales

However 'British' the surname may be, a surprising number of our ancestors were not born in England or Wales (some 4 per cent even in 1881, for example). The surname itself may be a clue to foreign origin, and a good dictionary of surnames should be consulted. The most obvious areas where immigration may have occurred in the nineteenth century are near the Scottish border and in the industrial north and Midlands, which drew large numbers of immigrants from Ireland, especially after the 1830s. A register of immigrants from Scotland has been compiled by the Anglo-Scottish Family History Society. Scotland, Ireland north and south, the Isle of Man (*Population Registration* 8.3) and Channel Islands (both Jersey and Guernsey) have their own registration systems (*FTM* 6.2 Dec 89). Scottish civil registration indexes can be seen, for a fee, at Kew. A more general source of information on immigration can be found in several websites under the phrase 'Moving here', and there is a National Archives digitisation programme on immigration, 1836–1960, due out in 2009. (For articles on immigration records, including those on line, se *Anc* 50 Oct 06 and 53 Jan 07.) Indexes of births overseas are available via www.findmypast.com (pay per view) and, from 1761, at www.familyrelatives.com. Alien registration cards, including photographs, for the London area, 1876–1991 (though fewer after 1960) can be seen at www.nationalarchives.gov.uk/documentsonline/aliens.asp, where there is an excellent introduction to the subject. The Civil Service Evidence of Age index (1752–1948) provides the origins of applicants for British positions, whether successful or not, if the applicant's birth was not in the GRO indexes (see *FTM* 24.4 Feb 08). The index, housed at the Society of Genealogists, is available at www.findmypast.com. For other immigration websites, see *FTM* 20.1 Nov 03.

If you suspect a birth of having been abroad (as must be the case with 'missing' Jewish birth entries, for example), see if the person appears later in the electoral registers, for aliens could not register to vote until they had been naturalised, for which subject see *NALD* 49. This is not an infallible guide, of course, as so many people have deliberately avoided electoral registration for quite different reasons. 'BS' in a census return normally means that the person has been born abroad but has become a British Subject, but there was no formal ceremony available to applicants for British citizenship until February 2004.

It has always been optional for British citizens (males only until 1983) to register the birth of their legitimate or legitimated children born abroad with a British consul or, from 1950, some High Commissions, which can register illegitimate children also. Registration in the host country may, of course, be compulsory. Certificates of British nationality for children born outside the Empire were introduced by the Naturalisation Act of 1870. The National Archives (an amalgamation of the former Public Record Office and the Historical Manuscripts Commission) contains birth records from about seventy countries in registers listed by Bevan and Duncan (1990), and issues a family fact sheet *Tracing an ancestor who was an immigrant* (see *NALD* 50.) Those births which are registered with a consul are recorded in the Consular Returns and/or the Chaplains' Returns from 1849 or occasionally earlier. There is no time limit for such registrations. They are now in the National Archives, which also houses Miscellaneous Registers of births abroad. Many of them are in the National Archives' digitisation programme, due for completion in 2008. Births at sea, 1854 to 1890, are indexed on the National Archives website. The General Register Office has separate registers and indexes for births and deaths at sea from 1837, in the air from 1948 and, believe it or not, on hovercraft from 1972. As one wit has written, the next problems to solve will be the Channel Tunnel and British-registered spacecraft. The former was the subject of a prediction in *Yes, Prime Minister* (Vol. 2, 'A diplomatic incident'), but fact outstripped fiction when the British dug more than half way across, and the jurisdiction of Dover registration sub-district had to be extended in order to be able to register deaths in what would later become the French half!

The General Register Office will supply certified copies of the entries in these and in consular or High Commission returns for the same fee as normal certificates. See Yeo (1995) and *MRS* 11. Note that indexes to these miscellaneous registers in the General Register Office are now available on microfiche. Failure to have the birth abroad registered in England and Wales can cause some distress later in life – see *FTM* 3.6 Apr 87.

The Department of Trade and Industry is responsible for the General Register of Shipping and Seamen, Cardiff. Its records of births and deaths prior to 1890 have been transferred to the National Archives, and the more modern records are not open to the public. The Registrar General will, however, search his records for the appropriate fee. The GRO Marine Register Book gives births 1837–1930, while the National Archives has the records of births at sea, 1854–91, in a series which is still maintained by the Registrar of Shipping and Seamen. A useful list of these sources for shipping and seamen can be found in the *Journal of the Glamorgan Family History Society*, No. 8 (1985). See *NALD* 61, and Watts & Watts (2004).

Other normal ways to discover the birthplaces of those living in Britain but not born there include consulting the census (pp. 71–91) or military records (pp. 56–60) for the ancestor or his brothers. The 1901 census tends to be more detailed on this subject than its predecessors, and may provide the county, rather than merely the country, in the cases of Ireland and Scotland.

Births to any British citizens while they are in Spain are returned to the General Register Office under a reciprocal agreement since 1963.

There is a list of books and articles in English on the subject of tracing ancestors in some other countries at the end of the references. See *FTM* 16.9 July 00; for immigration websites, see *FTM* 20.1 Nov 03.

Index entry missed by the searcher
Sir Anthony Wagner used a phrase worth remembering on this subject which goes to the heart of the problem – 'An entry missed once is usually missed for ever.'

It happens only to other people, of course, until it happens to you – and it happens to the best. It is unnervingly easy to miss the entry you are seeking, especially if you are not used to searching indexes, or if you have already been at it for an hour or so continuously, or if the handwriting is not the easiest to read, or if the surnames are collected together under initial capital letters but not arranged alphabetically, or if you are researching more than one name at the same time. See also p. 122.

Note which quarter-years of GRO indexes you have already searched. It is quite common to find that someone else is using some of the microfilmed indexes, or website pages you miss, and a few minutes later you can easily forget which ones you have omitted to search unless you have kept a record. It is easy enough to prepare a list of years, with quarter years M, J, S and D against each, which can be ticked only when that index has been searched. This can be especially useful on line, when sometimes a particular quarter is unavailable. Check for handwritten additions at the foot of each page – those below the right hand column are the cause of apparently missing pages in the GRO indexes on Internet sites such as www.ancestry.co.uk.

The indexes are arranged by date of registration, not by the date of the event, and births can be registered up to six weeks after the event. Thus a birth at the end of one year can be indexed in the first quarter of the next. Only recently, events in one year registered in the next have been included in both indexes. If the child was unnamed at the time of registration it will be indexed under the surname only, as 'male' or 'female'; if an entry is subsequently made in column 10 (or space 17), it is reindexed using the correct name. The Registrar General had the power to allow registration up to six months after a birth from 1837 to 1874, up to seven years from 1874 to 1922, and at any time after the birth ever since. If a late registration of an illegitimate child was preceded by a marriage, the mother will be described as 'now the wife of ...'. For conditions laid down see MRS 26.

If an expected birth is not found in the index, try the entries at the end of the relevant section for 'male' or 'female' in the right district. These are children either not expected to live so the parents were reluctant to name them; or, more likely in my view, the parents had not decided on a name at the time of registration. Apply for such a certificate, but give the anticipated parental names to make sure it is the one you are looking for.

Misleading clues
Hearsay from relatives is notorious for providing incorrect information. Officials in register offices will tell you that this is the commonest reason why you may fail to find the entry you are looking for. Any wrong element – surname, forename, date, place – can be leading you into a blind alley, and each should be rechecked if possible. For example, at South Shields in 1868 Edward Arthur married Jane Benton, then aged eighteen. There is, however, no birth certificate for Jane Benton because she was actually called Jane Bentham, born 13 May 1849 in South Shields. Both the birth and the marriage certificates are correctly indexed as the names appear on the respective certificates. An incorrect name may appear for several reasons: perhaps the person was registered under one name but was called, and even baptised, another. In the above case Jane was illiterate and could not check what had been written on the marriage entry. Just as misleading can be to make assumptions about age, for example – one witness to a marriage as young as ten years old is recorded.

Many hours were spent unsuccessfully trying to find the birth in 1857 of William Dearnley until a 1935 obituary was unearthed in Australia, where he had emigrated in 1880: 'When the whirl of business was resumed on Monday morning in Taree, many old friends heard with regret of the death the previous afternoon, about 4.30, of Mr Abel Henry Dearnley, better known for many years on this river as "Bill" Dearnley.' With that clarification the enquirer could be slotted into an existing pedigree with eight previous generations. My own mother was known as Pat throughout her life but was registered as Martha. Variants of forenames are quite common, of

FD 297541

CERTIFIED COPY of an ENTRY
Pursuant to the Births and
Deaths Registration Act 1953

Registration District Chorlton

1914. BIRTHS in the Sub-District of Didsbury in the County of Manchester

No.	Columns:— 1 When and where born	2 Name, if any	3 Sex	4 Name and surname of father	5 Name, surname and maiden surname of mother	6 Occupation of father	7 Signature, description, and residence of informant	8 When registered	9 Signature of registrar	10 Name entered after registration
358	Eleventh April 1914 49 Stevenson Street Longsight South Manchester R.D.	Mary Veronica	Girl	George William Mitchell	Margaret Mitchell formerly Breen	Warehouseman	G.W. Mitchell Father 49 Henry Street Longsight (Printed) Withington	Twenty second May 1914	Twenty fair st Rosser Registrar	—

BAD696289

CERTIFIED COPY OF AN ENTRY
Pursuant to the Births and Deaths Registration Act 1953

DEATH	Entry No. 55
Registration district Manchester	Administrative area Metropolitan District of Manchester
Sub-district Manchester	
1. Date and place of death Sixth April 1998 Fenton House, 2 Higher Ardwick, Ardwick Green	
2. Name and surname Veronica Mary MITCHELL	3. Sex Female
	4. Maiden surname of woman who has married —
5. Date and place of birth 11th April 1914 Manchester	
6. Occupation and usual address Teacher (Retired) Fenton House, 2 Higher Ardwick, Ardwick Green, Manchester	
7.(a) Name and surname of informant Theresa MORRIN	(b) Qualification Occupier
(c) Usual address Fenton House, 2 Higher Ardwick, Ardwick Green, Manchester	
8. Cause of death I.a. Old Age. Certified by DR. K. Sreedharan MBBS	
9. I certify that the particulars given by me above are true to the best of my knowledge and belief T Morrin Signature of informant	
10. Date of registration Seventh April 1998	11. Signature of registrar A P McMahon Registrar

Certified to be a true copy of an entry in a register in my custody.
J McAllister {Deputy *Superintendent Registrar ~~*Registrar~~ Date 13/3/08
*Strike out whichever does not apply

CAUTION: THERE ARE OFFENCES RELATING TO FALSIFYING OR ALTERING A CERTIFICATE AND USING OR POSSESSING A FALSE CERTIFICATE. ©CROWN COPYRIGHT

WARNING: A CERTIFICATE IS NOT EVIDENCE OF IDENTITY.

Figure 1. This lady preferred to use her second forename during her lifetime.

course, and if you are in any doubt about them, consult the *Oxford dictionary of English Christian names* for details. Fred, for example, may be short for Alfred rather than Frederick. See Bardsley (2004) for a much fuller list.

There are many other reasons why you may be looking in the wrong part of the index. If you fail to find the birth entry of a woman whose name you have obtained from the marriage indexes only, bear in mind that she may have been a widow or divorced at the time of marriage. If you are looking in vain for a fairly rare surname, and the index has been retyped, try looking at the adjacent surnames. Perhaps the person you are looking for had two or more forenames, only one of which you are aware of; go through all the first names in the indexes in order to find a possible double-name entry. (I have been told that Welsh people in particular use their second forename for everyday use.) Similarly, a reputed source of error is the reversing of two forenames, so that the registered Mary Veronica Mitchell became Veronica Mary Mitchell (because she hated the name Mary) causing problems of estate distribution following her intestacy in 1998! Again, the last letter of a forename might be erroneously added to the start of the surname for the many people who were not able to check the entries in the nineteenth century. Thus, Philip Richards might have been recorded as Philip Prichards.

Over the years the General Register Office has changed the way it indexes forenames. In the indexes of birth, the following are normally provided:

- 1 July 1837 to 31 December 1865: all forenames in full, but where the original has been transcribed into typed form, there is no guarantee that any other than the first forename will appear in full.
- 1 January 1866 to 31 December 1866: the first forename in full, plus the initials of other forenames.
- 1 January 1867 to 30 June 1910: the first two forenames in full, plus the initials of other forenames.
- 1 July 1910 to 31 December 1965: the first forename in full, plus the initials of other forenames.
- 1 January 1966 to date: the first two forenames in full, plus the initials of other forenames.
- 1 April 1969 to date: Mc and Mac merged.

Some illegitimate brides and grooms have been known to invent a father's name, or to use the name of their stepfather or even their grandfather, to put on their marriage entry, giving a totally misleading clue to identifying their birth.

Normally you will know if the date which you have tried is based on guesswork, for example 'His eldest child was born in 1865, so let's start in 1850 and work backwards to find his birth.' Sometimes, however, a marriage certificate or a census record can suggest a misleading year of birth, though it should not be too far out unless there was a wide disparity in age between the parties – in which case they often made the gap look smaller. Joseph Seigel of Pendleton was three years old in the 1901 census, but his birth was recorded as 30 March 1901, only one day before the census was taken. However, it was registered 42 days later – it looks as though they just avoided the fine for late registration, so he was probably three days, or three weeks old on census night. (His parents were Russian immigrants whose English might have let them down at this point!)

Ages on death certificates are more prone to error, and many military recruits lied about their age when joining up. When elderly widows or widowers die, sometimes leaving the informant to guess the age at death, gross errors may easily creep in. National Health Service records since the Second World War now help to minimise this problem, but people still often supply the wrong year of birth, even though they are correct as regards the day and month. Gravestones can also give the wrong age, because many are erected or inscribed years after the death. It is also easy to misread figures on the gravestone, confusing 1 and 4, 3 and 5, and 6, 9 and 0. Even worse, masons sometimes corrected errors with mortar which has since eroded faster than the stone! 'Twenty-one' on a marriage entry can mean 'over twenty-one', and in general the onus is on all but the youngest couples to tell the truth about their age, without the need to prove it. (Lying about one's age on a census or marriage entry is a well-known source of problems. See an article on the subject in *Anc* 38 Oct 05.) GRO guidance used to be that anyone under the apparent age of twenty-three should provide evidence of date of birth when a marriage was being arranged. Nowadays, all IDs are checked. In a census return, children are described as son or daughter of the head of the household – if this is a man, they are not necessarily the children of his current wife.

See *GM* 22.2 for an article about errors on certificates issued by the GRO in 34 out of 1,330 in the sample. Some might have been misleading but for the keen eye of the author of the article. 'Carry-over' mistakes, in which the writer incorrectly repeats an earlier name on the entry, are not uncommon (see pp. 124–5).

Illegitimate children will normally be indexed only under the surname of the mother unless the father's name appears on the entry, so that, if the child subsequently grew up using the name of the father or of the man the mother married, finding the entry will not be easy. If that has happened, search under the mother's maiden name in the indexes. Ellen, daughter of Joseph and Elizabeth Spruce, was baptised in 1878, but the birth was registered as Ellen, daughter of Joseph Duncalf; Joseph was illegitimate, his mother being Mary Duncalf, who later married George Spruce (*Duncalf Dossier*, 1.7; the *Dossier* is a newsletter issued privately by Anne Cole of Lincoln). The name on the marriage entry of an adopted child will normally be that of the adoptive father, and the fact of adoption will not be indicated. The remedies for all the above problems are obvious, though in some cases it may take a long time to find the correct entry. Try applying for a birth certificate of a known brother or sister; be less willing to believe everything that is written down; seek further evidence to help confirm a doubtful case – for example, find the name of the father and mother first from a census entry before you apply for the child's birth certificate.

In many cases the real date of birth does not correspond with the date on the certificate, the latter being the effective date for the purpose of indexing. The reason is either that the informant, especially if it was the father, could not remember the date or, more likely, that the birth was registered late, outside the six-week time limit allowed, in which case there was a strong temptation to falsify the date of birth. This can cause some distress when, years later, the child reaches pensionable age! There has always been provision for the very late registration of births, up to twelve months after the event by the registrar, afterwards only through the Registrar General. In such a case the phrase 'On the authority of the Registrar General' should appear in the margin. *Whenever you find that phrase on a copy certificate, by the way, you will know that something rather unusual has happened.* (For the official process of late registration, see *MRS* 26.)

Child was adopted
Before 1927 there was no such thing as legal adoption, though the word itself was often used of guardianship or foster-parenthood. Thus Fielding's hero was 'Your adopted son, sir, that Jones' (*Tom Jones*, Book XVII, chapter i), and there were adoption societies formed during the First World War. The status was not automatically recorded and, in theory, there should have been no change of surname from the original birth entry, but some children (sometimes called 'nurse children' in

the eighteenth century and even earlier) were undoubtedly brought up with the surname of their foster parents. For children 'adopted' before 1927 who assumed a new surname, the original parents are usually impossible to trace unless the family has preserved an individual record of the event, or unless it was under the auspices of the Poor Law Union. Thus, when John Turner married in 1939, he gave his father's name as Richard Turner (and was even baptised as such a month earlier); but he had been born as Jack, son of Henry and Ada Jones, in 1910 and misled his family later by telling them that he had been adopted. Luckily, the original birth entry was still in the family's possession, and (not surprisingly with that date of birth) an inspection of the birth entry showed no marginal note indicating adoption.

The Poor Law Guardians were responsible for boarding some children out from 1871. They could be *in loco parentis* from 1889 and could oversee childminding under infant life protection legislation in 1897. For the period before 1927 see also workhouse records (p. 70), the census (pp. 71–91), miscellaneous probate records (p. 258), health records (pp. 65–7) and Currer-Briggs (1979).

Since 1 January 1927 over three-quarters of a million children have been adopted, and for them now or, in turn, their own children there are two main problems – how can anyone tell whether they are adopted, and how can they discover their natural parents? Most parents have the good sense to bring such children up in the knowledge that they are adopted, and the full adoptive certificate, issued by the Registrar General after the court proceedings, shows the date and court of the order, the new name and surname legal from the date of the order, the child's sex, the name, surname, address and occupation of the new parents, and the date and district of birth. Country of birth was introduced in 1950, and the English or Welsh registration district of birth on 1 April 1959. The index to the present day is at Kew, but is also available in digitised form at Smedley Hydro, Southport. Microfiche copies of the index, 1927–2007, may be found in some libraries and record offices. A search is offered by www.ukcertificates.com.

If registrars receive an application for a copy certificate of the original entry, they will first try to establish, as discreetly as possible, whether the fact of adoption is already known by the applicant because it will be shown as a marginal note. They cannot refuse to issue such a certificate, however, so may try to break the news to the applicant before it is issued.

In the absence of this full, adoptive certificate one only sure way to distinguish an adoption is by interpreting the short birth certificate if issued before the 1990s. This will have been issued by the Registrar

General, not by a Superintendent Registrar, and will have an Adopted Children Register reference number, instead of the normal volume and page or, after 1939, National Health Service number. See *MRS* 4. Additionally, until the Adoption Act of 1958 adopted children were sometimes rebaptised as though the adoptive parents were the natural parents. Section 25 of the Act laid down that the entry should be marked 'Adopted son or daughter of ...', but I assume that this applies only to the Church of England because it amends George Rose's Act of 1812.

Almost all legal ties between natural parent and adopted child are severed by this procedure, including (since 1950) rights of succession on intestacy. From 1927 children being adopted, as well as the new parents, had to be both British and resident here; the child had to be under twenty-one years old and those adopting at least twenty-five years old (and normally more than twenty-one years older than the child being adopted). Numbers rose from only 3,000 in 1927 to over 21,000 in 1946, falling again to about 14,000 in the 1950s, then rising to about 25,000 in the 1960s. (Numbers have now fallen dramatically to a few thousand per annum, especially those involving children under 1. *MN* 23 Mar 99). For several genealogists, therefore, it may now be not only themselves or their parents who were adopted but also their grandparents.

Adopted persons unaware of the details of their original birth entry can request the Registrar General to arrange a counselling interview at which the information will be given, as laid down in the Children Act 1975 and subsequent legislation. (This is compulsory for those adopted before 12 November 1975.) A social worker who provides this counselling should try to obtain information to form the basis of advice about the personal problems involved, the circumstance of the adoption, and whether the natural parent has expressed to the Registrar General or social services department a willingness to be approached by the adopted person.

The original birth entry both at the General Register Office and at the Superintendent Registrar's office will have been marked 'Adopted' in the margin if the adoption has taken place in the United Kingdom, the Isle of Man or the Channel Islands, together with the UK country of adoption if different from that of birth, and this will be put on any copy of a full, not short, certificate issued. (Services and consular birth entries are marked in the same way.) The GRO birth index itself will also be marked, though not with the word itself. Only the Registrar General has the complete national index (to which few staff have access) which will connect the adoption certificate with the original birth entry, though the information will be held by an adoption society, the National Health Service, a social services department and, of course, by the court of adoption for a minimum period of time. The courts themselves have been instructed to keep adoption records for seventy-five years.

Adoption societies have had to be registered only since 1943. (For the whereabouts of adoption records, see Stafford, 1993, and *GM* 25.5.) Fuller files giving guardian *ad litem* reports showing the background to the adoption are commonly available only since the Adoption Act of 1958. Earlier agency reports are often missing, however, and some local authority files were reportedly lost during reorganisation in the 1970s. For the work of this section of the General Register Office see *MRS* 4 and *MN* 35 Spring 07.

Making contact with natural parents can then be quite difficult, even when you know their name, because of the long period of time which has elapsed since and the probable subsequent marriage of the mother, 75 per cent of adopted children being originally illegitimate. It is especially difficult if the adoption took place before the substantial social security systems developed after the Second World War. Some knowledge of whether the mother wishes to be approached can be obtained from the Adoption Contact Register, started by the General Register Office in 1991 – your local register office will have the details. Parents and children can apply to be placed on Part A (for a fee of £15.00), other relatives by blood or marriage on Part B (£30.00), and the applicant can now request no contact by specified persons – for example, wishing to contact a sibling but not a parent. The only contact allowed is through the person adopted. By 2001, there were about 20,000 names entered on the first part, and about 8,000 on the second. For background advice on this process, see www.gro.gov.uk/gro/content/adoptions/adoptioncontactregister/ondex.asp, and www.adoptionsearchreunion.org.uk. Changes to the system can be accessed via www.gro.gov.uk.

To contact those adopted, the Adoption and Children Act of 2002 allowed only approved organisations working in an intermediary capacity to apply, on behalf of a client, for the agency and court which had handled the adoption, together with details enabling the adoption entry to be traced. They must establish whether the adopted person wishes to be contacted before bringing them into contact with birth relatives, and there are extra safeguards if the adopted person is still a minor.

Access to an original birth entry, described above, applies only to an adopted child over the age of eighteen. In exceptional circumstances

[Printed by authority of the Registrar General.]

CK 334466

B. Cert.
S.R.

CERTIFIED COPY of an ENTRY OF BIRTH
Pursuant to the Births and Deaths Registration Act 1953

Registration District Manchester.

1843. Birth in the Sub-District of Hulme in the County of Lancaster.

Columns:—	1	2	3	4	5	6	7	8	9	10*
No.	When and where born	Name, if any	Sex	Name, and surname of father	Name, surname and maiden surname of mother	Occupation of father	Signature, description, and residence of informant	When registered	Signature of registrar	Name entered after registration
126	Thirty first of December 1842 at Hulme	Campbell Wood	Boy	Campbell John Pegus	Ellen Rosa Pegus formerly Wood	Retired officer of Marines	Campbell J. Pegus Father 105 Wilmott Street Hulme	Eleventh January 1843	John Rowan Registrar.	George Sydney boy baptism on 11th August 1843

*See note overleaf.

Certified to be a true copy of an entry in a register in my custody.

R. Cook Superintendent Registrar

30 January 1997. Date

CAUTION—It is an offence to falsify a certificate or to make or knowingly use a false certificate or a copy of a false certificate intending it to be accepted as genuine to the prejudice of any person, or to possess a certificate knowing it to be false without lawful authority.

WARNING: THIS CERTIFICATE IS NOT EVIDENCE OF THE IDENTITY OF THE PERSON PRESENTING IT.

Figure 2. Change of name following baptism. Both names should be found in the indexes.

(e.g. a court case) if any other person (e.g. a grandchild) wishes to gain access, application should be made not to the Registrar General but to the original court issuing the adoption order or the High Court for a direction under S. 50.5 of the Adoption Act 1958. (The Act refers also to the Westminster County Court, but this has changed its name and is therefore excluded from the process.) I have been advised that it is unlikely to be granted for genealogical purposes. An application can be made for any person to acquire information from the full file under the current Magistrates' Rules or High Court Rules, according to where the adoption order was first granted. The clerk of the court will ask a magistrate or judge to authorise the release of information, and although it can be refused there have been plenty of successful applications.

Change of name after registration
One of the commonest refuges of the bad amateur is to jump too quickly to the conclusion that an ancestor whose birth entry cannot be found must have changed his or her name during their lifetime. Unless you have some direct evidence that it happened, try some of the other explanations first. It has been popular at certain historical periods – French people living here during the Napoleonic period, for example, or Germans during both world wars.

There are several ways of changing a surname. The most famous, and probably the commonest, is by deed poll, which may be enrolled in the Supreme Court as a permanent record. Deeds poll (from 1999 known as 'Change of Name Deeds') were entered in the close rolls until 1903, but indexed by previous name, with cross-referencing only in later indexes; thereafter they are in the Supreme Court enrolment books (see also Phillimore & Fry, 1905, available on CD). British citizens living in the United Kingdom can change their name by such a deed. (It can even be done online, via www.nedgen.com.) Access to the records is in person at the Filing Department of the Central Office of the Supreme Court. Names have also been changed by Act of Parliament and by royal licence. All these methods record only intent; what really matters is usage, and legally a change of name requires nothing else. For example, a major change of circumstance early in life was the probable cause of Herbert Caldwell Blakeley becoming Herbert Victor Morris, a boxer in the 1930s, and as we all know many do not play on the stage or screen using their original name (see, e.g., Atkinson, 1987; Clarke, 1977; Room, 1981). They are now in good company, as I understand a former Registrar General was not registered with his current forename.

[Printed by authority of the Registrar General.]

CERTIFIED COPY of an ENTRY OF BIRTH

Pursuant to the Births and Deaths Registration Act 1953

Registration District **Manchester.**

1877. Birth in the Sub-district of **Ancoats Manchester** in the **County of Lancaster.**

Columns:—	1	2	3	4	5	6	7	8	9	10*
No.	When and where born	Name, if any	Sex	Name and surname of father	Name, surname and maiden surname of mother	Occupation of father	Signature, description, and residence of informant	When registered	Signature of registrar	Name entered after registration
67	Twenty fifth October 1877 4 am 11 Back Factory Street.	Joseph	Boy	Nicholas BRABAZON	Catherine BRABAZON formerly RONAN	Carter	X The mark of Hannah Ronan Occupier 11 Back Factory Street Manchester	Thirtieth October 1877	William Royston Registrar.	

*See note overleaf.

Certified to be a true copy of an entry in a register in my custody.

R. Clark *Superintendent Registrar*

3rd January 1997 */ Date*

CAUTION—It is an offence to falsify a certificate or to make or knowingly use a false certificate or a copy of a false certificate intending it to be accepted as genuine to the prejudice of any person, or to possess a certificate knowing it to be false without lawful authority.

WARNING: THIS CERTIFICATE IS NOT EVIDENCE OF THE IDENTITY OF THE PERSON PRESENTING IT.

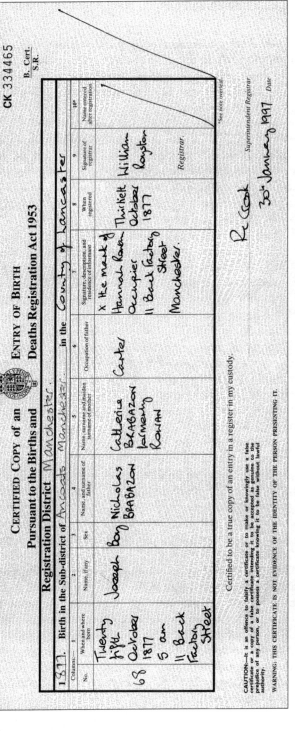

Figure 3. Twins with the same name. If it was a registration error Joseph's brother will not be found in the indexes.

Since 1961 Anglican registers can be annotated following the reregistration of the child. If you simply start using a new name, with no intention to defraud, then you have legally changed your name. See *NALL* 32, and Josling (1985). Palmer's indexes to *The Times* include a section on 'Changes of surnames'.

People who want to change their name have commonly announced their intention in local newspapers, or in the *London Gazette*. However, documentary evidence of the change is required for certain official purposes and it may be that this is the easiest way to discover the fact – for example, through passport or bank records. Many people will have obtained their evidence by swearing a declaration before a JP or commissioner of oaths.

Some lawyers believe that a Christian name given in baptism cannot be changed, only added to in the way that Churchill added 'Spencer' to 'Winston Leonard'. In the debate leading to civil registration in 1837 the Church claimed that a child should be named only through baptism, and that therefore the state registration service should not do so. However, all this has not prevented people from changing forenames. The Church of England gives the right to change the baptised name at the time of confirmation, and the Roman Catholic Church allows additional names to be given to the original baptismal name; see Burn (1824). Records of confirmation, by the way, tend to be modern – i.e. twentieth-century – but the *Herefordshire Family History Society Journal* 2.10 (1985) has some interesting examples from Llanwarne in the 1830s, including many adults; the ages ranged from sixteen to sixty! We have also seen that it is possible to change the forename on a birth certificate up to twelve months after the birth has been registered by using column 10 of the old certificate (space 17 since 1 April 1969). The entry is then reindexed. However, as few people know about this procedure it is not often used, and the surname, indicated in the entry only since 1969, cannot be changed anyway. It is not uncommon for the name given at baptism to be different from that on a birth entry.

Indeed, the only restriction on changing a forename through column 10 of the birth certificate is where the child has been baptised with the name with which it was originally registered. This facility was introduced in 1837, the General Register Office warning parents that such a change of name following baptism would involve 'trouble and expence'. In this respect the Births and Deaths Registration Act of 1953, section 13.1, provides an unusual incursion of religious ritual into a civil process. It is therefore not in the interest of parents who may wish to change the registered name of their child either to baptise it or to admit to having done so. In the same way, children known to have been baptised before adoption should not be rebaptised later.

If the child was given a name after the initial registration, and the registrar was not informed, the GRO indexes will include the child simply as 'male' or 'female' at the end of the list of the relevant surnames; see also p. 28.

Another means of confirming a change of name is by using the marriage entry, which often has the phrase 'formerly known as ...'; see p. 26.

Finding more than one possible birth

When I applied for the birth certificate of Sarah Hargreaves, my grandmother, born in 1858, the Superintendent Registrar replied that she could not help because two girls with the same name had been born in the same district within a couple of days of each other. (Being in bed with Sarah is my earliest memory, so finding the right one was quite important!) If I had not known the registration district in advance, this problem could have been magnified several times in the GRO indexes. Our current National Insurance records include over 6,000 people called John Smith!

In such cases – and they are very common indeed – it is essential to have more information than the name, year and place of birth. If the child's birthday can be discovered, for example, from an education, hospital or workhouse record, or from a gravestone, it will usually solve the problem, but not always.

Identification may be facilitated if you can supply the Superintendent Registrar with the signature of the probable informant from, for example, a will or marriage entry.

If the child's father or mother can be named in advance – for example, from the census or a marriage certificate – this will also help the registrar to identify the correct one – though it is often just to obtain that information that you are asking for the certificate in the first place! Knowing the child's later occupation can occasionally help, especially in trades, such as that of blacksmith, which tended to be passed from father to son – but this can never be conclusive in itself.

An exact address also helps. Although impossible to get for many country areas in the last century, it is perfectly possible for towns (see pp. 77–85). If an informant was found to have given the wrong address (in order to avoid having the child vaccinated after 1853, for example), a new entry might be created and the old one struck through as an error. Both will appear as normal in the GRO indexes, but it is not permitted to issue copy certificates of entries struck through, for whatever reason, because officially such entries do not exist.

The formal process of reregistration since 1927 will give the same child two entries in the indexes (see p. 29), sometimes many years apart. A copy certificate may be issued from the first entry, and should contain a marginal note indicating the fact.

The General Register Office and Superintendent Registrars may verify a correct entry if you supply enough information to make identification possible from among several index entries; the fee is £3.00 per entry. An illegitimate child will be indexed under both surnames before 1 April 1969 if the father's name appears on the entry. In modern times, an event at the end of one year but registered in the next will be in both GRO indexes, making it look like two events.

Negative evidence may be very useful in eliminating one of the possible births, and that is sometimes easier to obtain than positive evidence in favour of the correct one. For example, infant mortality remained high throughout the nineteenth century. Perhaps you can show that one of the two possible children died young.

It should also be added that, until 1929, when boards of guardians were abolished, registrars were paid by the number of entries made, and in the early years of the system, when they were paid 2s. 6d. for the first twenty entries in each year and 1s. thereafter, there were a number of scandals – at South Shields and Marylebone, for example – in which the same entries appeared, and were presumably indexed, more than once. Other entries proved to be fictional – see MRS 12 and GM 25.7. (Anyone interested in the history of financing the system should see MRS 10.) In other instances from 1839 to the 1950s, parents could claim the 'King's Bounty', a payment of one guinea for each child of a multiple birth above two, but some invented births which had not in fact occurred! (See MN 15 Winter 92.) Another unfortunate consequence was an unseemly dispute between two registrars wishing to record births in Buckingham Palace, which straddled their two areas (Anc 43 Mar 06).

If your problems cannot be solved by any of the methods described here, you will need to use the alternative strategies described in the next section.

Indexes or certificates not accessible: alternative sources

Perhaps you cannot find an entry in the indexes; perhaps you can find too many. Perhaps, even, the General Register Office cannot find the entry if the district has been incorrectly copied or coded during the indexing process. Perhaps, alas, you find a local registrar uncooperative.

In some ways registrars could be a law unto themselves because, until recently they have had no legal employer though they are paid by local authorities. In practice, however, their actions are controlled rigorously by the Registrar General's office, and since 1844 have been supervised by an inspectorate created to put a stop to various irregularities which he himself had uncovered, and which had led to dismissals early in the system. (For the background see *MRS* 4 and 5, repeated in *MN* 4 Jun 87. Since the introduction of RON, the traditional inspections have been abandoned.) On the whole registrars carry out their duties in a most conscientious and professional manner. However, Superintendent Registrars have been known to refuse access to their indexes, saying simply that the public has no right to use them. If this happens to you, ask the Superintendent Registrar to refer to the current *Handbook for registration officers*, s. 31(2) of the Births & Deaths Registration Act (1953) and s. 64 of the Marriages Act (1949). In the unlikely event that you have further trouble you should complain to the Registrar General.

It is worth mentioning at this point that genealogists can help to make life easier for themselves, as well as for the registration service, by taking certain precautions. Some of the smaller register offices are staffed on a part-time basis – by solicitors, for example – and are not open during the whole of normal working hours. Nowadays, however, these part-time registrars are not being replaced when they retire, and their districts are being merged with other registration districts. It is also worth remembering that even Birmingham, the largest of the register offices, will not welcome genealogical searchers on a Saturday, because so many staff are busy conducting marriages on that day (more people now marry in register offices than in churches) or on a Monday, when a large number of weekend births and deaths have to be registered. Try to avoid lunchtimes if possible, when a reduced staff have to deal with more than the normal number of clients. Ideally, confirm the hours of opening and let the office know in advance which indexes you wish to search. Do not write to a registrar by name, except via the Superintendent Registrar 'for the attention of ...' And, to establish at least minimum credibility, don't call it a 'registry' office! (See p. 20)

Most of the current trends in genealogy are making the hobby easier and cheaper, as more records are now open to the public, and more entries are being computerised. Historians are increasingly interested in demography and more and more people from all walks of life are becoming anxious to trace their ancestors. However, the rising charges of the Registrar General are running counter to these other trends, and the cost of certificates makes the period from 1837 the most expensive to research out of the last four centuries. Fees may seem high for copies of documents, but Bill Davies's article on what it is like to be a searcher in the GRO entry books (*MRS* 14) may go some way to counter that feeling. Some genealogists are already finding it hard to raise the cost of several certificates and have to find cheaper ways of obtaining the same information. While the current Registrar General's fee policy lasts, postal requests to the General Register Office by those without access to the Internet must be minimised – but that means many unnecessary letters to Superintendent Registrars, letters which are frequently unprofitable to both parties. Sources which cut costs include church registers, the census, gravestones and wills. All these are dealt with later in this volume, but many other sources make identification of age and place of birth easier, and can even replace the birth certificates altogether. These sources are discussed below.

Marriage and death certificates

Marriage certificates give the age at marriage and the name of the father for both bride and groom. Roman Catholic marriage records, indeed, can sometimes provide the maiden names of the mothers. Death certificates give the approximate age at death until 1 April 1969, since when exact date and place of birth should be entered, together with the maiden surname of a married woman. Both types of certificate therefore provide a basis for calculating the year of birth. This calculation should be repeated from the burial record and should not necessarily be taken at face value. A marriage entry in a local newspaper may also provide parents' names and addresses. So will an entry announcing a birth. For further discussion of marriage and death certificates see pp. 164–80 and 209–16.

Note that when these events take place in some other countries, such as Scotland, Australia or the United States, perhaps to a sibling who has emigrated, more detail about parents is entered than can be found in England and Wales.

Records of the armed forces

The size, political status and mobility of the British armed forces have created a separate world of documentary sources. Almost all those with public access are in London, either in the General Register Office or in the National Archives, and date from before 1920. Those between 1914 and 1920 not damaged by enemy action during the Second World War are slowly being transferred by the Ministry of Defence. (See Rogers, 1986, for more modern records, but there have been changes of address since that publication. For example, modern Ministry of Defence army records are at the Army Personnel Centre, Historical Disclosures, Mail Point 400, Kentigern House, 64 Brown Street, Glasgow G2 4TX.) Those presented below are only the tip of a documentary iceberg available about individuals. A number of writers have detailed these sources with a genealogical eye – see in particular Bevan & Duncan (1990), Colwell (1992), Fowler (2003, 2006), Gardner & Smith (1959, II), Herber (2005, chapter 19), Holding (1991 a-d), Rodger (1998), Watts & Watts (1995), and Wilson (1991); see also *FTM* 21.3 Jan 05. The National Archives publishes Family Fact Sheets on tracing military ancestors, and a series of information leaflets, including No. 2 (*Admiralty records as sources for biography and genealogy*), No. 13 (*Air records as sources for biography and genealogy*), No. 59 (*British army records as sources for biography and genealogy*), No. 74 (*Royal Marines records in the National Archives*), and Nos 123 and 125, covering pensions of all three services. (Texts of these and the National Archives' Family Fact Sheets on tracing military ancestors can be seen on the Internet, together with information on the National Archives' research service – see Preface.) Records of civilian employees of the MOD are also archived – see *FTM* 19.5 Mar 03 and 20.3 Jan 04.

There are some military records, including a medal search facility, available online at www.DocumentsOnline.nationalarchives.gov.uk, and pension records from the First World War have been made available at the pay site www.ancestry.co.uk.

The discovery of parentage can be assisted by a number of different records, arranged until modern times according to the service concerned. Those in the General Register Office are available on microfiche in some local libraries.

Army. There are three series of records of births to army personnel in the General Register Office, separate from the main civilian series. One runs from 1761 to 1987; another, based on regimental records, from 1761 to 1924 (see *Anc* 53 Jan 07). The index to the former gives name, place, year and regiment. The third series, compiled by chaplains from 1796 to 1880, includes baptisms also, and is solely for events overseas – it continues as Army Returns from 1881 to 1965, since when they have been in the general UK High Commission returns of births abroad. The cost of GRO certificated copies is the same as for civilian entries. All other army documents named below are in the National Archives.

The names of the parents of soldiers are included in relatively few documents – notably when entered as next of kin in the post-1882 discharge documents, or in casualty papers (1797–1910), arranged by regiment.

The names of children (of officers only) can be found in widows' pension applications (1755–1908) and compassionate payments (from 1773) when dependants were involved. Children of other ranks can be found in Soldiers' Documents, but from 1883 only. They can sometimes be found entered in army marriage registers (see p. 182), or in muster and pay books (1868–83) if the children were in married quarters.

For officers, see FTM 23.2 Dec 06, 23.8 Jun 07 and 23.9 Jul 07. Baptisms of officers, with index, are available for 1755–1908. The baptisms of soldiers' children can be found in a few regimental registers (largely nineteenth- and twentieth-century, but from 1691 for the Royal Chelsea Hospital).

Records of First World War soldiers are being put on line – see FTM 23.9 Jul 07 and 24.1 Nov 07 for a good introduction. Soldiers' birthplaces are given in description books and casualty lists (1809–57). The Casualty Returns 1797–1910 give place of birth and next of kin, and include deserters (1809–1910). Place of birth can also be obtained for any ancestor who died in the First World War from the War Office publications, *Officers died in the Great War* and *Soldiers died in the Great War* (see p. 234). Details of the age and birthplace of other ranks are normally found through the records of the Royal Chelsea Hospital Soldiers' Documents (1760–1913), arranged by date of pension. They are alphabetical only from 1883; for the previous ten years they are in the four main corps, but before 1873 they are by regiment. They are also in muster and pay books and description books. The Chelsea Pensioners series, 1760–1915 is part of the National Archives' digitisation programme, due for completion in 2009.

Thus, for other ranks, locating the regiment is very important. See Kitzmiller (1988) for the means of doing so and Swinson (1972) for the history of individual regiments and their amalgamations. A website, giving dates of regiments since lost or amalgamated, is at www.regiments.org. Swinnerton (*FTM* 17.1 Nov 00, 17.5 Mar 01, 17.8 Jun 01, 17.10 Aug 01, 17.12 Oct 01, 18.1–7 Nov 01-May 02 and 18.9 Jul 02) has a series of articles on this subject. Briefly, the regiment of a soldier can be found in GRO birth, marriage or death certificates, a pension payment (1842–83, though most end in 1862), the records of dead soldiers' effects (1810–81) and the absent voters' lists of 1918–19 which also give the army number. (These are normally found in the main series of electoral registers for those years.) If it is known where a soldier was stationed it is possible to find the regiment in the Monthly

Station Returns for the British Army in the *United Services Magazine* (*Journal*) from 1829 to the 1870s. Deserters (see above) are described physically in *Hue and Cry* from 1773 which became the *Police Gazette* in 1827 where their birthplace and regiment are given.

Royal Air Force. The General Register Office has a separate register of births abroad to RAF personnel, 1920 to 1965, the index to the final years (name, station and year) being merged with that for the other armed forces; from 1965 they are in the general UK High Commission returns of births abroad. See *GM* 27.5 for the records of First World War airmen.

Indexes to RAF and WAAF personnel are being compiled; see *FTM* 5.6 Apr 89 and Wilson (1991).

Royal Navy. Births to Royal Navy personnel abroad are in the Marine Register Book from 1 July 1837 (which includes both merchant and naval ships), and in the Services Register in the General Register Office from 1956; from 1965 they are in the general UK High Commission returns of births abroad. Most Royal Navy records, however, are in the National Archives, including the Compassionate Fund papers 1809–1921, which contain reference to children of officers killed in action. Children of Royal Navy personnel could attend the Royal Hospital School, Greenwich, which has registers from 1728 to 1883. See *FTM* 20.12 Oct 04 for Internet sources for the Royal Navy. The Navy List, 1793–1815 is on CD-ROM.

Baptismal certificates for some new officers are available from around the mid-eighteenth to the mid-nineteenth centuries, and for ships' masters from 1691 to 1832 in their passing certificates. The ages of prospective lieutenants are available for 1795–1832; dates of birth are in the series of surveys of naval officers between 1816 and 1859.

The names of parents of officers and ratings are in their post-1853 service registers (which are indexed) together with age, place of birth and parental consent if joining as a minor; those after 1891 are still with the Ministry of Defence, however. Pre-1914 disablement files on some ratings provide marital and parental status, age, birthplace, names of parents and siblings, and religion. The age and place of birth of ratings from 1764 to 1877 are in ships' musters, so you will need to know which ship an ancestor served on; one way to find out, if it is not in the family's own record, is by using the pay books of each, which are indexed. Much quicker is the use of Greenwich Hospital pension records from 1704 (with earlier pension lists from 1675); some include baptismal certificates.

There is an article about Royal Navy ancestors in *Anc* 38 Oct 05.

Records of the mercantile marine

From 1835 to 1857 and again from 1913 to 1972, the government maintained a register of seamen in case they might be needed in time of war – a useful replacement for the earlier press-gang system. The records are in the National Archives. Crew lists 1863–1913 are available on CD.

Merchant Navy records supply the date and place of birth or baptism, but most from before the nineteenth century have been lost. The date and place of birth of all seamen, 1844–56, for example, are in the National Archives, which has digitised seamen's wills from 1786 to 1882. The records of merchant seamen, 1840–44, can be seen at the paysite www.theoriginalrecord.com. Trinity House petitions, submitted by distressed sailors or their widows, are now in the library of the Society of Genealogists; see *FTM* 19.2 Dec 02, *FHM* 100 Jan 04, and *Anc* 41 Jan 06. See also Herber (2005, chapter 20), Watts & Watts (2004) and, for fishermen, *FTM* 5.8 Jun 89; see PRO Records Information Leaflet No. 5 (and *MN* 10 Summer 90) for the records of the Registrar General of Shipping and Seamen, and No. 8 for HM Coastguards. Internet sites are outlined in *FTM* 20.6 Apr 04.

Education records

Most of our ancestors in the last 100 years attended elementary schools, the pre-1944 forerunners of primary schools. These go back for well over 400 years, but it is rare to find any records surviving from before the nineteenth century. One set which is now in the Cheshire County Record Office is for a charity school called Seamon's Moss, near Altrincham. It illustrates the type of information which such records may contain. In addition to the normal trustees' minute books, which rarely name children or parents, there is a detailed school register which gives the names of children and parents, ages, dates of admission, periods of absence and even reasons for absence. My favourite entry is for ten-year-old George, son of George Podmore of Dunham Massey, who in 1788 'informed me that his mother had leave ... for him to absent from school 3 weeks to take care of the family while his mother assisted Mr Carter to make hay. But they took 10 days more. NB This Account being false.' Poor little George then disappears from the register.

Such registers are the source of most genealogy using school records, and Anthony Camp (1978, p. 37) gave examples of tracing several generations using only this source.

From the middle of the nineteenth century, the survival rate of educational records increases so considerably that a proposed Gibson Guide on the subject had to be abandoned because of the amount of documentation in record offices. From 1833, the state gave Church schools substantial financial aid, and voices were raised in Parliament in the 1850s calling for increased accountability to go with such grants. From 1862, therefore, schools receiving state aid were made subject to a 'payment by results' system, which was designed to make education either cheaper or more efficient. This system is now anathema to the teaching profession, but it opened up an Aladdin's cave for the genealogist. Because it became far more important than before to keep accurate records – after all, the teacher's salary now partly depended on them – registers began to include the names and addresses of children and parents and the children's dates of birth.

Since 1880 local authorities have had a duty to ensure that children in their area are being suitably educated. Some have done so since 1870. The 1876 Act allowed authorities to establish a database for this task by requesting information for all births in the area from the registrar. Stockport Public Library has a good run of these lists from 1880 to 1948 with gaps, containing for every child born in Stockport name, date of birth, address and parental names and occupations. See *GM* 21.6.

Unfortunately, local education authorities no longer seem to acquire this information, with the result that none which I have consulted is able to say with certainty which children in its area are of school age, or pre-school age; unless neighbours inform the local education authority that children are not attending school, there seems to be no way of ensuring that all children are being educated. Legislation remains in force, however, by which the education authorities are entitled to receive information about births (and indeed deaths) in their area.

Even if the school register has not survived, you should ask to see the school log book which was and still is kept by the head teacher to record the curriculum and any unusual day-to-day events. A very large proportion of a school's population can sometimes be found in these log books. I have looked through those for where my mother went to school at the turn of the century, and found her brothers and sisters winning prizes, being naughty, being late, ill with smallpox, off school for the potato picking and many of those other activities which will take you back to your own childhood. In the log book, or sometimes in a separate register, you may also find punishments, which will give the name of the offender, the nature of the offence and the punishment inflicted.

Very few of these documents have ever been published, so finding the originals is essential if you wish to consult them. The first problem to overcome is that very few records, outside the educational institutions themselves, will tell you which schools your ancestors attended. Contemporary town or county directories (see p. 80) will tell you which schools existed close to where they lived. If it was in a rural area, it is probable that there was only one school within reach – almost certainly Anglican. The real problem comes in the towns and cities, where there may have been several schools within walking distance (or the safest walking distance) of the child's home. He or she might have attended the nearest, the nearest of one particular denomination, or the cheapest – the established Church complained that Protestants were sending their children to Catholic schools because their fees were the lowest. Perhaps the child continued to attend a more distant school in an area from which the family had moved; perhaps he or she did not attend school at all.

On the question of school attendance, I have doubts about relying on the word 'scholar' when used of a child in the census. Since 1851 the censuses have recorded at least minimum information about schooling. Enumerators were asked to record which children were educated daily at school. In the 1851 census this was limited to children over five, those being tutored at home being designated separately. However, I believe that you should not automatically assume that 'scholar' meant that a child was certainly on a school register, or even formally educated at home; correspondingly, I am sure that some of those who were not described as scholars were actually at school. The 1851 urban census returns for scholars are higher than the contemporary, and separate, school census of 1851 would suggest, though I must confess that the census officials themselves thought that the number of real scholars was underrepresented (see Wrigley, 1972, chapter 9, and Higgs, 1989, chapter 11).

Perhaps part of the explanation lies in Sunday schools. Between 1780 and 1880 the only form of education for many children was in a Sunday school, which at that time taught the fundamentals of reading and writing as well as religion. This was particularly true for those young children who were at work during the rest of the week. Some of the Sunday schools in urban areas were remarkably large. For instance, the one in Stockport catered for over 3,000 children. Its registers, running from 1780 to 1920, provide names, ages, dates of admission, class, educational attainment and date of leaving. Other Sunday school registers such as those of Tintwistle, now in Derbyshire, also provide parents' names.

Records of all types of elementary school, of whatever denomination, have sometimes found their way into county record offices. Many schools, as well as those of the Church of England, could survive the nineteenth century only with such substantial state aid that they had to be taken over by the local education authorities. Their records, together with those of the councils' own schools, are now normally kept in the local education authority archives. These, in turn, are often to be found in the local library or archive office. Many other schools have never centralised their records, especially the log books. In this situation an approach should be made direct to the head teacher or, if it is a Church school, the local clergyman. There is no charge for consulting school records, but nor does the public have any right to do so. In my experience, head teachers are only too pleased that someone is taking an interest in their old records, and will deny access only to the most recent of them – certainly to those compiled within the last generation. Record offices, however, may operate restrictions of up to fifty years on access to deposited school records.

Thus there is no easy way to locate the records of individual schools, and advice should be obtained from the county archivist, the local education offices or the schools section of the religious denomination concerned. There has been a welcome call for the compulsory deposit of all log books into county record offices (*Local Historian* 18.1). The search is well worth the effort, as the log books in particular provide the most fascinating insights into the social and educational attitudes of the time, as well as putting some flesh on the bones of your family tree.

Until the twentieth century, separate institutions for older children consisted almost entirely of grammar and public schools, though it should be remembered that, even until 1944, most children spent their entire school career in elementary schools. Grammar schools existed in surprisingly large numbers as early as the seventeenth century, when most market towns possessed one. Strangely enough, their records are not as illuminating as those of the post-1862 elementary schools. However, the grammar schools run by local education authorities since 1902 have log books and there are usually trustees' or governors' minute books, and often the register. Only the last need normally be consulted by the genealogist.

A number of grammar and public school registers have been published. County lists are available in articles in the *British Journal of Educational Studies* (Wallis, 1965, 1966); see also Jacobs (1964). These list only the published registers; others are to be found either in the schools themselves, in education offices or the county record office. The published versions often have the double advantage of having editorial annotations about the child's family or subsequent career, as well as an alphabetical index, but published so-called 'registers' from before the eighteenth century are sometimes misleading because they include only those pupils who went to university; you should check in the introduction whether this is the case.

Over the centuries, grammar schools tended to generate many other records which can be used by the genealogist. For example, petitions to trustees or to those who had the right to appoint the teachers sometimes provide long lists of local residents. Eighty inhabitants of Farnworth near Widnes complained in 1631 that the teachers – 'old Weaknes', Francis Hawarden, the headmaster, and 'yong Idlenes', Robert Williams, his assistant – had turned the springtime of their school into an autumn – 'the little plants wee send there are no sooner budded but blasted'; see pp. 108–16 for the genealogical use of such records.

University records are the easiest of all education records to use, but it is only in very modern times that even 10 per cent of the population has attended. When, in addition, you remember that the only universities in England and Wales before the 1820s were Oxford and Cambridge, your reaction may well be that none of your forebears will be found there. However, for a number of social and religious reasons these two universities expanded the number of undergraduates dramatically in Elizabethan times so that, by the early seventeenth century, a greater proportion of children were attending university than at any time before the 1950s. There was a marked decline after the middle of the seventeenth century. A large number of families will therefore find at least one of their ancestors in the Oxbridge records, and the search is so easy that it is well worth the effort. This might even include a marriage in a college chapel – see *FTM* 16.7 May 00.

Foster (1891–) and Venn (1922–27) contain the known students at Oxford and Cambridge, arranged in alphabetical order. Foster is not as full, or as accurate, as Venn, but, using the two works, you can hope to obtain the names of the students, their parents, their home town, their age, where they went to school and even the names of their schoolteachers, as well as editorial information about their subsequent careers. These registers should be found in large municipal libraries. Starting with London in 1828, and Durham in 1836, other cities in Britain developed universities, often based on earlier technical colleges; their registers have been published until relatively modern times (see Jacobs, 1964). You can contact the registrar of the university concerned with a specific enquiry. Some of the directories referred to on pp. 81–2 provide clues concerning which university your ancestor attended.

Many institutions other than universities have catered for post-school education or training. Catholic children, for example, were often sent to colleges on the Continent, and their 'Responsa', or replies to the admissions questionnaire, have been published by the Catholic Record Society. Puritans and Dissenters sometimes sent their children to Scottish, Irish or even Dutch universities, which also have published their registers, or, after 1662, to the growing number of dissenting academies. The students of the earliest, Rathmell in Yorkshire, are listed in Oliver Heywood's diary (see Turner, 1881–85), but few other registers have survived. The Glasgow University register 1727–1897 is also available on microfiche and disk. Records of eighteenth- and nineteenth-century colleges, such as Owen's in Manchester and Manchester College, York, are kept by the universities of which they later became a part. Military and naval colleges have similar records, but these must normally be consulted in the National Archives or in the colleges themselves.

For further reading on educational records, see Chapman (1991), FHM 23.7 May 07, and (for teachers) FTM 24.3 Jan 08. The National Archives has a series of leaflets on educational records – start with NALD 119.

Health records

Records of birth in each area are collated from general practice, hospital, clinic and midwives' reports, births notified to the district medical officer within three days and the lists of births sent to the relevant superintendent registrar of births. In turn, the civil registration system has, since the Public Health Act of 1936, informed health authorities of births being registered. Both the registrar and the health authority are then in a position to chase up events which appear in only one list – discrepancies can lead to those failing to register a birth being discovered and, occasionally, to baby snatchers and abandoners being identified.

Meanwhile the health visitors maintain a file on each individual, starting with their copy of the notification of birth. The most thorough health authorities record parental occupations, previous confinements of the mother, the social conditions under which the children are being raised, the subsequent medical records of the children at the formal stages of vaccination and pre-school examination, the schools attended and all the addresses at which that individual lives until the age of twenty-five. At that point, however, the file ends and will be destroyed, which is a great pity from the point of view of our historically-minded descendants. The public has no right of access to these files except via a court order. As this record will also state whether a child has been adopted – though probably the original name will have been erased – it may be possible for an individual to discover the fact of his or her own adoption on personal application to the district health authority concerned.

Incidentally, general practitioner National Health Service patient records are the property of the Department of Health and are centralised and destroyed three years after the patient dies. An individual practice, however, may decide to keep computerised records longer.

If the child you are tracing was born in hospital, there will be yet another record of the event in the hospital's own archives. Hospitals usually keep their own records, but an increasing number are now being persuaded to deposit them in a local authority archive office. Even when this is done, the records are not open to public inspection until they are 100 years old, health professionals being obsessively paranoid even about records of the deceased. There is a Hospital Records Project computer database – London entries are listed in *GM* 24.3, and *FTM* 19.12 Oct 03 has details of hospital records on the Internet.

We are all aware of the existence of the National Health Service records above, because they are the tip of the iceberg visible to patients. The heart of the NHS record system is its Central Register (NHSCR), which contains a record of all individuals from birth to death, distinguishing each by a reference number which will be found on their medical card. It is kept at the Smedley Hydro in Southport, requisitioned during the Second World War as safer than London, and still retained by the Crown! The NHS number started as a security identification number allocated as a result of the enumeration of the United Kingdom on 29 September 1939 – see Appendix 3. From 1939 all those registered at birth, and all immigrants registering with an NHS doctor, have been issued with such a number, which has been added to the Central Register copy of the national birth indexes since 1966. Access to this system is strictly limited for a few legitimate purposes within the NHS, and for the most dire emergencies – of which genealogy is not one, however obsessive about it you may have become. It is mainly used for the calculation of doctors' pay, but it is also involved with the provision of new identities, movement in and out of prison and the armed forces, research (especially into cancer), and a variety of authorised social events. As the deceased are not removed from the system, it is the largest database of individuals in the country, but it appears to be little-used by the NHS to confirm, for example, patient entitlement to dental treatment. Since 1 April

2008, the NHSCR is part of the NHS Information Centre – see www. ic.nhs.uk.

As the old NHS number can no longer be used for fraudulent purposes, I see no reason why former practice cannot be revived, and you should ask for the old NHS number when applying for a short birth certificate for anyone born between 1939 and 1995 – one day it will be useful to have in your file. All genealogists should record the old pre-1995 NHS numbers, for one day they will give a direct reference to their place in GRO indexes and the 1939 National Register.

For all the above, see Rogers (1986), though since then an all-digit computerised system has been introduced which has given us all a new number, starting with the newly born on 4 December 1995 and now allocated by maternity departments in the NHS instead of the registration service, with the result that the number is no longer a direct link to the registration of birth (see *MN* 35 Winter 06/07). I have to say, however, that although 470 699 1528 is more efficient, the old equivalent (NWRP228/3) has lost its soul.

Meanwhile it is anticipated that the NHSCR will remain in Southport, following its transfer to the new NHS Information Centre for Health and Social Care on 1 April 2008. The GRO will also remain in Smedley Hydro for the foreseeable future.

Pension and insurance records

Place and date of birth should be obtainable from pension records, both public and private, because every individual claiming a pension will, at some stage, have had to prove his or her age with his or her own birth certificate. Indeed, in the early days of the state's old age pension scheme, which started in 1908, some applicants had been born before birth began to be recorded in 1837 and were therefore required to produce a certificate of baptism. Years ago, one of my students learned when and where her great-grandfather had been born by this method, but only a small minority of early pension records has survived. On the other hand, war pension records of the MOD occupy 42 miles of shelving!

However, please note that the Benefits Agency has informed me that it will no longer pass on to any living person in the United Kingdom a letter of enquiry about the family as described in Rogers (1986). (The change of policy was a result of the increased volume of demand.)

Some textbooks recommend consulting private insurance records, which are still largely in the hands of the insurance companies themselves. However, unless you already know with which firm your ancestor was insured such a search is probably not worth the effort needed to locate the records. There is some guidance in articles in the *Journal of the Chartered Insurance Institute*, and indexes to some early policies are now available; see *Local Historian* 17.4, *FTM* 19.6 Apr 03, *FHM* 122 Oct 05 and *Anc* 37 Oct 05.

Affiliation orders

One of the most annoying situations for a genealogist is to see your friends galloping back to the eighteenth century while you have been saddled with a modern bastard – often a genealogical non-starter. If the father of an illegitimate child is not named on the birth entry, his name and changes of address can sometimes be obtained from bastardy files resulting from the Poor Law Amendment Act of 1844, which introduced the concept of maintenance for single women and widows into statute law. There was further legislation in 1872 and 1914, when the term 'affiliation order' was adopted. Magistrates' courts could grant such an order at the request of the mother, the legal guardian or the Poor Law Guardians if the child had become chargeable. The orders should have been copied to the Clerk of the Peace, and thence to the Home Office. Some lists, 1844 to 1859, are in county record offices. Guardians' records should be consulted, therefore, if the court affiliation orders are not available. Application had to be made within a specified time after the birth (one year at first, later increased to three years) and maintenance could be awarded while the child was of school age. At the turn of the century under a quarter of the fathers of illegitimate children were successfully taken to court, but this figure fell below one in ten after the Second World War (Rose, 1986). The father's changes of address during the period of maintenance should have been recorded, which is very important from the point of view of one day finding him in a census.

Affiliation order files are not open to the general public, but that should not prevent you from enquiring. They are kept in the archives of the magistrates' courts, or handed over to a local archive repository, normally in the area where the mother lived at the time, and you should make a formal approach to the Clerk to the Justices to have them inspected. What you may be asking for, however, is a long search through dirty piles of documents in a remote part of the court buildings by hard-pressed staff who have no statutory duty to oblige you!

Trade union and friendly society records

Documents about individual members of trade unions rarely survive from before the mid-nineteenth century. The most useful are apprenticeship and membership registers. The former provide the boys' signed declarations and their addresses; the latter are more useful, as they provide names, addresses, ages and marital status. More rarely you may find names, addresses and numbers of dependent children in the records of benefit paid during strikes or short-time working; you may also pick up the names of many of the more active members from the minute books.

Locating trade union records is not straightforward, however. Many of the smaller unions have been amalgamated into larger organisations, some of which are not necessarily familiar with their separate individual histories. A list of these smaller unions, together with the names and addresses of head and district offices of the larger ones into which they have been amalgamated, has been published in Eaton & Gill (1981). The local city or county record office will advise whether the records of individual union branches have been deposited with them; it is most likely to have happened in areas where there are active local projects which encourage such a transfer, for example in the Calder Valley, Coventry, Manchester and Newcastle, where calendars of deposited records are being compiled. A pamphlet, *Trade union and related records* (1981), published by the University of Warwick, and an index to material about trade union records in the *Bulletin of the Society for the Study of Labour History* are also useful. See also Trough (1990). It is unlikely that there will be more than a thirty-year restriction rule on access to deposited trade union records, and probably there will be no restriction at all. The University of Warwick library has a modern record centre with some research space, and will answer postal enquiries.

If the records have not been deposited, you should apply to the district secretary of the union for permission to approach the branch which you think your ancestor may have joined. It is probably worth going to the branch even if the district office thinks that the records you seek do not survive, though you may find it hard to discover the secretary's name and address.

Few friendly society records of individual members survive from before the twentieth century, and not all of those provide genealogical information. Occasionally, however, you can find in them a real gold mine. The admissions book of St Michael's Friendly Society, 1845–1941, in the Lancashire Record Office, gives each member's name, trade, place of birth, current address, date of joining the society and his age at the time.

Surviving friendly society records are either in the possession of the society itself or its modern counterpart, or are deposited in county or city record offices. See *FTM* 22.2 Dec 05, *FHM* 139 Jan 07, and

Local Historian 16.3. As an example, see Fisk & Logan (1994) on the Ancient Order of Foresters. For Internet sites relating to friendly societies, see *FTM* 23.9 Jul 07.

Poor Law Union records and the workhouse

Post-1834 workhouse admission books, usually in the city or county record office, give name, year of birth, parish of settlement, marital status, reason for seeking relief, religion and a physical description. Workhouses also kept records of the birth and baptism, and registers of the religious creed, of the inmates, each giving useful genealogical data. (See Gibson, Rogers & Webb, 1997–2008, for a fuller description of the records and a list of those which survive, and *FTM* 18.5 Mar 02 for Internet sources, particularly www.workhouses.org.uk.) For life in the institution, see Fowler (2007).

From 1871 duplicates of birth certificates, though normally excluding the mother's maiden name, had to be made under the Vaccination Act and sent to the local vaccination officers. Where these have survived they have found their way into the local record office, which may also hold other duplicates of birth and death certificates among the Medical Officer of Health records. Some surviving in Cheshire are as recent as 1935, and the series in Cambridgeshire lasts until 1948. Smallpox vaccination before the age of three months was made compulsory in 1872, and each vaccination certificate is dated a few months after the birth itself. An estimated 85 per cent were vaccinated in the early years of the system. After 1898, however, when parents could refuse vaccination for their children on grounds of conscience, the number fell to below two-thirds. Surviving vaccination registers are listed in Gibson, Rogers & Webb (1997–2008), and there is a photo of a compulsory vaccination notice in *FTM* 23.12 Oct 07. See also *FTM* 24.4 Feb 08.

Lunatic asylums, regarded almost as criminal institutions in their day, have records giving name, age, parish of settlement and discharge notes (see Hawking, 1992). Deserters from workhouses were listed in the Poor Law Unions' *Gazette*.

Criminal records

Hawking (1992) has given an excellent description, with many examples, of criminal records, taken particularly from the nineteenth century, and a vast amount of additional material can be gleaned once you have the excitement of knowing that one of your ancestors was incarcerated. In the context of looking for family relationships, transfer papers give next of kin, age and marital status. Prison registers, available for London and Middlesex from 1791 and for the rest of the country from 1805 to 1892, give name, place of birth and date of death if in prison, evidence of identity, physical description (in case of escape or reoffending), residence, and sometimes place of birth, marital status, number of children, religion and, in the case of juveniles, name and residence of parents. Calendars of prisoners who were accused persons, usually with a name index, give name, crime, age, trade and state of literacy; quarter sessions depositions contain name, address, occupation and signature. There is a list of Internet sources for crime and punishment in *FTM* 18.11 Sep 02 and 18.12 Oct 02; see also *NALD* 88.

Local newspapers should not be forgotten in this context – they have always delighted in reporting the scandalous, even if only to increase sales.

Miscellaneous records

It is possible to work out when a voter reached the age of twenty-one from a study of electoral registers (pp. 78–9). Notices of birth have appeared in newspapers for over two centuries, but only in relatively modern times have these been on a large scale. Similar notices of marriage can provide parents' names, and even obituaries (p. 228) can be useful in pinpointing date and place of birth. It is worth asking if there are indexes available. Many old newspapers will be found archived in the nearest large public library, but if the one you want is not there try the huge British Library archive – there is an index available at catalogue.bl.uk. See also *NALD* 123.

Various religious denominations have maintained a 'cradle roll' or equivalent, listing children who would eventually be expected to attend Sunday school.

Jill Wye, The Sampler Coffee Shop, 17 Nun St, St Davids, Pembrokeshire SA62 6NS maintains a register of surviving samplers which contain genealogical data.

Names of parents, and the maiden names of wives, can sometimes be found through gravestone inscriptions (*q.v.*).

The census, 1801 to the present day

The genealogical importance of the census is twofold – the fact that it lists whole families (or at least all those together on the same night), which is very rare in British records; and the detail it shows on each individual, especially age and place of birth.

Most recent books on genealogy give directions about using the census to find ancestors, and Higgs (1989) has provided a very useful analysis for genealogists as well as for historians, answering many questions of detail. It is enough to say here that the national census in England and Wales (including the Isle of Man and Channel Islands) was first taken in 1801. Earlier attempts failed in Parliament because of religious and libertarian opposition; some enumerators still felt in need of police protection in 1841. For the methods by which the exercise was carried out see Higgs (1989) and the *British Medical Journal*, 7 April 1951. Since 1801 a census has been taken once every ten years (excluding 1941, though there was a full enumeration on 29 September 1939) and a 10 per cent sample in 1966. There was also a National Registration Act in 1915 which used the administration of the GRO to list 22 million names – see Appendix 2 .

There is always a firm undertaking that the returns naming individual people will be regarded as confidential for 100 years, though a statistical analysis of the material is published as soon as possible. For the first four censuses the returns themselves were destroyed, and there are some interesting stories about the survival of many of them (*FTM* 18.3 Jan 02). Once the enumerators' returns are 100 years old, they are transferred by the Registrar General to the National Archives; they may be seen on microfilm free of charge at Kew. So we are back to London again, normally out of the reach of most genealogists except on rare occasions, unless they have Internet access. All returns, 1841–1901, and soon 1911, are available on the Internet – see below. The story of the survival of, and access to, the census records is told by Anthony Camp in *FTM* 18.3 Jan 02; see also *FTM* 20.5 Mar 04, for census websites.

Census material divides into three distinct periods, each of which presents different problems. For general and detailed background see Higgs (1989) and Lawton (1978).

Censuses less than 100 years old

Strictly speaking, it should not be possible to obtain information from these records, but during the 1960s the Registrar General was prepared to release information about named individuals from the census of 31 March 1901 or earlier. (I am unclear as to the level at which this decision was taken. In 1966 the Lord Chancellor determined that all censuses should be closed for a period of 100 years, because they contained personal information supplied by citizens about themselves – yet in 1970 I could buy information from the 1901 census.) Because of the furore surrounding the census of 1971 (when a campaign maintained that it was an infringement of civil liberties) this facility was withdrawn for a time, but it is now possible to obtain details from 1911.

Censuses 1841–1911

The easiest way to access the census returns for these years is through the Internet, various commercial enterprises being used in order to present both the original page images and complete (well, nearly complete) indexes. Try www.ancestry.co.uk, for example, for 1841–1901.

For those without Internet access, it is not necessary to travel to London in order to see the census returns for these years. For many years now, local libraries have been buying microfilm copies of returns for their own areas and it is normal for a city or county record office to have film of all six censuses taken between 1841 and 1901. These usually cover the whole county. Exceptions include Lancashire, whose enormous nineteenth-century population makes the procedure very costly – it would also mean duplicating holdings already in the large towns and cities within the county. Regrettably, census copies are one of an increasing number of records for which some record offices are now having to make an access charge. The National Archives sells small area copies (registration sub-districts) of the 1891 census on microfiche – contact the Reprographic Ordering Section, National Archives, Ruskin Avenue, Kew, Surrey TW9 4DU, for details.

An excellent source for all local historians is Gibson & Hampson (2001), who list the years and areas of copy census material in local reference institutions. See also Gibson & Hampson (2008/9) and Gibson, Hampon & Raymond (2007).

For those without Internet access, there are name indexes for many parts of the country in 1851, for example (plus an increasing number for 1861 and 1871), but 1881 should be singled out because of the relative ease with which individuals can now be found in it. Even at a time when all other censuses are available on line for a search fee, 1881 is still free. As a result of a massive project involving the National Archives, the Mormons (LDS), and the Federation of Family History Societies, transcription of the whole census (including a checking and correction exercise) was undertaken by thousands of volunteer genealogists, and the result is available on microfiche in the libraries of record offices and family history societies. There are two main sequences of fiches. One presents the whole country, county by county, in alphabetical order of personal names as they appear in the original returns. The data are rearranged, and the PRO piece, folio and page numbers are given, as well as the name of the head of household, for each person; on the other hand, only the place, rather than the exact address, is included. For rare surnames, the family can be pieced together using these reference numbers, but it is normally more convenient to cross-refer to the second sequence of fiches which present individuals in the same order as they appear in the census itself – in order of exact address. The project also makes 1881 available arranged by place of birth and parish, each presented in order of surnames, and there are single surname and birthplace indexes for the whole country. The transcription has been issued on fiche and CD-ROM, and is available at www.familysearch.org. It is also the basis for the wonderful surname atlas issued on CD-ROM by Archer Software. (For an assessment of the quality of the LDS 1881 census transcription (now used by www.ancestry.co.uk, by the way), see *FTM* 15.8 Jun 99, 19.1 Nov 02, and 19.10 Aug 03.) This mapping facility is now available at www.thegenealogist.co.uk paysite, and at www.nationaltrustnames.org.uk where a 1998 equivalent can be seen, both on the basis laid out by Rogers (1995).

For the cost of postage Mormon family history centres will make available to any visiting member of the public a specified census reel, not just from England and Wales but from anywhere in the world where census microfilming is permissible. Requests should be sent to the librarian in advance of a visit, as the reel may have to be ordered from stock or copied in Salt Lake City. It should be added that genealogists owe a considerable debt of gratitude to the Mormons for opening their facilities to the general public in this way. For lists of LDS family history centres see 'Archives and Libraries' in www.genuki.org.uk, or in your local phone book.

The normal arrangement in filming the nineteenth-century censuses is by the 'piece number', each with an individual National Archives reference number, which can occupy several reels of microfilm. Within each one there are several enumeration districts which were the responsibility of individual recorders at the time of the census itself. Finally, each page filmed is known as a 'folio', and has two sides, both of which must be checked if you have a specific reference obtained from a modern index.

1841 was the first census which attempted to record the names of the whole population of England and Wales. Householders had to complete a schedule (instead of a much more expensive method of door-to-door enquiries) which was then copied into enumeration books by clerks. The purpose was still (and remains today) statistical, but the inclusion of names meant that enumerators could not cheat! The information available for England and Wales for each person in the 1841 census is as follows: township or street; names of all living persons in the household; age, normally rounded down to the nearest five years, except in the case of those under fifteen, for whom exact ages had to be given (exact age could be given for adults if they so preferred, and some evidently had their age rounded *up*; it is believed that the elderly sometimes rounded down to the nearest ten); occupation, in order of importance if the individual had more than one; and whether the individual was living in the county of birth. The answer to the last question is quite unhelpful; a 'yes' may mean born in the same house or at the other end of the county; a 'no' may mean a hundred yards away across the county boundary or at the other end of the country. An improvement made in 1851, and in subsequent censuses until 1951, was to ask for place of birth. The naturalised foreign-born were distinguished from 1861. In 1961 and subsequently, however, the question again asked for country instead of place of birth. Another improvement in the 1851 returns is that everyone had to give their exact age and state their relation to the head of the household. Any relationship between visitors in the same house is not always clear, however, and Higgs (1989) quotes one agricultural labourer stating his relationship with the head of the household as 'friendly'!

There were significant changes in 1891, when questions relating to occupation, number of rooms occupied, and the speaking of Welsh were added (see *Local Population Studies* 4; and *Local Historian* 22.4). In 1901 there was a question about disability – whether the person was deaf and dumb, blind, a lunatic, an imbecile, or feeble-minded, but sometimes a mere tick will not distinguish between these categories.

A consolidated list of abbreviations used in Victorian censuses is as follows:

Ag Lab	Agricultural labourer (1841–81)
Ap	Apprentice (1841–61)
B	Being built (1861–91)
Cl	Clerk (1841–61)
daur	Daughter
F	Foreign parts (1841)
F	Female (sex column)
F-in-law	Father-in-law
FS	Female servant (1841)
HP	Soldier or sailor on half pay (1841)
I	Ireland (place of birth column). I have heard it said that some Manx immigrants referred to their homeland as 'the island', and were mistakenly entered as Irish; a distinctive surname may provide a clue in such a case.

Ind	Of independent means (1841)
J	Journeyman (day labourer, 1841)
M, Mar	Married
M	Male (sex column)
M-in-law	Mother-in-law
M	Manufacturer (1841)
MS	Male servant (1841)
m	Maker (1841)
N	No (place of birth column, 1841)
NK	Not known
Rail Lab	Railway labourer (1851)
S	Single (marital status column, 1891)
S	Scotland (place of birth column). 'S' can mean anywhere north of the border, sometimes referred to as 'North Britain'.
serv	Servant (1861)
Sh	Shopman (1841)
U	Uninhabited (1861–91)
U, Un, Unm	Unmarried
W, Wid, Wid'r	Widow(er)
Y	Yes (place of birth column, 1841; the question was 'Are you living in your county of birth?')

In 1911 the census was disrupted as part of the suffragette campaign. Punch had a cartoon showing a lady hiding from the enumerator behind her lace curtains. The caption read, 'The women of England have taken leave of their census'. Emily Wilding Davison did so by hiding in the 'Guy Fawkes' cupboard in the cellar of the Houses of Parliament! (Records of the suffragists and suffragettes, by the way, are in the John Rylands Library in Manchester – see www.library.manchester.ac.uk/specialcollections.) This census is being made available for a partial release in 2009, to be fully available at the start of 2012. Large cities will be released first, the remainder progressively, but infirmities will be blanked out until January 2012. You can already send for entries for a specified address, through www.nationalarchives.gov.uk/1911census, but the cost is £45! The big difference in 1911 will be the availability of the householders' schedules, not just the enumerators' books, for the first time, making it several times larger than any previous census at 0.5 petabytes! For its content, see the photograph in *FTM* 23.11 Sep 07, and for more technical detail, *FTM* 24.3 Jan 08.

The way to obtain ages and places of birth of individuals from the 1911 census is to write to the Registrar General, enclosing the following: the fee, since 1 July 1996 £45.00, including VAT (hence £34.05 for overseas applicants); your reason for wanting the information – genealogy is acceptable; a statement saying either that the person about whom you are enquiring is dead and that you are a descendant, or that the person is still alive and has given written permission for the enquiry to be answered; and that the information will not be used in litigation. You should state the name and exact address of the person at the time the census was taken, though the entry for the whole household can be requested. To discover the exact address, use the same techniques as for censuses 1841–1901.

When using the census, you should try to copy the names of all the people in the same house, and, if possible, in the adjoining houses, if the occupants have the same surnames. Households at the same address are normally separated by a single (1851) or double horizontal line. If you can spare the time, look through adjoining streets also, and note all occurrences of the same surname; if you cannot spare the time, do so anyway! It was common for relatives to live quite close to each other, but the relationship between households will not be clear from the census itself. Those described as 'visitors' or 'servants' may be more distant relatives, so make a note of their details also. The information may fall into place only after subsequent research. Copy the entries exactly as written – even ditto marks can be important because they are sometimes associated with clerical error through over-use. (The *Manchester Genealogist*, 29.3, 1993, reported that a volunteer for the 1881 census transcription project had found the same house enumerated twice in different districts, and some of the entries showed marked differences because of the misuse of ditto marks!)

Thus, almost at the very point, 1837, before which there are no birth certificates, the census will tell you where everyone was born and how old they were, as well as the identity of parents of children who were living at home at the time. Needless to say, it all sounds too good to be true, and once again there are many reasons why this source of information can fail to give you the answers you want.

Finding addresses in the census
The need for this has been considerably lessened by the introduction of excellent (though not perfect) indexing systems, especially on line. If you do not know the exact address already, it can be obtained from a registrar's certificate, the place of the event or the address of the informant, from baptismal and burial records, or from a number of

other sources, such as education or cemetery registers. Victorian Britain never made anyone report a change of address. Enumeration districts were based on registration districts which were, in turn, associated with the boundaries of Poor Law Unions. Each enumeration district will have a description of the area it contains, with the main streets named.

Electoral registers, which are now held in town halls or record offices and can be consulted free of charge, should survive from 1832 (see Gibson & Rogers, 1990). There are just a handful of earlier ones. Until 1939 they contain both home and qualifying addresses, where these are different, and occasionally include a former address if there had been a recent change. Relatively few people are found in them until 1867, when there was a large increase in the number of urban voters – still men only, however; from 1884 almost all men over twenty-one appear in them, and from 1918 women over thirty. Women over twenty-one were given the right to vote in 1928, though they can be found in the local government election burgess rolls after 1869 if they had the necessary property qualification, and in the registers of parochial electors, 1894–1914. Those who fell on hard times and sought poor relief were, in consequence, deprived of the vote.

Since 2002, there have been two versions of the register, the fuller one being open to the public only after ten years. Constituency boundaries 1885–1972 are given in Craig (1972), with modern boundaries available at www.election-maps.co.uk.

Between 1867 and 1918 there was a year's residence qualification before an elector could appear on the register. No electoral registers were published in 1916–17 or 1940–44. See also poll books (p. 113).

Normally, electoral registers are now in street order, but there are name indexes available for some London boroughs before the Second World War, and many pre-1884 registers are in alphabetical order of surname, ward by ward. However, there were many reasons why eligible electors were excluded from the registers; see Seymour (1915/1970). Don't forget to look in the right-hand column – some tenants (who did not necessarily have the right to vote) may be listed as a means of identifying the qualifying property.

Some names in the electoral registers have a code against them, and I have even seen two people of the same name and address in modern times distinguished by their NHS numbers. The following abbreviations have been used during the twentieth century:

§   Not entitled to vote in local (later, metropolitan borough, urban district, or parish) elections

†	Not entitled to vote in county council elections
‡	Not entitled to vote in rural district elections
date given	Entitled to vote from that date
a	Absent voter
BP (Bw)	Business premises qualification (women)
D (Dw)	Spouse's occupation qualification
E	Not entitled to vote in local or parliamentary elections
F	Not entitled to vote in local elections
G	Citizen of Europe, entitled to vote in local elections only
HO	Husband's occupational qualification
J	Juror
JS	Special juror (as defined by the Juries Act 1870 ss. 6 and 11 – esquire or above, bankers, merchants, and anyone owning property of more than a certain value)
K	Citizen of Europe, entitled to vote in local and European elections only
L	Not entitled to vote in parliamentary elections
M	Merchant seaman
N	To be included in the next register as a voter
NM	Naval or military voter
O (Ow)	Occupational qualification (women)
R (Rw)	Residential qualification (women)
S	Service voter
U	Citizen of Europe, entitled to vote in European elections only
x	Not entitled to vote in parliamentary elections
Y	Entitled to vote in the following year

Early telephone directories are rare. They date from 1880 and contain relatively few individuals before the Second World War, the whole country being covered in one volume before 1900. My copy of the local 1935 telephone directory covers, in one volume which is smaller than two of the present London directories, the whole of Lancashire, the Isle of Man, Cumberland, Westmorland, Durham, Northumberland, Yorkshire and much of Cheshire. Only one household in twenty was then on the phone. British Telecom itself has a full set of these directories at 135 Queen Victoria Street, London EC4V 4AT. They welcome postal enquiries. A further set is in the British Library, and all directories 1880–1984 are available at www.ancestry.co.uk.

Of greater use for obtaining addresses are the town or county trade directories, of which Kelly's is the most famous. These directories do not normally pretend to list all householders, let alone all inhabitants, though the town ones are fuller than those covering a whole county. In Sheffield, for example, 42 per cent of householders are to be found in the 1852 directory of the city. (Those in more modern times often exclude council property.) They were first developed in the seventeenth century in order to give commercial salesmen an idea of where potential customers lived. The earliest annual publication for London is 1734, and by the 1770s they were being published for large towns such as Liverpool and Manchester, where the notorious Mrs Raffald combined her interests in running a boarding house for commercial travellers with producing the town's first directory. By the nineteenth century most towns and counties had directories issued at regular intervals. Acquiring them is now an expensive undertaking for the antiquarian book collector. Lists of known directories have been compiled – see Goss (1932), Atkins (1990), Norton (1950) and Shaw & Tipper (1988) – and most public libraries and record offices possess at least a few nineteenth-century editions for their own area. Several hundred before 1920 have been digitised by the University of Leicester, and are freely available at www.historicaldirectories.org. (The project is currently on hold, however, through lack of funding.) Kelly's Directories Ltd keeps a copy of all its own publications at Windsor Court, East Grinstead House, London Road, East Grinstead, West Sussex RH19 1XB, where they can be consulted for a fee. For their content and reliability see *Local Historian* 13.4 and 18.4. Don't ignore the occupational lists in such directories – many jobs run in families.

There are also more specialised directories which are useful to those who have ancestors in certain trades, occupations or professions. The earliest are those for law, the Church and officers of the armed services, but in the nineteenth century other professions followed suit. They often have the added advantage of including academic qualifications and where they were obtained; reference to the educational records (see pp. 60–5) can then lead to more information, including parents. It should always be borne in mind, however, that many are reliant on individual submissions. John Parker, editing the 1925 *Who's Who in the Theatre*, wrote in exasperation of

the extraordinary difficulty which I experience in persuading a great many members of the Profession to give anything like accurate details of their early theatrical careers. Players of both sexes seem to have an inordinate dislike of revealing facts and dates, and quite a number appear to have no compunction in striking years off the date of a production in which they have appeared, ignoring the fact that I am able to trace these incorrect statements quite easily, from my files. Others, quiet calmly, inform me that I must have mixed them up with someone else of the same name, but somehow these other persons always seem to disappear.

The list which follows is not comprehensive, but it includes series which were being published regularly before the Second World War. The year given for each entry is the earliest date of publication.

Annual register of pharmaceutical chemists, 1842
Army list, 1642, annual from 1702 (officers only)
Catholic directory, 1837
Chemical industry directory and who's who, 1923
Congregational yearbook, 1847
Crockford's clerical directory, 1858 (on CD for 1929)
Dentists' register, 1879
Directory of directors, 1880
Directory of insurance brokers, 1922
Directory of shipowners, shipbuilders and marine engineers,
   1903
Dod's parliamentary companion, 1832
Electrical Contractors' Association yearbook, 1918
General Assembly of Unitarian and Free Christian Churches'
   yearbook, 1890
Incorporated Brewers' Guild directory, 1924
Incorporated Society of Musicians: handbook and register of
   members, 1900
Institute of Actuaries yearbook, 1928
Jewish year book, 1896
Law list, 1775
Lloyd's Register of Shipping: register book, 1764
Lloyd's Register of Shipping: register of yachts, 1878
Masonic year book, 1775
Medical directory, 1845
Medical register, 1859
Methodist Church, 1847
Navy list, 1772 (officers only)
Register of architects, 1932

Register of pharmaceutical chemists and chemists & druggists,
   1869
Religious Society of Friends: book of meetings, 1801
Royal College of Veterinary Surgeons: register and directory,
   1844
Royal Society of London: yearbook and list of fellows, 1898
Royal Society of Tropical Medicine and Hygiene, 1908
Salvation Army yearbook, 1906
Schoolmasters' yearbook and directory, 1903
Solicitors' diary, 1844 (on CD for 1900)
Who's who in the theatre, 1912 (on CD for 1922)
Wisden, 1864

If you suspect that your ancestor was a member of any form of society, trade union, association or profession, you should always contact its modern headquarters in order to find out whether there is any information (e.g. on education or pensions) unpublished but nevertheless accessible on request to the general public about individual members – for example, for entertainers born before 1920. See Gibson (1988), *FTM* 15.4 Feb 99, Herber (2005, chapter 21), and Raymond (1997) for other occupational sources. The police (*FTM* 6.12 Oct 90; 8.6 Apr 92; and *FHM* 128 Mar 06), Post Office and British Telecom, for instance, can be very helpful with information about former employees. Records of former railwaymen are in the National Archives at Kew, among the British Transport Historical Collection; see Richards (1989) and *NALD* 82. See *FTM* 17.3 Jan 01 for an article about the records of Anglican clergy, 17.4 Feb 01 for medics, 20.6 Apr 04 for Customs and Excise officers (see also *NALD* 38), 23.12 Oct 07 for nurses (see also *NALD* 79), and Mar 17.5 01 for lawyers, described by David Hey (2004) as 'the best recorded profession' (see also *NALD* 36). *Anc* 58 Jun 07 has an article on Internet sources for the theatre, and the National Fairground Archives can be accessed at www.shef.ac.uk/uni/projects/nfa. Football league players from 1888 are in Joyce (2004) and Hugman (1998), and there is an equivalent www.cricketarchive.com for the whole world. There are several published dictionaries of artists, clergymen, doctors, musicians or architects, but some professional bodies charge for providing non-confidential information from their files – for example, the Royal Institute of British Architects (RIBA) asks for a fee. Details of former freemasons can be obtained from the secretary, The United Grand Lodge of England, Freemasons' Hall, Great Queen Street, London WC2B 5AZ. For many of the above – for example the police and railwaymen – some records may be found in the appropriate city or county record office.

We put addresses on a wide variety of documents during our lifetime, of course, but a large number, such as most income tax returns and Benefits Agency records, are destroyed. Among those which do survive, however, are rate books of many kinds which may exist from the last three centuries. Rates have been known under other names – assessment, ley and mize, for example – and are usually thought of as a local tax, but a rate is a collection for a specific undertaking whose cost is calculated in advance and divided between those rateable, so a rate could be national and a tax could be local. The oldest rate books are those of the parish officers, and are to be found in the parish chest. They are well described by Tate (1983) and Darlington (1962) and include the poor rates, collected by the overseers of the poor, the church rates, collected by the churchwardens, and the highway rates, collected by the constables or highway officials. These early, separate rates for various purposes were merged with the poor rate in 1739. The rate books will normally provide details of who paid, or was due to pay, the rates concerned and will perhaps also describe the property which formed the basis of the assessment. It should also indicate whether payment was being made by the owner or the occupier. Church rates were abolished in 1868, by which time most of their functions had been taken over by local government. Most old rate books have been transferred to county record offices at the same time as the parish chest.

By the nineteenth century, however, when the question of addresses becomes more acute for the genealogist, the county or borough rates are of much more use. Local authority rate books can provide exact addresses sometimes decades before they become available in directories or electoral rolls. They are normally to be found in the archives of the rating authority concerned, whether it be county or borough. The archivist can advise you about which books exist and how to locate any one person within them from information you already possess.

Addresses are also given in the published *National roll of the Great War*, a curious work which seems to be official but was very incomplete. According to a letter in *FTM* 5.12 Oct 89, the volumes were compiled following door-to-door enquiries, with entries guaranteed for anyone whose relatives promised to buy one! Being in alphabetical order, they are easy to use, but don't forget to look in the addendum pages at the back of the volume. Towns covered were Bedford, Birmingham, Bradford, Leeds, London, Luton, Manchester,

Northampton, Portsmouth, Salford and Southampton. Some air force, naval and civilian personnel are included. Reference numbers against each entry are no longer meaningful in our context.

Addresses are also provided on jurors' lists among quarter sessions papers in the city or county record offices. Jurors were aged twenty-one to seventy until 1823, when the upper age was reduced to sixty; the lists are of males only, drawn up annually by churchwardens and overseers, and made public by being pinned to church doors. They were divided into common and 'special' jurors, the latter being identified in a succession of Acts affecting juries (e.g. s. 6 of the 1870 Juries Act) as being of superior social status – presumably to shelter those of such status who found themselves in the dock. Addresses are also available on dog licence applications (see Dowell, 1965), in trade union records (see pp. 68–9), in school registers (see pp. 60–5), in cemetery records, in post-1858 probate calendars and in boards of guardians' outdoor relief lists; see Gibson, Rogers & Webb (1997–2008) and *Local Historian* 16.1. In the years leading up to the First World War the Commissioners of Inland Revenue compiled returns of duties of land values, in alphabetical order of addresses with named occupiers. The National Archives has now transferred these returns to the relevant city or county record offices. There is also a well-known return of freeholders of land, published in 1873, the so-called 'Domesday' book, which can be seen in hard copy or microform.

Both drivers and vehicles were licensed from 1903 until 1973, but only on a local level (county or borough), so records can usually be found in the appropriate record offices for that period. How fortunate that making the ancient European custom of driving on the left compulsory in 1835 was a national decision! Records since 1973 are held by the DVLA in Swansea, which has strict rules about the provision of information. (Their register for older vehicles – those not subject to road tax – closed in 1983, though old unregistered vehicles can still be registered today as a special concession to motorists who missed that cut-off date.)

It should be added here that hitherto unpublished directories of people in particular trades have been, or are being, compiled by interested individuals who are usually pleased to give, as well as to receive, information about them. With all requests for information, please enclose a stamped, addressed envelope or international reply coupons. For details, see Gibson & Hampson (2008/9).

Failure to locate individual addresses in the census
Knowing the address you are looking for is one thing; finding it is quite another. In rural areas, where addresses were often not used in the nineteenth century, the fact that no address is known will create few difficulties because it takes relatively little time – under an hour – to search the census returns for whole parishes with up to 4,000 inhabitants. For urban areas, the census abstract may help to locate the registration district of a particular township. For towns of over 40,000 inhabitants, in some cases occupying up to 30,000 census sheets, street indexes are available. These are listed by Gibson & Hampson (2001). In addition, individual libraries have often prepared their own street indexes. These will tell you which enumeration district, and hence which reel of microfilm, contains the address you want. Such indexes are not infallible guides, however, and you sometimes need to use other methods in order to locate 'missing' streets. These methods are described below. If you are working from a page reference from another source, such as an index, note that each 'page' in the census covers *two* sides of an original sheet.

The main problem, clearly, for those without Internet access is those towns with a large population but which, because they are somewhat under 40,000, have no street index. In the last ten years many have been indexed by local librarians or enthusiastic members of family history societies. If you have plenty of time to spare, of course, you will simply require patience and reasonable eyesight. A short cut is to apply for a detailed map which marks the boundaries between enumeration districts, and to locate the address where your ancestors lived, on a contemporary map if possible. Once the enumeration district has been identified by using the two maps in conjunction, the address can be found relatively quickly from the reel list which the librarian will have. However, such maps do not exist for all urban areas. At the start of each enumeration district in the census you will find a description of its geographical boundaries.

The address occasionally cannot be found by this method because some small streets are unnamed on maps; in that case, consult a contemporary town directory. This should have a full street index, normally in its first few pages. Small streets can then be found, next to the larger streets off which they run; you can then find the larger street first in the census. Alternatively, see if the surname index also contains a separate street index, noting that page numbers refer to *two adjoining sheets* in the original.

There is a slight possibility that the enumerator himself missed the household or even the street altogether, as apparently happened to Grosvenor Square in 1851, that some of the returns have either been destroyed or were in too fragile a state to microfilm; or that the National Archives has missed a section during microfilming, which is happening to perhaps one page in a thousand. Or once again, you have missed the address through tiredness, eyestrain or the illegibility of the microfilm copy. The latter is a particular problem with the 1861 census. You should also remember that when the National Archives makes a microfilm copy it is of the returns based on geographical boundaries as they existed at the time of the census concerned. Subsequent boundary changes must be taken into account, and your librarian or archivist will advise you how to find out what changes there have been.

Finding houses in more remote, country areas may be helped by the techniques described in Rogers & Smith (1991, pp. 89–90, 109).

Even when you have found the street, you may be unable to find the number of the house. There are three basic reasons why this happens. Firstly, the census enumerator sometimes failed to enter the house numbers, and indeed in 1841 it was not normal for them to be included at all. Marks in the edge of the columns containing people's names (/ or //) are the only indication where family groups and households end. Do not be confused by the number in the extreme left-hand column; it is an enumeration number, not a house number. Secondly, it was normal for the enumerator to start another street before he had completed the previous one. A main road would be covered down one side only until a side road was reached; the side road might then be completed, after which the main road would be resumed. Searching for an inhabitant of the main road therefore may mean having to pass over the returns from several side streets before your number is reached. One long street might be in more than one enumeration district, and you may have to consult several reels in order to cover it from end to end. Consult the description of the enumerator's itinerary at the start of each district, or plot the route using methods such as those described in Rogers & Smith (1991).

Thirdly, it is worth remembering that Victorian cities grew very rapidly, that streets changed their names, and that sometimes they had more than one house sporting the same number. There was a major renumbering of houses during the 1850s in particular, over 40,000 being changed in Liverpool during 1856 alone. The National Archives has an index of changes in London street names. Newly developing local authorities also flexed their muscles by creating and changing street names (made compulsory in towns from 1847) as well as house numbers. Arthur Harry Pole was born at 4 Mycock Street, Manchester, in May 1862; at the time of the 1861 census the street had not yet been built and by 1871 its name had been changed. Finding his family in the microfilmed census would be impossible unless the change is recognised.

British ships in port or in navigable rivers on census night should be found in 1851 and later censuses, but not in 1841; see *Local Population Studies* 38.

Failure to locate individuals in the census
Even if you find the street, and find the house, you still may not find the person you are looking for. The usual reason is that the family was not living there, for the chances are only one in over 3,650 that the source of the address – a marriage certificate, for example – will have the same date as the census. If the whole family has moved, you might consider buying another certificate, that of the birth of an ancestor's sibling, for example, closer to a census date. There was an astonishing amount of movement in Victorian towns, before the days of mass home ownership and council housing. Even today the average family moves once every ten years, with high mobility in London and the south, and the lowest in Wales and Yorkshire. Residential mobility is particularly high at times of marriage, child-bearing, widowhood and nowadays divorce. Young couples were likely to be living as lodgers with relatives, especially if they had low-income occupations. If the address has been obtained from a directory or electoral register, it is worth remembering that such documents were compiled months before the date which appears on the title page. Find a directory for 1872 or even 1873 if your ancestor was not living at the address shown in an 1871 directory at the time of the 1871 census. Michael Anderson (1971) found that over 80 per cent of people over the age of ten in Preston in 1851 were not at the same address ten years later, though half were living in the same or an adjoining enumeration district. Migrants who had been born in the same place as each other tended to cluster in the same neighbourhood.

Failure to find individuals should now be overcome by reference to any of the national indexes unless they had emigrated or died, but don't rely on them completely. If you expect a person to be in a particular place, and there is no index entry, still look at the image itself because there are omissions and mis-readings. Notoriously, the entry for Karl Marx in 1881 has been transcribed as 'Karl Wass'. See *FTM* 19.1 Nov 02, for example, for an assessment of the accuracy of one transcript of the 1881 census.

The census is taken on a particular date, which changes from decade to decade, in the spring. In 1841 this was 6 June; in 1851, the evening of 30 March; in 1861, 7–8 April (this was Easter, so some people were away from home); in 1871, 2–3 April; in 1881, 3–4 April; in 1891, 5 April; in 1901, 31 March; and in 1911, 2 April. The enumerator's schedule should show those who were actually at the address on the date in question, not those who normally lived there. Occasionally the same individual was entered at two addresses – but a genealogist's usual problem is not finding the entry at all. If he had died the night before; if she was visiting relatives; if he was in jail, hospital or the workhouse, or was a sailor at sea; if she was working as a domestic servant living in the house of her employer; in short, if anything had taken your ancestor away from home that evening, the entry should not be found with the rest of the family. In 1841 there was no provision for including night workers, householders were not told whether to include boarders or lodgers, and merchant vessels were not included. All these categories should be found from 1851, however. (On the age at leaving home, an important consideration when searching for teenagers in the census, see *Journal of Family History* 22.4, 1997.)

The statistician John Rickman, who had a major hand in designing and analysing the first censuses, objected to holding them on a Sunday because so many Londoners were 'out of town', and the first four were held on a Monday. In and since 1841 the census has been taken on a Sunday evening, but the late date in 1841 meant that many were away on holiday. A few families even moved before the enumerators could collect the schedules which had been distributed to them. At Hollingworth, Cheshire, for example, an unnamed family in the 1861 census had 'removed and taken the schedule with them', and one of my students discovered an ancestor recorded simply as 'occupant found dead'. Conversely, the recently deceased may sometimes be found as if alive, because the forms seem to have been filled in long before the required date!

In order to aid frustrated genealogists whose ancestors had moved far from their origins on the night in question, the Federation of Family History Societies co-ordinates the production of a National Strays Index, only part of which is the voluntary listing of individuals whose birthplace was in another county, submitted by the strays co-ordinator in the various member societies. This index is microfiched at intervals and given to each society.

There were other causes of omission. There was a widespread belief that very young infants, particularly those not yet baptised, should not be included in the returns, and it has been estimated that up to 4 per cent of children under five years old are missing from the 1841 census and perhaps 3 per cent from the three later ones. At Nether Thong, in the West Riding, there was an 'infant not baptised' and therefore not named in the census, although he was four years old. From all censuses until 1911 up to 6 per cent of all children under the age of one year were omitted. Very few individuals actually refused to complete the schedule, but sometimes the number of children returned is smaller than the actual number in the family in order to avoid accusations of overcrowding. Gypsies, shepherds, fairground people, and those living in overcrowded areas were often missing, as were (I understand) clients in brothels to whom enumerators seem to have turned a blind eye. If the whole family is missing, they were simply living elsewhere at the time; if individual members were missing, it should not be assumed that they had died, or that you have found the wrong family – though of course this is possible. It was very common for teenage girls to be living away from home in the mid-nineteenth century, and for boys to have left home altogether by the time they were eighteen, especially from poorer families. (On tracing hired hands, see *PFH* 94 Oct 05.)

Children of remarried widows should be entered under their original surname, but are sometimes to be found with their stepfather's surname (see p. 44).

If the address you have is from a marriage certificate, you should realise that a large number of brides and grooms married from their future partner's home address, or from an address of convenience, in order to appear to fulfil residence requirements. There has never been a requirement that the address given at the time of the banns or marriage notice must be shown to be correct. (Nowadays, a third of partners marrying, especially females remarrying, give an identical address, but this is probably due to pre-marital cohabitation; see *MN* 3 Dec 86.) From 1853 some informants on birth certificates are known to have given an incorrect address so that the vaccination officer would not call. If the address is from a death certificate, remember that the deceased may not have died at home – and in one instance I know of the place of death was incorrectly stated anyway. A funeral director of my acquaintance once helped to carry a corpse from a public house (where the deceased's wife had forbidden him to go) to the house of a friend, whose address then appeared on the death certificate.

Other mistakes arise from the fact that, from 1851, the enumerators had to rely on a schedule which was completed by the head of each household or, in the case of institutions such as prisons, by the head of the institution, who often recorded individuals by initials instead of full names. Unfortunately for the genealogist, these schedules were destroyed many years later by the General Register Office, so we are left with the enumerators' interpretation of what the householder had written, or what he was told by those too illiterate to complete the form. Enumerators were actually instructed to alter what they thought was 'manifestly false'; the supervising district registrars often made 'corrective' changes, and so did the clerks at the census office who did the final counting. The last, by the way, are responsible for those marginal ticks which sometimes mislead you into thinking that your ancestor was recorded as deaf and dumb in the final column. It was not unknown for Victorian enumerators themselves to be accused of being poorly educated (they were supposed to be between eighteen and sixty-five, to be literate and to have some knowledge of the area of between twenty-five and 200 houses which they each covered); they certainly varied markedly in their ability to follow the instructions, though the variations are more serious for the historical sociologist than for the genealogist. One survey shows that a quarter of the forms in Manchester had to be filled in by the enumerators because the respondents were illiterate, and that in one subdivision the proportion was as high as two-thirds (see *Local Historian* 13.8).

If the address you find turns out to be non-residential premises such as a shop, try looking in the corresponding electoral register – they sometimes provide the home address of the owner.

If there was more than one street of the same name, they may be indexed together, giving the impression that only one of them appears in the census, whereas both should be found if all the references are followed through. Thus, in 1861, there are two places known as 27 Chapel Street, Salford, in two separate streets but the two are incorrectly merged in the index. If you did not know that there were two such addresses you would probably miss the second one, having found the first.

Last, but sometimes first, most of us access the census via the use of indexes, either published or on line, and we are therefore entirely reliant on the index having been accurately compiled. The indexing of the censuses of 1881 and 1901 leave no doubt that such reliance may not be well founded, and the genealogical journals are full of examples – Altrincham being Altrinham, John Smith senior becoming John Smith Senior. The use of transcribers who are not native English speakers did not help. The index should transcribe the name as given in the return – but this can be a nickname, or at best the name by which a person was then known, rather than the name given at birth or baptism (see Bardsley, 2004).

Censuses 1801–31

I have already mentioned that these censuses required the return of numbers, rather than everyone's name in which, as Higgs (2004a) has shown, the state took no great interest unless connected with taxation or warfare. However, various local copies of the original returns have come to light, together with additional data collected at the time. Those which have been housed in record repositories, or written into parish registers, are listed by Gibson & Hampson (2001). Compared with later censuses, however, these early returns contain less information, as from 1811 only the head of the household was named. The census dates were 10 March 1801, 27 May 1811, 28 May 1821 and 30 May 1831. The armed forces, registered seamen and convicts were not to be enumerated.

Because the surviving documents are not those officially returned, and are not always in the form requested, they vary in content. At the least you should find the names of all householders in 1811, 1821 and 1831 arranged in order of named streets, the number of families living in each house and information about occupations. In 1821 the ages of all males and females are given separately in groups of five years. This question was voluntary for enumerators to ask and respondents to answer, but it seems to have elicited a 90 per cent completion rate. Some large towns in the north and Midlands and many parts of London did not make this return, however. The 1831 census is less complete, providing simply the number of males aged twenty or over.

It is clear that the enumerators – the Overseers of the Poor – went to the trouble in some areas of finding out the names and ages of all the inhabitants, as at Winwick in Lancashire, even though in 1801 they were not asked even to name anyone in their official returns. See Laxton (1981) for a photograph of one of these early survivals, that of Liverpool in 1801, and Rogers & Smith (1991) for a transcript of Croston in 1801, which includes a record of dog owners! See also *Local Historian* 18.1 and *GM* 23.3.

Church baptism, 1538 to the present day

We are now reaching back in time before the state attempted to exercise control using the institutions of central government, relying instead on what were essentially locally based organisations. Most of the records are still held locally, and in consequence are more difficult to find on the Internet. The most important documents which can be used to trace parents prior to 1837 are records of baptism. Quakers, and sometimes Baptists, recorded births. It is perhaps worth stressing that baptismal registers continue down to the present day. While it is true that before 1837 you have to rely basically on Church records, it is perfectly possible, especially in country areas where there may be only one or two local churches and where the influence of the clergy remained much stronger than in the towns, to trace a line of ancestors back to the sixteenth century by using parish registers alone. I have done it, though Elizabeth Silverthorne has some cautionary words on the subject (*FTM* 3.9 Jul 87). The proliferation of churches in urban areas makes these registers more difficult to use in the nineteenth century, but town and county directories, as well as *Crockford's clerical directory*, should indicate the foundation date of each church, and the *National index of parish registers* (Steel, 1968–) and GENUKI will provide the dates covered by the registers themselves.

Whatever your religion now, it is most probable that your forebears attended the Church of England if they lived in England over two centuries ago. The further back in time the truer this becomes until, in 1700 and earlier, probably 95 per cent of the population are to be found in Anglican records. Strictly speaking, the phrase 'parish register' applies to the Anglican registers of baptism, marriage and burial, though it is nowadays colloquially but incorrectly applied to similar registers kept by other denominations (see pp. 135–8), the 'non-parochial' registers.

Whole books have been written about parish registers, so once again I do not propose to go into historical detail, which may be obtained from Burn (1862), Waters (1883/2000), Steel (1968–) , Tate (1983) and Cox (1910/1974). There are, however, some basic features of these documents which the genealogist should know, as without this information you cannot use the registers properly.

In common with most handwritten documents of the time, registers in the sixteenth and the greater part of the seventeenth centuries are written in a form of handwriting called secretary script. At first, the beginner may scarcely recognise the words as English, but with remarkably little practice it becomes legible without undue difficulty. *Amateur Historian* 1.5, Gardner & Smith (1956, III), Hector (1980) and *Anc* 56 Apr 07 may help at first with acquiring the skill, but there is no real substitute for attempting to read the real thing without guidance or transcription. Record offices will supply relatively cheap photocopies of secretary script of varying difficulty which you have identified. I taught myself by reading an old deed that I'd framed under the glass of a coffee table. Distinguish between f and s, c and r, u and n, C and T and that is half the battle. An on line tutorial is available at www.english.cam.ac.uk/ceres.

Another problem, which appears far worse to the beginner than it really is, is the fact that many of the earliest registers – up to the middle of the seventeenth century and a few beyond – are written in Latin. Surnames are not normally Latinised, however, and the Latin words for the months of the year are easily recognisable. Days of the month are in roman numerals, with the final i usually written as j; the years themselves are in our 'own', normal Arabic numerals. The only problem, therefore, is in translating Christian names, occupations and such phrases as 'son of', widow' and so on. Even here, many are easily recognisable, but a very useful list is found at www.nationalarchives. gov.uk/latin/beginners/lesson09/default.htm. Don Steel (1968, I, p. 34) even quotes entries which were made in cipher.

Most textbooks on tracing family trees give forewarnings about spelling. Before the nineteenth century officials were not very scrupulous about the way in which people spelt their names; illiteracy was common anyway, and dialects were stronger. The result is that the same person might have had his or her name written in various ways, even in the same document, so that it will be a very unusual family tree which has a surname that never varies. Mander (1984) counted thirty-six ways of spelling Dixon, and one of my students, surnamed Pridgeon, has found forty-five variations of his name, excluding one used by a lady who called him Mr Prartridge! Over time, variations of spelling and pronunciation might even change the name of a family. The grandfather of 'my' Sarah Hargreaves normally called himself 'Hargreave' but his grandfather was called 'Hargrave', which has quite a different origin. On the other hand, it is possible that, when names were very similar, those who wrote the registers were more particular than usual about spelling in order to distinguish one family from another.

Until 1752, New Year's Day was celebrated on 25 March ('old style'), not 1 January ('new style') so that December 1700 was followed by January 1700 in the registers. In a Christian country, of course, it was quite logical to use the day of Christ's conception as the beginning of the New Year, though most of continental Europe had changed in 1582 with the introduction of the Gregorian calendar. A proposal to change the calendar here was defeated in Parliament a year later. Several nonconformist denominations had been already using the new style for several decades.

In 1751 eleven days were lost at the time of the changeover, the third of September being the same day as the fourteenth of September, with some odd results. May blossom has since appeared in June, rumour persists that Christ was really born in January, and people alive on 2 September 1751 could celebrate two birthdays a year. On 27 June 1800, James Woodforde wrote in his diary, 'this Day I entered my sixtieth Year being born (old Stile) the sixteenth of June in the Year, 1740'. Renewal of annual contracts, and reaching the age of majority, appeared to be eleven days late. More pertinently for us, a child might appear to be born before the marriage of the parents even though it was legitimate. The new style had long been recognised as an alternative way of expressing the date. Ralph Josselin, the diarist cleric, referred to 'Jan. 1: Newyears day' in 1639; Pepys wrote 'So ends the old year' on 31 December 1663/64. For much of the late seventeenth and early eighteenth centuries, dates from 1 January to 24 March were given two years, one written over the other.

It was long believed that the loss of eleven days provoked rioting by a populace too ignorant to know better, but R. Poole (1995) has shown that this is a myth, based on Hogarth's famous cartoon.

The information contained in baptismal records has varied over time and there was no standardised form of entry until 1 January 1813. From their starting date in 1538, many contained the name only of the child, but perhaps this was the result of the order of 1597/98 which asked for all the older entries to be copied up in a book of parchment. As no pay was provided, it would be understandable if some clergymen copied only the barest essentials – the names of the children. Others took another easy way out; they seem to have done the minimum requested, and copied the old registers only as far back as the start of the reign of the then queen, Elizabeth I, 1558; others did nothing at all. Oddly, the 1538 injunction (repeated in 1547) was originally for a 'book or register' rather than the slips of paper which seem to have been used all too commonly. In Anglican registers it has never been the custom to include the names of godparents, apart from a short period in the 1550s when they were subject to strong Roman Catholic influence, and the rewriting of 1597 tended to ignore earlier 'popish' entries.

Family reconstitution studies have indicated the not unexpected errors of transcription – for example, the transposition of Christian names of parent and child, or the parent incorrectly being given the child's first name. From the early seventeenth century, however, if not before, parental names – the essential information for genealogists – begin to be included in the baptismal entry; as the next two centuries passed, other information also appeared. At first we are perhaps given the name of the child's father, then of the mother (often from the 1650s), and later of the township within the parish, especially in the large parishes of northern England which contained several townships.

It must be stressed that this is not necessarily the way in which each register changed over time – there might be a regression to scant information when the incumbent changed, and there is often a wide discrepancy of styles between parishes. A typical baptismal entry from Whitegate in Cheshire reads 'William, son of Jonathan and Mary Nickson, baptised 24 January 1779'. At the same time at Witton, a chapelry in the adjoining parish of Great Budworth, the register is much fuller: 'Ellen, daughter of Samuel Walley of Witton, labourer, the reputed father son of John and Katherine Walley of Witton and Betty Ravenscroft daughter of Ralph and Ellen Ravescroft of Witton, born 13 December 1778, baptised 6 January 1779'. The north of England has a number of these very full 'Dade' registers, especially in the Archdiocese of York between 1778 and 1812, following a directive from the Archbishop, William Markham, in 1777. (Markham was by all accounts a tall, arrogant, overbearing man who had once taught the young Jeremy Bentham; he married a rich Dutch woman, who bore him thirteen children. He had noticed and evidently admired the system being used by the Revd William Dade, a clergyman in York.) These registers are, of course, a goldmine for demographic, as well as genealogical, research. See *Local Population Studies* 23, 73 and 76 for background references.

George Rose's Act of 1812 led to baptisms in the Church of England being entered on a standard form in printed books from 1 January 1813. (Rose's main interests seem to have been in warfare and finance, but he was also a keen advocate of vaccination, helping to found the National Vaccine Institute in 1809.) Most, though not all, parishes adopted the new forms, which are still in use to the present day, with significant amendments in 1978 and 1992. Following the introduction of a stamp duty in 1783, and up to 1813, a few parishes were already using printed forms which provided a space for date of birth as well as baptism (see *Local Population Studies* 26 and 76). For some parishes, standardisation in 1813 was a retrograde step, because the new forms required less information than the parish had entered in its pre-1813 registers. This, together with the standardisation, led to J. S. Burn's opinion (1862) that they were now 'greatly devoid of interest' and he proposed a significantly improved form which, sadly for the genealogist, was never adopted. At Witton in Cheshire, however, a vestry meeting decided that their own system was so superior to the new one being introduced by Parliament that they would maintain the old in tandem with the new, and they did so until 1862. A typical George Rose entry reads 'Sarah, (daughter of) Thomas and Sarah Smith, joiner, of Witton, baptised 10 January,

1819'; the auxiliary register gives this as 'Sarah, daughter of Thomas Smith of Witton, joiner, (son of) John and Betty Smith of Northwich and Sarah daughter of Samuel and Betty Wilcockson of Witton, born 20 December 1818 and baptised 10 January 1819'. Thus two entries from this auxiliary 'Dade' register could cover six generations of the same family. It will be noted, by the way, that the George Rose registers have no columns for the child's surname, or for its sex, which has to be inferred unless the scribe thought fit to include it.

Entries for illegitimate children in parish registers before 1813 normally name only the mother. They often contain an additional term of disapprobation of the child, such as 'base', 'bastard', 'B', 'byeblow', 'chanceling', 'dropped child', 'filius/filia populi', 'unmulierly begotten', 'populi/vulgi/terrae/meretricis', 'illegal', 'lamebegot', 'lovebegot', 'merrybegot', 'nothus', 'spurius', 'viciatus', 'scapebegot', 'uniuscuiusque', and even 'dratsab'. Steel (1968, I, p. 50), lists a number of others in English and Latin. Sometimes it is the mother who is implicitly blamed by being referred to as 'fornicator', 'adulterer' or 'harlot'. It is not uncommon for the name of the reputed (or 'supposed') father or fathers to be given also, especially after an Act of 1634 which required the recording of the names of both parents at baptism. (Incidentally, M. Vincent-Northam, in *PFH* 110 Feb 07, suggests that 'reputed' fathers had acknowledged paternity, whereas 'imputed' had not.) In the seventeenth century an illegitimate child might carry an 'alias' in his or her surname when an adult, a practice which survived into the nineteenth century (see *GM* 15.14, 17.6). Thus John Smith alias Jones would have a father and mother who were not married to each other, one called Smith and the other Jones. John Smith alias Jones might then grow up, marry and have children who themselves would carry the surname Smith alias Jones, and occasionally so might his grandchildren. There seems to have been no strongly applied convention that one or the other should come first. In more modern times illegitimacy has been the origin of some hyphenated surnames. (For others see *FTM* 3.4 Feb 87, and Steel, 1968, I, pp. 92–6, who notes that hyphenation became 'widespread' in the nineteenth century including, for example, through marriage or remarriage. The practice has many elements in common with the use of an alias – see below.)

Don Steel and others have expressed the view that a few children entered as 'illegitimate' may have been so classified because they were the offspring of Dissenters.

References to illegitimacy within marriage are very rare, but J. S. Burn (1862) found a saint in Stepney whose wife had a child 'begotten as she affirmed in the field this side the mud wall near the Gunne, about 9 of the o'clock at night; the father she knew not, but the said [husband] by them that brought the child to be baptised, requested that it might be recorded in his name – October 23, 1633'.

An alias, often abbreviated to 'als' in the registers, did not always denote illegitimacy, however; see Steel 1968, I, pp. 89–96, and *GM* 24.4. It has also been used on marriage, or on the remarriage of a widow to denote 'formerly'; to recognise changes of name, including some following immigration; to signify a common-law marriage; to differentiate between different holders of common surnames; to acknowledge a personal inheritance from outside the family; and to indicate stepchildren or fostered children, often in order to preserve rights inherited from their original birth family; occasionally, to indicate an occupation; or to indicate a commonly used nickname or occupational name for the individual concerned. For example, 'Nicholas, son of Nicholas Jackson alias Nogg' was baptised at Burnley in December 1668; as Nogg does not appear as a local surname, it rather looks like a nickname. There are many aliases in the diary of Nicholas Blundell of Crosby, 1702–28, which suggests that Roman Catholics were in the habit of using them for security during their years of persecution. Before the seventeenth century, and especially in the sixteenth, a place of dwelling was also used as an alias. Discovering the reason for an alias, therefore, is not straightforward, and each case has to be treated on its merits. Even where illegitimacy was the cause, there is no rule for whether the father's or mother's name was given first, and there are cases in which the individuals changed them round on different occasions! See Redmonds (1987) on the subject of aliases.

There were large numbers of illegitimate children in the days of our forefathers, and a great deal of research has investigated the phenomenon. It was once thought to be related to a high average age of marriage, or to other economic factors or social customs such as 'bundling', or trial marriage, a practice which lasted into the nineteenth century as a means of establishing whether a marriage would prove fruitful. See Stone (1977), and *Journal of Social History*, 35. (This is rather contentious among family historians, by the way, and it is certainly the case that many marriages were apparently childless.) However, the pattern of illegitimacy has not yet been fully analysed, and the reasons for it seem to be more subtle than any of the above explanations. For one thing, it was more common in some areas than in others – counties from Gloucestershire north to Lancashire had higher rates than the rest of the country, long before the industrial revolution. The national rates have varied over time, with a peak of up to 5 per cent in 1590, a dramatic fall in the 1650s, the time of the Puritan ascendancy, a slow rise to 6 per cent by 1800 and to almost 7 per cent by 1845. To put those figures in perspective, the 2000 rate was about 40 per cent! It was unconnected with urbanisation, with the average age of marriage or with the ratio of men to women at any one time. The biggest mystery lies in the fact that the proportion of illegitimate children varied with the actual number of children born – the greater the number of births, the greater the proportion of bastards.

Servants in rural areas were particularly likely to be mothers of illegitimate children. They were away from parental control, often denied the normal formalities of courtship, and prone not only to the attentions of their masters but also to those of their fellow servants. Parson Woodforde recorded on 4 March 1789 a neighbour's

> Man Servant James Atherton having been too familiar with his two young Servant Maids, Lizzy Greaves, an old Servant Maid of Mine about 23 years of age, and another Girl by name Mary, both of which are with Child by James. The former Maid Lizzy, was married Yesterday to James, and the other discovered her Situation only last Night. James also had kept Company with Lizzy's Sister, Sukey ...

See Turner (1962).

Before the New Poor Law of 1834, the fathers of illegitimate children were often included in a baptismal record, but rarely thereafter; they might also be named in workhouse records. Fathers were sometimes made to pay for the apprenticeship of their children (*FTM* 17.7 May 01), at a time when orphans or pauper children could be made to serve as parish apprentices (too often a euphemism for cheap labour). If your ancestor was illegitimate, you can normally trace the tree only through the female line, but there are a few ways to discover the father even if he is not named in the register. It should be admitted, however, that most fathers who are named anywhere at all are to be found in the parish register entry, and occasionally more than one possible father is given! The most common way is through bastardy papers, which are to be found among the parish Poor Law records (see *FTM* 24.4 Feb 08 for an example). The mother of an illegitimate child who might require poor relief from the parish was interrogated in order that the father could be named, the onus of paying for the child's upkeep placed upon him, and he could even be forced to marry, until the practice was made illegal in 1844. Unfortunately, as well as the father, any of the four grandparents might sign the indemnity bond pledging family support for the child. In the seventeenth century the father might have been identified for ecclesiastical trial, and therefore be found in the 'presentments' in the appropriate Diocesan Record Office. Quarter sessions papers and vestry minute books also refer to the problems caused to the parish by individual cases, the former being asked to issue maintenance orders on the fathers, and a few parishes have registers of bastards. The *Manchester Mercury* published the names of those fathers of illegitimate children who had failed to answer recognisances, stating residence, occupation, and the name of the mother. There are also cases of parishes paying men to marry the mothers of illegitimate children in order to get them off the rates. For relevant legislation see Davey (1922) and Tate (1983) and the discussion of baptisms in other parishes on pp. 102–16.

With foundlings, unfortunately, you are almost always at a dead end. Such children had to be given names, and often these tell a little story in themselves about the child's circumstances. For example at Nantwich on 13 March 1735 a child was baptised and recorded as 'Hannah Tuesday, a foundling'. I wonder how many other people whose names contain days of the week or months of the year are descended from foundlings. Monday is by far the commonest, followed by Friday and Sunday. An entry for 1 February 1593 in nearby Acton is the baptism of 'Matilda ignoramus' – 'Matilda [whose surname] we do not know'. There must be plenty of people surnamed Lawrence who are descended from St Lawrence Jewry foundlings in London, but that is not the reason why the surname was omitted from Weekley's books of surnames – D. H. had run off with his wife! For foundling names see *GM* 21.4, and for specific cases a newspaper search is recommended (*Anc* 59 Jul 07).

To look after these unfortunates, Captain Coram founded the nation's first foundling hospital in 1741. He accepted unwanted children who were left in a basket suspended from the perimeter wall, taking children from all over the country until 1760, when a grant from the government was discontinued. See *GM* 23.3 and 27.5, *FTM* 2.4 Jan 86 and 16.8 Jun 00, and Saul (1995) under 'Children's societies'. Not all who found their way there were foundlings, however – some were the product of broken marriages. Most were fostered in the country, then educated and apprenticed in London. Patrons and fundraisers included Hogarth and Handel.

Less well known than the hospital itself, however, is the inability of the new civil registration service in 1837 to provide any birth certification for the children, and the hospital had to provide their own equivalent until 1953! The Thomas Coram Register, now in the care of the Corrections section of GRO, was compiled to include all children who entered from 1 January 1853 to 29 January 1949. This

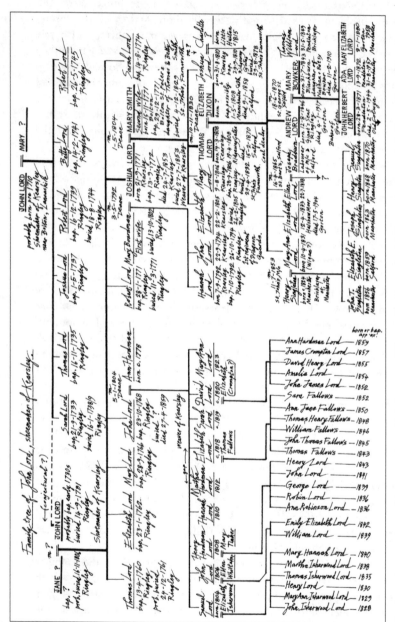

Figure 4. A common problem: proving a link between different family trees which may be connected. Use a dotted line for tentative connections.

is treated in a way similar to the Adoption Register, the GRO holding a confidential linkage to their original birth where known. See *MN* 18 Oct 94 for photos of the relevant documents.

Failure to find an Anglican baptism

Following a family through several generations in a parish register is often quite easy. Until the end of the last century the baptisms of several children to the same parents (usually with an average of two years between each child, though intimacy normally recommenced a month after childbirth) will have been preceded by a marriage which, in turn, arose from two baptisms twenty to thirty years earlier. It all sounds very simple until the genealogist is forced to conclude that long before the twentieth century – indeed, long before the industrial revolution – there was much more geographical movement among the population than most people realise. Family reconstitution studies usually find the baptism of only about a third of brides and grooms, though genealogists can improve on that figure through zealous pursuit of their particular family's records. There are several reasons why you may not find the baptism you are looking for and, in each case, various possible courses of action to take. Sooner or later, however, you will encounter an apparently insuperable problem, but the fascination is, of course, that you never really know whether it can be solved or not. Reference to Volume 3, Chapter 10 of the wonderful *Genealogical research in England and Wales* by Gardner & Smith (1956–64) gives an excellent introduction to the ramifications of the pursuit of this particular truth.

There is one important piece of advice that will help you to decide which course of action to take. You should make a note of all the occurrences of the surname you are looking for in the probable parish, and in those which surround it, building up their individual family trees just before and during the time when you expect to find your 'missing' baptism. This will establish the likelihood of a local birth and may reveal clues as to where the child was baptised. Note also whether the register provides evidence of mobility, and where the migrants came from. A gap in the regular two-yearly production of children probably means an early death or miscarriage, but there may be other explanations. Conception was more likely if the mother was not breast-feeding the previous child. It should be noted that there was often a surprisingly large interval between the date of marriage and the birth of the first child, for a number of different reasons, but only rarely (and in rich families) might it be through the bride having been very young at the time, often revealed by reference to Consistory

Court papers (see Rogers & Smith, 1991, p. 163). Figure 4 illustrates this stage of research into the origin of an ancestor whose baptism could not be discovered.

Baptism in another parish
Do not be surprised, therefore, if your ancestors moved from parish to parish even before the industrial revolution. Peter Spufford (*GM* 17.8–10) concluded his research into seventeenth-century mobility by suggesting that very large numbers did not live where they had been born, and that almost half the population did not die where they had been born. Baker (1973), for example, found that 55 per cent of the heads of Cardington households in 1782 had been born over five miles away. The most mobile appear to have been unmarried people aged over fifteen, as, before the nineteenth century, at least half were farm servants hired for the year. Movement was largely limited, however, to a twenty-mile radius, and could be much less if the geography of the area was not conducive to travel. Celia Fiennes noted, 'You are forced to have Guides as in all parts of Derbyshire, and unless it be a few that use to be guides the common people know not above 2 or 3 mile from their home' (*Journeys*, 1949, p. 101). On the other hand, London has been known to attract young migrants, especially male, for several centuries. From 1813 incumbents should have received notice of baptisms of their parishioners elsewhere but did not necessarily record it. Baptism in another parish is therefore a very common problem before 1851, when the census began to include place of birth – see Camp (1987). This was especially acute in large towns, London having over a hundred parishes in the seventeenth century.

It is worth looking at an actual case in order to see how it can be solved. Thomas Darlington married Mary Houghland at Frodsham in 1745, but a search of the Frodsham register shows no record of his baptism – indeed, there was no Darlington family in the parish when Thomas was baptised, probably about 1720. If only he had been given a more unusual name, like the Valentine Darlington who was born at Whitegate, nearby, in the late seventeenth century! Alas, he had to be a Thomas, and several possible baptisms can be found in the notional twenty-mile radius. A helpful list of churches at specified distances is being developed on the Internet at www.genuki.org.uk. Fortunately Frodsham is on the coast, which reduces the search somewhat. (My father was born there, on Ship Street, named when the town was a port!)

The first assumption to make is that Thomas Darlington was born in a neighbouring parish and that his baptism took place in the parish of his birth, although this rule, like so many others, was sometimes broken. Research through the registers of a series of parishes can nowadays be much easier than it once was (just how easy depends on which county you are searching) if you use the massive index being compiled by the Mormon Church, about which more later. Even if you can find only one potentially correct baptism, you should then answer the following questions, in sequence, in order to reduce the likelihood of error to a minimum:

Did the child die before reaching adulthood? (In London especially, this might involve a burial in the parish of a wet nurse up to forty miles away! See *GM* 23.3.)
Was the child later married in its parish of birth?
Did the child in turn have children in the parish of birth?
Did the child's father or other relative leave a will, making identification possible? (Local family history societies might have indexes of surnames, other than those of the testators, found in wills.)
Does your ancestor's age at death accord with this baptismal date?
Did other members of the family also move to the new parish?
Is there a monumental inscription (see p. 225) which would provide the names of other relatives?
Do census entries for surviving relatives provide clues?
Is the officiating minister, named in baptismal and burial entries after 1812, from a distant parish?

In Tarvin, a parish bordering on Frodsham, one Thomas, son of Thomas Darlington, was baptised in 1719, twenty-six years before the marriage concerned. Was this the correct baptism? The Thomas baptised in 1719 did not die as a child; nor did he marry at Tarvin – so hopes rise that he is the right one. In the Tarvin baptismal register for the 1740s and 1750s however, there he is, having children himself – so he has to be eliminated, as he cannot have been the man who married in 1745 at Frodsham.

Meanwhile the International Genealogical Index (IGI) has produced three other possible baptisms, each of which will have to be checked in turn in the same way. This index is a massive undertaking by the Church of Jesus Christ of Latter-Day Saints (LDS) to computerise the extant records of birth, baptism and marriage. The 1992 edition had 56 million names for England alone, and 2 million for Wales. Members of the Church may have the satisfaction of knowing that their deceased ancestors can, after the appropriate ceremonies, have the choice of becoming a Mormon or not. (See *GM* 24.7–8, for a much fuller explanation of the background to this edition of the index.) The most up-to-date version of the IGI should now be found on the www. familysearch.org website. (See Nichols, 1993; Young, 2002.)

For genealogists without Internet access the end product of this indexing is a set of microfiches on which, in the case of England, each county is presented separately, with the entries arranged in alphabetical order of surname. All Welsh entries are indexed separately either by surname or by Christian name, and require some care in using – see Gibson (1987) – especially as they are based on bishops' transcripts (BTs) rather than the registers themselves. (For BTs see below, p. 140) Some family history societies and libraries have the fiches for the whole country, and they are available at the Church's genealogical family history centres (listed at www.genuki.org.uk/big/LDS/centres. txt), where the whole world's index can be consulted. They also may have the index on CD-ROM, where the whole country, not just separate counties, can be viewed in alphabetical order. Large public libraries and record offices normally have copies for their own and adjoining counties, and many have facilities for issuing printouts of individual pages. Gibson (1987) gives the most complete list available for the location of International Genealogical Index copies. Individuals and organisations can buy the index, county by county, at remarkably modest prices from the Family History Department, 50 East North Temple Street, Salt Lake City, Utah 84150, USA.

The Church of Jesus Christ of Latter-Day Saints has long welcomed visitors who are not Church members, and hopes that they will contribute their own research findings to two other files of very substantial proportions – Ancestral File™ and Pedigree Resource File – though by their very origins these entries are not as reliable as those in the main Index. These entries have not been put through the normal form of baptism in temple ceremonies. They should be thought of rather as a self-help database for any genealogist to use, and are available to purchase in the form of a package which can run on MS-DOS or on a Macintosh (see *FTM* 12.9 Jul 96). Directions on how to input the data will be found on an information sheet at the Church's family history centres.

Using the International Genealogical Index is very easy. If I am looking for, say, the baptism of a John Sladen in Nottinghamshire in the 1750s, I look up the surname in the county microfiche, perhaps finding it mixed up with variations such as Sladdin and Sladin but nevertheless with the spelling identical to that in the original register.

The information I expect to find against each entry is as follows: name; name of parents or name of spouse in the case of a marriage entry; sex; husband or wife; date and parish of the event; type of entry (A for adult baptism, B for birth, C for christening, M for marriage, and so on); three columns relating to the Mormon religious ceremonies (the word 'cleared' in these columns means that the temple ceremonies were still pending at the time of computerisation, whereas 'uncleared' in the column means 'father unknown'); and references to the batch and serial sheet from which the entry has been taken. If the tenth column reference contains only digits, no letters, the first two will refer to the year and the next three to the day on which the entry was computerised from information submitted by an individual. Making a note of all such entries will quickly indicate whether anyone has submitted several entries for the same surname. If the third number is less than four you can write to the Church for a copy of the original information sheet, available for a modest fee, which will include the name and address of the person who was interested enough in the entry to have it put into the index, and perhaps get in touch with the person concerned to exchange information. You should send the relevant batch and serial number, with the county and name of the individual entry concerned, to the English Division, Genealogical Department, 50 East North Temple Street, Salt Lake City, Utah 84150, USA. Following a long, unsuccessful attempt to find the deaths of my great-great grandparents, I contacted relatives in the United States by using the index, and they were able to tell me that most of the family had emigrated to Idaho in the early 1870s. The index can also be used in slightly less obvious ways. Siblings can be picked out quickly by searching the column showing parental names; so can the movement across parishes and even across county boundaries.

If you are using the website, and have identified a particular entry in the IGI, copy the batch number from the foot of the page, open the main enquiry page again and, instead of entering another name, enter the batch number and place. This will provide all the names and dates in that batch, in alphabetical order. A very useful alternative is to use http://freepages.genealogy.rootsweb.ancestry. com/~hughwallis/IGIBatchNumbers.htm which lists all the churches on the IGI individually, with their batch numbers and dates covered.

The index has its drawbacks, however, and it is particularly important to know what they are if the entry you are seeking seems not to be on it. The proportion of surviving baptisms and marriages incorporated into the index varies considerably from county to county. (Consult the Parish and Vital Records List for which places and periods have been included, and remember Peter Park calling the IGI the 'Incomplete Genealogical Index'.) Figures published in 1983 suggest that in the City of London you can expect to find over 90 per cent but in Herefordshire and Somerset only 4 per cent. The average is about 25 per cent (see *GM* 21.3). Naturally, in an undertaking so large, human error is unavoidable; in the International Genealogical Index such errors can take several forms. Occasionally entries from one parish have been placed in the wrong county, such as those of Formby, Lancashire, which appeared to be across the entire north of England, and all the pre-1813 West Drayton entries, which were scattered elsewhere; in some cases, names have been transcribed incorrectly – for example, Apolline Winstanley, who was married at Middlewich in 1686, appeared as Apolonia Whinston, and is indexed under Whinston, with the result that no one looking for Apolline Winstanley would find her, except by accident. (She is still missing.) Similarly, some Worrall entries for Great Budworth appear transcribed as 'Merrill'.

Pauline Litton's article in *FTM* 14.10 Aug 98 shows some of the difficulties of interpreting names in the IGI, including the merging, or otherwise, of Mc and Mac, and the disappearance of O'. The LDS does not have the manpower to correct errors even after they have been reported. It has been estimated that up to 12 per cent of the Ilfracombe entries were incorrect. Part of the blame must lie with the employment of some transcribers who are not native English-speakers. Again, 'John sone of Thomas and Mary Smith Carpenter' might have been misindexed with 'Carpenter' as the surname. 'Josh' is almost certainly 'Joseph' in earlier times if written as Jos[h] in the original register.

Some 10 per cent of entries in the current edition for England and Wales have been taken from information supplied by individuals, a percentage much greater for other countries and likely to increase in future British editions. If the batch number appears to antedate 1990 it is worth writing for copies of the original sheets, as above, but beware if the batch number begins with the letter F, or if the third digit is 0, 1, 2, or 3, as they are less reliable than others.

Other problems for the genealogist arise not necessarily from faults within the index but from failure to understand what it offers. The IGI contains almost no burials, so that, unless the word 'infant' appears in columns 5 or 6, there is no way of telling whether the person survived to marriageable age. No date of birth is included with a baptism, even when the original source provides both, so that an adult baptism could be overlooked by the searcher because it occurred at an unlikely date. The list of parishes included in the index, listed by county on a separate microfiche or print-out, can be misleading; for example,

'Runcorn baptisms 1700–50' may mean that all the baptisms between these dates have been included, or only a few. You should suspect undertranscribing if the reference number in column 10 begins with a digit rather than a letter.

In some areas, the IGI contains copies of the BTs rather than the registers themselves, for which they have been refused copying rights. Like some other religions, the LDS claims exclusive rights of access to heaven for their members, causing some Anglican bishops to have reservations about allowing interference with the souls of those already baptised. (This is genealogically unfortunate – either the LDS is correct, in which case we should all be grateful; or they are not correct, in which case it doesn't matter anyway.)

Finally, a word of warning about the arrangement of the names in the index in the microfiche format. I think that the merging of different spellings of the same surnames is admirably arranged, though even here the separate indexing of, for example, Tickle and Tittle could be a reason for overlooking entries. So long as the transcript is correct, there should be few problems in finding the surname you want if you search the obvious variations. Within each surname the Christian names are arranged alphabetically, and events concerning each Christian name are presented in the chronological order in which they occurred. However, each variation in the spelling or even an abbreviation is treated as a separate Christian name. Eliz, Eliza, Elizabeth, Elizth, Betty, Liza, Betsy, Bess and so on are given separate lists, strictly as the transcriber read the original register. Even Eliz and Eliz. are kept apart. Between Ino and John, two common forms of the same name, many other names would intervene, so that several names have to be passed over if you are to be sure that you have searched all the variations under which the entry you are seeking might have originally appeared. A considerable portion of the alphabet lies between Anne and Hannah, or Ellen and Helen.

It must always be remembered that, even when an entry has provided the answer you were seeking, this is still only an index and not a substitute for looking up the record in the original parish register, where additional information will often be found.

If the above methods fail to locate the baptism you are seeking, and there is no census or gravestone record to help you identify the place of birth, the search has to be extended geographically to cover even more parishes, though if the couple concerned subsequently emigrated, there may be a short cut in seeing what is on the death certificate. Some, such as those in Australia, include information about birth or baptism. Searching many parish registers becomes very tedious and is an obvious danger point at which the less committed may give up hope. However, even with a Smith or Jones of which there were rarely a large number in any English parish before the industrial revolution, there are always ways of narrowing the search. Many of the documents dealt with in Chapters II, III and IV can help in locating families of the surname you are seeking when the baptism probably occurred. Your choice, of course, will depend on the period in which your missing baptism occurs, but the fullest are the GRO indexes; see Camp (1987).

The earliest sources normally used by amateur genealogists to locate individual family names are probably the tax returns known as lay subsidies (see pp. 161–3). Most of the returns are among the Exchequer records in the National Archives, where there are also certificates of residence (1547–1685), completed so the subsidy payer was not charged twice if he had changed address. The earlier subsidies can be very difficult to read, but many have been printed by local record societies or in works on topographical history. Some have copies in city or county record offices, surviving to the seventeenth century – see *Amateur Historian* 3.8 and 4.3 for an historical introduction. It is always worthwhile noting the land held by the lord of the manor, which might provide a good lead in tracking movement.

Additionally, several other documents which list inhabitants prior to the full 1801 census can give an indication of where families with certain surnames lived at different times. The earliest known to contain ages is one for Ealing in 1599 (see Allison, 1963), but the first on anything like a national scale is the Protestation of 1642, a petition signed by most of the males in the country over the age of eighteen (and occasionally females), and some over sixteen, which attempted to avert the Civil War. Those who could not write marked a cross against their name; those who did not wish their name to be seen in support were also listed. The original is in the House of Lords, and the places covered are listed in the fifth report of the Historical Manuscript Commission (1876, pp. 120–34), obtainable in the largest public libraries. The fullest is claimed to be that of Cornwall, with over 30,000 names. Many of the returns have been published, and a list may be found in *GM* 19.3. See *Local Population Studies* 55 and 56, *Local Historian* 14.3 which has an article about this and other petitions from the same period, and *Local Historian* 21.9 for the Collection for Distressed Protestants, also in 1642. The Free and Voluntary Present (1661–62), celebrating the restoration of Charles II, covered anything from 25 per cent to 90 per cent of householders, and provides name, status, occupation and amount of gift; see *GM*

22.1. Two volumes in the 'Gibson Guides' series (Gibson & Dell, 1991; Gibson & Medlycott, 2001) list the extant documents for the seventeenth century.

The hearth tax returns are a very useful source for finding families with particular surnames (see *NALD* 32). Note that there is a difference between the hearth tax and the incorrectly named 'chimney tax', as some old houses in the seventeenth century were built before the relatively new practice of installing chimneys. The returns are also interesting, though indirect, evidence of your ancestors' wealth, the interpretation of this aspect being related to where they lived, there being a marked difference between a one-hearth house in urban and rural areas (see *Local Population Studies* 67). Probably about 80 per cent of people lived in a house with only one fireplace (many of their descendants living in one *room* in industrial towns two centuries later). This was especially likely to be the case in the countryside. The tax was collected every six months at a flat rate of 1s. for each fireplace in the house occupied (not necessarily owned, though the owner should be listed if the house was unoccupied). For the periods 1662–66 and 1669–75 lists of assessments or actual taxes paid are in the Exchequer records in the National Archives. Except in 1662, those too poor to pay are listed separately at the end of each roll, and normally amount to some 40 per cent; if they do not do so, you should suspect significant omissions. Thereafter, however, until the tax was abolished in 1689, the government employed private tax collectors who were more interested in profits than in keeping meticulous records. Many city or county record offices and libraries have microfilm copies of the lists associated with their area, so you need not rely on a visit to London. Some even have contemporary copies of the returns, and an increasing number are being published. See Gibson (1996), Schurer & Arkell (1992), and the useful introduction in Webster (1988). The Roehampton Project, digitising and publishing all hitherto unpublished hearth tax returns, using the fullest from each county, is being undertaken at Roehampton University – four volumes have been issued so far (see www.roehampton.ac.uk/hearthtax/).

The hearth tax was a very unpopular levy because, in the words of the Act which abolished it, its collection 'exposed every man's house to be entered into and searched at pleasure by persons unknown to him', and one of William of Orange's promises *en route* from Torbay to London after his invasion in 1688 was to get rid of it. In abolishing it he also lost the revenue, and hence developed the window tax from 1696 to 1852 (with an associated house tax to 1834), which could be assessed without entering the house. There are two main difficulties in using these records, however. Very few are available locally – most are in the National Archives once again; and the basis of assessment changed at frequent intervals, which makes interpretation difficult. For a full discussion of the tax, see Dowell (1965); the surviving records are listed in Gibson *et al.* (2004). Dowell also lists an astonishing range of other taxes collected during the eighteenth and nineteenth centuries – taxes on people keeping male servants, on people keeping female servants, with bachelors charged double (!), on persons possessing silver plate, carriages, horses and dogs, on clocks and watches, on people wearing hair powder and so on. Most of the returns for these taxes are in the National Archives. Rate books, however (discussed on p. 83), are more easily available for the purpose of locating families. See also the poll tax (p. 146).

In 1694 a tax was imposed on all births and marriages, and on bachelors over the age of twenty-five, by the Marriage Duty Act. Many clergymen, who were responsible for collecting the relevant information, compiled lists of existing parishioners which could be used as their baseline for assessing future changes; indeed, they were supposed to list all persons by name, social standing, marital status and property ownership. Lists have survived in relatively small numbers, however, and will be found with the other parish records either in the parish chest or in the diocesan record office. The tax was levied until only 1705, being hard to administer. See *Local Population Studies* 31 and Schurer & Arkell (1992).

The National Archives contains the Association Oath lists of 1696, in which all MPs, freemen, military and civil officers of the Crown, gentry and clergy in England and Wales swore loyalty to the house of Orange. Some areas have published their lists. See *GM* 21.4 for a useful list of the areas in which the oath rolls survive; see also Gibson (1996). Macfarlane (1977) is optimistic about how far the oath also covered all residents, including the poor.

In addition to the above, there are potentially many other listings which may be available in individual parishes; local printed histories or the county archivist will yield clues about which ones exist in the parishes and periods you wish to search. Muster rolls should list all able-bodied males between sixteen and sixty; lists of militia (from 1757 until replaced in 1908) can be found among the earlier constables' accounts (see Tate, 1983; *GM* 23.2; *MRS* 17; Gibson & Medlycott, 2004). Muster rolls from the sixteenth century are usually in the National Archives, but later ones may be found in the parish chest (see *NALM* 2 and 7). An act of 1803 required all men between the ages of seventeen and fifty-five to be recorded, with their age and occupation, whether they had children, and whether they were willing to volunteer. The militia, a 'reserve' force which lasted until 1908, was subject to regular listings which have normally survived in local record offices. They are especially common for the period of the Napoleonic Wars, when most men between eighteen and forty-five, 5′ 2″ or more tall and having no more than two lawful children should be found in them. They contain name, age, place of birth, physical description and occupation, though true age was easy to conceal. The 1777 militia list of Northamptonshire has been published as an excellent example, showing sizes of families and occupations; see *NALM* 18.

Ad hoc censuses are rarely to be found, and very rarely on bases as wide as a county – the only one I know was of Westmorland in 1787, which has been published. Pew rents, in the churchwardens' papers, give a very good indication of local surnames. The pew papers for Chesham, Bucks., in 1606 appear to list all the heads of household at the time (see *Local Historian* 22.4). Parishioners were allowed a choice of pew at a fixed rate, so that often plans would be drawn up, indicating who was entitled to sit in which part of the church. Half the pews had to be free in urban churches built after 1856. You can infer social status from the distance of a pew from the altar or pulpit. There are articles about pews in *FTM* 10.1–3 Nov 93-Jan 94.

The Test Oath of 1723, which should have been signed by all male adults, except officials who had already signed an earlier version, can be found in some city or county record offices, probably arranged by main town centre in the order in which people came to sign it. Those who refused to do so are also listed, but it is clear that both lists are far from complete (see *FTM* 24.4 Feb 08).

Taxation records are useful for identifying where families of specified surnames lived at various periods, as well as giving an indication of the wealth of our individual ancestors. (For those on line, see *FTM* 20.4 Feb 04.) Land tax records are of considerable use to the genealogist looking for surname distribution and the wealth of known ancestors. Though started by an act of 1692 and terminated in 1963, the tax gave rise to easily accessible returns mostly from 1780 to 1832, when the record of payment was copied to the Clerks of the Peace as a qualification for voting, and the avoidance of a fine! (Payment was sometimes by the owners rather than occupiers who from 1780 were included for the first time.) The tax was levied at the rate of one-fifth of the yearly rent paid to landowners, with Roman Catholics charged double before 1831. The records are normally to be found in the city or county record offices and supply the names of landowners, land occupiers and the amount of tax payable. They are sometimes arranged in annual bundles for large areas; hence a search through the land occupation history of any one parish may be awkward. Notice the value of the property, and the sequence of entries, which provide clues as to change of occupancy in subsequent years. See Gibson *et al.* (2004) for surviving returns, *Amateur Historian* 6.5, *GM* 16.6, and *FHM* 126 Jan 06.

Income tax was levied from 1799 to 1816 when it was abolished and the records ordered to be publicly destroyed. Duplicates were kept, however! (See Higgs, 2004a.) The tax was revived by Sir Robert Peel in 1842, and has enjoyed a long and prosperous run ever since.

Tithe schedules provide a slightly later source for similar information, but with the additional bonus of very large-scale maps which pinpoint exactly where your ancestors lived and perhaps worked. The tithe – an illegal (i.e. unparliamentary) tax of one-tenth of a man's annual income, payable in kind to the Church of England – had been a source of irritation for centuries, as Shakespeare and many other writers testify. The same feeling may be seen in Austria today, where tithes are still payable. The right to collect tithes under common law lasted well over 1,000 years. With the growth of Nonconformity and industriali-sation, the reforming Whig government of the 1830s finally devised a way of eliminating it without suddenly undermining the financial support of Anglican incumbents. Indeed, the tithe still survives in a few small areas, and was a continuing source of aggravation into the twentieth century (see Twinch, 2001). (Nonconformists sometimes satisfied their religious and social consciences by paying tithes as a gift; see Blundell's diary, 10 April 1710, or Josselin's diary, 20 July 1674, for example.) In establishing a firm basis for a gradual change over the next 100 years, detailed maps of each parish in which tithes were payable were drawn, showing every house, garden and field. The accompanying schedule listed all landowners and land occupiers, the state of cultivation, acreage and the amount of tithe payment. Three copies were made during the next twenty years. The original was eventually lodged in the National Archives, which also has tithe files which may be useful in those areas not covered by tithe maps; one copy stayed with the incumbent of the parish, with whom it should still remain unless it has been deposited in the diocesan record office (though many are now lost) and the third went to the bishop, who will normally have placed his copy in the diocesan record office. (In Wales, this last copy has normally been deposited in the National Library of Wales (NLW).) The National Archives has a leaflet on the subject – see *NALD* 41. The diocesan copy is the most convenient to use. Several parishes can be seen together; there are the facilities of a map room; and the schedules, which were originally stitched into the right-hand end of the map, have in many cases been separated for ease of consultation. There is a search fee for consulting documents which are still in the custody of the incumbent. See *FTM* 19.3 Jan 03, Evans (1993) and Kain & Prince (1985) for good accounts of how tithe documents can be used by historians and geographers. See also *Local Population Studies* (42–3) for Easter books, with associated lists of parishioners.

The Cheshire Record Office has put its collection of tithe maps (together with later OS maps) on line, at http://maps.cheshire.gov.uk/tithemaps.

In a few parishes the clergyman's tithe account books have survived from long before 1836, giving the income from tithepayers in the parish (see *Local Historian* 14.1). The Great Tithes were payable to the rector but, as he was sometimes the lord of the manor, receipt books for tithes may be found in manorial records. Where the amount payable was fixed it is possible to detect changes in land holding from year to year.

Genealogists, incidentally, have another reason to be grateful for the tithe system. It is still the way the Mormon Church funds its activities, including the International Genealogical Index.

In parishes where the tithe had already been changed into regular cash payments, about one-fifth in all, the tithe commissioners did not carry out this detailed recording procedure. The East Midlands, for example, has fewer tithe documents than other areas. But in some parishes enclosure maps, surveys and schedules may have survived. These, together with estate maps and any accompanying documents, which may go as far back as the seventeenth century, can provide very similar information about land use and surname distribution. Those dating from before 1801 will probably be in local archive offices, but there is a collection from 1836 to 1845 in the National Archives (see *GM* 24.8). Land ownership was also the subject of the *Returns of owners of land* (1873), published as book, microform and CD-ROM. For a list of surviving enclosure maps, see Kain *et al.* (2004).

Among this long list of sources for locating the whereabouts of families with certain surnames at different periods there are also voting documents. Until the introduction of the secret ballot in 1872, voting at general elections was open and the results were written down; many were even published, the largest collections being in the British Library, at the Institute of Historical Research, and at the Society of Genealogists. The Kent Family History Society has set a good example by reprinting about two dozen for that county on microfiche, and

Stuart Raymond issues a series of them. The poll books list each voter, the candidate they voted for, and their address and occupation. Often those who did not exercise their right to vote are also listed.

The original documents are in city or county record offices, and a list of all those known can be found in Sims (1984) and Gibson & Rogers (2008), which should be used in conjunction with each other. See also Vincent (1967) and Drake & Finnegan (1994, vol. 4) which includes a table of changes in the franchise. From these documents you can gather not only surname distributions but also the way in which your ancestors voted – or perhaps the way in which their employers or landlords expected them to vote! (Benjamin Shaw's diary records his thirteen-year-old daughter Agnes being dismissed by her employer merely for shouting the name of a candidate he did not like during the election of 1826.) Occasionally canvassing registers of the political parties survive, showing the names and addresses of those who had promised support, or otherwise, together with an indication of how they had voted at the last election. Since 1832 there are also electoral registers (see pp. 78–9).

For the rarer surnames even modern telephone directories can be useful. Your public library should contain directories for the whole of the United Kingdom, representing up to 50 per cent of households in the country. If you put a dot on a map to represent each telephone rented by those with the surname you are tracing, you may be surprised how far this method can be used for pinpointing the geographical origins of surnames. Most families will be represented in the main industrial centres, in London and across the south coast; but try to spot those parts of the country where the surname seems to be over-represented compared with the population size. You can examine areas as small as a county with useful results; see Rogers (1995). This type of research has now been greatly assisted by Steve Archer's CD-ROM *The British nineteenth century surname atlas.*

We have still not exhausted the ways of locating baptism in an unknown parish, and the available sources are well summarised in *Family History*, November 1982. For London and the Home Counties the location of nurse children (who were fostered by others, often relatives, for their first few years) may help; see GM 21.9. If the mother's parish is known, you should try there for the baptism of at least her eldest children. This is believed to have been a common practice, perhaps because new mothers-to-be liked to 'go home' to have their first child, or because parents felt, particularly between 1662 and 1744, that it would give the child a little more security under the Act of Settlement. Paul Hair (1970) found no evidence of this phenomenon, however, and there are several possible reasons why there was an unexpected gap between wedding and first child – stillbirth, abortion or miscarriage, for example. Equally, another parish may have been used simply for geographical convenience.

The Act of Settlement and subsequent acts relating to settlement gave rise to another set of documents which may be useful in tracing the place from which a family moved. From 1662 until, believe it or not, 1948, each person 'belonged' to a particular parish, in the sense that it was responsible for poor relief payments if he or she fell on hard times. Normally it was the parish of birth or place of real estate ownership, though other property could be provided as security by those who wished to change parish. Thus births to paupers were a potential drain on the ratepayers and pregnant girls were often 'encouraged' to give birth elsewhere. This practice was stopped in 1744 by the simple device of recognising the legal parish of an illegitimate child to be that of the mother. Until that date, it was important to record births to 'strangers' (those not belonging to the parish) and some parents seem to have travelled to extra-parochial areas in order to avoid consequences of the settlement law. From 1691 legal settlement in a new parish could also be obtained through apprenticeship, being in service for a year or paying rates in the new parish. The settlement laws were not uniformly enforced, as it was often in the interests of employers to maintain a local free, unemployed labour force. Until the mid-nineteenth century a parish of settlement might pay another parish to keep its emigrants rather than have them back. Formal proceedings were held in disputed cases; Peter Pownall's diary records on 11 May 1787, 'Sarah Marslands resedenc tryed at Stockport she is made a Bramhall woman.'

Settlement certificates were given to those leaving a parish, either temporarily or after 1696 permanently, acknowledging the continuing responsibility of the parish of origin. The certificates were then lodged with the officers in the receiving parish and were sometimes copied into the parish books. If the new parish was later unwilling to give poor relief, and the pauper was unwilling to return to his own parish, he or she would be examined by a magistrate and possibly removed by force. James Clegg's diary for 6 December 1751 records seeing 'a poor woman brought by a [travel] pass in a wagon. She had strong labour pains on her when she was brought, and was delivered the next day after,' thus landing legal settlement firmly on the doorstep of his parish and not the parish which had successfully removed her! The procedure gave rise to Examination Papers, which sometimes contain extremely detailed biographical data, and Removal Orders. These survive either in the parish chest or in quarter sessions papers – see

FTM 18.7 May 02, 18.10 Aug 02 and 24.2 Dec 07, Tate (1983), Steel (1968, I), and Gibson (2007) – and survival rates vary considerably from county to county, and even within a county. You should ask the county archivist's advice about where they are for any particular parish. The great majority of such certificates have been destroyed, so other local clues, such as the minutes of Quaker meetings, victuallers' licences (see Gibson & Hunter, 2008) or conveying back to parish of settlement by the constables in their accounts should be sought. On settlement, see *FTM* 18.5 Mar 02.

Sometimes, church or chapel membership lists will record where a new member had come from, or indeed where an old family had gone to. Another way to discover where families migrated from is to look at other 'new' names appearing in the parish register and, in the nineteenth century, the census, in order to see if there is a clue pointing to where others had come from. It is rather a long shot, of course, but not too difficult if the register has good indexes. I have the impression that agricultural labourers tended to move in single families or as individuals, but that industrialisation could bring about the simultaneous movement of many people engaged in similar trades when major new developments such as canals were being undertaken. (See *Anc* 29 Jan 05 for south–north migration.) In more rural areas, it has been possible to find the place of baptism by discovering which other parts of the county were held by the local lord of the manor, and searching there. Manorial records (pp. 144, 156) sometimes also contain lists of freemen and tenants for individual years. Certificates of baptism had to be produced when couples took out a licence to marry between 1 August 1822 and 26 March 1823, and should be found with the bonds and allegations; see pp. 195–6; see also *GM* 21.3. Ordination papers of clergymen should include baptismal certificates, and the National Archives has parentage for most solicitors (called 'attorneys-at-law' before 1875) from their articles of clerkship, 1730–1835. Gravestones, obituaries and wills can also provide useful clues to geographical movement.

The general drift of population from south to north in England was matched by the north to south movement in Wales to work in the newly industrialised areas. Parliamentary Sessional Papers 1843, Vol. XLV, list a couple of thousand individuals who had moved from specified agricultural areas to industrial centres, but such numbers are, alas, only the tip of the iceberg. Many moved in the wake of relatives or friends who could recommend jobs or living accommodation.

Baptism not recorded

Some children were simply not baptised, even before the industrial revolution, and finding reference to such children in the wills of the parents is not an uncommon experience. It seems to have been particularly true of the very large parishes in the north of England in which families might be living several miles away from the parish church (see *Local Population Studies* 24). Of course, many of these missing baptisms were of children who died young anyway. Probably between 2 per cent and 5 per cent of children died within the first few days of life in the sixteenth and seventeenth centuries. However, as we shall see, others were baptised together as a whole family and it is difficult to escape the conclusion that some families never got round to baptism at all. Many others were baptised in non-Anglican churches (see pp. 135–8), and it has been generalised that reference to individuals naming (unusually) birth or 'interment' rather than baptism and burial in a parish register is a sign of Nonconformity. Some refused to baptise during the imposition of stamp duty, 1783–94, a sort of 'poverty trap' encouraging the exclusion of those slightly too wealthy, or too proud, to be shown as exempt as paupers (indicated by the letter P in the margin). A few parish registers recorded births in the early eighteenth century, and they are much more numerous than baptisms in those parishes. In Childwall, for example, only 75 per cent of those born between 1700 and 1725 were baptised; see Edwards (1976).

Additionally, some Anglican baptisms were not recorded. The scribe either forgot, or was too lazy to enter the event in the register. Gypsies were normally outside the Anglican net, but when they were 'caught' they were sometimes given occupational surnames (see Floate, 1999; GM 26.6; FTM 20.9 Aug 04). Steel (1968–) notes that illegitimate children were commonly not baptised, or at least the ceremony was not recorded. Scraps of paper which the clergy used for a 'first draft' of the entries were sometimes lost. In the 1806 register for Woodhead, in the Pennines, there is a note to the effect that the previous baptisms, from 1780, were 'taken from the Notes found amongst the papers of the late Reverend Joseph Broadhurst, Minister of Woodhead, dec'd'. The very act of writing up the register from daily notebooks could cause difficulties. In Frodsham nineteen entries from 5 July to 1 December 1727 are repeated from 28 June to 1 December 1726, and it is evident that six months' baptisms, or thereabouts, are missing. It was to prevent such abuses that George Rose's Act required the recording of baptisms and burials within seven days of the event, but needless to say it seems to have been widely ignored. Peter Razzell concludes (*Local Population*

Studies 64 and 77) that about three-quarters of the events in his sample parishes are found in the Anglican registers, a number that would greatly decrease into the nineteenth century. Most of the omissions he puts down to clerical negligence rather than Nonconformity.

If you are unable to find a baptism, particularly when you can see families with the same surname living in the parish earlier still, I would always recommend constructing a histogram. Count the annual number of baptisms for a matter of decades on either side of the expected date, and represent the numbers on a graph, with time along the base axis and the number of events determining the height of each column. The appearance of the graph will tell you immediately whether there are likely to be a significant number of entries missing from the register whereas only the most obvious omissions would be evident to a cursory glance through the text itself.

It is difficult to generalise about the extent of underregistration because it varies from parish to parish, and in some parishes over time. According to Razzell (1972), about one-third of children born in forty-five rural parishes between 1760 and 1845 were not baptised where they later said, in the census, that they had been born. The registers of Wales, including Monmouthshire, are notoriously defective, some having more marriages than baptisms!

Some registers have deteriorated over the centuries to such an extent that parts are either illegible or missing altogether. Through poor storage conditions, fire damage, or the eating habits of rodents, illegibility is an all-too-common problem, but in many cases an ultra-violet light reader, which record offices usually possess, will help. Unfortunately the machines are often too small to use with bulky parish registers, and perhaps repositories should consider a mobile ultra-violet light such as those used by veterinary surgeons for identifying skin complaints.

Vandalism has affected registers as well as the church fabric. It has been known for visitors to cut entries out while the clergyman's back was turned. Stories from the nineteenth century include those of the parson who threw away an old register because no one could read it, a parish clerk who was the local grocer and used some of the leaves as wrapping paper, leaves being used to back books in the church school, and so on. Whole registers have disappeared. A useful list was produced as part of the 1831 census, which investigated the state of each parish register. However, registers continue to be lost through fire, negligence and (especially after 1812 when wooden chests holding the parish documents were replaced by iron ones) damp. Lord Teviot reported to the House of Lords in 1976 that 2,400 volumes had been lost since 1831 – one every three weeks! J. S. Burn complained that 'the most ancient Registers are yearly disappearing or becoming illegible for want of proper care and preservation', and Gatfield (1897) told some sad stories of how this was happening.

One result of poor security is the existence of forgeries (see Steel, 1968, I, p. 17), but I suspect these are far less common than late entries in a parish register, in which baptisms in particular have been entered much later than most of the others. They are easy to spot, and must be distinguished from late baptisms, being squeezed between existing lines, or in the margin, or in a different handwriting, and a good published transcript should indicate whether such is the case in the original register. My guess is that the majority are quite genuine but must be regarded with suspicion, especially when they are not repeated in the BTs (see below).

One of the objectives of the Parochial Registers and Records Measure 1978 was to give these documents greater security. As a general rule, if a register was missing in the 1831 list it is most unlikely to turn up now; if, however, it was there in 1831 but is now missing, seek the advice of the relevant county archivist. He or she will tell you either that it has been lost through some known disaster or that its loss is news – in which case the city or county record office will almost certainly search for it. This has happened to me twice and the registers were found.

Counties vary considerably in the extent to which sixteenth-century registers have survived – the subject of an interesting article in *GM* 24.2 – and there is no doubt that, for this reason alone, your ability to trace ancestors for 400 years or more becomes a bit of a lottery, depending much on where they lived at the time. The 'census' of parish registers, published in 1831, listed only forty in the whole country which had entries earlier than 1538.

'The gap' is the notoriously difficult period in the 1640s and 1650s during and after the Civil War. It has been estimated that about one-sixth of all baptisms are missing in this period. The war itself is often blamed for the fact that whole years are omitted from the registers. During the 1650s registration was taken out of the hands of the clergy, and civil clerks – often schoolteachers, for example – who often covered more than one parish by merger, were required to record births as well as baptisms, and from 1653 to charge a prohibitive 1s. fee for doing so; indeed, an ordinance to do so had first been passed in 1645. Rather confusingly, these clerks were called 'registers', not 'registrars'. John Evelyn wrote in his diary for 11 October 1652:

My sonn Jon Stansfield was borne, being my second child, and christned by the name of my mother's father, that name now quite extinct, being of Cheshire. Christen'd by Mr Owen in my Library at Sayes Court where he afterwards churched my wife, I always making use of him on these occasions because the Parish Minister durst not have officiated according to the forms and usage of the Church of England, to which I always adhered.

Although Wrigley & Schofield (1981) have shown that baptismal registers in the 1550s were over twice as defective as those of the 1650s, in general the quality and survival rate of the registers do decline at this time. Moreover, some of the main ways of overcoming the problem in other periods (see the discussion of alternative sources to parish registers on pp. 138–51) are not available. For tracing soldiers in the Civil War, see *GM* 25.8.

Since the revised canons of 1948 the Anglican Church will not marry a couple if neither party has been baptised, and may make stipulations in cases where only one party has been baptised. Before then, however, I can find no rubric on the matter, so that an Anglican marriage does not necessarily imply baptism on the part of the bride and groom. Even since 1948, so long as the baptism is in the name of the Trinity, it has not mattered by whom the child is baptised, and private baptism has long been held to be just as acceptable as church baptism – indeed, private baptism or 'half-baptism', is sometimes distinguished in the records from public christening. According to canon 70 in 1603, a clergyman should have recorded all baptisms in his parish, and indeed it is not uncommon to find the letter P or 'Priv.' in the margin of a register of baptisms. From the middle of the sixteenth century some clergy had refused to baptise except in church, in order to counter Nonconformity. On 12 April 1689 John Evelyn complained in his diary of 'the baptising in private houses without necessity' which proceeded 'much from the pride of women'. He accused ministers of receiving 'considerable advantage and gifts for baptising in chambers', a practice which he described as 'novel and indecent'. The practice is said to have been particularly popular in eighteenth-century London, where it probably originated. The 1801 census listed private baptism as one of the major reasons for deficiencies in parish registers and estimated that up to one-third of entries were missing in Northumberland for that reason. However, private baptism saved many children from being refused a proper burial (see pp. 241–2). Some clergy evidently waited for the public baptism before making the entry (a phenomenon which can be proved by observing the chronological sequence of dated events in the register) but paupers, it is said, could not afford the cost of either the ceremony or the party which was expected to accompany it. The registration of private baptisms is supposed to have improved after 1812.

Occasionally, odd pages of the original register may have been missed by the technician doing the microfilming – page numbers or the sequence of dates should be checked if omissions are suspected.

For solutions to all the problems thrown up in this section see the alternatives to registers discussed on pp. 138–51. Lest the impression created by this whole section is too gloomy, it should be added that research into pre-industrial communities suggests that only a tiny minority avoided being recorded altogether (Macfarlane, 1977). Most of the solutions which follow assume that you have already taken the advice on p. 101 above and tried to piece together the rest of the family from other sources, such as parish register entries or the census, to find potentially related survivors of earlier generation(s) and first-name patterns in order to get round the problems of misinformation or lack of information.

Baptism not in England or Wales

It is beyond the brief of this book, and the capacity of the author, to describe parallel recording systems in other countries for those who discover, to their amazement, frustration and curiosity, that they are descended from immigrants. The references on pp. 292–302 suggest reading, in English, on how to undertake genealogy in some other countries.

The National Archives has details of the naturalisation of aliens from 1789, but they are not available until they are 100 years old (see *FTM* 6.8 Jun 90). Naturalisation papers in the National Archives should include residence, marital status, occupation and country of origin. Certificates of arrival of aliens 1836–52 are also in the National Archives. Their names were published by HM Stationery Office from 1844 (when naturalisation could be granted by the Home Secretary as well as by private Act of Parliament) until 1900, in one volume; from 1961 the job was taken over by the *London Gazette* (see National Archives Records Information Leaflet 70). 'Denization', the granting of only some of the privileges of naturalisation, was by letters patent, and allowed children born subsequently to inherit property. Jews naturalised between 1609 and 1799 are in the *Jewish Historical Society of England* 22 (1970) and the oaths taken by foreign Protestants upon naturalisation 1708–12 have been printed by the Huguenot Society. See Colwell (1984, chapter 5) and Bevan & Duncan (1990). The IGI has a fiche entitled 'Births at sea'.

There are several immigration societies based on country of origin

– Anglo-German, Anglo-Italian, Anglo-Scottish, the Huguenot Society of London (www.huguenotsociety.org.uk), and so on. Many have their own website. See *GM* 27.10.

Entry missed by the searcher (see also pp. 38–9)
There are several potentially dangerous circumstances in which a baptismal entry can easily be missed:

If you are reading the same set of records continuously for more than an hour.

If you are using registers in which baptisms, marriages and burials are not separated but written in the chronological order in which any of those events took place. Sometimes the clerk put small marks in the margin in order to distinguish baptism, marriage and burial entries from each other. Baptisms are occasionally written as burials, and vice versa; in many registers the odd few entries are written entirely out of chronological order, or even on the flyleaf of the register book.

If you are using a microfilm copy of the register. It is all too easy to forget that some entries are too difficult to read, and to fail to check them later in the original register. In fact once a register has been microfilmed you may have some difficulty in persuading the archivist in charge of the original to allow you to use it. The 1978 Measure, however, gives an enquirer the right to see the original if the illegibility is due to poor filming rather than a poor original.

If you are using a register which has been rebound. Entries are sometimes located in the wrong part, or detail hidden in the tighter spine.

If you are looking for entries for families of more than two surnames at the same time.

If you have eyesight that is less than perfect. Muscular strain is automatically relieved by a temporary alteration of focus, without the sufferer being aware of it, until the fault is corrected by an optician. The result is that the eyes do not allow sufficient concentration on each entry on the page.

Misleading clues (see also pp. 39–44)
You will normally be searching for a baptism with no positive indication of the place of birth, unless it has been obtained from the census. The

first assumption must be that the baptism occurred in the parish where the marriage, or the birth of later children, took place. There are two basic reasons why your search may not prove fruitful. As we have seen, the population was quite mobile, even in pre-industrial times, and the twenty- or thirty-year interval between birth and marriage was ample time for a family to move, perhaps more than once. And the registers themselves may be faulty.

You may also be looking in the wrong direction if the basis of your information is misleading you. There is, for example, a period between about 1780 and 1837 when some clergymen, particularly but not exclusively in the new industrial areas, stated incorrectly that the bride and the groom were both 'of this parish' when they married, the real place of residence being concealed. It is not clear why this happened, and it did not affect marriages by licence as much as marriages by banns.

You should also bear in mind that many of the sources which have given you a clue to the date of birth – age on a marriage bond or gravestone, for example – are not necessarily accurate, especially in the case of those who claimed to be centenarians, or those who claimed to be twenty-one at the time of marriage. Beware of gravestone inscriptions if they were not inscribed immediately after the earliest burial. Baker (1973) found that almost a quarter of ages given on early Cardington gravestones were wrong by a factor of five years or more! Even knowing this, it is not easy to accept a baptism in, say, 1722, when the age at marriage in 1748 is given as '22 years and upwards', and the strategy adopted on p. 103 should be adopted as a test of identification. Always look at as many documents as possible in order to confirm the first data, and if you find conflicting ages for the same person, it is normal for the earliest date to be correct. Daniel Broadbent and Martha Cheetham took out a licence to marry in 1780, both claiming to be aged '21 years and upwards'. The Mottram marriage entry itself, having the word 'Behold!' in the margin, shows Daniel to have been twenty-three and Martha to have been eighty-three years old. Their married bliss lasted for two years, Martha dying in 1782.

An American family, descended from emigrants in the 1790s, had inherited a detailed history showing descent from the marriage of John Bennett and Mary Cheetham in 1783, John being shown as the son of one Horatio Bennett, after whom one of their own children was named ten years later. All other details were shown to be entirely correct, and much time was spent searching the records of over four counties for John's baptism. Imagine the family's mixture of shock and delight,

AA 279981

M. Cert.

S.R./R.B.D.

CERTIFIED COPY of an 👑 ENTRY OF MARRIAGE

Pursuant to the Marriage Act 1949

Registration District **MANCHESTER**

18___. Marriage solemnized at ___ Church in the Parish of Manchester in the County of Lancaster

No.	When Married.	Name and Surname.	Age.	Condition.	Rank or Profession.	Residence at the time of Marriage.	Father's Name and Surname.	Rank or Profession of Father.
32	January	Thomas Carlile		Bachelor	Grocer's Manager		Hugh Carlile	
		Frances Philpotts		Widow		Margate Street Heaton Brough Fordmans		

Married in the ___ Church according to the Rites and Ceremonies of the Established Church, by ___ Banns ___ or after ___ by me,

This Marriage was solemnized between us,

Thomas Carlile
Frances Philpotts

in the Presence of us,

William Booth
Alice Williamson Walsh

Certified to be a true copy of an entry in a register in my custody.

VALERIE F. LANG

Deputy Superintendent Registrar   30 . 1 . 1997   Date

CERTIFIED COPY OF AN ENTRY OF MARRIAGE

Given at the GENERAL REGISTER OFFICE

Application Number R007981c

Registration District **Manchester**

1854 Marriage solemnized at **St. Johns Church**
in the **Parish** of **Manchester** in the **County of Lancaster**

No.	(1) When married	(2) Name and Surname	(3) Age	(4) Condition	(5) Rank or profession	(6) Residence at the time of marriage	(7) Father's name and surname	(8) Rank or profession of father
32	January Second	Thomas Carlile	Full	Bachelor	Book Binder	mangle St.	Hugh Carlile	Spinner
		Frances Pickford	Full	Widow	-	mangle St	Hewron Brough	Cordwainer

Married in the **above church** according to the **Rites and Ceremonies of the Established Church after banns by Henry Sayers Curate**

This marriage was solemnized between us, | Thomas Carlile | in the presence | William Booth |
| Frances Pickford | of us, | Alice Williamson X mark |

CERTIFIED to be a true copy of an entry in the certified copy of a Register of Marriages in the District above mentioned.
Given at the GENERAL REGISTER OFFICE, under the Seal of the said Office, the **17th** day of **February** 1997

MB 466010

This certificate is issued in pursuance of section 65 of the Marriage Act 1949. Sub-section 3 of that section provides that any certified copy of an entry purporting to be sealed or stamped with the seal of the General Register Office shall be received as evidence of the marriage to which it relates without any further or other proof of the entry, and no certified copy purporting to have been given in the said Office shall be of any force or effect unless it is sealed or stamped as aforesaid.
CAUTION—It is an offence to falsify a certificate or to make or knowingly use a false certificate or a copy of a false certificate intending it to be accepted as genuine to the prejudice of any person, or to possess a certificate knowing it to be false without lawful authority.
WARNING: THIS CERTIFICATE IS NOT EVIDENCE OF THE IDENTITY OF THE PERSON PRESENTING IT.

Form A513 Dd 8103197 433308 160 9/95 McCorquodaleTRRU

Figure 5. An extraordinary 'carry-over' error in which one element of an entry is incorrectly repeated. The local index and the GRO quarterly copy name the bride as Frances but the original error remains uncorrected.

however, when they eventually examined the 1783 marriage allegation (see p. 195). A clerk's note was found at the foot which read: 'This is to certify that I, Thomas Bennett ... do give my full and free consent for my son John Bennett to marry Mary Cheetham.' Evidently the existence of a later Horatio (before Nelson became famous) had made someone jump to conclusions. Incidentally, we all owe a debt to one of the direct descendants of this marriage, Ralph Bennett, OBE, who was instrumental in developing microfilming in the United States, and whose baby son Ralph has been known ever since as 'Mike'!

At a census teenage girls and women in their late twenties show a tendency to present themselves as being in their early twenties, but on the whole people under thirty do not overstate their age. On the other hand, many over thirty pretend to be younger than they are, and research suggests that women are up to five times more likely to do so than men. (For an example see the *Midland Ancestor* 8.1, 1986.) Probably under 1 per cent of ages given in censuses are wrong by more than five years, but up to 10 per cent show an error of over one year. *FTM* 19.10 Aug 03 has an interesting article on how some of these errors have arisen. Coincidentally, 10 per cent of people entering hospital twice in the 1960s gave a different date of birth on each occasion, and most of the errors involved the year of birth. People over the age of fifty have a propensity to overstate their age, a tendency which increases with age! Guessing a child's age from the parent's will involves recognising that in earlier times all the boys were named first, followed by the girls, in descending order of age.

Be careful to note whether an age in the census has 'mo' against the age figure, indicating months instead of years. The 'mo' is sometimes placed inside the next column, and can be missed. Ages given on marriage licence documents can also be wrong. A study of such documents suspects that ages are overstated and has spotted a curious tendency to give an age divisible by two, especially thirty. Demographers call this tendency 'heaping'. Young children in census entries might be the grandchildren of the head of household, erroneously appearing as children either through the incautious use of ditto marks or from the desire to disguise an illegitimate child of a teenager. A 'grandmother' appearing after the children may of course have been the mother or mother-in-law of the head of the household, not his grandmother.

The census can also be misleading by quoting a county and place for a birth, but there might be more than one place of the same name in that county. Additionally, it is important to consult all census entries for the same person, in case a different birthplace is given. Our ancestors did not always know where they were born.

There are many other reasons why your base information may be misleading. Have you automatically assumed that a John Smith junior must be the son of the local John Smith senior or that Robert Jones the younger is the son of Robert Jones the elder? It will not necessarily have been so. He may have been a half-brother, or even closer (see *FTM* 7.7 May 91). Place of birth as given in the census should not be taken for granted, any more than age. A comparison of answers by the same people in the 1851 and 1861 censuses shows a 14 per cent discrepancy. Always look in more than one census, if the individual was still alive, and if the census is accessible to you. Another odd feature of the census is that, when people moved parish, they tended to give their new parish as their place of birth at the next census – then to tell the truth in later ones. Higgs (1989) suggests that this may have related to the needs of the Poor Law – many would not accept that the census really was confidential. The spelling of distant and therefore unfamiliar place names by a clergyman or census enumerator sometimes leads to curious variations and therefore to false conclusions about the place of birth. A census can mislead in several other ways also. A well known place *near* the true place of birth may have been given; the use of ditto marks should always be regarded with suspicion, especially when there are rather a lot of them; the name given in a census schedule may have been a nickname or a second forename. Some first names, quite popular in the eighteenth and nineteenth centuries, can be mistaken for a rank – Squire, Major, Judge and Doctor are not unusual, for example.

Before the twentieth century 'Mrs' might refer to social rank rather than martial status. Thus Ralph Josselin recorded in his diary that, on 8 May 1683, 'Mr Spicer married my youngest daughter Mrs Rebekah', though she was a spinster (Macfarlane, 1977). Similarly, 'cousin' might mean 'relative' rather than 'child of an aunt or uncle' and a 'widow' could be simply an 'old woman'. 'Widow Smith' might be a spinster, though 'Mary Smith, widow' (or 'relict') should have a deceased husband. 'Son-in-law', even as a census entry, may mean 'stepson', and 'brother' may mean 'brother-in-law'. When Josselin wrote that, in his childhood, 'my father was a widdower, and my corrupt heart feared a mother-in-law' he meant a stepmother. The use of 'son' for 'grandson' was common, and in the seventeenth century 'nephew' or 'niece' was used of a related descendant or even grandchild. The phrase 'natural son' was formerly used for a genetic male offspring, whether legitimate or not. Roger Lowe refers more than once in his diary to his 'father', Raphe Stirrope, who was actually his godfather. For a discussion of titles used in registers see Steel, 1968, I, Appendix 2.

The same person might be accorded a different status in different, though contemporary, sources (Macfarlane, 1977), and of course many changed their occupation during the course of their lifetime. 'Parish of settlement' can also be misleading, because it was not always the place of birth (see p. 115). 'Twenty-one and a day' or twenty-one and a half' can both mean simply 'over twenty-one'. Do not assume that anyone leaving a will, or even being an executor, must therefore have been over twenty-one. Before 1837 testators could be fourteen (males) or twelve (females); since 1970 the lowest age has been eighteen, even if the testator is married, unless he is on active military service. Wills sometimes omit the eldest child (see p. 252) or even all the children if the property was being left entirely to the widow or had been distributed before death. Equally, a will might omit the youngest if it had been written some years before death. If you are looking for the baptism of a bride, remember that she may have been a widow already (see also p. 204) and that before 1754 the marriage register would not necessarily have recorded her marital status. See p. 168 for minimum age at marriage. The 1841 census can suggest misleading information because relationships and marital status are not given. For census errors see Wrigley (1972, chapter 3) and Higgs (1989).

Earlier registers sometimes Latinised Christian names, but not always. If you have found the marriage of a Silas you may need the baptism of a Silvanus – or vice versa. (For a list of Latin equivalents of forenames see Steel, 1968, I, pp. 110–12.) Odd spellings of normal names, especially before the industrial revolution, can cause confusion. On 26 September 1670 'Henry the sone of Eliz Nutter de Monkehall' was baptised in Burnley, but was not illegitimate – he was the son of Ellis Nutter! Consult the *Oxford dictionary of Christian names* and Bardsley (2004) for the variations which can occur between baptism and later life. Nanny, for example, might have been either Ann or Agnes. Will'son is probably Williamson rather than Willson.

Other problems can arise because of a relative lack of punctuation in many registers. What should we make of this burial entry in Salford on 22 March 1780, for example – William Christopher Roper? Roper was William's occupation!

After the start of the industrial revolution, and until birth certificates give more specific information, a certain type of baptismal entry can give quite a misleading direction to your search. On 26 February 1810, at Seathwaite in Furness was baptised Mary, daughter of Matthew Jackson and Sarah Allison. The immediate impression is that Mary was illegitimate, and the later baptism of Ann to the same parents in 1812 is insufficient to dispel such an interpretation. A check through the marriages, however, reveals that Matthew Jackson Allison married

Sarah Tyson in 1807. (The introduction of printed form registers from 1813 should have removed the ambiguity (as would probate records), but published transcriptions can still be misleading thereafter.)

Using any copy of a register (bishop's transcript, fine copy, published version, etc.) lays you open to being misled. One of the commonest errors of copying is the transposition of first names, so that 'John, son of Thomas Smith' can become 'Thomas, son of John Smith' or, more commonly, 'John, son of John Smith'. Two entries in the burial register of Heywood read:

Oct 29 1820: John Barot of Rochdale, 52 years
Oct 29: Joseph Strandring of Heywood, 18 months

but the BT has these same entries as:

Oct 29 1820: John Barot of Rochdale, 52 years
Oct 29: Joseph Strandring of Heywood, 52 years

It is clear that the clerk copying the register has made a significant error, not uncommon for adjoining entries. If only the BT had been consulted, the baptism of Joseph would not have been found.

Change of name after baptism (see also pp. 49–53)
I suspect that informal changes of name after baptism were at least as common 200 years ago as in our own day. With the earlier age of adult deaths, fostering led to new surnames being adopted, and being orphaned was another occasion for a change of name, though it was not a universal consequence by any means. (London and Bristol have records of orphans who were cared for by the municipal authorities.) Case law built up concerning the legality of banns, marriage licences and even marriages using names with which the bride or groom had not been baptised in the first place. (Only an intention by both parties to deceive would invalidate the marriage. For a discussion of the fraudulent exploitation of this process see *GM* 22.4–7.) Logic indicated that using the original baptismal name for banns could subvert their purpose if the person was normally known by another name, so that marriages were not always in the same names with which the people had been baptised. Both names could, of course, appear in the marriage entry, though I am not sure what to make of 'Sarah Richardson, commonly called Peter', who married Maria Sprosten at Middlewich in 1750. Often, however, the change would have been one of those common alternative versions – Peggy instead of Margaret, Bill instead

of William – which can be found listed in Withycombe (1988), which also provides an indication of when individual names were first used or were fashionable in Britain. See also Steel (1968–), and Hanks & Hodges (1990). Alan Bardsley (2004) has produced an extremely useful booklet which deals with this very subject.

There have been many motives for changing a surname. The Churchill and Cromwell families adopted theirs in order to associate with a well-known set of ancestors; others have changed their name, or introduced a hyphen, in order to avoid racial or foreign overtones, to facilitate inheritance or to break with another branch of the family. The reasons may be found recorded in appropriate entails of landed family settlements (see GM 24.10). The London Foundling Hospital changed the surnames of some children so that they would easily be recognised later in life (see GM 23.3; see also 7.7 for change of surname.) In the same way, charity schools invented children's uniforms so that the founders could recognise the recipients of their benevolence.

Change of name at the time of confirmation was not unusual, and was accepted practice. It was encouraged for children who, it was felt, had had the misfortune to be baptised with an unfortunate name (Macnamara, 1881, p. 129).

Late baptism

With the exception of Mormons, Quakers, Jews, Muslims and Baptists, almost all sects in Britain baptise in early infancy. Collective baptisms, however, in which several brothers and sisters may be baptised on the same day, are not uncommon, a phenomenon especially noticeable when families moved parish, a more zealous incumbent took up his post or the religious equivalent of a loss-leader was on offer. When the date of birth is not given, rights of inheritance later were difficult to prove – probably more important than Nonconformist pressure as one of the main reasons for the 1836 Registration Act. It is said that a multiple baptism might also indicate a change in religious belief on the part of the parents. Baptism at the age of twenty-one, just prior to marriage, or shortly after the death of a parent, was not unknown, and at Rochdale in 1659 we find baptised on the same day James Chadwick and his own great-grandfather, James Stocke. Maybe he was one wishing to be baptised on his deathbed, rather than one of the many others who went through the ceremony shortly before marriage.

The 1662 Prayer Book said that infants should be baptised within fourteen days of birth, but detailed local studies suggest that parishes continued to differ quite markedly in how rigidly they adhered to the guideline. The number of adult baptisms rose after 1660, and they were also common in the last few days before civil registration began on 1 July 1837 (when over 360 a day were baptised in Manchester Cathedral). The median age at baptism seems to have increased from about one week to one month between the middle of the seventeenth century and the eighteenth. In Bedfordshire there were mass baptisings once a year on the day of the saint to whom the parish church was dedicated. To be safe, you should assume that only 75 per cent of those born were baptised in the first month of life. See *Local Population Studies* 24 and 65 for a series of articles and references on this subject. My own analysis of seventeenth-century Lancashire registers indicates that children who were illegitimate and children of the gentry were the two categories most likely to have been baptised late.

Before 1813 the age of people being baptised as adults is not always given, but a good indication is that the name of the parent is not supplied. Such an entry needs to be treated with caution, however, because it may record a burial which has been entered in the wrong part of the register! The title of George Rose's Act in 1812 included reference to births, but there was no enforcement of the registration of births in its clauses.

There is no easy route to the discovery of a late baptism, unless the register has been published. The ideal, for every baptism, is to start looking about five years before the estimated year of birth until the day of marriage!

Finding more than one possible baptism
(See FTM 4.4 Feb 88)
The techniques used to solve the problem of baptism in another parish, on pp. 102–16, will sometimes lead you, as we have seen, to more than one candidate for the honour of joining your family tree. You may, on the other hand, have already met the problem in the parish where you expect to find the baptism, and genealogists are normally grateful when one, and only one, such child comes to light within the probable time scale of between twenty and thirty years before a marriage. Believing that you should never look a gift horse in the mouth, few bother to check whether the child baptised and the adult married were one and the same person. The professional searcher would never dream of adopting such a casual approach, and if you are looking as closely as possible for 'the truth' you must exploit all the evidence before confirming the identification. A late baptism can sometimes repeat an earlier one in a different denomination. Before you start to research the problem, however, make sure that it is not a false duplicate (on the IGI, for example) resulting from a computer recognising small,

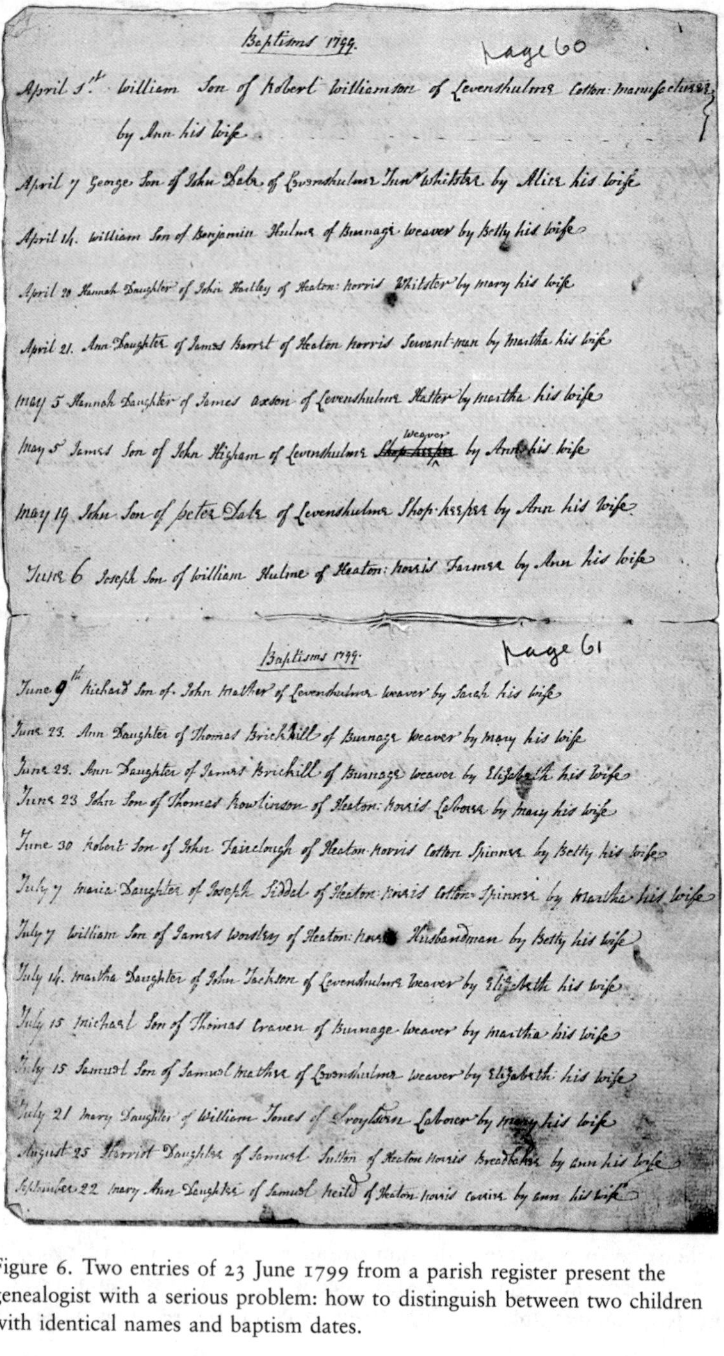

Baptisms 1799. Page 60

April 1st William Son of Robert Williamson of Levenshulme Cotton: manufacturer by Ann his wife

April 7 George Son of John Dale of Levenshulme Junr Whitster by Alice his wife

April 14. William Son of Benjamin Hulme of Burnage weaver by Betty his wife

April 20 Hannah Daughter of John Hartley of Heaton: Norris Whitster by Mary his wife

April 21. Ann Daughter of James Barrat of Heaton Norris Servant-man by Martha his wife

May 5 Hannah Daughter of James Axson of Levenshulme Hatter by Martha his wife

May 5 James Son of John Higham of Levenshulme ~~Shop keeper~~ Weaver by Ann his wife

May 19 John Son of Peter Dale of Levenshulme Shop-keeper by Ann his wife

June 6 Joseph Son of William Hulme of Heaton: Norris Farmer by Ann his wife

Baptisms 1799. Page 61

June 9th Richard Son of John Mather of Levenshulme weaver by Sarah his wife

June 23. Ann Daughter of Thomas Brickhill of Burnage weaver by Mary his wife

June 23. Ann Daughter of James Brickhill of Burnage weaver by Elizabeth his wife

June 23 John Son of Thomas Rowlinson of Heaton: Norris Labourer by Mary his wife

June 30 Robert Son of John Fairclough of Heaton Norris Cotton Spinner by Betty his wife

July 7 Maria Daughter of Joseph Siddel of Heaton: Norris Cotton Spinner by Martha his wife

July 7 William Son of James Woolley of Heaton: Norris Husbandman by Betty his wife

July 14. Martha Daughter of John Jackson of Levenshulme weaver by Elizabeth his wife

July 15 Michael Son of Thomas Craven of Burnage weaver by Martha his wife

July 15 Samuel Son of Samuel Mather of Levenshulme weaver by Elizabeth his wife

July 21 Mary Daughter of William Jones of Droylsden Labourer by Mary his wife

August 25 Harriet Daughter of Samuel Sutton of Heaton Norris Breadbaker by Ann his wife

September 22 Mary Ann Daughter of Samuel Heild of Heaton-Norris Carrier by Ann his wife

Figure 6. Two entries of 23 June 1799 from a parish register present the genealogist with a serious problem: how to distinguish between two children with identical names and baptism dates.

inconsequential differences in the way the same entry has been put in by different sources.

Such evidence must be employed when two or more baptisms are found in the right place at the right time, a not uncommon problem. When looking for the baptism of Thomas Darlington's bride, Mary Houghland (see p. 102), it was somewhat disconcerting to find Mary, daughter of William Houghland, baptised in 1715 and Mary, daughter of William Houghland, baptised in 1717. Because the children had both had William as their father, they might have been sisters, but there was more than one William Houghland with a wife of a child-bearing age living in the area at the time.

The first way through this sort of problem is to study the burial register of a parish for the days, and if necessary the years, following the date of the two baptisms. Until the end of the nineteenth century, it has been estimated, up to half the children born did not live to be adults. The figure was especially high in the early eighteenth century. The easy solution, therefore, is to find that one of the two Mary Houghlands died as a child. One of my students had a similar problem, followed this strategy, and found that both had died! In the case of Mary Houghland, however, neither was buried in Frodsham, so I had to have recourse to other methods. Did a William Houghland leave a will after 1745 naming Mary Darlington as his daughter? Do other Darlington or Houghland wills (of cousins, for example) provide sufficient evidence for identification? If the marriage had been after 1753 a relative might have been named as a witness, or might have been married within a short time. Did the 'other' Mary Houghland marry in such a way as to provide evidence? Does the bishop's transcript include the burial of the first Mary, missing from the register itself? Can any of the other documents listed below on pp. 138–51 be used to help? Was either Mary buried in an adjoining parish? Does the burial entry (or more likely the monumental inscription) for Thomas Darlington's wife indicate her age at death? Between 1696 and 1832 jurors' lists in quarter sessions papers state the ages of those qualified to serve, as well as their occupation, their place of abode and the location of their estate.

Try following both candidates, who apparently survive adulthood, to their own marriages, and see whether the naming patterns of their own children can help to distinguish between them. (For sixteenth- and seventeenth-century naming patterns see *GM* 23.8.) Might school or apprenticeship papers help to distinguish them?

When all other possibilities have been tried and found wanting, try ignoring the two children for a moment, and concentrate on the

ancestry of the two fathers. If you have people of the same surname
living in the same parish, at the same time, it is quite possible that
they were siblings or cousins. If you can accept a temporary fork
in the trunk of your family tree you can thus bypass an otherwise
insurmountable obstacle, which is surely far better than the record
coming to an early end.

If the problem occurs immediately prior to 1841 the census may
provide the name of a brother or sister of your ancestor who was born
after 1 July 1837. In that way, discovering two possible baptisms, as
well as a missing baptism, can be overcome by tracing known siblings
instead. For an earlier period the relevant wills may provide similar
evidence. It should also be pointed out, however, that it was not
unknown for couples to have more than one child alive with same
Christian name as each other, especially before the early eighteenth
century. James, son of William and Jane Bradshaw, was baptised at
Standish on 20 November 1664. Fourteen months later (bearing in
mind old style and new style) on 7 February, James son of William
Bradshaw 'the second James' was baptised, with no burial between.
Gardner & Smith (1959, II, p. 134) give a probate document of 1570
showing a man with three children each called John. One theory
suggests that they were each called after a godparent. Peter Razzell
has shown, however, that this phenomenon must have been very rare
(see *Local Population Studies* 64).

Some genealogists advocate careful study of the sequence of
forenames among the children in a family in the belief that choice of
name may have been determined by the first names of their parents
and grandparents. Such a closely defined system is most common
among the Sephardim Jews. It is certainly true that the eldest boy was
sometimes given the name of his father or grandfather, but it is equally
true that many families followed no such pattern. If there is really no
other evidence, I suppose it is something to fall back on; it is certainly
useful when the forename in question is an unusual one.

A 'hypothetical' or 'conditional' baptism was when there was some
uncertainty about whether a previous ceremony had been legitimate, or
orthodox. A late baptism, on the other hand, can sometimes repeat an
earlier one in a different denomination, but occasionally, children were
baptised twice in the same one. There are many instances of a private
baptism being recorded first, then a public christening some weeks later
or when the mother was 'churched' or purified after childbirth. This
subtle difference between baptism and Christening was often ignored
even in the parish registers, however (much as 'genealogy' and 'family
history' are used interchangeably today). Parson Woodforde's diary for

1 October 1777 records 'Harry Dunnell behaved very impertinent this morning to me because I would not privately name his child for him, he having one Child before named privately by me and never had it brought to Church afterwards. He had the Impudence to tell me that he would send it to some Meeting House [i.e. Nonconformist] to be named etc. – very saucy indeed.' Hey (2004, p. 146) notes the practice of Nonconformists to baptise in both their own denomination and Anglican. The two baptisms might even have been in different parishes, if the parents had moved, or if they had property in the second parish. James Woodforde again, 22 September 1784: 'Before Dinner I publickly baptized their little Boy at home, which I did not much like, but could not tell how to refuse – He was privately named before at Norwich I believe.' Occasionally the name might change! An entry in the register of Rivington reads '24 March 1800 Mary, daughter of George Makin of Rivington (private baptism, but was later christened Harriot on April 27th 1800)'. Illegitimate children admitted to the London foundling hospital between 1756 and 1760 are known to have been baptised twice with different names on each occasion.

Non-Anglican baptism

Whatever your own religious persuasion, it is increasingly likely that, as you trace your ancestors back over the last 400 years in Britain, you will find them in Church of England records. It should always be remembered, however, that some parts of the country remained staunchly Catholic, despite the Reformation of the sixteenth century, and that Protestant Nonconformity was common in other parts from the middle of the seventeenth. It soon became impossible for the Anglican clergy to obey canon 70 of 1603, which directed that they should register all baptisms, whether of believers or not, in the parish. In the main, however, Nonconformist registers become numerous only after 1780. Wrigley & Schofield (1981) suggest that Nonconformist baptism tripled in the last thirty years of the eighteenth century, from about 2 per cent to about 6 per cent of all baptisms. Many denominations ran their own newspapers, which can carry useful birth, marriage and death notices. (For a convenient breakdown of the bewildering variety of Nonconformist denominations see Pelling & Litton, 1991, and an introduction in Anc 46 Jun 06.)

Nonconformist registers which are housed at Kew are in the National Archives' digitisation programme, due for completion in 2008. They are available at the paysite www.BMDRegisters.co.uk, and include clandestine marriages.

Even in south Lancashire, where the gentry ensured the relative continuity of Catholicism through the sixteenth and seventeenth centuries, the earliest surviving Roman Catholic registers, those of Wigan, date from 1732, and a series of records specific to that denomination need to be located. ('Recusant' rolls, however, can include Puritans also, and are not complete.) Many of these documents, including registers, have been published by the Catholic Record Society; see Gandy (2001, 2002) and Gandy (1993) which lists all surviving Catholic registers. Internet sources for Roman Catholic records are listed in *FTM* 20.7 May 04; see also www.catholic-history.org.uk, and *NALD* 66. Nonconformity grew with the industrial revolution, so that by the early nineteenth century a large number of non-Anglican churches and chapels flourished, especially in the swelling towns of the Midlands and north and also in certain rural counties such as Cornwall and Norfolk and in Wales. By 1812, in settlements with over 1,000 inhabitants, there were normally more Dissenting places of worship than Anglican. Where new churches or chapels were built closer to home, don't be surprised to find your ancestors changing their allegiance – if necessary across denomination boundaries! (To see those churches and chapels still standing, try www.imagesofengland.org.uk.)

The records of these different denominations have been very well described by Steel (1968, II–III), who covers Jewish, Roman Catholic and a host of Protestant Nonconformist – or 'non-parochial' – registers. Subsequent volumes in this series indicate which such registers are known to exist for individual counties. With the main exception of Jews and Baptists, most denominations record parents' names at the baptism of infants. Quakers, probably the earliest of the Nonconformists to record their own vital events, recorded birth rather than baptism, and numbered the months rather than naming them, but before 1752 the 'first' month was March rather than January. Quaker 'digests' of births, from the mid-seventeenth century until 1959, are kept at Friends' House library in London, but may be found on microfilm in the local CRO. (See www.qfhs.co.uk; Milligan & Thomas 1999; *FHM* 112 Dec 04.) They are one of the denominations which have their own newspaper, which carry birth, marriage and death notices. Some Nonconformist registers supply additional data such as the names of the godparents.

The fullest records are probably those made by some Lady Huntingdon's chapels – eighteen entries to a page, noting the names and parish of parents, the maiden name of the mother, her parish before marriage and the date and place of the birth and baptism. Additionally, there were some private chapels, often Anglican, attached to large manorial estates, which gave baptismal facilities to estate workers.

Surprisingly little has been written about Mormons in Britain. According to Gardner & Smith (1956–64, I) about 52,000 (or 40 per cent of the total) emigrated to America in the century after 1837, among them two of my ancestors; see *FHM* 120 Aug 05.

For Jewish ancestors, see www.jgsgb.org.uk, Gandy (1995), Mordy (1995), and Wenzerul (2000, 2002).

There are several ways to discover the existence of Nonconformist places of worship. Some books, for example, advocate a careful study of the number of baptisms and burials in the local Anglican registers; where the number of baptisms falls to the same level as, or below, the number of burials, that can be taken to be an indication of Nonconformist baptisms in the area. The odd year or two in which it happens normally indicates a higher than normal mortality rate, or a failure to record the baptisms which had been celebrated. For most genealogists, however, this is too complicated. Early town or county directories (p. 80) will provide the dates at which most churches or chapels were founded, as will the yearbooks or directories of the denominations concerned. Even simpler, however, is to ask the advice of the local history librarian in the nearest large public library, or the archivist in the relevant city or county record office, who should have this knowledge at his or her fingertips. Between 1754 and 1837 one clue to the Nonconformist allegiance of individual families is to find an Anglican marriage and no subsequent baptisms of children, though of course the family may have moved, or have been childless.

I have seen it said that the use of the word 'interred' instead of 'buried' implies Nonconformity on the part of the deceased (or excommunication, suicide, or Catholicism), but I've not had any experience of such an interpretation.

The local record office, indeed, should not only be able to tell you which non-parochial registers exist, and where they are; it may even have some of the originals, and will almost certainly have a microfilm copy of most surviving pre-1837 registers. Following the start of civil registration in 1837, all non-Anglican denominations were approached with a view to having their registers centralised with the Registrar General for safe keeping. This had already been suggested by some Nonconformists as a way to give their records more authority in an age when evidence of birth and baptism was becoming socially more desirable (*Journal of the Society of Archivists* 2, pp. 411–17). By 1859 over 8,800 were in the General Register Office, but only one, from St Petersburg, came from outside England and Wales. They were transferred to the Public Record Office in 1961. Synagogues and most Catholic churches declined to deposit. On the whole their records, together with the modern non-parochial registers, are still in their places of worship, though some Welsh Protestant registers are in the National Library of Wales (see Ifans, 1994), and some Catholic registers have been transferred to city or county record offices, via the diocese. Many early Baptist registers are with the Baptist Union (see *FHM* 144 Jun 07), and some Congregational registers are in the United Reformed Church headquarters at Westminster College, Maddingley Road, Cambridge CB3 0AA (see *FHM* 147 Sep 07). Registers of closed Methodist chapels usually go first to the safe in the relevant Circuit headquarters, and are not in the Methodist archives in the John Rylands University Library of Manchester, contrary to popular belief (See *FHM* 140 Feb 07 and *Anc* 63 Nov 07).

For the genealogical use of non-parochial registers see Steel (1968, II–III), and *GM* 22.5. Additionally, there are a number of booklets describing the search for ancestors of particular denominations: Breed (1995), Clifford (1997), Gandy (1995), Leary (1993), Milligan & Thomas (1999), and Mordy (1995). For Catholic ancestry, see also *News and Digest* 8.1, and Gandy (1993, and in *FHM* 131 Jun 06, and 134 Sep 06).

As with the Anglican registers, modern transcripts sometimes exist locally, and there are almost no bishops' transcripts (see p. 140; relatively few non-parochial registers have been printed, though the Catholic Record Society has published a number of early Catholic registers for Lancashire and Hampshire.

The Mormon International Genealogical Index pp. 86–8 contains a very large number of entries taken from the non-parochial registers, including those in the National Archives.

Registers not accessible: alternative sources

The Parochial Registers and Records Measure of 1978 (amended from 1 January 1993), affecting only the Church of England, has had the effect of hastening a development which had been going on for years – the centralisation of parish registers and other documents from the parish chest to diocesan record offices (see Anon., 1992). Those affected are registers of baptism and burial in which (1) any entry is more than 150 years old and (2) all entries are more than 100 years old. The public already has right of access to those registers which are housed in local authority institutions – most commonly where the diocesan record office and county record office share the same organisation and facilities. For the contents of UK archive offices, see Foster & Sheppard; for Wales see National Library of Wales (1986); also Steel (1968, XIII), and Moulton (1988). For the

location and addresses of record offices in England and Wales see
Gibson & Peskett (2002).

As in register offices, genealogists can help themselves to get better
service in record offices by taking certain precautions. Cuts in local
government spending, and the substantial increase in the public's use
of record offices, are resulting in deteriorating services and increased
charges for access to records. Check the hours of opening and let the
archivist know in advance which documents you will require or send
a small, specific search enquiry by post. Be as specific as possible, and
book a place in advance if necessary. Always use pencil when consulting
archives, never ink. Learn how to use the document reference system
yourself. Occupy an archivist's time as little as possible. If you have
to hunt in pairs, try to do so as silently as possible. And never eat or
drink in the search rooms! See *FTM* 5.6 Apr 89 for some good advice
on how to use record offices.

There are three private diocesan record offices, however, which are
allowed to charge the same search fee as incumbents (see below):
Canterbury, in the cathedral library; York, at the Borthwick Institute;
and Oxford, in the Bodleian Library. As time goes by, you will be
expected to consult more of these registers on microfilm rather than
handling the originals. Any earlier difficulties concerning access to
registers deposited in diocesan record offices can now be overcome
by reference to section 20.2a of the 1978 Parochial Registers and
Records Measure, which allows searches to be made 'at all reasonable
hours'.

This measure still leaves some old registers, perhaps in up to 10 per
cent of parishes, in those churches whose parochial church council
has decided to invest in the equipment necessary to keep the records
at the appropriate temperature and humidity levels – BS 5454, the
same British Standard which is applied in record offices. The local
archdeacon has oversight of the procedures. Although there is a public
right of search, the incumbent can make a charge for inspection of
the registers or even, by judicious timing of his religious and social
calendar, effectively deny access altogether.

Crockford's clerical directory or the current diocesan handbook
in your local library will provide the name, address and telephone
number of the incumbent, and a little about his career. (The correct
form of address, by the way, is 'The Revd Mr Smith', or 'The Revd
John Smith', *not* 'The Rev. Smith'.) You should include a stamped,
addressed envelope in your request for an appointment to view his
registers. Better still, telephone for an appointment at his convenience
– do not ask to visit for the purpose on a Sunday! If the incumbent

is not accessible, the diocesan handbook also provides the names of the churchwardens and the secretary of the parochial church council. Ask about fees, for whatever textbook you are consulting may well be out of date.

Some genealogists may be deterred by the fees alone, first introduced in 1836. To search for specified events in registers remaining in church you can be charged £13.00 for the first hour in which you search the registers for any baptism or burial, and £11.00 for each subsequent hour, or part thereof. The same fee applies also to marriage registers only before 1837, but the incumbent may make any charge for inspecting his marriage registers later than that year; the fee for a general search of the registers is also negotiable. A single fee is payable for early registers which contain baptisms, marriages and burials in the same volume. A certified copy of an entry of baptism or burial is included in the fee but is not normally required by the genealogist, who needs only the information. Each additional copy costs £13.00, but the fee for a copy of a marriage entry after 1837 is £7.00, the same as a registrar's fee. You may even find that some parishes impose an extra charge in the form of a churchwarden's fee, but I am not sure about the legal basis of such a levy.

It is thus still important to find alternative ways of acquiring information about baptism, even when the register still exists, and, as we have seen, there are many other circumstances which make the quest for such alternative sources essential. It is an all too salutary experience to compare the known starting dates of churches and chapels with the dates of their earliest surviving registers – at any time before the nineteenth century there is a risk that no record of the ceremony will have survived.

Bishops' transcripts

By far the commonest way around these difficulties for Anglican registers are bishops', or episcopal, transcripts, occasionally called 'register bills', and affectionately known in the trade as BTs. Some date from as early as 1561, when at least the diocese of Lincoln believed that annual copies of the parish register entries should be sent to the bishop. There are other early survivors in the dioceses of Canterbury and Norwich, the former starting in 1558 and having some sent in at six-monthly intervals following a visitation, with a duplicate set of transcripts to 1812. The Church opposed Lord Burghley's bill of 1590 which would have founded a General Register Office to hold all such copies, and itself issued the order of 1597. Parishes in England and Wales should have provided duplicates of the previous year's entries, written on a single sheet of parchment. Not surprisingly, some did not do so, and other copies were lost in transit. 'Peculiar' parishes, exempt from many normal procedures, had to return them to their bishop only after 1812, however (when all returns should be found on standardised forms, by the way) though many had sent bishops' transcripts in earlier.

There are advantages and problems in using BTs. Bishops have their own record offices, which, in many cases, but not in all, coincide with a city or county record office. Most Welsh BTs are in the National Library of Wales at Aberystwyth, but none there antedates 1662. At these institutions you can see, usually free of charge, copies of a succession of parish registers, and all this in the comfort of an office which is purpose-built, equipped and staffed. Before the nineteenth century BTs regularly contain entries which are not in the original parish register, and indeed it is suspected that some registers are actually a copy of the BT, or that they are each copies of an earlier rough draft. For example, names omitted in the original may sometimes be found in the BT, but there is no guarantee, for example, that both surnames in an alias will have been transcribed for the bishop. Whatever the cause of a discrepancy, the extra entries and the extra information sometimes found in BTs make them well worth consulting, whether the local register is missing or not. Remember the important general principal – if the evidence is there, use it – and you are advised against relying wholly on the BT if the register still exists. See *GM* 11.6, and, for a detailed analysis of one chapelry (Worsborough in South Yorkshire) *Local Population Studies* 55.

Unfortunately, there are snags. Most pre-1813 BTs have been stored tightly folded, making many entries illegible at the crease. As usual, the church provided no extra money for the work, and the result is an intermittent rather than a continuous series, especially before the eighteenth century. Postage was supposed to be free, at least between 1812 and 1840, but if Post Office officials did not recognise the exemption the parcel was destroyed because no one would pay for it to be delivered. Even worse, there were several dioceses where the submission of annual BTs never became established practice, or the records were not preserved if stored outside the diocesan registry. The worst offenders were Bath and Wells, London, Rochester and Salisbury. Bishops' transcripts are normally submitted a year at a time on a single sheet of paper, including returns from chapelries within the parish, but the largest parishes found this impossible, and a Manchester BT was characterised in the last century as 'nearly as large as a church Bible' (Burn, 1862, p. 204, who lists the state of these records in various dioceses).

Some clergymen submitted BTs during an episcopal visitation, which was not necessarily held at the start of a new year. Notice, therefore, which months are covered – some entries may be missing for that reason. Even after 1812 the BT could be submitted within two months of the year's end. From 1754 to 1812 marriage BTs normally record the names of only the bride and groom, not the full parish register entry. It also goes without saying that the transcripts are subject to individual quirks. Some baptisms (and, at Ashton in Makerfield, some fathers) of illegitimate children are known to have been omitted from the BTs. At Kencot, in Oxfordshire, marriages where both parties were not 'of the parish' were not included, and in late seventeenth-century Chorley neither stillbirths nor the marriage of parishioners in other parishes were transcribed into the BTs. Stretford excluded either of the two surnames of parents with an alias in the PR. Incidentally, entry in a BT was never accepted as legal evidence of baptism, a fact which led to some curious wrangles concerning legitimacy and inheritance.

In those dioceses which did have a tradition of sending in the BTs, the practice continued for most of the nineteenth century, dying out gradually rather than ending suddenly, with some parishes sending returns well into the twentieth century. (The series for Croydon, Surrey, extends to 1970!) The exception to this seems to have been marriages, entries for which do not continue long after civil registration began in 1837. The BTs are no automatic solution to 'the gap' in the 1640s and 1650s, for bishops themselves were abolished in 1646, and BTs are often missing for some years before that. However, some bishops, including those of Carlisle, Lincoln and Chester, when they were reappointed in 1660, ordered that some or all of the missing BTs should be submitted; see Gibson (2001).

Many record offices have embarked on schemes for copying BTs into microform, and you will be expected to use a reader rather than the original where this has happened. The Church of Jesus Christ of Latter-Day Saints took an early lead in this process, having microfilmed all surviving Welsh BTs by the mid-1950s.

Other copies of parish registers
According to George Rose's Act of 1812, the bishop's registrar who received the BTs should have compiled alphabetical indexes for each parish, and made them available to the general public. J. S. Burn (1862), who scarcely has a good word to say about the 1812 Act, complained that this part of it was not being complied with because of shortage of money. These registrar's transcripts do exist in some

areas, and are to be found in the diocesan record offices. You may find, however, that the names of only the children are entered.

A few parishes, as we have seen, possess their own second copy of the registers. In London at least, there are parish clerks' or sextons' transcripts, which appear to be the rough notes, day books or memoranda books from which the registers and perhaps BTs were compiled. As such they are sometimes more detailed than the register itself (*GM* 20.2 and *FTM* 19.8 Jun 03). George Rose's Act of 1812 tried to stop such rough registers being compiled.

It is also possible that the register has been published, and in that case you will normally have the advantage of a name index. Counties vary widely in the extent to which their registers have been published, because in some there are parish register societies which have been undertaking the task for a century or more. The most fortunate counties are Bedfordshire, where all the pre-1813 Anglican registers have been printed, Cornwall, Cumberland, Durham, Lancashire, Lincolnshire, London, Northumberland, Shropshire, Staffordshire, Sussex, Westmorland, Worcestershire and Yorkshire. (John Titford lists the publishing bodies in *FTM* 15.10 Aug 99.) The current parish register project in Cheshire, transcribing on to a computer at the University of Liverpool, is improving the situation immeasurably in that county. (See www.csc.liv.ac.uk/~cprdb.) When using printed registers, note whether the dates in the title apply to baptisms, marriages and burials, whether the index is comprehensive at baptism (for example, some name only the children, not the parents) and whether the register has been collated with the BTs before publication – the preface should inform you. Are surnames with different spellings collated in the index or presented separately? Does the index include both groom *and* bride? If an entry you are expecting to find is not indexed, it may be worth looking through the text itself to double-check. Indexing a parish register is not only a time-consuming and thankless task; it is also prone to errors of omission and, I would guess, rarely checked before submission to the printer. If there are gaps in the published register, check to see whether they are a faithful reflection of the original, or an editorial error which was discovered too late to be corrected in the printed version. For example, Volume 138 of the Lancashire Parish Register Society series omits in error seven years of baptisms for the 1730s. When a register has been published the baptisms and marriages will be entered in the next edition of the International Genealogical Index, we may hope.

If the register you are seeking has not yet been published, it may have been transcribed already with publication in mind, possibly with an index added. Such transcriptions are widely scattered. Many are in private hands and some are in the possession of the local parish register society. The county archivist should be able to advise you on which exist. Occasionally you will find an index available without transcription.

An increasing number of registers are being microfilmed, but these are indexed relatively rarely. Any difficulty in reading the original because of natural wear and tear is quite literally magnified on microfilm. It is therefore much easier to miss an entry, so extra care should be taken during the search and you should make a note of the location of the illegible entries. Microfilming of parish registers was started during the Second World War to help preserve the records from enemy action (see GM 9.8) but, ironically, any lists made of those parishes where it was done seem to have disappeared and the films themselves have been scattered. In more modern times, microfilming is done to protect the original registers from overuse; individual incumbents and diocesan record offices can make use of convenient microfilming facilities, often in large public libraries which then keep a copy themselves for their readers. Microfilming is also an essential part of the programme of the Mormon Church as part of the compilation of their International Genealogical Index (see pp. 103–7).

There is already some pressure to get the parish registers themselves onto the Internet once civil registers and censuses have been digitised, but there are many problems to such a project, including size, ownership and legibility.

Manorial records

It has been argued that for the genealogist this class of record is second in importance only to parish registers. Such may well be the case in those areas where access to them has been eased. They are most useful in the period before the industrial revolution, though many continue into the nineteenth century, and some into the twentieth. Manorial documents are scattered in a number of private and public repositories, and are being listed in the Manorial Documents Register on line at www.mdr.nationalarchives.gov.uk – so far, Wales and a limited number of English counties are included. (Title deeds are not included, however. The National Register of Archives, Quality House, Quality Court, Chancery Lane, London WC2A 1HP, will give advice on their present location, though you should be specific about the parishes and dates which are the subject of your enquiry. See www. nationalarchives.gov.uk/nra/. Most city or county record offices have a copy for their own county.) Even when you locate the records you will find that, apart from the period of the Protectorate, 1653–60, they are written in Latin until 1732. Anita Travers suggests that one-third of manors have no surviving records, and that less than one-fifth have a good sequence from before 1700; see *GM* 6.3, 14.1, 21.1. In too few areas (Middlesex and the three separate ridings of Yorkshire) there are copies of enrolled deeds through which the holding of property can be traced in documents as far back as 1535. The Wakefield repository, holding deeds from 1704 to 1970, can be accessed through www. archives.wyjs.org.uk. The North Riding Record Office holds a register of one and a quarter million deeds from that area. (see *FTM* 20.9 Jul 04; *FHM* 122 Oct 05). See *NALL* 9 and 25, Park, 2002, and *FTM* 20.7 May 04 for manorial record websites.

The luckier searchers will find that the manorial records they want have been translated into English; some are even published. Then you can see the old manorial courts at work. The records sometimes provide lists of tenants and inhabitants above a certain age, the 'view of frankpledge', rentals and surveys. Manorial records are often more efficient than even probates in identifying acts of inheritance and succession. Also listed are absentees from the court, or Essoins, and lists of jurymen in the court leet, which dealt with a wide variety of minor offences and disputes. Most important from the genealogist's point of view, they also record the transfer of property and leases as they affected the interests of the lord of the manor in the court baron. Leases for a number of lives (usually three) are especially useful, as they normally record if the individuals were related to each other. Such leases were especially common in the western half of England; the person taking one out would also name two future recipients, and the lease could be renegotiated at the time of the death of a leaseholder by agreement with the landholder. They were giving way to leases for twenty-one years in the more prosperous parts of the country by the mid-seventeenth century; see *GM* 17.6. Any tenant's death since the previous meeting led to an investigation into his holdings, his heir (including age) and whether any forfeit was due to the lord upon transfer. The information contained in the records of such cases can be used to distinguish between people in the parish who had the same name.

References to 'mortuaries' can sometimes be found in burial registers, or even in separate books. A mortuary was the value of the 'second-best beast' payable to the minister following the decease of a parishioner owning goods worth over £30. The best beast, however, went to the lord of the manor, so among the manorial records are 'heriots', which give basically the name of the deceased but can also supply the inheritor of the lease. At a period for which the parish register has not survived, a Glossop heriot reads, '1599, after the death of

Nicholas Hadfield, one black cow sold for lvs [55s.], his son Alexander is now possessed' (i.e. had inherited Nicholas's property – except for one black cow, of course). Heriots can be found in separate books, or tucked away in the annual accounts.

Military records and school registers
These have already been discussed on pp. 56–60 and 60–5.

The poll tax
Governments are fond of taxing essentials rather than luxuries, but records concerning taxation (see above, pp. 108–13) normally provide no direct genealogical evidence. One exception is the poll tax – 'poll' being an old word for a head. This medieval tax was revived by Charles II in his desperate search for money after the Puritan rule of the 1650s, when Ralph Josselin complained in his diary, 'I paid it once formerly in '41 as I remember, this rate unusual twice in an age'; by 1677/78 he had other taxes to contend with: 'wee are a people peeled and polled'. The poll tax was collected seven times before 1698, when it remained on the shelf until taken down and dusted by Mrs Thatcher in the 1980s. The original returns are in the National Archives, but their survival rate has been uneven across the country. Copies can sometimes be found in local record offices, and a few have been published. See Gibson (1996) for extant copies, and Schurer & Arkell (1992). The tax returns list families together. Wives and children are named as such, the different rates they paid whenever it was collected, and exemptions given to those too poor to pay. Normally, the children listed are over fifteen years old.

The poll tax, of course, was no more unpopular than any other form of taxation. It is therefore hard to believe the story found in the diary of Oliver Heywood, a Nonconformist preacher (a rich source of unusual entries in the registers – see *GM* 29.3), who wrote in 1678:

> In Cheshire, not far from Maxfield [Macclesfield] a woman killed too of her children, the third run to his father in the barn, who coming in met his wife in the doore, who sd I have saved thee two shillings and if the other had stayed I had saved thee three, meaning she would have killed that lad, for fear of paying the pole-money for them, wch at that time was imposed. (Turner, 1881–85)

Records of the College of Arms

While the use of heraldry was common by 1200, there was systematic, centralised control through the College of Arms only some two centuries later. Since then, the College has been responsible for approving and/or designing the visible insignia of a person's gentility – a process assisted and policed by the Heralds' visitations from 1530 to 1686.

The genealogical significance of the heraldic devices for any one family is far too complex to illustrate here, and for the sixteenth and seventeenth centuries the data are available in the form of family trees anyway. For earlier and later periods, however, it is perhaps sufficient to note that

> Coats of arms are granted to individual persons ('armigers').
> The description ('blazon') of what each contains is very exact, with its own terminology. The blazon should contain a description, not an interpretation, of the arms. Woodcock & Robinson (2001), both authors being Officers of Arms in the College, includes a useful glossary.
> Children inherit the blazon, but in the process it is modified according to prescribed rules according to the holder's place in the sibling sequence of each sex ('cadency'), legitimacy, marital status, and nowadays even adoption.

A proper reading of the full heraldic device ('achievement') can lead to much greater accuracy concerning the genetic forebears than a mere association of names, but there are many caveats which should deter even the most cavalier novice from trying to interpret this without reference to anyone skilled in the art. Most ancestors were excluded because of the need for design simplicity. Sometimes elements were incorporated more from a desire to honour a (potential) benefactor than from any urge for genealogical accuracy. The maternal line normally disappeared except following marriage with an heiress (and even she had an effect only on the shield of the next generation). Cadency was often ignored. The design could be augmented in recognition of some event during the holder's lifetime. Crests were not regulated until the sixteenth century, and mottoes were not inherited by right, were not used regularly until the eighteenth century, and were not really a formal part of the grant of arms.

Coats of arms may be identified by using *Papworth's ordinary of British armorials* (1874, 1961) which is arranged by blazons, or Burke's *General armory*, arranged by families. Crests may be found in *Fairbairn's book of crests of the families of Great Britain and Ireland*, and mottoes in *Elvin's handbook of mottoes* (1860, revised by R. Pinches). The Harleian Society has listed those who had grants of arms from 1687 to 1898. Heraldry sources now feature on the Internet, at http://digiserve.com/heraldry/, for example. See also Humphery-Smith (2003), and *FTM* 21.7 May 05, 22.11 Sept 05, and 23.1 Nov 05.

From 1528 to 1686 a tour of the nation's gentry was made on behalf of the College of Arms, county by county, on average every thirty years or so. This was used by the Tudor and Stuart monarchs as one means of maintaining their political control over that class by verifying claims to gentility. After 1583 lists of gentry were drawn up from the jury lists kept by the county sheriffs. All who had the right to bear arms were listed, together with their ancestry for three generations. A list of disclaimers for those families which had descended from grace or fallen on hard times was normally included, though not always printed. Such lists are preserved by the College of Arms. The county visitations are listed in Sims (1856). Richard Sims, who worked in the British Museum, also compiled an index of the pedigrees included in these Heralds' visitations. This index has been reprinted (Sims, 1856/1970), and there is a list of all the visitations in the Society of Genealogists' library in *GM* 28.4.

A large number of the visitations have themselves been printed, often by a record or historical society in the county concerned. Mullins (1958, 1983) lists these society transactions; Squibb (1978) lists the printed visitations, and the *Genealogical research directory* for 1994 lists all those published and filmed. These family pedigrees are not infallible, by any means, because of the sources of information on which they are based (see e.g. *GM* 6.12; there is a suspicion, for example, that Catholics and criminals were deliberately omitted), but gift horses in the shape of a 'free' set of parents and grandparents must never be overlooked. Of course, the information they provide should not be taken for granted, and must be checked wherever possible. Remember that, as well as the families concerned directly, the records also contain input on the female side from many other ancestors. On the other hand, they are rarely comprehensive even in their coverage of the immediate family of the 'key man' on whose status the pedigree was based.

From 1567 until 1688 it was also the practice for any herald from the college to record the details of all the funerals which he attended. The record included the date of death, the place of burial, the deceased's parents, spouse, in-laws, and children, their ages, to whom they were married and their arms and crest. Mourners and friends in the funeral procession are also listed.

Once again, these are records which relate only the wealthier, law-abiding, Anglican classes. Indeed, after the late seventeenth century they are confined to royalty and a few great noblemen. Not a lot survive; but, once again, many have been printed by local societies devoted to the publication of old records.

Inquisitions post mortem

These somewhat grim-sounding documents provide useful genealogical information from the thirteenth century until the late 1640s, when they decreased in use until they were finally abolished in 1661. See *NALL* 10. They describe investigations into landholding when a landowner had died, and were instigated by the Crown because, in certain circumstances, the land could revert to the monarch. The inquisition recorded evidence concerning the acquisition of the land, the deceased owner's family, his heirs and his age. If the heir was a minor, there is often a 'proof of age' document.

There is a typed index to inquisitions in the National Archives, where most of these documents are housed, but because a copy was kept by the family concerned, many are also in city or county record offices. Inquisition summaries have been published by local record societies, and the archivist or librarian in the county where your ancestor lived should be consulted for advice. Some will be very difficult to read in the original form. (See below, p. 156, and *Amateur Historian* 1.3).

Freemen rolls

From the Middle Ages until modern times, cities or corporate towns have had the power to grant 'freedom' to certain categories of people, and this was not necessarily confined to those who lived in the borough concerned. They could be: the sons of other freemen or, after 1835 (when corporations which had not done so were compelled to keep the relevant records), direct descendants of freemen along the male line; anyone who had been an indentured apprentice in the borough, though not all trades seem to have used the facility; anyone who wished to purchase such a freedom; and those who had received an 'order of assembly' for the freedom to be given as an honour. Freemen are sometimes called 'citizens'. The benefit to the freemen included being allowed to be self-employed in the town, exemption from tolls, business protection, a share in the borough administration, influencing the price and quality of goods, and the right to vote, all of which made it an attractive proposition, you would think, for any tradesman to take up. Additionally, and very useful for the fortunate genealogist, several boroughs had the right to care for freemen's orphans; see Carlton (1974).

Ideally, the rolls record parentage, date of admission, the name and trade of the master in the case of a former apprentice, the amount paid, the father's residence and whether the master or parent was dead. It should be stressed, however, that their quality varies considerably. They are normally kept in town halls or archive offices, if they have survived at all. Those for London, to which there is a unified index, are in the possession of the City of London Record Office (see *GM* 23.4). Some have been printed, and if so they are worth consulting; but annual admissions cover under 1 per cent of the borough's population, so do not be surprised if your ancestor is not among them (see *FTM* 9.3 Jan 93).

London freemen were usually members of one or more of the various livery companies (listed by FitzHugh & Lumas, 1998), or guilds. Most of their records may be seen in the Guildhall Library.

Apprenticeship records

From 1563 until about 1835 a seven-year apprenticeship was the normal period and method of training craftsmen, though each trade developed its own set of regulations governing the entry of new members. Hey (2004) notes terms of up to sixteen years! Records have survived in large numbers from 1710, when a tax was imposed on the indenture, and include the boy's name, his father or mother and, occasionally, their trade, the master to whom the boy was being apprenticed, the trade and the fee. They became briefer after 1760 when the poorer boys were exempted from the tax, along with those paying less than 1s. for the indenture. See *Local Historian* 14.7 for pauper apprentices, *PFH* 66 Jun 03, and *FHM* 148 Oct 07. John Titford analyses apprenticeship indentures in *FTM* 24.3 Jan 08.

Apprenticeship indentures have survived in many places, a surprisingly large number remaining with individual families. These family copies have often found their way into libraries and record offices, and some may even be bought in antique shops. During the period when the tax was levied, a copy of each indenture was kept by central government, and thousands are now recorded in the National Archives, indexed by the name of the master and the apprentice (see *NALD* 80).

Unless the genealogist has access to London, or to a London searcher, these records are very much a hit-and-miss affair – mostly miss. In more modern times, however, when it becomes possible to identify the firm for which an apprentice worked, the firm's own records should be searched – some, such as Metrovick's in Manchester, have even been printed as an index. See also trade union and friendly society records (pp. 68–70, *FTM* 1.3 Mar 85 and *GM* 23.4).

The Society of Genealogists has an index of apprentices in England and Wales, 1710–74, giving name, name of father (or mother if widowed), name of master, trade, amount paid, and sometimes the residence of father and master. However parish apprentices, and those paying under 1s. for the indenture, are not included. Apprentice records of London companies may be found in the Guildhall Library (See *GM* 28.3, Oct 04).

Royalist composition papers
These are available for only a short period in the seventeenth century, but they sometimes give the names of the heirs and relatives of the individuals whose estates were being confiscated.

The Middle Ages, *c.* 1300–1538

General problems
In our quest to push back the knowledge of our genetic forebears, 1538 marks a much more significant watershed than 1837. The two periods examined so far, those dominated first by civil registration, then by parish registers as sources, have one thing in common which does not apply when we try to trace our medieval ancestors – a system which at least attempted to keep a permanent record of marriages and the start and end of individual lives. Imagine how difficult it would have been to reach back almost five centuries without them – yet that is what characterises our last great genealogical adventure. Welcome to the Middle Ages! There are other reasons why relatively few genealogists have broken through the 1538 barrier.

> Many will have already experienced the same problem in Elizabethan times, or even later, in the majority of parishes which have no extant parish registers or bishops' transcripts going back to the sixteenth century, so they know what it is like. Most prefer to opt for the easy life, continuing research on the many other branches of their family.
> Few textbooks give advice on how to tackle the period. Some, indeed, do not explain the sources available. (A notable exception is John Unett, first edition 1961 (see also Unett & Tanner 1997), who devoted half his book to them while excluding civil registration altogether!)

The sources are often unpublished, difficult to read, normally not in English, and many are available only in the National Archives, which publishes Records Information Leaflet 28 (*Genealogy before the parish registers*). There is a very useful website, www.medievalgenealogy.org.uk, with many cross-references to different sources, and *FTM* 23.1 Nov 06 has an article on Internet sources.

Apparently alien social customs and expectations are expressed in alien terminology, requiring a glossary for the beginner. Dates are expressed in regnal years (as all legislation was until the 1960s), the death of each monarch marking the end of a sequence. A key is given in FitzHugh & Lumas (1998), and Cheney & Jones (2004).

It is probable that, with the exception of very few years in those three centuries which we are about to enter, the majority of people alive at any one time will not appear in the extant written records. It will come as no surprise, however, that the minority include the wealthy and the criminal. Even if they do, the great majority of men (some 80 per cent according to David Hey) shared only five Christian names.

Part-way through this period (the time depending on which part of the country, and what type of surname, you are researching) inherited surnames are genetically preceded by non-inherited byenames.

Sources for Wales (where the English practice of inherited surnames was adopted only from the Act of Union in 1536) are even poorer than those for England.

Thus the genealogical jigsaw now has the majority of its pieces missing, and none too clear a picture on many of the ones which are in place!

Those contemplating this step into the unknown will already have put a lot of time and effort into tracing their family tree, and will typically have had varying degrees of success with different branches. Already it will be clear that the majority of ancestors, alive as the Middle Ages died, will never be individually known. Many genealogists will be trapped in the eighteenth or even the twentieth century, unable to solve particular problems in some of those branches.

For the tiny minority who have successfully traced more than one branch to the mid-sixteenth century, however, a question we considered at the start of the book may re-emerge – 'Which branch should I try to trace?' The original answers still stand (the rich, and those who lived reasonably close to where you can undertake the research). Now, however, a third criterion should be considered – the type of surname. My personal inclination would be to explore first those which are based on a (hopefully, rare) place name ('locative'), rather than on a personal name, a nickname, an occupation or a topographical feature, all of which have a greater degree of unpredictability as to their spread and origins.

The 'rarity' of locatives refers to the number of places which bear the same name, rather than to the number of people who carry that surname. The more geographically restricted distribution, based on a seventeenth-century survey, will be another useful indicator of which to choose first. The survey is best achieved using the protestation and hearth tax records, but these must be replaced by other sources in some counties (see Rogers, 1995).

Every textbook on genealogy, including this one in the early stages, recommends that genealogical research is undertaken step by step, generation by generation, moving back in time only when genetic relations have been satisfactorily established. That *modus operandi* must now be abandoned, to be replaced by the assembling of as many data as possible, arranged chronologically place by place. Within that framework will be relationships, tax payments, jury appearances, witnesses and a wide variety of instances in which the same surname occurs over a 200–300 year period. In the absence of an automatic source for details of parents and marriages, it is the act of assembling these data into a coherent framework which will form the basis of most genealogies, and at first (and even at the last) the relations between individuals may not be clear. It is what one writer has called 'a long and laborious procedure' (*GM* 12.16).

The difficulties already indicated are in themselves sufficient encouragement to enquire how much information has already been accumulated by previous researchers, only a few of whom will have been genealogists. The works of Marshall (1903), Barrow (1977) and Whitmore (1953) have already been noted, and should be re-examined for references to the medieval period. The International Genealogical Index should be searched by date in order to extract all the pre-1538 entries with the individual surname, county by county, and the files of the Society of Genealogists can be expected to contain a wealth of references. From the genealogist's point of view, Col. Swinnerton's articles in *FTM*, starting Aug 02, are useful. See Chambers (2005).

In this round-up of gift horses one beast needs to be ridden with great care. Deficiencies in the Heralds' visitation pedigrees have already been noted. It should be emphasised here that they are magnified in the Middle Ages. Some of the printed versions are not taken directly from the originals at the College of Arms. All rely on data supplied by the gentry themselves since the early sixteenth century, and each may therefore be on a spectrum somewhere between the totally accurate and the totally fanciful. The pedigrees are characterised in the medieval period by the absence of firm dates and the absence of quoted sources. They may be anything from three to twenty generations long, and the marriage of ancestral siblings is often included, which makes them always worth consulting even by non-gentry families.

Doubts about the accuracy of visitation pedigrees suggest that we should not make them the central core of a family tree, except in the absence of any other evidence – and, even then, each item needs a mental question mark to be attached. On the other hand, the data cannot be ignored, for they are, at minimum, how a publisher has printed a transcription, sometimes of a transcription, of what the Heralds recorded as information supplied by the families concerned from unknown sources.

Corroborative evidence must be sought from the sort of documents described below, but before turning to them there is one further piece of research which should be recommended. Works on topographical (commonly called 'local') history have been popular for well over a century, and until relatively recently interest in named individuals was quite marked. In Victorian times particularly, the interests of antiquarians and genealogists overlapped, with the result that a large number of family trees can be found in their works. Furthermore, the *Victoria County History* series long had a policy of providing early instances of families with local, locative surnames, as well as the history of the gentry in medieval times.

The authors often took considerable pains to access both local and national archive collections (sometimes even amassing them themselves) in their efforts to provide the early, nominal history of their area, and as a result we were able to piece together the broad outlines of my wife's maiden name over a 250-year period (1332–1580) with comparatively little effort. As the great majority of these works are indexed, they can provide another excellent starting point for data collection. Soon, however, you will need to turn to the major sources themselves to provide more evidence of genetic relationships and surname distribution.

Looking for parents

Looking for parents in more modern times has normally involved finding a record associated with the specific event of birth or baptism.

Before 1538 you will be very lucky to find a similar record, and you must therefore seek out other sources which provide at least the names of the fathers concerned, with mothers' names, dates, places and occupations to be regarded as bonuses. Luckily, the range of those sources available nationally is surprisingly large.

Baptism
With hindsight it is easy to see the social and personal advantages of a system which records the ceremony of baptism, in the absence of one recording birth. The need to be able to establish age and relationship suggests that it was in everyone's interest that it was done, and done in a way which was accessible decades later. With that in mind, the possibility that such recording *did* take place, and that the records were taken out of the country to the Vatican, and elsewhere, at the time of the Reformation, is very exciting. Such a prospect is summarised in correspondence to the *GM* in March and June 1992, in which 'actual registers' are mentioned, as well as notes kept marginally in other volumes.

The excitement, however, must be tempered not only by the relatively limited availability of these records but by their content even if they were to be brought out into the public domain. It seems that many are of undated events, with no surnames or no parental names, versions even more basic than those of some parishes in Elizabethan England. It seems plausible that only baptisms in the wealthier families would seem to need recording because of considerations of inheritance. Furthermore, if there had been an extensive system of recording baptism in the Middle Ages, people would not have had so much difficulty proving age and relationships.

Nevertheless, there *are* some such records, the best known being the annotations found in service books surviving here and abroad. There are also some in missals, primers and psalters owned by the laity, akin to those in family Bibles in later centuries after the invention of the printing press. They have found their way into many national and local repositories, but the extent of their survival is unknown, and published church histories would not necessarily have them transcribed. Events in the lives of some laymen may also be found in the chronicles of some of the smaller monasteries.

In summary, it would seem that such records as exist cover only a tiny fraction of the millions of baptisms which took place in the three centuries before 1538.

Manorial records (see pp. 144-6)

Free tenants gave military service or paid rent for 'their' land; bondsmen or villeins had to pay for the privilege by working on the land of the lord of the manor until that arrangement was commuted into cash payment. The manor court rolls (which David Hey has called 'the most important sources for the history of the family and local history in the two or three centuries before parish registers begin') record the passing of land from one tenant to another, with the occasional surveys and 'extents' being taken, and the appointment of local officials.

It is rare to find a long series of records available for any one manor, however, and the heart of a professional provincial genealogist, commissioned to trace a family before 1538, sinks when it is discovered that no manorial records survive for the relevant area. Anita Travers estimates that the records of only 4 per cent of all pre-1538 manors survive (*GM* 21.1). These, more than any other source, provide evidence of a genealogical line for most families. There are also clues to the timing and direction of geographical movement, especially those between parishes in different parts of the same estate.

While there are many manorial records in the National Archives, the majority are held in regional, local, and even private repositories. Where known, they should be recorded in the National Register of Archives. See Mullins (1958, 1983) and West (1982). Most in the National Archives are listed in 'List and Index of Court Rolls' (Lists and Indexes VI), and 'List of Rentals and Surveys' (Lists and Indexes XXV and Supplementary XIV).

Inquisitions post mortem *(see p. 149)*

Following the death of anyone holding land directly from the monarch (i.e. tenants 'in chief' or 'in capite') an official called an escheator investigated the family circumstances in order to see whether the land should revert to the Crown. (This would happen if the deceased had been outlawed, or died without heirs.) Many of the witnesses were of less exalted status, however. The palatine counties of Chester, Durham and Lancaster, incidentally, had their own chanceries and escheators, and do not appear in the main series of calendars. The various writs involved have been conveniently listed by FitzHugh & Lumas (1998) and Steel (1968, I, pp. 367-8), and the inquisitions *post mortem* themselves have been published up to 1422.

The Crown might alternatively enjoy the profits from the land if the heir had not yet reached the age of twenty-one. When a minor came of age, a fine (or 'relief') was paid to the king, a practice imitated by lords of the manor in turn to sub-tenants. It was thus important to establish the age of the heir so as to fix the date at which adult entry to the estate ('livery of seisin') would take place. Contained within the series of inquisitions *post mortem* are 'proofs of age' documents in which the date (often just the year) of the birth of an heir is recorded according to the memories of the jury and the information they could collect (see Bedell, 1999; *Past & Present* 162). Steel (1968, I) argues that proofs of age 'are the only large class of mediaeval documents which set out, however imperfectly, to establish dates of birth'. Confirmation that Ralph was the son of Richard Basset of Weldon in 1321 was the subject of twelve different attestations. John de Cracroft was stated to be twenty-four years old on 13 March 1359, as his godfather had caused the baptism to be recorded in the missal of Hoggesthorp church, with confirmatory reports concerning the date of a first Mass, his father going on a dated pilgrimage, someone else's birth date, the death of another whose date was written into a calendar, the date of a flood, and of someone becoming a nun.

Inquisitions *post mortem* applied to land which was inheritable by the next generation ('in fee'). The series runs from 1235 to 1662, with a miscellaneous series from 1219 to 1422. There is an index of inquisitions in the National Archives, but, because a copy of the inquisition was kept by the family concerned, many are also in city or county record offices. Inquisition summaries have therefore been published by local record societies also (see Mullins 1958, 1983 and a list in West, 1982), and the archivist or librarian in the county where your ancestor lived should be consulted for advice. Some documents will be very difficult to read in the original form (see *Amateur Historian* 1.3).

Final concords (or 'feet of fines')
These are not to be confused with Fine Rolls. Transfers of land (or of other hereditable rights) were properly recorded from very early times if they had been the subject of a genuine dispute heard in court, and the existence of such a record had so many advantages that from 1195 fictitious lawsuits developed as a device to avoid loss, destruction or forgery resulting from more casual practices. The series lasts to 1834, recording the transfer of property from the seller (or 'deforciant') to a buyer ('querent') on a specified date. Three copies of the concords (agreements) were written on the same sheet, one part going to each of the two parties and the third, written at the foot (hence 'feet of fines') was sent to the Treasury or, if appropriate, the palatinate authorities. They are normally in the National Archives (see *NALL* 2), with Welsh ones transferred to the NLW.

They can be useful to genealogists because the transfers were often between relatives, and the recent descent of ownership, or occupancy, of the property is sometimes described, three generations being not unknown.

Indexes and calendars of the feet of fines have been drawn up by local organisations – see Mullins (1958, 1983)

Education records

Very occasionally, school registers survive from before the sixteenth century, but the best used series are the published lists of graduates by Foster (for Oxford) and Venn (Cambridge) described above (p. 64). Some students were sent from England and Wales to Ireland or Scotland, where published medieval registers are available for the Universities of Aberdeen (from 1495) and St Andrews (1413).

Patent rolls

'Patent' as used here means 'open' or 'unsealed' letters, issued by the Court of Chancery on a very wide variety of subjects, including grants to individuals and organisations concerning licences, wardships and the right to use land. More domestic matters such as sewers, keeping the peace and gaol delivery may also be found. In published form the calendars are normally available in large libraries, though the earliest text (1202–16) is in Latin. To date, sixty-six large volumes cover the period 1216–1587, though those for 1509–47 are to be found in the series *Letters (foreign and domestic) of the reign of Henry VIII*. See also *NALD* 2 and *NALL* 42. Those in the palatinates of Chester and Lancaster are covered separately through their own Courts of Chancery.

On 12 May 1397 a pardon was issued 'to Geoffrey, son of Geoffrey de Bockelegh [Buckley] of his outlawry for not appearing in the King's Bench to answer Geoffrey, son of John de Dernelegh, in a plea of mayhem and breach of the peace, he having surrendered to the Marshalsea prison, as is certified by Walter Clapton, chief justice'. This entry was excellent confirmation of a relationship at a specific date – but it is the only reference to the Dearnley family in all sixty-six volumes, possibly because they lived in the palatinate of Lancaster.

Close rolls

'Close' here meaning, essentially, closed or sealed. They are in the National Archives, from 1205 to 1903, and cover a very wide variety of subjects, including deeds, wills, leases, naturalisation and changes of name. They are especially useful for deeds of sale. Most of the medieval period has been calendared, and published to 1509, with full texts for 1227–72.

Fine rolls

'Fines' in this case were payments for privileges – e.g. to enter land being inherited, liberty from knight service, safe conduct, pardons, etc. They run from 1120 to the execution of Charles I, the earliest being known as 'oblata' rolls. Calendars are published to 1509 in twenty-two volumes. Those from 1216 to 1234 can be seen, with translation, at www.finerollshenry3.org.uk.

Charter rolls

From 1199 to 1517 (after which they are in the patent rolls), charter rolls contain grants of land and privileges to organisations, and are in the National Archives. Calendars are available for 1226–1517, with full texts for 1199–1216.

Curia Regis rolls

These are cases before the King's Bench and Court of Common Pleas, containing many pedigrees establishing plaintiffs' rights. They are in the National Archives, and the printed calendar is from 6 Richard I (1194/5) to 1242. Plea rolls from 1273 to 1875 contain several pedigrees among the actions heard in the Curia Regis; many of the early rolls have been published by the Selden Society.

Miscellaneous deeds

It is difficult to convey the extent of private, family deeds which have now found their way in very large numbers into our local record offices rather than being enrolled in the great national collections listed above. Until the formation of the Land Registry in 1862, there was no automatic central recording of changes of land ownership, for example. A large number are also in private hands. Such deeds include transfers of land and property (title deeds), moneylending, gifts, leases, fines (private copies of the feet of fines, above), bonds, agreements and 'quitcalms' – deeds by which anyone with a claim on an estate following transfer would waive the claim, so making the transfer more secure. Deeds vary considerably in the amount of genealogical information they contain. For details of deeds generally, see Alcock (2001).

A not untypical deed of 1306 among the De Houghton deeds in the Lancashire Record Office includes 'Ad[am] s. Rog[er] s. Willy de Ribbelchestr' grants to Rob[ert] s. Ad[am] Moton in marriage with

Alice his sister a part of his land in Ribbelchestr wh. he had by gift and feoffment of Rob[ert] s. Rob[ert] s. Christian de Ribbelchestr ...'
Thus three generations of two families are supplied within a couple of lines, at a time when surnames were just becoming inherited in that part of the country. Typical also is the fact that the deed itself is undated, and amateur reliance on expert help or edited transcripts is considerable.

Probate (see pp. 251–9)
Parentage is often at the core of the making of a will, by which parents try to ensure that their named (or even as yet unborn) children are recognised as their rightful heirs. The series of wills extends back before 1538 in most counties:

> Prerogative Court of Canterbury (PCC) from 1383
> Prerogative Court of York (PCY), 1389
> Bedfordshire, 1480
> Berkshire, 1391
> Buckinghamshire, 1483
> Cambridgeshire, 1449
> Derbyshire, 1516
> Devonshire, 1532
> Essex, 1400
> Hampshire, 1502
> Hertfordshire, 1415
> Huntingdonshire, 1479
> Kent, 1396
> Leicestershire, 1485
> Lincolnshire, 1506
> London, 1374
> Norfolk, 1370
> Northamptonshire, 1510
> Nottinghamshire, 1500
> Oxfordshire, 1516
> Shropshire, 1516
> Staffordshire, 1516
> Suffolk, 1354
> Surrey, 1480
> Sussex, 1479
> Warwickshire, 1516
> Wiltshire, 1528
> Worcestershire 1451

See Gibson & Langston (2002) for their whereabouts. There are occasional survivals in other counties, such as Lancashire. For those with property in London, the Court of Hustings, run by the City's Corporation, proved appropriate wills (as well as recording land transfers, for which there is an index of buyers and sellers). It was possible here to have more than one valid will for the same individual.

In the early Middle Ages, when wills in the modern sense started, the Crown jealously guarded its interest in land, so the civil courts retained the final decision in disputed cases. Wills involving only land were nevertheless valid without probate and could be used as evidence in a temporal court of law. Again, wills involving only cash or personal property such as clothing, jewellery or furniture did not need to be proved. Wills should be distinguished from testaments until 1540, when the two were merged. (The survival of the phrase 'last will and testament' for over 400 years seems astonishing.) A will proper was the means by which leasehold land was effectively passed from the deceased to his successors. The testament contained bequests of personal property ('personalty') which developed the common format found in later centuries of one-third to the widow, one-third to the children and one-third distributed idiosyncratically. I remember the look of horror when I told my family that I intended to adopt this formula in my own will!

Guilds and freemen (see pp. 149–50)

The records of the guilds of medieval Britain can most conveniently be found through West (1983) but they are likely to be rather disappointing, as few contain records of the membership. Try the accounts, however, which can contain individual applications. It is probable that, before the seventeenth century, membership of a particular livery company did imply that the person followed that occupation. In Preston the roll of membership itself starts in 1397.

Freemen rolls of periods before 1538 have been published for Canterbury (from 1297), Chester (1392), Great Yarmouth (1429), King's Lynn (1292), Newcastle-upon-Tyne (1409), Wells (1377) and York (1272).

Lay subsidies (see p. 108)

These were taxes on movable property paid by the laity (clergymen *per se* paying clerical subsidies), levied by the monarch to pay for the armed forces in wartime. Surviving records are in the National Archives, and can be accessed through www.nationalarchives.gov.

uk/e179 (see *NALD* 10). This lists extant records, not who is named in them, but does have references to publications relating to each record. E179 is not, as you might think, a suspicious-looking food additive, but a code for a wonderful series of 25,000 taxation returns in the King's Remembrancer series, 1198–1688 (see *FHM* 123 Nov 05). Those with individuals listed are identified. The earliest to be denoted by this phrase was collected in 1275, and they were thereafter raised at regular intervals, and in different forms, until the seventeenth century. After 1332 (1334 in the case of Kent alone on a county-wide basis, though there are occasional later survivors – Horton and Stone in Buckinghamshire for 1336, for example) there are no individual names, only village totals for 200 years until the Great Subsidy of 1524/25. Wales was exempt from lay subsidies until 1543, and northern English counties until 1603 (Hoyle, 1994).

For detailed, historical accounts of lay subsidies, see Willard (1934), Beresford (1963), Jurkowski *et al.* (1998) and, for a list of those published, Rogers (1995). The principle was to tax individuals at a fraction of the assessed value of their movable goods, the fraction varying from year to year and even (after 1294) from place to place. There was a difference between urban and rural areas as to which goods had to be assessed and which were exempt. In 1327 the fraction was one-twentieth, whereas five years later it was one-fifteenth in the countryside and as high as one-tenth in towns.

There is a well researched connection between the lay subsidies and social class, as they always contain a minority of the population – those who were wealthy enough to be assessed – though Peter Franklin, editing the Gloucestershire lay subsidy of 1327, advises against the automatic assumption that all those of poorer rank would be excluded. On each occasion, the poor were formally exempt, a minimum payment usually being set – in 1327 it was 6*d*. The Church was also exempt, except in so far as some clerics owned lay property after 1291. Others who escaped the collection were 'moneyers' (workers in the royal mints), inhabitants of the Cinque Ports and, alas, the counties palatine, Cheshire and Durham. Tin miners in Cornwall and Devon were also exempt, but their names are included in the Devon subsidy roll of 1332. On the other hand, individuals having property in more than one small area (the 'vill') might appear more than once in the record. Simon Blake paid the 1327 tax on property in three different Essex vills, for example.

From 1290 and 1332 (1334 for Kent only), the returns provide individual names, but for the next two centuries only village totals are given. Then in 1524, when the annual value of land was taxed at 20 per cent and goods at 28 per cent in the pound, names reappear and continue until the lay subsidy died out.

The poll tax (see p. 146)

This was technically another lay subsidy, but is now classified separately because of the character of its format. It is by far the most likely medieval document to contain the names of our ancestors. Poll tax returns are available for almost all English counties but, as with so many other medieval documents of this nature, the Palatinates of Cheshire and Durham were excluded. The returns normally include the names and payments of some 60 per cent of the whole population, several times more than may be found in the earlier lay subsidies. The poll tax was levied in 1377, 1379 and 1381, the basis being slightly different in each case. That of 1377 targeted more taxpayers than the other two, although the records of only a few counties and cities have survived. In 1377 everyone not exempt aged fourteen or over was to pay one groat (4d.) to the Crown; but in 1379 a grading system, related to social class, was introduced for men and single women aged sixteen and over, extended to every lay person aged fifteen and over in 1381. Relationships (spouses, children) between taxpayers are often stated, and occasionally occupations. No county return is complete, and the returns vary from place to place in content. The poor were always exempt, and servants and spinsters both seem to be underrepresented, partly for that reason. Servants were often given only their Christian name, however.

Oxford University Press has published all the existing poll tax records for the British Academy, edited by Dr Carolyn Fenwick; they are indexed by place, but not by name.

Hundred rolls

These are the result of enquiries into the rights and properties of the Crown. Although they are available for many counties from 1273, the surviving 1279 returns are extremely detailed in a few cases – Bedfordshire, Buckinghamshire, Cambridgeshire, Huntingdonshire, Leicestershire, Oxfordshire, Suffolk and Warwickshire – which list the names of all tenants, including the humblest. J. B. Harley's useful article (1961) includes a map indicating the extent of coverage within those counties, and which have been published.

III *Looking for marriages*

There are basically two reasons why genealogists need to search for the marriage of their ancestors. Before 1 July 1837 a record of marriage is normally the only way to discover a bride's maiden name, which you need to have in order to find her own birth or baptism. Recourse to a marriage may also be needed in order to confirm the age of one of the parties or the name of one of their parents.

Marriage records are among the more satisfying of those which genealogists use. Among the birth/baptism, marriage and death/burial series they are probably the least susceptible to omissions. The reasons for this are that marriage establishes the legitimate rights of future children and widows, and that the number of entries you have to search is far smaller than the number of births, as it takes two to marry, and many never did. The discovery of a marriage brings evidence of a whole new family series which can then be linked with your own – indeed, it *is* your own, and (for women) more likely to provide your own genetic history than your male line!

Marriage certificates, 1837 to the present day

Since 1 July 1837 the Registrar General has had a duty to record all valid marriages in England and Wales, no matter what the form of ceremony involved. Since that date the state, represented by a Superintendent Registrar of marriages, has been able to conduct marriages itself. However, the fact that both church and state can conduct marriages complicates the recording and indexing process considerably at the local level.

In the case of civil ceremonies, the recording process is similar to that for births (see pp. 18–19). There are again two entries, one kept locally by the Superintendent Registrar, the other centrally by the General Register Office. If the wedding takes place in church, the same will apply when a Registration Assistant is present, and both church and civil certificates are completed immediately after the ceremony. The latter is kept by the registrar and a copy is sent to the General Register Office. However, registrars have not been present at Church of England, Jewish or Quaker marriages since 1837, and since 1898 other denominations have been able to apply for this relatively privileged status for individual church buildings. (For the procedure, see *MN* 3, Dec 86.) In that case an 'authorised person', usually the priest or a member of the congregation, is the sole recorder and sends copies of each marriage quarterly to the Superintendent Registrar and the General Register Office. Following industrial action by registrars in the 1980s, a majority of places licensed for marriages have now applied for authorised person (AP) status. Only some 20 per cent of marriages as recently as the 1960s were by APs – whose work is subject to the registration inspectorate, by the way. A number of mosques are in the process of applying for this status.

For the basic prohibited degrees of marriage see below, pp. 189–90. The list allows some surprising unions. A woman caused some consternation in 1894 by successfully proceeding with a marriage to her stepfather's brother, against the advice of the registrar.

The only addition to the list of prohibited degrees in the twentieth century is that of a child with its adoptive parent, though marriage with an adoptive sibling is permitted. (A bill to remove all obstacles to marriage within degrees of affinity – i.e. non-blood relationships – in 1979 failed.) For a detailed list of legal changes and their implications see Wolfram (1987); see also *MRS* 6 and *MN* 3 Dec 86. Since 1960 you have been able to marry the sibling of your divorced spouse, and the 1986 Marriage Act permitted a man to marry his mother-in-law (if his wife and his father-in-law were dead), a change of considerable interest to the comedian Les Dawson! It also permitted a stepparent/ child marriage, provided there has been no 'child of the family' relationship.

In 1907, for the first time, a man was allowed to marry his deceased wife's sister, though a clergyman can still refuse to conduct the ceremony. Before then, this had been the commonest form of invalid marriage. From 1921 he could marry his deceased brother's widow and, from 1931, nephews and nieces by marriage. Since 1960 a divorce(e) has been able to marry a former sister- or brother-in-law.

Until 1835 any marriage which had been inadvertently contracted within the prohibited degrees was voidable; Lord Lynhurst's Marriage Act made void any contracted after 1835, at the same time removing the power of ecclesiastical courts to annul marriages. Not until 1837 were Jews and gentiles allowed to marry one another. In 1770, however, Parliament unfortunately drew the line at making null and void any marriage which resulted from a woman luring a man by 'scent, paints, cosmetic washes, artificial teeth, Spanish wool, iron stays, hoops, high-heeled shoes, or bolstered hips ...' (quoted in *MRS* 4).

Many genealogists like to be precise about stating cousin and cousin-derived relationships. Children of siblings are first cousins, their own children second cousins, and so on. Each generation gap between cousins is denoted by a number of times 'removed'.

Civil marriage, available in Britain before 1837 only for a short time in the 1650s, grew slowly in popularity, though surprisingly large numbers used this option after 1837 in the far north of England, the south-west and Wales, and in urban areas, and it was more common among the under-twenties and over-thirties. About half of the original registrars of marriage were also RBDs, but unlike the latter were not confined to subdistricts for registration purposes. In 1841 under 2 per cent of all marriages were by civil ceremony, about 90 per cent being Anglican. In 1976 civil marriages overtook religious ceremonies in popularity. In the 1990s the two were about equal in number until the 1994 Marriage Act liberalised the 'approved premises' regulations, though that seems to have had little effect statistically. In 2008, preliminaries for marriage were entered on line (RON) for the first time; the entries themselves will be registered on line from 2009.

Some churches had very few marriages indeed, and it was often many years before the Superintendent Registrar received his copy of the marriage certificate. In his diary for 6 August 1873 Francis Kilvert tells the story of Llanlionfel:

> It is long since the Church has been used, though weddings were celebrated in it after it was used for other services. There is a curious story of a gentleman who was married there. Some years after his marriage, his wife died, and it happened that he brought his second bride to the same Church. Upon the altar rails she found hanging the lace handkerchief which her predecessor had dropped at the former wedding. The church had never been used nor the handkerchief disturbed in the interval of years between the two weddings.

Sooner or later, therefore, the state receives two copies of the details of each marriage celebrated since 1 July 1837, one in the General Register Office, the other locally. Indexing is by the names of both bride and groom, in alphabetical order, strictly according to the spelling on the entry. At the General Register Office the index is national, covering England and Wales; in the Superintendent Registrar's office, however, each church is normally indexed separately, which makes the task of locating any one entry extremely laborious unless you know in advance where the marriage took place – or at least under which denomination it was likely to be. Only in the large cities, starting with Manchester in 1950, are marriage indexes now unified annually; in most districts there are still many indexes to search. Furthermore, some marriage books might not have been centralised – the register for St Paul's, Hensall, lasted from 1856 until 1999 when it was centralised with some blank pages remaining; Allhallows, Medway, and the appropriately named St John in the Wilderness, Todmorden, were still in use in 2002!

In these circumstances access to the GRO indexes saves even more labour in the case of marriages than it does in the case of births. The old index books themselves have gone into GRO storage at Christchurch, and enquirers now have to use microfiche copies, or go on line. (The books are far fewer in number, but still occupy about 200 yards of shelving. They are bound in green, in contrast to the indexes for births in red and deaths in black. Each quarter is contained in only a few volumes – in only one for certain years for which the original indexes have become so worn that they have had to be typed and rebound.) Unless you do not already know the names of both parties, it is rare to be faced with more than one possible marriage, though the degree of mobility by young persons during the Second World War can make those six years somewhat more difficult. The normal technique is to search for the rarer of the two surnames; each time the full name occurs, look for the name of the spouse in the same index in order to see whether the reference numbers coincide. If they do, then almost certainly that is the entry you require. You can then apply for a copy of the certificate, using the green application form or direct on the Internet at www.gro.gov.uk.

Once the MAGPIE system is in place, these indexes will be available (on line only) showing the spouse's surname from 1837 (after 1911 till then) so that cross-checking will no longer be necessary. (See A note on presentation, p. xxiii above.) Only occasionally, e.g. Liverpool, 1837–54, can you find such cross-referencing in local indexes. In the case of the remarriage of a widow, her earlier married name should be indexed but not her maiden name; the certificate, however, should provide both. Divorcees remarry using the name by which they are then commonly known, but I have seen no research to suggest whether this is normally the maiden name or previous married name – probably the latter if there were children in the dissolved marriage. This might be a useful investigation for a family history society to undertake.

Yet another advantage of using the GRO indexes is that they can be consulted free of charge, whereas the local indexes may be searched for only a five-year period without incurring the prohibitive 'general search' fee. Normally, you will know the names of both parties from the birth certificate of one of their children, but that will not have told you whether the child was the eldest or the youngest in the family, so that a long search may be needed before the entry is found (unless the marriage ended in divorce; see pp. 182–5). It is particularly at this point that family 'information' about the probable year of marriage can be misleading. The cost of searching for, and purchasing, marriage certificates is identical with that for birth certificates (see p. 19). It should be remembered, however, that an application to a Superintendent Registrar's office in a large city may require a long search unless you can provide the denomination or probable location in advance. Do not be surprised, therefore, if you are politely advised to do the search yourself, or apply to the General Register Office instead.

The copy certificate

The certificate itself provides the following information for both bride and groom: date and place of the marriage, name, age, condition, rank or profession, residence, father's name and occupation and the names and signatures of the bride, groom and witnesses. Bilingual marriage entries have been permitted in Wales since 1 April 1971.

The name is that by which the bride or groom are commonly known at the time of marriage. There is provision for alias names to be added, joined by 'otherwise', though not against the wishes of the party concerned. Both would be indexed.

The entry in the age column is all too often given as 'full', meaning twenty-one or over, a word actually used in the 1837 sample of how to fill in a form! Giving the correct age was not compulsory, and a few did not provide it even in the mid-twentieth century. (The figures are 4 per cent in 1838–39, about half in the early 1850s, falling to almost everybody giving their ages by 1900.) Nowadays, however, all brides and grooms are asked to provide ID, including age and address.

Giving the wrong age or condition does not in itself invalidate the marriage, though willful deception might lead to a prosecution for perjury. 'Minor' or 'under age' meant between twelve and twenty inclusive for a girl, or between fourteen and twenty for a boy, until 1929 when the lower age limit was raised to sixteen for both parties. A consent form should be signed by the parents of minors but the system involved is still easy to subvert. Evidence of consent is still sought, but the record does not normally survive. (No one already widowed has been classed as a minor, no matter what their age.)

The average age of marriage was partly related to social status, the upper classes having a higher average marriage age. Professional men married at almost thirty in 1871, but manual workers at about twenty-four. Women have always tended to marry, on average, about two years younger than men during the last few centuries.

'Condition' in this context means marital status – bachelor, widow, etc. – rather than weak at the knees. ('Spinster' and 'bachelor' were replaced by 'single' for civil register marriages on 5 December 2005.) This entry is usually correct as stated, but occasionally widowers or divorcees will describe themselves as 'bachelor'. Between 1858 and 1952 a divorced bridegroom should be described as 'the divorced husband of ...', his former wife's maiden name being given; a divorced bride is 'the divorced wife of ...' with the additional phrase 'from whom she obtained a divorce' only in the case of the respondent. Since 1952 the condition of a divorcee is simply 'previous marriage dissolved'. A divorced woman, by the way, must remarry under the surname by which she is then known, which will not necessarily be her earlier married name or even her maiden name. After the annulment of a marriage the parties reverted to their previous status until 1971, when their stated condition became 'previous marriage annulled'. Widowhood status is ascribed to those remarrying after the *presumed* (as well as the actual) death of a spouse.

There are several possible explanations of why the surname in the 'father's name' column can be different from that of the bride or groom, in particular the remarriage of the mother, the illegitimacy of the bride or groom, or the remarriage of the bride. If the column is blank, however, it usually signifies that the name of the father is unknown, for whatever reason, or (incorrectly) that he had died. Brides and grooms are asked if their fathers are still alive, but I don't know when the practice started. In the latter case the word 'deceased' should follow his name. The 'father's occupation' column will sometimes indicate that he was already dead, but sometimes the name and occupation of a dead father are given without any indication that he had died. There has never been a legal requirement to record whether a father is dead or alive. When an adopted child marries, the father on the entry can be the adoptive or the natural father, with the fact of adoption indicated in the entry if the surnames differ. (Oddly, if only the mother had adopted the bride or groom, her name should appear in the father's name column! The name of a mother entered, incorrectly, in the father's column, or the absence of a father's name, more usually means that the child was illegitimate.) By choice, the name of a stepfather can now be given instead of a birth father.

Addresses in towns are notoriously inaccurate, often being for the convenience of avoiding payment for two sets of banns. Marriage of a bride and groom from the same address should be regarded with suspicion. If two addresses appear, it probably means that the party moved between banns or between notification and the ceremony itself. In more modern times, however, cohabitation before marriage is much more common, accounting for about one-third in the 1980s. A new study of the falsification of addresses at marriage is being undertaken – see *Anc* 58 Jun 07.

Few marriage entries at the General Register Office contain original signatures of brides, grooms and witnesses. Brides are required to sign in the name they used immediately before the ceremony. If it is important to check a signature, you should therefore approach the Superintendent Registrar or the minister of the church or chapel where the marriage took place to see whether he will consult the records for you. Many Anglican registers have been microfilmed by local libraries, in which case the signatures are easy to check for yourself. In the mid-nineteenth century some 31 per cent of men and 45 per cent of women marked rather than signed. By 1875 this had fallen to 16 per cent for men and 22 per cent for women. See *MRS* 27.

Witnesses can be minors, so long as they appear to be 'of credible age', and one as young as ten years old is on record at Lewisham. They are usually of the same age group as the bride and groom, being of an age to bear witness to the event for a long period if required (which might prove necessary, for example, in court at a later date if the register was not preserved).

Failure to find a marriage entry in the indexes

This problem is rarer with marriage than with birth certificates, but even so it does happen, and once again there are many reasons why. Some of the reasons are similar to those which sometimes make birth certificates so elusive. See Foster (2002) who found up to 5 per cent missing from GRO indexes. If the marriage was terminated by divorce (see below) many of the problems can be solved through the record of a decree absolute which will give the date of the original ceremony. Both former surnames should be checked in the case of a divorcee remarrying.

Registration in another district

If the national indexes are being consulted, this will not be a problem. If you are sure where the bride and groom lived or worshipped, but cannot find the marriage indexed in the areas concerned, then it is almost certain that the marriage was elsewhere. There are several ways to discover where, though access to the national indexes is by far the easiest.

The solution may be found in the Anglican books of banns in the known parish of the bride or groom. (These are sometimes called 'proclamations' or 'publications'.) All marriages other than Anglican have their equivalent of banns, known as 'notices of marriage', which are publicly posted before the ceremony. Indeed, if an Anglican clergyman is reluctant to call banns (for a remarriage, for example) a registrar's certificate of notification can be accepted instead. They should have been copied into Marriage Notice Books, which were open to the public, in the 1840s at least. From 1837 to 1840 these notices were sometimes read out at the board of guardians' meetings, and so may be found in their minute books. The Superintendent Registrar is not obliged to keep these notices longer than five years, but many do, and a few notices have survived among the local Poor Law Union records (Gibson, Rogers & Webb 1997–2008). They have also been required for a marriage between a British subject and a foreign national in a foreign country since 1906, and between two British subjects in a foreign country since 1915. The notices must, in any case, be written up into permanent notice books. Irregularities in these preliminaries to marriage are analysed in MN 21 Winter 96. The public's right of access to the old notices in the custody of a Superintendent Registrar has been denied by the General Register Office.

The Superintendent Registrar also issues certificates as an 'authority for marriage' which have been an alternative to Anglican banns since 1837. These are returned to the Superintendent Registrar in all cases where a registrar was present at the marriage ceremony. The certificates from 'authorised person' marriages (p. 165) are returned to the Registrar General quarterly. They are kept for a minimum of two years, but again many districts keep them much longer. The Superintendent Registrar's licence, which is quicker than a certificate, is not acceptable for a Church of England marriage, and since 1856 Anglican clergy have been able to refuse to accept a registrar's notice as an alternative to banns. A Registrar General's licence since 1970 allows a marriage to take place at a deathbed and is not, therefore, the civil equivalent of an archbishop's special licence; see p. 194. Other ways of discovering a 'missing' marriage involve trying to find the parish of the partner, as that is where it was probably performed. In the nineteenth century the place of birth of an adult is available from the census (pp. 71–91) or from military records (pp. 56–60). Place of birth has been on death certificates since 1 April 1969. Even if the place of birth is discovered, of course, there is no guarantee that the marriage took place there. The date of a Roman Catholic marriage can sometimes be found in the margin of the subsequent baptismal entry of the children.

Discovering which churches were licensed for marriages is not easy. A town or county directory should help, and the Registrar General regularly publishes an official list of certified places of worship which celebrate marriages.

If the marriage was in the Jewish or Quaker faith it should be remembered that it could take place anywhere in the country, whether the premises were registered for marriages or not. A person authorised to register Jewish marriages in Leeds may record a Jewish marriage in someone's front room in Penzance, provided that the groom is a member of the synagogue in Leeds.

Marriage not registered

While this is a theoretical possibility, it is more likely to be the refuge of a bad amateur genealogist, or at least one without much wit or stamina. One exception will be the unfortunate bride and groom who, perhaps unwittingly, have gone through an unorthodox marriage, a rare practice which is still alive in modern times in, for example, witches' covens. On the whole, if the marriage was not registered, it was not performed. There were plenty of couples who simply lived together as man and wife, knowing that the law puts the burden of proof on those who would challenge such a 'marriage' as invalid. If you cannot find a second marriage, make sure that the first spouse was actually dead or divorced. Living in sin was perhaps preferable to committing bigamy (which carried a penalty of two years in jail, seven years' transportation, or even – after 1795 – death), and I guess led to many 'wives' being deserted. Many 'common-law' wives have described themselves as widows when registering their 'husband's' death, making it difficult for the real widow to draw a pension, and there have been cases of informants being convicted of falsifying the surname. In 1877 the penalty for this offence was a £5 fine or a month in prison.

Another exception to come to light in the latter half of the nineteenth century was recent immigrants who refused to go through the established procedure for Jewish marriages, which had given the Board of Deputies a virtual monopoly. This was effectively stopped in 1906 (see *GM* 24.3).

In 1837 some bishops failed to inform the Registrar General about chapels licensed for marriage, so it is possible that, in the early days, some marriages after 1 July 1837 were recorded by the Church but not by the new registration system (see *MRS* 8).

Marriage incorrectly indexed (see pp. 34–5)
I have been told that the correct spelling of their names is not the first priority of brides and grooms, and of course many in the last century were unable to spell accurately. If the entry is wrong, the index will be wrong also, and in 1869 the Registrar General admitted to using 'aliases' in the indexes because the original clerks' handwriting was so hard to read. Standards in this century are, hopefully, much better, and on one occasion prevented the marriage of Elsie Dawn Hobbs as Elsie Doorknobs! With the advent of computerised entries, such problems should be a thing of our quaint, but so interesting, past.

Marriage not in England and Wales (see p. 200)
Scotland, Ireland, the Isle of Man and the Channel Islands each have their own registration system, and if your ancestor lived in Britain but married abroad, there will not be an automatic copy returned to our national records. Marriages of Britons abroad are, of course, subject to the laws of the country where the ceremony takes place. The National Archives has registers of marriage from about fifty different countries, listed by Bevan & Duncan (1990). However, the couple can voluntarily inform the British consul, who will then include the marriage in the consular returns, which are at the General Register Office. They sometimes include a version of the banns system, and one of my students discovered such a record which postdated the marriage itself! If a British chaplain conducted the ceremony, the entry should be in the Chaplains' Returns, again at Kew. They have been housed with the Registrar General since July 1849. The indexes, together with those of military personnel marriages, are on the open shelves. See Yeo (1995), *FTM* 16.9 Jul 00 and *MRS* 11. The marriage abroad of a British resident might be recorded in the marriage notice book, or book of banns, if a certificate of no impediment had been required (see p. 171). The General Register Office indexes of marriages overseas may be on microfiche in some local libraries, and are available via www. findmypast.com (pay per view). Those at sea on British vessels can be accessed via www.theshipslist.com; see *NALD* 61. The register is from 1854 to 1972.

Index entry missed by searcher (see pp. 38–9)
I think the commonest cause is not realising that the maiden name of a mother, obtained from a birth certificate, is not the surname she used at the time of the marriage concerned.

Misleading clues

If the spelling of a parental name on a birth certificate is incorrect, you may be looking at the wrong part of the marriage index. Even if you have the correct name, however, you may still be misled. For example, the bride or groom may have had a double forename of which you are not aware; your John Smith might be Wilfred John Smith. The provision of information about the forenames of individuals in the marriage indexes is as follows:

1 July 1837 to 31 December 1865: all forenames in full.

1 January 1866 to 31 December 1866: the first forename in full, plus initials of other forenames.

1 January 1867 to 30 June 1910: the first two forenames in full, plus the initials of other forenames.

1 July 1910 to date: the first forenames in full, plus the initials of other forenames.

Do not make the mistake of thinking that a marriage should be at least nine months before the birth of the child. Search all quarter-years, including that of the birth concerned. Indeed, it might be found dated after the birth of the eldest children, even seven years, perhaps, in the case of women whose first husbands had deserted them. In the first half of the nineteenth century almost one-third of all brides were pregnant (Wrigley & Schofield, 1981). Sometimes indentures forbade marriage during an apprenticeship. Births of siblings can occur outside the normal twenty-year period; a teenage bride could have given birth at any time during the next thirty years. Charles Darwin's wife Emma was 47 when her last child was born, having married at 31.

The maiden name of the child's mother is not necessarily the name she married under; the further back in time, the greater the proportion of weddings which involved the remarriage of a widow – 10 per cent in the middle of the last century. The birth entry of one of her children may indicate both her maiden name and her earlier married name, but a space for this information was introduced only in 1969. A later census, which may include her children by an earlier marriage, should also provide useful clues, because those children should have the surname of the mother's former husband. Again, the marriage will not necessarily be found just prior to the birth of the eldest child recorded from the census; it often happened that teenage children were not living at home when the census was taken, thus making a 'middle' child look like the eldest. Similarly, the census will not tell you how many children of a father were born to the wife named in that census.

Until 1875 the informant could name anyone as the father of an illegitimate child. Such cases, which were more than distressing to the named father when the attribution was incorrect, did occur, and some may deceive you (not to say the child) into thinking that the birth had been legitimate. It is all too common for a man to have lived with a woman other than his wife, and for her to describe herself as his widow when he died. A search for that 'marriage' would be in vain, as would that for an unmarried mother who, as informant, pretended to be married in order to make the child appear legitimate. Before remarriage, widow(er)s have to provide evidence of the death of the earlier spouse, though there has been provision since 1603 for remarriage after the disappearance of a spouse.

If a father married more than one wife with the same forename, and had children by each, the marriage to the women whose maiden name appears on the birth entry of his younger children will not be found before the birth of his eldest!

See above (p. 29) for the process of reregistration following legitimation, which can give a misleading clue to the date of a marriage since 1927.

Don't reject a marriage purely on the basis of apparent literacy, especially in the nineteenth century. There is plenty of evidence that some individuals marked when they could have signed perfectly well had they chosen to do so. When Elizabeth Moffit married at Colton on 27 March 1824 she signed the register, but marked the bishop's transcript which was evidently written at the same time!

I cannot detect any significance in either age or sex, in the order in which names within the same household appear in an electoral register, so assumptions about relationships in the household cannot be made from this source.

Change of name before or after marriage (see pp. 49–53)
If marriage followed a change of name by deed poll, and the fact was declared to the registrar, only the new name should appear on the entry, with the phrase 'name changed by deed poll'. 'Formerly known as ...' or 'otherwise ...' can also indicate change but will be entered only if the registrar was informed at the time of marriage and the party did not object to its being entered.

Finding more than one possible marriage
Once again, this misfortune is much rarer with marriages than with births, and normally the place of the marriage given in the index should resolve it anyway. You can confirm the correct entry by

AA 268043

M. Cert.
S.R./R.B.D.

CERTIFIED COPY of an ENTRY OF MARRIAGE
Pursuant to the Marriage Act 1949

CAUTION:—It is an offence to falsify a certificate or to make or knowingly use a false certificate or a copy of a false certificate intending it to be accepted as genuine to the prejudice of any person or to possess a certificate knowing it to be false without lawful authority.

WARNING: THIS CERTIFICATE IS NOT EVIDENCE OF THE IDENTITY OF THE PERSON PRESENTING IT.
[Printed by the authority of the Registrar General.]

Registration District (Liverpool)

18 56. Marriage solemnized at Trinity Church in the Parish of Liverpool in the County of Lancashire

No.	When Married.	Name and Surname.	Age.	Condition.	Rank or Profession.	Residence at the Time of Marriage.	Father's Name and Surname.	Rank or Profession of Father.
469	October 18th	George Mearns	full age	Bachelor	Master Mariner	Lawrence Week	James Mearns	Gentleman
		Alice Turton	full age	Spinster	—	Mill Street	William Turton	Miner

Married in the Church of St Philip according to the Rites and Ceremonies of the Established Church, by me, B. Lawrence

This Marriage was solemnized between us,
George Mearns
Alice Turton

in the Presence of us,
Keith Turton
Thos Maddock

Somerset Deputy Supt Registrar 19/5/97 Date

Certified to be a true copy of an entry in a register in my custody.

CK 546023

B. Cert.
S.R.

CERTIFIED COPY of an ENTRY OF BIRTH
Pursuant to the Births and Deaths Registration Act 1953

Registration District West Derby

1946. Birth in the Sub-district of Toxteth Park in the County of Lancaster

No.	Columns:— 1 When and where born	2 Name, if any	3 Sex	4 Name, and surname of father	5 Name, surname and maiden surname of mother	6 Occupation of father	7 Signature, description, and residence of informant	8 When registered	9 Signature of registrar	10* Name entered after registration
18	Twelve April 1946 6.0 a.m. 121 Stanhope Terrace Upper Stanhope Street	Alice Maria	Girl	George Pryer STEAINS	Alice STEAINS formerly TURTON	Collector of Government Taxes	Geo P Steains Father 121 Stanhope Terrace Upper Stanhope Street	One May 1946	George Edgar Registrar.	

*See note overleaf.

Certified to be a true copy of an entry in a register in my custody.

.... Barrowdale .... Deputy Superintendent Registrar

19 5 T 46 .... Date

Figure 7. The father added a forename and changed his occupation between marriage and the birth of his daughter.

CERTIFIED COPY OF AN ENTRY OF BIRTH

GIVEN AT THE GENERAL REGISTER OFFICE

Application Number: G008253

REGISTRATION DISTRICT Mansfield

1909 BIRTH in the Sub-district of Blackwell in the County of Derby

Columns:	1	2	3	4	5	6	7	8	9	10*
No.	When and where born	Name, if any	Sex	Name and surname of father	Name, surname and maiden surname of mother	Occupation of father	Signature, description and residence of informant	When registered	Signature of registrar	Name entered after registration
59	Seventeenth October 1909 70. Colliery Blackwell No. 3	Raymond Roy	Boy	Charles Warren	Elsie Warren formerly Heathgrave	Coal Miner	Elsie Warren Mother 70. Colliery Annetts Blackwell	Twentieth November 1909	Constance N. H. Dobbs Registrar	

CERTIFIED to be a true copy of an entry in the certified copy of a Register of Births in the District above mentioned.

Given at the GENERAL REGISTER OFFICE, under the Seal of the said Office, the 14th day of May 19 94.

BXBZ 597322   *See note overleaf

CAUTION:- It is an offence to falsify a certificate or to make or knowingly use a false certificate or a copy of a false certificate intending it to be accepted as genuine to the prejudice of any person or to possess a certificate knowing it to be false without lawful authority.

WARNING: THIS CERTIFICATE IS NOT EVIDENCE OF THE IDENTITY OF THE PERSON PRESENTING IT.

Dd 8995412 2PD160 50000 2/94 Mcr235596

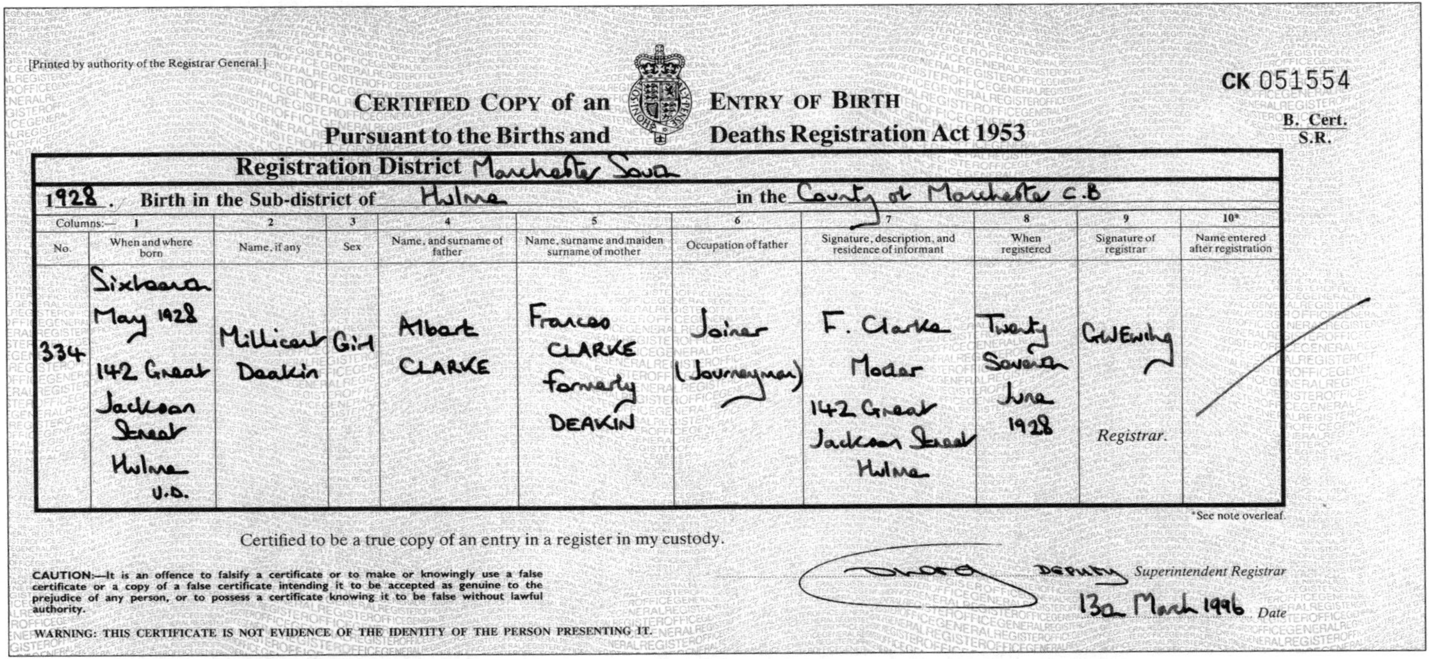

Figure 8. Two apparently normal birth entries which, because they contain incorrect information, will not lead to the previous marriage of the mother and father.

checking the name of the father of one of the parties to the marriage against their birth certificate or other source such as the census, and supplying this information when you apply for the marriage certificate. A signature can be a very useful means of identification, but normally you can see it only on an original or microfilmed AP marriage entry, not one from the General Register Office. Very occasionally confusion may arise because the reference number given in the index refers to a page of marriages in the register book, not to an individual entry. If your friend John Smith married Elizabeth Jones, and on the same page in the register another John Smith married Elizabeth Taylor, then both John Smiths, Elizabeth Jones and Elizabeth Taylor will all be given the same reference number. If one of the parties marries under two different names, using an alias, the other party will of course appear twice in the index. Don't think it happens only to John Smiths! There are apparently two Francis William Clark marriages in 1859, and two Rosina Ullah marriages in 1973, each pair having exactly the same reference number.

In the rare event that you find more than one possible marriage in the index, the verification fee is £3.00 per entry. Marriages known to be bigamous are now marked with a marginal note in the registers after information from the GRO, and copy certificates may be issued, annotated accordingly. Remarriage after the absence of a spouse for seven years (following the case of Prudential v. Edmonds, 1877), however, was not classed as bigamy.

Occasionally, presumably in a fit of enthusiasm, a couple will remarry each other. When that happens the date and place of the previous marriage should be found in the second entry. Like the increase in marriages following the outbreak of the First and Second World Wars, it reflects the uncanny ability of twentieth-century hormones to triumph over reason. (Earlier wars had the opposite effect – see MRS 11.) Since 1875 if not earlier, the regulations also allow a couple to marry twice in different venues on the same day, thus reducing the chances of religious rivalries, or suspicion of civil ceremonies, devastating the happy event. In such cases, each ceremony should be conducted as if the other did not exist, and each should be indexed, giving the appearance of two marriages.

Civil partnerships

Since 5 December 2005, same-sex couples have been able to obtain legal recognition of their relationship. While such partnerships, by definition, cannot in themselves give rise to genetic issue, the entries will have relevance to genealogy for several reasons – to those who wish to trace all relatives, or to trace beneficiaries, and from the fact that the legislation gave adoption and succession rights to the couples concerned. Furthermore, the partners might already have children.

These civil ceremonies require a fortnight's notice, and are conducted by the registration service before two witnesses. The same list of prohibited degrees applies – you cannot enter into a civil partnership with your own sibling, for example. The data provided in the entry are identical with that in a marriage entry, with the addition of the mother's name and occupation for each participant. Entries are indexed separately from marriage, and a certificate may be issued to any applicant – though the address(es) of the partners will not be shown unless already provided by the applicant. (The cost, however, is £7.00 even for a recent event, instead of £3.50 for a marriage certificate.) Access to the indexes is the same as for other vital events.

Indexes or certificates not accessible: alternative sources
(see also pp. 54–71, 207)

The options open to those who cannot afford to go to London, or even to obtain marriage certificates locally, are fewer than in the case of birth certificates. However, copies of marriage certificates are sometimes cheaper from the incumbent of the church where the ceremony took place. The marriage may also have been recorded in local newspapers (pp. 228–9), which will often provide evidence of denominational preference and place in a sequence of siblings. Churches retain their own records of marriages, unless they are so few in number – as in the case of non-AP Nonconformist chapels – as to make the keeping of a marriage register something of a luxury. However, the church entry would be difficult to locate unless the approximate date and place were known (see p. 167). As duplicates of the civil ceremony do not exist outside the registration system, apart from a copy which may be retained by the couple themselves, recourse should be had to any other documents which supply the name of the bride, such as a child's birth certificate. In that way the marriage can be simply bypassed altogether. To the genealogist the marriage certificate is only a means to an end – and sometimes that end can be reached more quickly and more cheaply.

Records of the armed forces (see pp. 56–60)

Army. The General Register Office has certificates of marriage of army personnel from 1761 separate from the main series of civilian registers. Marriage registers from some regiments are in the National Archives, but they are all nineteenth- or twentieth-century, except those of the Royal Chelsea Hospital, 1691–1856. (See *FHM* 142 Apr 07 for an article about Chelsea Pensioners.) Also in the National Archives are reports between 1830 and 1882 containing certificates of marriage. There will also be a reference to the marriage in pension applications from officers' widows, and in lists of widows from 1713 to 1892. Marriages of other ranks are contained in muster and pay books 1868–83.

Royal Air Force. Marriage registers of RAF personnel are in the General Register Office from 1920.

Royal Navy. The Marine Register Book in the General Register Office, from 1 July 1837, includes marriage on board naval and merchant ships. Marriages of sailors abroad should be found in the normal consular returns. According to *FTM* 19.2 Dec 02, the belief that captains are able to perform marriage ceremonies at sea is incorrect – only the clergy can carry out this function.

The National Archives has registers of marriages aboard naval vessels from 1842 to 1889, and names of wives and dates of marriages are in the officers' service registers. Marriage certificates had to be submitted by widows claiming a pension (officers only, 1797–1829), or claiming the royal bounty (a year's pay for those killed in action) 1672–1822.

The Registrar of Shipping and Seamen has a record of marriages at sea 1857–1972.

Divorce

Records of divorce may provide another means by which information about the original marriage can be obtained. For an introduction, see *NALL* 43 and 44, *FHM* 106 Jul 04 and *PFH* 120 Dec 07. Between 1700 and 1857 the only legal means of obtaining a divorce were by Act of Parliament or (except for Jews) through the ecclesiastical courts. For the latter, the bishops' registers should be consulted in the diocesan record office. (See Steel, 1968, I, p. 323, for acceptable grounds for divorce, women being given the same rights as men only in 1923; Stone, 1977, and *FTM* 18.4 Feb 02 for the history of post-

1858 divorce and its indexing. For the very interesting history of post-1858 Jewish divorces see *GM* 24.3–4.) However, very few people actually obtained a divorce before 1857, a situation that led some desperate men to sell or exchange their wives. The wife's consent had to be obtained. (See *Amateur Historian* 6.6 and Menefee, 1981, who suggests that purchasers were well known in advance – sometimes too well known for the husband's liking, as many wives had committed adultery with someone of higher social standing!) Although frowned upon by the authorities, the practice was not uncommon at markets and fairs in the sixteenth and seventeenth centuries, but dying out by the nineteenth century – carried into towns thereafter by families migrating for work. Some, like the diarist Ellen Weeton, were forced to agree to a deed of separation, which at least gave some relief from intolerable conditions in the marital home. A legal separation could be obtained on grounds of cruelty or adultery, the former being defined in 1790 (Evans *v.* Evans) as actual bodily harm. Cases can be found in the Court of Arches records, 1660–1913 (Index Library vol. 85).

Olive Anderson (1999) has shown that late nineteenth-century England had the lowest divorce rate in Europe, but the highest separation rate! Magistrates could accord women a sort of 'semi-detached' status, affecting almost 4 per cent of couples – perhaps twenty times the divorce rate – giving them all the advantages of divorce but without permission to remarry. (On cohabitation and bigamy, see *Journal of Family History* 22.3, 1997.) Davey (1922) pinpoints the Summary Jurisdiction (Married Women) Act of 1895 for an easy and cheap way to obtain maintenance for desertion – better than a prosecution under the 1824 Vagrancy Act which had a very narrow definition of 'running away'!

Until 1858 the Registrar General did not even issue instructions on how to describe the condition of a divorced person at remarriage. The number of divorces after the 1857 Act (which enabled divorce only for adultery) remained small, some hundreds each year (though that is in contrast to three a year before then), presumably because many potential applicants did not realise that court fees could be waived for people with low incomes. In the twentieth century, from 8,000 per year in 1939 the number jumped to 160,000 by 1985. In the 1860s, 70 per cent of divorces were granted to men, the reverse of the position in the 1980s.

Case records are kept in the court where the divorce proceedings were heard, and, if the proceedings resulted in a decree absolute, copies of the final certificate may be obtained, by post or in person, by any member of the public. The decree absolute includes the names of the two parties, the date and place of the marriage being terminated and until recently the name of any co-respondent in the case. Many other documents, including a record of the hearing, the dates of birth of any children of the marriage and the final settlement, are confidential to the two parties concerned and their solicitors. Despite this, I would recommend making an approach to the court for access to the papers if you can show that the parties have given permission or are dead. The files are kept for fifty years, and are then destroyed, but the Lord Chancellor's office has directed that files on cases over fifty years old can be preserved if they relate to matters of general public concern, throw light on social or economic change, illustrate new or revised legal procedures or legislation, relate to cases published in the annual all-England law reports, or are generally of wide public interest.

There are no geographical boundaries to the jurisdiction of each court, so it is by no means obvious where a divorce took place. Somerset House will tell you, for its index is national. It seems extraordinary that the public have no direct access to any recent indexes of divorce, either local or national, and I still believe that a good social case can be made for divorce being registered and indexed also by the Registrar General.

Index records of all decrees absolute since 1857 are kept by the national Divorce Registry, through which copies may be obtained. (Write to Section 5, Divorce Branch, Somerset House, Strand, London WC2R 1LP.) There is a fee of £25.00 for a ten-year search, and the full forenames of both wife and husband are needed. A questionnaire will be sent to you, consisting largely of all those questions which you need answering by buying a copy in the first place! There may be a few days' delay, because the copies are issued directly by the court where the proceedings were heard. Case details of those between 1938 and 1960 have been destroyed – only the decrees absolute remain.

Divorce indexes for 1858 to 1958 are now available on microfiche at the National Archives, Kew. Their arrangement is not straightforward, but there is an excellent guide to them in FTM 18.4 Feb 02. Many case files survive from 1858 to 1937, but more modern ones can be destroyed after 25 years, thanks to Lord Denning's Committee report of 1966; see FTM 16.6 Apr 00. Those from 1858 to 1903 are available on pay per view at www.nationalarchivist.com. A ten-year search facility is offered by www.ukcertificates.com, and the index for 1858–1903 is on the paysite www.nationalarchivist.com.

Copies of all decrees absolute, from 1858 to the present day, are kept at the Principal Registry of the Family Division, First Avenue House, High Holborn, London WC1V 6NP. They are not open to the public, but a ten-year search can be undertaken, and a copy of the decree supplied, for £25.

Civil partnerships can be dissolved by court order (the equivalent of divorce), or by annulment in cases where there was something legally wrong with the ceremony.

Marriage in church, 1538 to the present day

Marriage records of the Church of England form a very useful series indeed, whatever your religious persuasion nowadays. They start at the same time as the baptismal records (see pp. 91–101) and have a similar history before the mid-eighteenth century. They are subject to the same vicissitudes, especially in the 1640s and 1650s, when it has been estimated that over a third of all marriages were unregistered. In Mary's reign a century earlier, the figure was almost as high (Wrigley & Schofield, 1981). In 1653 the right of performing marriages was removed from the clergy altogether and temporarily given to justices of the peace. Between 1657 and 1660 either JPs or clergy could marry people. During this period, couples had to find a parish where a JP was available, and in consequence some parishes had far more marriages than in normal times, as couples could marry there for convenience. Again, in the decades before 1754 some parishes seem to have had far more than their fair share of weddings. Were some clergymen accepting reduced fees, I wonder, or were an increasing number being given surrogate rights to issue marriage licences?

From the late seventeenth century the Anglican Church was ignored by an increasing number of Nonconformists as well as Roman Catholics, though sometimes their extra-parochial activities are reported in the Anglican parish register. The vicar of Bowdon, for example, recorded that Roger Simpson and Mary Harrison 'of this parish married about 21 November 1699, but do not tell where, when, or by whom they were married. This said by Mr John Brown, not in Holy Orders.' In the early eighteenth century the Church of England began to regain some of its former popularity for marriage, but even so a significant proportion of weddings – including some 10 per cent in Wales, according to Brown (1976) – were held elsewhere. It is believed that some Anglican clergy were ignoring the requirement of banns or a licence as a prerequisite.

Until 25 March 1754 marriages were normally entered in the same book as baptisms and burials, usually as a separate list, but sometimes together with baptisms and burials, the events all in a single, merged, chronological order. Since 1754 until the present day, marriages have been entered in a separate book, normally consisting of printed forms (see *FTM* 4.10 Aug 88, p. 21 and 12.12 Oct 96, pp. 19–20). This change was brought about by Hardwicke's Marriage Act, 1753, which was passed in order to prevent a series of abuses, especially in the 'marriage shop' parishes which had scandalised the more socially responsible (as well as endangered the ambitions of the wealthier classes for their sons and daughters) for decades, and there was a rush of marriages before the Act came into force. 'Irregular' marriages were those which took place either (1) with neither banns nor licence, or (2) in a parish church that was in neither the bride's nor the groom's parish. 'Clandestine' marriages were both (1) and (2), and appear to have included apprentices marrying without their master's consent. (On banns, see *FTM* 17.6 Apr 01.) As Lord High Chancellor, Harwicke took this subject seriously – the bill included the death penalty for anyone using a false marriage licence or destroying a marriage entry book.

The most notorious were the marriages conducted within the area of the Fleet prison in London by laymen who were not particular about who were being married so long as the fee was forthcoming, and some of whose certificates proved to be forgeries anyway. The Fleet marriages have been published by Mark Herber. (See *GM* 22.10, 23.9; *FTM* 16.5 Mar 00, 19.12 Oct 03; Steel, 1968, I, chapter 4, who lists the churches known to be irregular; Burn, 1833; Outhwaite, 1981, chapter 6.) Anthony Benton (*GM* 23.9) says that in the two decades before 1754 over half the weddings in the whole of London were at these locations, and finds that the abuses even extended to marriage by licence. Until 1754 canon law recognised vows before witnesses, and subsequent consummation, as the only necessities for a valid marriage – see Stone (1977, chapter 1, section iv). This fascinating issue was revived in 1996 when a couple were 'married' in an Anglican church by a person not ordained. A minister could tell Moll Flanders (1722) 'that her marriage by licence in an inn "will be as firm here as in a church; we are not tied by the canons to marry nowhere but in the church; and as for the time of day, it does not at all weigh in this case"'. By the time *The vicar of Wakefield* was published in 1766, however, Goldsmith's Olivia could observe that 'I knew that the ceremony of our marriage, which was performed by a popish priest, was in no way binding' (chapter 21). Clandestine marriage registers at Kew are part of the National Archives' digitisation programme, due for completion in 2008.

The centre of abuses shifted to the Gretna Green area and the Channel Islands after the passing of the 1753 Act. Gretna retained its popularity until the Marriage (Scotland) Act of 1939, though Brougham's Marriage Act of 1856 introduced a three-week residential qualification for at least one of the parties. In some years of the mid-nineteenth century over 1,000 English couples married in Scotland. Scotland and the Channel Islands were exempt from Hardwicke's Act, so that, for example, the marriage of a minor which took place there remained valid without parental consent. All such areas advertised their liberties, with some success. It is somewhat ironic that Hardwicke himself was well known for some anti-Scottish legislation, and it is fortunate for everyone that he had more success with this Act than with his attempts to stop the Scots from wearing tartan! His Marriage Act had several other important consequences for the genealogist.

From 1754 until 1 July 1837 only Church of England, Jewish and Quaker marriages were valid. Statistically, Quakers formed a tiny minority, falling from 1.1 per cent in 1680 to 0.2 per cent in 1800 and 0.7 per cent in 1861 (Wrigley & Schofield, 1981). In effect, other denominations had to go through an Anglican marriage ceremony if they wished to live in lawful wedlock, if they were to have legitimate children and if a widow were to be able to claim pension rights. Note that the property of any bastard dying without children himself could revert to the Crown! These penalties made it very desirable for couples of all persuasions to go through a valid ceremony. Thus James Livesay of Walton and Ellen Riding of Houghton, Lancashire, who married in Brindle Roman Catholic Church on 2 February 1755, also married in Walton le Dale Anglican church the next day in order to legalise their union. Statistically, therefore, deficiencies in Anglican registers between 1754 and 1837 must be very small indeed, an estimated 2 per cent.

Hardwicke's Act also limited the number of buildings in which marriages could be performed. It is thus quite common to find chapels in outlying townships having marriages before 1754 but not afterwards, unless they achieved parochial status. Even those which did retain or acquire the privilege were supposed to have their records from 1781 integrated into the register of the mother church. To retain the facility of marriage, an episcopal licence had to be obtained. For the genealogist this requirement means that the search for a marriage entry in the two generations following 1754 is easier than before or after, though a few clergymen, such as Mr Hadfield in Mellor, Derbyshire, continued to conduct marriages without such a licence. The requirement that weddings have to take place in daylight hours also dates from Hardwicke as a symbol of the openness with which the ceremony was to be conducted in future, and he effectively invalidated infants' marriages by licence. Witnesses, by the way, could be of either sex, and even minors, but most were adult males. In days when a wedding did not attract the presence of hordes of relatives, these witnesses were often local functionaries – look at adjoining entries, and the same names will recur in that case; but if the names appear to suggest otherwise, the first assumption is that they are relatives of the bride or groom (often one of each), and normally a sibling.

From 1754, you will come across marriages being described as 'by certificate', sometimes 'from' a named person. This means that one of the parties had had the banns read in another parish, the proof of which was contained in the said certificate. If you take the trouble to identify the person named, usually a clergyman, you have a major clue to the former residence of the bride or groom. The system applies only to marriages by banns, of course. Both banns and licences lasted three months, after which they were void.

Before 1754 only the names of the bride and groom were normally given, sometimes with their township of residence. It is very rare to find marriage registers such as those of Glossop in the early seventeenth century in which the names of the bride's and groom's parents were also recorded. The Act itself did not require forms, only entries on ruled lines; George Rose made the forms compulsory from 1 January 1813 (see GM 22.9). Occasionally you may come across chapels which continued to use the old style of register book after 1754, without the printed forms – this happened at Daresbury and Waverton in Cheshire. The printed forms widely adopted after Hardwicke were of two kinds, according to which printer produced them, it seems (FTM 12.12 Oct 96), and can be found with either three or four entries to a page before 1813 and with three to a page afterwards until 1837. One kind incorporates a space for banns (see pp. 192–4), the other does not. Each asked for the names of both parties, their parish, whether the marriage was by banns or by licence and the names of the witnesses, who might be relations but equally might be the parish clerk or other 'regular' witnesses who performed the function for many couples. Occupations sometimes appear, though this was voluntary, perhaps for the purpose of proper identification. Oddly, Hardwicke's Act had not laid down the actual content of a marriage entry!

Hardwicke made provision for a marriage of a minor (under twenty-one) by licence (not banns) dependent on written permission. The marriage form was modified on 1 January 1813 to include a consent section for the marriage of minors. At first, many incumbents completed this section even when both parties were over twenty-one, as they do not seem to have understood that it was for minors only. Consent should have been given by (in priority) the father if alive, guardians, mother if unmarried, or guardians appointed by the Court of Chancery. Consent by guardians, therefore, does not necessarily mean that both parents were dead; guardians could be appointed while the mother was still alive – for example, by the Court of Probate (see pp. 258). Marriages have never been void if solemnised without consent, and formal *consent*, as opposed to defaulting lack of *dissent*, was not required. A form claiming that consent was forthcoming was made subject to perjury. Dissent, however, voided the banns, and banns entries without a corresponding marriage are found quite commonly.

Subsequent to 1 July 1837 the Anglican marriage register takes a similar form to the record of civil registration (pp. 168–70) and includes the name and occupation of the father of both bride and groom. Attention should be paid to the signatures, not simply for an indication of literacy by those involved but for identification purposes, and it is always worthwhile spending a minute or two taking an exact copy (though *not* by tracing!). Since 1754 brides normally sign with their maiden name, even though they are already married. There is often a discrepancy between the clerk's spelling of a name and that of its bearer, but occasionally the name is quite different. When Mary Johnson married at Lancaster on 10 April 1774 the clerk spelled the bridegroom's surname 'Gardner', but he signed as 'Garnet'.

Over the years, several students have asked me variations of the same basic question which has arisen during their researches – which categories of people were not allowed to marry each other? From Archbishop Parker's statement of 1563, adopted as Canon Law in 1603 and written into the 1662 Book of Common Prayer, the list of 'prohibited degrees' remained unchanged until 1907.

A man was not permitted to marry his:	A woman was not permitted to marry her:
Grandmother	Grandfather
Grandfather's wife	Grandmother's husband
Wife's grandmother	Husband's grandfather
Father's sister	Father's brother
Mother's sister	Mother's brother
Father's brother's wife	Father's sister's husband
Mother's brother's wife	Mother's sister's husband
Wife's father's sister	Husband's father's brother
Wife's mother's sister	Husband's mother's brother

A man was not permitted to marry his:	A woman was not permitted to marry her:
Mother	Father
Stepmother	Stepfather
Wife's mother	Husband's father
Daughter	Son
Wife's daughter	Husband's son
Son's wife	Daughter's husband
Sister	Brother
Wife's sister	Husband's brother
Brother's wife	Sister's husband
Son's daughter	Son's son
Daughter's daughter	Daughter's son
Son's son's wife	Son's daughter's husband
Daughter's son's wife	Daughter's daughter's husband
Wife's son's daughter	Husband's son's son
Wife's daughter's daughter	Husband's daughter's son
Brother's daughter	Brother's son
Sister's daughter	Sister's son
Brother's son's wife	Brother's daughter's husband
Sister's son's wife	Sister's daughter's husband
Wife's brother's daughter	Husband's brother's son
Wife's sister's daughter	Husband's sister's son

From 1907, a man could marry his deceased wife's sister, and, from 1921, his deceased brother's widow.

These rules could be circumvented by the parliamentary personal bill procedure, though doing so may not be to everyone's taste. (Against the first in the list, one wit wrote, 'Lord have mercy upon us and incline our hearts to keep this law.') They have also been overcome by oversight or deceit, particularly between widower and deceased wife's sister, according to a Royal Commission in 1847. Ellen Weeton recorded in her journal for 1824 that 'Mr Hudson's second wife was sister to his first, and consequently, aunt to her first stepchildren. I felt greatly concerned when I heard of this, but made no observations to them about it.'

It was thus not only possible for first cousins ('cousins-german') to marry each other; it was also quite common, having been legalised in the 1540s, and has been particularly common among minority religious groups, reportedly with unfortunate genetic consequences. It might be related to the 'genetic attraction' well known to workers on adoption cases. Perhaps two or three in every hundred marriages were between first cousins, though the figure seems to have varied with place and time (see *GM* 8.6; Kuper 2002; *Journal of Family History* 11.3, 1986). I have no doubt that it was not only the Quakers who frowned on such a union, but it was probably more common before the industrial revolution improved the facility for mobility among a much increased population. Henry Fielding (in *Jonathan Wild*) pinpoints the ambivalent attitude towards cousins being 'in the eye of a strict conscience, somewhat too nearly related' for marriage. The absence of a satisfactory system of medical record linkage means that the genetic effects of close-kinship marriages are still a matter of some controversy, but the need for such a system will surely increase with the development of embryo technology. The risk of genetic malformations in children of a cousin marriage is twice that of a marriage between unrelated parties.

Failure to find an Anglican marriage

If you are interested in tracing only the male line, failure to find a marriage really does not matter, especially before 1837, when there is little hope that the entry will name the groom's parents. However, there are many genealogists, including the Mormons, who wish to trace all their recorded ancestors, so that the mother's maiden name, normally obtainable before 1837 only from a marriage entry, is important. There are several reasons why a marriage entry may be hard to find.

Marriage in another parish

This is a very common problem, though one good authority has suggested that almost all pre-industrial marriages were within a fifteen-mile radius. I suppose that, in the days before bicycles, most courting couples relied largely on shanks's pony for transport. Evidence points to the 1850s being the decade which marks a large rise in mean marriage distances, especially over thirty miles, as trains improved on the carrier's waggon and the more expensive stagecoach facility. Normally, you will know in advance the surname of only the father of a baptised child, and you will need the marriage record to discover the maiden name of the mother. This is on *some* records before 1837, however. The information can be obtained, for example, from a baptismal entry in a 'Dade' register (see above, pp. 95–6), or from the register of Dissenters, 1740–1837, in Dr Williams's library, part of the National Archives' digitisation programme, due for completion in 2008. Now, if a man married a woman who lived in the same parish, and their children were born there, the marriage should be found without much difficulty. Even in this simple case, however, it was not unknown for the couple to marry elsewhere. It sometimes happened even when the marriage was by banns. William Darlington married Betty Cookson by banns at Daresbury in 1803 (an entry omitted from the International Genealogical Index, by the way) despite the fact that they both lived in Frodsham. The marriage took place two months after the baptism of Betty's illegitimate child. Speculation suggests that William was the father; but why the need for secrecy, I wonder, implied by holding the ceremony at Daresbury? Had they incurred the wrath of the vicar at Frodsham? Had William's parents forbidden the marriage? But he was married twenty years and eleven months after his baptism, so perhaps he was already twenty-one?

Much more commonly, however, the problem of a 'missing' marriage arises because the groom married in the bride's parish. Occasionally they marry in the groom's parish, but live in that of the bride. The resulting problem is still the same, though the possible solution is slightly different. Often they married in the nearest large town (especially London) where a licence might be obtained, or on the road between there and where they lived. The attraction of large cities as a venue for weddings was still prevalent in the middle of the nineteenth century. Only a minority of adults living in any parish were both baptised and married in it. (See, e.g., Macfarlane, 1977; *Local Population Studies* 2 and 28.) From 1930, banns have been available in a parish where parties worship rather than reside, though they must be on the Church Electoral Roll there.

If the marriage took place after 1753, there should be a record of the banns or the licence, either of which should lead you to the parish where the wedding was performed. Indeed, marriage entries are occasionally to be found in the books of banns (see *GM* 23.1). However, only from 1823 has the law compelled banns to be read in both the bride's and the groom's parish where these were different (except during the period 1941–47). Also, not all books of banns have survived. In some of those which have, banns may have been recorded only where the marriage was to take place. In the middle of the nineteenth century there were complaints that some clergymen were increasing their revenue by marrying persons, even minors, neither of whom was their parishioner, and not bothering to check the addresses which the parties gave. But the abuse continued long after that.

Both banns and marriage licences have been used since the Middle Ages as means by which the church protected itself from performing invalid marriages, particularly those which involved close relatives (see pp. 189–90) or bigamy, made a crime in 1603, before which it was a matter of discipline by the ecclesiastical courts (see *GM* 19.7). At a time when the reading of banns – announcement of the intention to marry a named person – over three consecutive Sundays would be heard by the majority of the population of the parish of the bride and groom, it would be expected that normally someone would know the parties sufficiently well to be able to inform the clergyman if the ceremony should not take place.

From 1653 to 1660 a civil equivalent of banns, or proclamations, was read from either church or market place, and normally the readings are noted in the parish register itself, sometimes with the addition of a letter M (for marriage) in the margin. Apart from this short period, however, it is very unusual to find banns recorded at all until Lord Hardwicke secured the passage of his Act of 1753 making the recording of banns compulsory. Before then, at best, banns might be indicated by the phrase 'by publication'. (They were also known colloquially as the 'askings'.) Hardwicke himself had wanted all marriages to be by banns but, fortunately for genealogists, licences were continued.

From 1754 until 1812 banns were recorded on printed forms, which may be found in a number of different places in the parish records. Sometimes they are in separate books, or in a separate section of the main marriage register, each entry recording names, parishes and dates of publication. Some marriage forms, however, have a space for banns to be entered at the top, and I suspect that in that case, clergymen were reluctant to 'waste' a whole form on marriages which were to take place in another parish, and so did not enter them, being content to send a certificate to the church where the marriage was to take place. Occasionally, on the other hand, a parson would fill in one section of such a book with banns only and use another part of the book for the marriages. Also, from 1754, the marriage had to take place in one of the churches where the banns had been called.

After 1 January 1813 it is normal for banns to be in separate books, and in the mid-nineteenth century the Society for the Propagation of Christian Knowledge tried to prevent certain abuses of the marriage regulations by issuing books of banns forms which contained a space for street names and house numbers. Any separate surviving register of banns is usually kept with the parish register itself, so that when the latter is centralised to a diocesan record office, the associated books of banns will probably go with it. No search fees are laid down. There is, however, no legal obligation to preserve banns books permanently, which has allowed some incumbents to throw older ones away if they were thought to be cluttering up the vestry.

The existence of a set of banns does not prove that the marriage took place, but if the prospective bride's Christian name is the same as that of the later mother, then, in the absence of any other evidence, they should be accepted as one and the same person. This cannot be infallible, but it may be all the evidence you can find. You are the only person who can decide whether to accept it as sufficient proof; but note that it would not be accepted in a court of law! Sometimes the banns system was effective in preventing a marriage. For wasting the time of the Church, a fine could be levied if the marriage did not take place after the banns had been called. From 1837 banns could be replaced by a certificate from a Superintendent Registrar (see p. 171). Indeed, the Marriage Bill of the previous year had abolished banns in favour of universal civil preliminaries, but the Lords restored banns in the final Act (see *FTM* 17.6 Apr 01).

Marriage licences, or 'dispensations', could be obtained as an alternative to having the banns read. They were issued at a number of levels within the church hierarchy: by archbishops, whose special licences have been issued since 1533 for marriages which cannot be performed between 8.00 a.m. and 6.00 p.m. (these licences enabled a marriage to take place at any time and in any place, but the weddings should nevertheless be entered in the local parish register); by bishops, archdeacons, surrogates, deputies or clergymen in a 'peculiar' parish exempt from normal procedures, though the last were barred, in theory, by the canons of 1603.

The licence has always been a rather more expensive means of ensuring the legality of marriage, and for that reason it has never been as popular as banns. I believe, however, that a licence was more popular if the bride and groom came from different parishes. The 1603 canons said that a licence should be issued only to those 'of good state and quality'; it is still discretionary for the Church to issue one, whereas banns must be read for those who request them. In the seventeenth century licences were used for weddings during 'prohibited' seasons, such as Lent. Nowadays the issuing of licences tends to be discouraged unless banns appear to be inappropriate – for example, for a marriage between a British citizen and an alien.

The proportion of marriages arranged by licence has varied considerably over time and by area. In seventeenth-century Bowdon up to 30 per cent of marriages annually were by licence rather than by banns, but elsewhere the figure was normally much lower. Once a clergyman had become an episcopal surrogate for issuing licences, the proportion in his parish increased dramatically, Anthony Benton noting, for example, that virtually all marriages at St Botolph's, Aldgate in the early 1700s were by licence issued by the curate. (See Rogers & Smith, 1991, for other examples.) A licence was popular with certain families, especially those that did not wish to have their domestic affairs paraded before the other parishioners on three consecutive Sundays. These included Nonconformists of all shades of allegiance. It also had the advantage of relative speed and secrecy, and seems to have been particularly popular with sailors! A licence also facilitated a marriage during Lent, when banns should not have been called, and it saved Dissenters the embarrassment of having them called. See *Local History* 10.6 and Outhwaite (1973), who observes the use of the licence system by those with rude surnames. It must have been worth the extra cost in order to avoid guffaws, or even titters, when the banns were read out. (Nowadays, by the way, a registrar is entitled to refer proposed names for the newly born which might be deemed 'objectionable' to the Registrar General.)

A marriage of minors by licence (but not by banns) without the consent of parent or guardian was null and void after 1753, but that did not prevent the system being used when parents were known to oppose a match. It was also commonly used by persons marrying from different social classes, and by the wealthier Nonconformists to avoid having to use the local parish church more than necessary.

A visit to the clergyman issuing the licence resulted in three separate documents. An allegation or affidavit was sworn out, normally by the groom, to the effect that there was no lawful impediment to the marriage. By the seventeenth century allegations are on printed forms, with spaces for the relevant details, including the names, ages, marital condition, residence and occupations of the parties wishing to marry, the name of the church where the marriage was to take place and sometimes even the name of the clergyman who was to perform the ceremony. Licences issued in London from 1598 to 1619 contain even more information – see Outhwaite (1981, chapter 4). The age as stated cannot always be relied upon – see pp. 174–5.

Secondly, there is a marriage bond, which was a promise by two people – normally the groom and a friend or relative, though the second name is often fictitious – that, if the marriage proved to be invalid in the eyes of God or the law, they would pay the Church a very substantial sum of money, usually amounting to tens or hundreds of pounds, depending on the place and period. Such bonds became compulsory from 1579. Unfortunately, not all dioceses asked for bonds, which were no longer required after the Marriage Act of 1823, though they apparently continue in some areas. Both Allegations and Bonds are likely to be on printed forms after 1733, and there should be a consent for minors after 1754. The details were often written up into the bishops' Marriage Act Books, which are now in diocesan record offices. Although the evidence from surnames suggests that relatives often acted as bondsmen, it was unusual for the relationship to be stated on the bond itself, and some bondsmen were self-evidently fictional names, John Doe having offered more collateral than anyone else! Welsh bonds for 1661–1837 are indexed at http://isys.llgc.org.uk.

Finally, there was the marriage licence itself, but as it was given to the parties concerned it has not normally survived. The Church kept the allegation and the bond which, when they are now in diocesan record offices, can be consulted free of charge.

There are four ways to discover whether a marriage took place by licence. The easiest is to search the indexes which have been compiled and often printed in the last 100 years by a local record society – see Gibson, Hampson & Raymond (2007) for a list of those which have appeared in print. The indexes often supply the relevant details from the allegation and bond; reference to the original document sometimes adds nothing to what you already know, though that should not deter you from looking to the original papers for additional information. Secondly, for those areas or periods which have not yet been indexed, a long search through boxes of dusty documents, usually arranged chronologically or by year, will be necessary. Thirdly, the parish register itself will normally indicate by the letter L, or 'Lic.', or 'per lic.' that the marriage was arranged by licence rather than by banns. In that case the diocesan papers should be searched because of the extra information which the allegation and bond will give you. However, the diocesan record has not always survived, especially when the licence was issued by a surrogate. If the register does not indicate banns or licence, it is worth spending time searching the relevant period to see whether a licence was taken out. Finally, licences are entered into Act books in some areas (Gardner & Smith, 1956–64, I, pp. 220–1).

William Hallows and Eleanor Grice were married at Frodsham in 1763, and for some time I searched for Eleanor's baptism in the neighbouring parishes. The nearest I could find was Ellen Grice, baptised at Runcorn, an adjoining parish, in 1748, only fifteen years before the marriage. Though this would have been legal at that time, it seemed unlikely. Perhaps she was two or three years old when she was baptised? That was clutching at straws, which should be done only when all other evidence has been consulted. In this case the marriage was by licence, and the allegation told me that William was a thirty-year-old miller from Kingsley in Frodsham, and Eleanor was twenty-four years old and already a widow – so she had not been baptised Eleanor Grice after all!

It may be helpful to point out that changes in the rules governing the use of licences are relevant to the genealogist. Until Hardwicke's Act of 1753, for example, although a church and even a clergyman could be named on the documents, the licence was used in practice in churches other than those of the bride and groom, and by clergymen not named on it. I once searched in Bowdon for the marriage of Joseph Walton and Jane Ashley. Both had been born in the parish; the licence, dated 2 December 1709, mentioned St Mary's, Bowdon, and all their children were baptised there. But there was no marriage record. It was only years later that I came across it, quite by accident. They married at Daresbury on 4 October 1711. It was not unusual for couples to take out more than one licence; presumably they had had second thoughts about marrying the first time. However, after 1753 the church named on the licence (often in the town where it was issued) has been the only one for which the licence is valid. Other odd situations arose before Hardwicke's reforms. For instance, in 1631 John Meredith took out a licence to marry Ellen Nield four days after marrying her!

During the Civil War the office of bishop was abolished, so there is a gap in the marriage licence series between 1646 and 1660.

The next set of solutions is identical with that for missing baptisms (see pp. 101–30); that is to say, searching the marriage registers of neighbouring parishes, especially those which seem to have attracted a large number of marriages compared with the population of the place. If that search fails it has to be widened, turning first to those parishes containing families with the surnames you are looking for. Try looking also in the churches in the nearest town where marriage licences were issued. Once again, the International Genealogical Index (see pp. 103–7) may be a great help. If the marriage is in the index, you will learn the name of the spouse, the date and place of the event and a reference to how the information was included in the index.

If the couple concerned subsequently emigrated, check to see what is on the death certificate. Some certificates, such as those of Australia or Zimbabwe, include information about marriage.

The International Genealogical Index is the largest of many marriage indexes which have been compiled over the last century or so. The most famous is that of Percival Boyd, which covers sixteen English counties, being especially useful for Cambridgeshire, Cornwall, Durham, Essex, Northumberland and Shropshire; see Steel (1968, I). This is now being largely incorporated into the International Genealogical Index anyway. There are many others, often on a county basis. There are, for example, excellent ones for Hertfordshire and the Isle of Wight, and there is the Pallot index for London marriages from the 1780s. Sometimes there are copies in city or county record offices, but others remain in the hands of the compilers as a source of profit. A fairly recent list of these indexes will be found in the *GM* 16.6–7. See also Gibson, Hampson & Raymond (2007), and for Percival Boyd, *PFH* 72 Dec 03.

A famous series of marriage entry transcriptions was published early this century by W. P. W. Phillimore, but Don Steel points out that they are prone to error, as some were really undertaken by volunteers without the necessary level of palaeographic skill. Once again, use the original, in microform, wherever possible. The Phillimore series was not normally indexed, as Phillimore preferred his funds to go into the publication of the entries themselves. They are available on CD-ROM.

Marriage not recorded
Steel (1968, I) reports a remarkably high estimate of a quarter to a third of marriages in the first half of the eighteenth century having been 'clandestine'. The figure was especially high in London, where two-thirds of the chapels failed to continue into the nineteenth century. The children of such marriages were not always classed as illegitimate; see *Local Population Studies* 10.

There can be no doubt that, even in the relatively complete period from 1754 to 1837, some marriages in the Church of England went unrecorded through the negligence of the clergyman. Before 1754 many clergy seem to have been in the habit of keeping the relevant notes on scraps of paper and entering the marriages *en bloc* later. Since 1754, fortunately, the bride and groom have been required to sign or mark the entry immediately after the ceremony. Even so, the printed forms were not universally adhered to, as we have already seen.

There are several standard ways to overcome the problem of a missing marriage entry. If the bishop's transcript (pp. 140–2) or non-parochial register does not yield the information, then, before 1837, you must use more indirect evidence, mainly sources which relate to preparations for the event rather than the ceremony itself including, as we have seen, banns and licences. Desperation may prompt enthusiasts to take an even longer-term approach – to seek the wills (made after the likely date of the missing marriage) of the parents of girls born within five years or so of the groom's own baptism, hoping to pick up an inferred reference to the next generation which they have already traced.

The marriage, perhaps, never took place. There is plenty of evidence that the right of the poor to marry was hindered in the seventeenth century because of fears that their offspring would become a burden on the rates. The view that pauperism arose from inheritable character defects lasted well into the nineteenth century. Some of the early census draft returns record certain couples as 'not married'. See also Steel (1968) and Drake (1982, p. 111) for more information on unrecorded marriages. Wrigley & Schofield (1981) show that a fifth to a quarter of those surviving to forty years of age born between 1600 and 1650 never married. It has been said that the imposition of duties on marriages 1698–1703, and 1783–94 encouraged avoidance of the formal ceremony. Gillis (1985) suggests that the number of common-law marriages rose from the mid-eighteenth century and peaked in the 1840s, when some clergy took the unusual step of offering to perform the ceremony free of charge in order to reduce the number living in sin.

Once a girl was pregnant anyway, attitudes might change. Parson Woodforde wrote in his diary on 22 November 1768:

I married Tom Burge of Ansford to Charity Andrews of C[astle] Cary by License this morning. The Parish of Cary made him marry her, and he came handbolted to Church for fear of running away, and the Parish of Cary was at all the expense of bringing them to, I rec'd of Mr Andrew Russ the overseer of the Poor of Cary for it 0. 10. 6.

Another entry, 25 January 1787, reads:

married one Robert Astick and Elizabeth Howlett by Licence ... the Man being in Custody, the Woman being with Child by him. The Man was a long time before he could be prevailed upon to marry her when in the Church Yard; and at the Altar behaved very unbecoming. It is a cruel thing that any Person should be compelled by Law to marry.

In this, of course, Woodforde was technically incorrect: but the Bastardy Act of 1733 effectively made marriage the only alternative to imprisonment or financial indemnity to the parish, which would otherwise have to support the mother and her child.

Marriage not in England or Wales (see also pp. 121, 245–58)
Occasionally you may find the word 'abroad' in a parish register – for example, the baptism of a son on 1 January 1671 at Standish of a man 'being a poore man going abroad for almes'. It almost certainly means in another parish rather than in another country. If you suspect it really meant what we would take it to mean, remember that you can see the International Genealogical Index for many other countries, via the Latter-Day Saints' family history centres.

Entry missed by the searcher (see pp. 122, 173)
Between 1754 and 1837 marriages by licence were sometimes recorded separately from those by banns. This can cause you to miss a whole register (especially if you are searching on microfilm) unless you ensure that both methods are recorded in the one you are using.

Apart from the usual causes (tiredness, searching too quickly, failure to decipher handwriting correctly and so on) there is a further cause which can sometimes be easily rectified after 1753. If the clergyman wrote down the name of the bride or groom incorrectly, you may still be able to check through the signatures themselves, which occasionally show discrepancies between the names signed and those written by the clergyman. Many, of course, marked rather than signed; but if you have good reason to think that the marriage should have been in a register, and you have not found it, try going through the signatures at the end of the forms, just in case. John Handford apparently married Nelly Ashton at Mottram in 1790, but her signature – actually written under her mark – gave her real name, Nelly Ashworth. Some brides, applying impeccable logic, signed with their new married name.

Some missing marriages may be found entered, incorrectly, among the books of banns. Equally, some clergy did not waste a register entry containing the dual banns and marriage forms if the marriage (for whatever reason), did not take place in that church. Instead, the second half of the form might be used for a marriage arranged by licence, and that can be missed if you see only the names in the banns part of the form.

Misleading clues (see also pp. 174–5)
The three main elements in a marriage entry, from the genealogist's point of view, are names, a date and a church. We have seen already how a marriage licence document earlier than 1754 may be misleading if it names the church where the marriage was to take place. It is also possible that, if you cannot find the marriage you are looking for, you have been misled about the date and even the name. The spelling

of an unfamiliar surname by a clerk in a distant parish can result in some extraordinary variations. If the wife's maiden name has been obtained from a birth certificate, remember that your ancestor may have married her when she was already a widow. It is sometimes useful to know that Roman Catholic marriage entries try to include the mother's maiden name.

Probably the commonest garden path up which you may be led, however, arises from an interpretation of an unusual forename among the children of the marriage you are seeking. One of my great-great-grandfather's children was baptised John Hignett Rogers, and my first assumption was that Hignett had been his mother's maiden name; but I was wrong. Then I thought that the child, like myself, had been given his paternal grandmother's maiden name; but I was wrong again. That left only his maternal grandmother's maiden name; but I was still wrong! Then by chance, I came across Miege's account of the manners and practices of early eighteenth-century Britain; "'Tis rare for the English to have two Christian names ... but it is not unusual with them to Christen Children with the Godfather's surname.' One of my ancestor's sisters had married a Hignett. Samuel Taylor Coleridge is a later example, and Pepys, as a godfather, expressed some annoyance (29 May 1661) when the custom was not followed. (See *GM* 16.2 for naming after godparents.) Arthur Barlow Stubbs, born 29 April 1912, was given his middle name because both his parents worked at Barlow Hall. On this subject see Steel (1968, I) and *FTM* 6.6 Apr 90, where examples are given of children being named after the village doctor or minister; it might also simply have been after a good friend.

In short, always look for a reason why a child is given an unusual forename, though you might not always find it. How many, I wonder, could guess why a girl should have been called Lavaine?

It was not uncommon for illegitimate children to be baptised with the father's surname as a Christian name, but in Wales the other side of that particular coin is to avoid falling into the trap of thinking that the child must be illegitimate if the father's surname is different. Read up on the system of patronymics which survived in Wales far longer than in England; children could take the Christian name of their father as their own surname, 'son of ...' being understood rather than stated.

Incidentally, the use of a surname as a sole Christian name implies that the parents were mainstream Protestant rather than Puritan or Catholic. *GM* 23.8 has an interesting article about the influence of different religious groups on naming practices. It is a pity, genealogically, that more parents did not follow the example of one Thomas Smith, a schoolmaster in early nineteenth-century Cheshire, who was clearly so frustrated at having a common surname that he christened one of his children Edmond Frederic De Courcy Moleneaux Gerard Swinchatter Smith. There is no chance of getting *him* confused with someone else of the same surname. Smith is one of the commonest names to find hyphenated, presumably for the same reason.

If you have inferred a marriage from the 1841 census, you should bear in mind that no relationships were stated therein, and a 'couple' may have been, for example, a brother and sister.

Another cause of going astray is to make assumptions about the date of the marriage from other evidence. A licence issued, as we have seen, was sometimes not used, and a further one had to be taken out. We all assume that people are likely to marry in their early twenties, but the average age of marriage seems to have fallen from about twenty-eight for men and twenty-six for women in the early seventeenth century to about twenty-five and twenty-three respectively by the mid-nineteenth century. This average varied across different periods and different social classes. There is some early evidence that the gentry married earlier yet had fewer children than yeomen. Labourers married even later and had even fewer surviving children, but by the second half of the nineteenth century, the reverse was true. The lowering of the average age of marriage during the eighteenth century is believed by many historians to have been the major factor in the rise in population which characterised the industrial revolution, a theory currently being disputed.

Before Hardwicke's Marriage Act of 1753 there was no lower legal age of marriage, except during the 1650s when it was sixteen for 'men' and fourteen for 'women'. In 1753 it was fixed at fourteen for men and twelve for women, and remained at those ages until the Age of Marriage Act in 1929, which raised it to sixteen for both. Of course, marriage below the age of twenty-one (eighteen since 1969) should have had the consent of parents or guardians recorded on banns or licence, and on the marriage entry itself, but it was often omitted. A consent section on the standard form was introduced only in 1813. After 1835 marriage of minors without consent was not invalid, nor was the minister conducting the ceremony punishable if he had not been informed that one of the parties was a minor. There were, in fact, very few child marriages (Laslett, 1983), a practice which had been encouraged in the first place because it ended wardship (and therefore loss of income to the Crown) for one or both of the parties concerned; but it must be remembered that any first assumption about age at marriage can be wildly inaccurate for a specific event. See *Local Population Studies* 3 for an account of a virginity test on a widow of thirteen who wished to marry her own brother-in-law!

At the other end of the scale, births to women aged forty-five and over were not unknown – the oldest mother in my own family gave birth at forty-eight. It 'began to be time' for Moll Flanders (1722) 'to leave bearing children, for I was now eight-and-forty'. In 1980 one legal abortion in 240 was to women in this age group, and births to English women in their fifties, including two over fifty-five, have been authenticated.

Sometimes, when recording a baptism, a clerk would repeat the child's name in error instead of entering the name of the father or mother. Check the baptisms of siblings before seeking the marriage of the parents. It is unlikely that the error would have been repeated.

If you are looking for the previous marriage of someone whose status was described as 'Mrs', remember that the term may have been applied to a spinster, and that she may therefore not have been married before.

Before the easily obtained divorce of the twentieth century, many couples lived together even though one or both of them had a spouse living. Margery Pinchwife observes, in Wycherley's *The country wife* (1675, V, iv) 'Don't I see every day in London here, women leave their first husbands, and go and live with other men as their wives?' If your forebear seems to have disappeared, by accident or design, the marriage may have been seven years later than you expected, after a declaration of death.

Finding more than one possible marriage

If the names of both parties are known in advance, it will be very rare indeed for two possible marriages to be found. If it happens before 1837 you should find the parents of all four people and see if any of them subsequently left a will, which could provide a clue to the solution – naming grandchildren or places of abode, for example. So might a comparison of signatures on, for example, wills and marriage entries.

Before the middle of the eighteenth century, it is possible that you will not discover even the Christian name of the mother from the baptismal entries of children, which sometimes give the names of only the child and the father. In that case, the burial register or one of many other documents discussed in this book may help. Up to half the offspring of the marriage probably died as children anyway, and one of the burial entries may give the mother's Christian name. The mother herself should have been buried as the named wife or widow of the husband. Note, however, that widows were sometimes still called 'wife', which can add considerable confusion to the reconstruction of a family group.

If only one marriage of the right groom's name can be found, you will have to assume that the entry is the correct one, especially if it was within twelve months of the first child's baptism. At Davenham in 1748 Richard Greenaker married Mary Shaw, and in 1756, at the same place, Richard Greenaker married Mary Nickson. I am descended from Mary, daughter of Richard and Mary Greenaker, baptised in 1761; but which one? The first thing to check, once again, is the burial record, for it is quite possible that there was only one Richard Greenaker who married twice. Luckily for me in this case, his first wife died in 1756, and was buried on 10 May, less than four months before his second marriage. (Odd how genealogists sometimes have to wish death on people!) Otherwise, I would have to hope that the two potential fathers-in-law left wills, naming Richard as son-in-law. The ability to use a close relative to witness a will had been stopped in 1752, however.

By modern standards, this interval between the death of a first wife and the remarriage of the widower seems very short, and is often taken to indicate a certain coolness towards the first wife's memory. In the seventeenth century, however, the average interval was only three months (a bit longer in the eighteenth century), as men who had been left with young children to raise clearly looked for an early remarriage as the easiest and most socially acceptable way out of their predicament.

Very early remarriage was frowned upon, however. On 9 February 1645/46, Ralph Josselin wrote in his diary, 'A woman buried in our towne that intended: [on 12 February] to have married a man whose wife was buryed but on the 12 day of Jan: before, I perswaded him to the contrary, to stay a longer tyime, but God hath prevented itt for ever.' Needless to say, the average interval for widows to remarry was considerably longer. Men remarried twice as quickly (see Bonfield, 1986, chapter 5). If you find the phrase 'my now wife' in a will, it usually means that the testator had remarried.

If, however, there had been two Richard Greenakers, each of whom had married a Mary, it would require a careful study of the baptismal register in order to distinguish between them, unless they lived in separate townships. Once again, a will provides important clues if one was left by any of the eight parents, or even by the parties concerned. From 1754 comparison of the signatures on the two marriage entries can provide further evidence, as can manorial records. It was, however, considered unlucky for a bride to sign if the groom had marked with a cross, or, in the case of Jews, a circle. The signature on a will should be genuine, even if someone other than the testator had written the main text. Thus, on 19 April 1729 James Clegg 'visited Elisabeth Wright again, writ over the copy of her last will, which she seald and signd'.

It should be observed at this stage that the pattern of second marriages has changed drastically over time. In the sixteenth and seventeenth centuries up to 30 per cent of all marriages were a remarriage for one of the partners (see, e.g., Bonfield, 1986, chapter 5). By the mid-nineteenth century, the proportion had fallen to 10 per cent and after the Second World War it sank to less than 5 per cent, but it is now rising as a result of the increasing number of divorces. The decline is not fully understood, but the type of remarriage which became less popular, oddly enough, was that of a bachelor marrying a widow. Peter Laslett's analysis of 100 English communities found that there were four times as many widows as widowers.

One more word of warning about remarriage; a study of the Bowdon marriage licence documents from the seventeenth century shows that some widows were entered as 'spinster' in the parish register itself. Equally, however, spinsters of the wealthier classes could be described as 'Mrs' when they died. For example, 'Mrs Ann Parr, spinster', the daughter of a local attorney, was buried at Salford on 12 February 1744/5.

In the late seventeenth and early eighteenth centuries, especially in the Commonwealth period in the 1650s, it was not unknown for couples to marry each other twice, in two different Anglican churches on different dates. I do not know the reason for this, unless the couples were from the two parishes concerned. It has certainly caused considerable debate in the genealogical press. Occasionally, but not always, it may have been a case of one clergyman making a note of a marriage in another parish. Don Steel (1968, p. 66) believes that the main reason was that the first marriage was clandestine. Pauline Litton adds the possibilities of a 'remarriage at 21 if consent had not been previously obtained for a minor', or by a couple having lied about both being 'of this parish'. Although the Commonwealth marriages of 1653–60 were regularised by statute, couples are known to have remarried 'just to make sure'. John Wilcoxon of Over and Ann Young of Whitegate took out a licence on 19 February 1696, the wedding to take place in either church. But two days later they married at both Whitegate and Witton, a chapelry in a neighbouring parish. On the other hand, the reason for the remarriage of John Stringer and Eleanor Ashbrooke at Daresbury in October 1769 was clearly stated in the register; 'heretofore married

on the 14th day of April, 1768, as appears on the 81st page of this
Register, by one Jones an Impostor who took upon himself the Office
of a Minister not being in Holy Orders'. One possible explanation of
'double' marriage entries is given in a Mottram register entry:

> John Hollinworth of this parish and Mary Ann Holinworth or
> Sidebottom of this parish having been married at the Parish Church
> of Doncaster on the 8th of January 1827 but as they were then
> and still are generally resident in this parish it has been deemed
> expedient to repeat the ceremony were married in this Church by
> Licence this sixth Day of April 1831.

Non-Anglican marriage

The location and extent of non-parochial registers have already
been briefly described (pp. 135–8). Until 1837 most of them contain
baptisms and burials only, but a few churches of all denominations
included marriages as well. Between 1754 and 1837 marriages other
than by Church of England, Jewish or Quaker ceremonies were not
illegal; they were simply not valid.

Marriage registers from closed Methodist churches are usually sent
to local record offices. Often, however, marriages in Nonconformist
churches were not recorded if the 'authorised person' was absent and
the registrar attended instead, or if there was no 'authorised person' at
all. This has not been true of Roman Catholic marriages.

Where Roman Catholic registers survive, even from before 1754, the
names of formal witnesses are given, a practice which was extended by
the Quakers to include all present at the wedding, with relatives and
friends on separate lists. Unfortunately, the relations of witnesses to
bride and groom is rarely stated. In 1837 Jews and Quakers adopted
a printed marriage form, providing information identical to that in
the civil registers, but the Quakers maintained their earlier tradition
by issuing another, much fuller and larger, certificate to the people
concerned which still lists all those present at the ceremony.

It may be possible to find transcripts of Catholic marriages with the
relevant Catholic diocesan authority after 1850. Subsequent baptisms
often provide the mother's maiden name.

Registers not accessible: alternative sources
(See pp. 181–5)

Marriage notices in newspapers are common for the eighteenth century, and can include an estimate of the bride's 'portion', or dowry. There are also notices of elopement, including maiden names. Marriage settlements are discussed in *Transactions of the Royal Historical Society* xxxii (1950); see also *FTM* 19.5 Mar 03.

A coat of arms can provide a major clue to the family into which an armiger married, for during his lifetime he combined the elements of each. Only if the wife was, or became, an heiress to an armigerous family was the merged blazon carried through to the next generation, however.

Evidence of a remarriage can be gleaned from hatchments (see below, p. 259).

Finding a marriage before 1538
(See pp. 151–63)

There was no systematic recording of marriage in England and Wales before 1538, and in the overwhelming majority of cases the date and place of the wedding remain undiscoverable even when both bride and groom are known with certainty. Medieval documents already referred to can be used into order to establish the fact of a marriage, including service books, missals and psalters, clerical annotations, heraldic records, Chancery records, inquisitions *post mortem*, wills and many others. Deeds can include marriage contracts, for example. (Then, as now, reference to brothers and sisters in a will often implies that the testator is unmarried.) Knowing a wife's Christian name is, however, only a first step to discovering the family into which a man married, and can be found in the incidental survival of the type of document where the relationship between the families was important. Heraldry is the obvious example, but there are many other instances, particularly those involving property, in which the two family surnames are brought together in one source.

There was no minimum age for marriage, but stories of child marriages, and the sale of the right to approve a child marriage along with wardships (see *GM* 12.9) should be regarded as an aberration rather than as typical of the great majority of our ancestors. Fines may have been due at the time of a marriage, and appear in rentals or other manorial records (see, e.g., *GM* 6.10).

IV *Looking for deaths*

Death is of less importance, genealogically speaking, than birth or marriage. Once you have been born, married and had children, your life is over, the remainder being of no direct genetic consequence. Death is no more than a vestigial triviality, except for the release of pressure on resources. As my time approaches in 2030, of course, I reserve the right to change my mind. Certainly you can trace your ancestors without knowing anything about the death of any of them, and the absence of date of death is a normal feature of family trees.

Why, then, are genealogists known for that peculiar perversion, an attraction to things which normal people consider morbid? Why should one family history society have arranged a trip to a local cemetery for those who did not want to watch yet another royal wedding on television? Who but a genealogist would ask for a death certificate as a birthday present? I remember receiving a most odd stare from a lady living opposite a graveyard where I was feverishly clearing snow from a set of stones (though I must admit to going a bit too deep to find a stone which was not actually there!). More than one of my students has found it hard to get used to the idea of looking at other people's wills. Yet such records are not only interesting in themselves: they can save you a great deal of time, effort and money, and can provide information which is unobtainable elsewhere.

I had a good start: my father-in-law was in the death business, with a fleet of hearses. He was fond of bringing his wife flowers, until she discovered where they came from. He used to talk about Burningham and Droppingham, and for a long time I wondered where they were! In other words, he had developed that hardness towards death, the degree of realism to insist on extra-strong handles for his own coffin, which comes to all those professionally involved with it. Genealogists soon feel the same.

There are two main reasons, apart from interest, why the genealogist applies for a copy of a death certificate. Age at death will suggest the approximate year of birth; and an address can be used to locate the family in the census. Death away from home should nevertheless provide the usual residence by address, though since 1904 not by name of institution, unless it appears on a coroner's certificate.

Death creates probably more records than any other event in our lives, if you see what I mean. There is the doctor's certificate centralised to the General Register Office; possibly a hospital record; the bills of the undertaker and other tradesmen involved; the state registration of death, duplicates of which may be found in the Medical Officer of Health records; a grave register entry; an order for cremation, with the cremation record; a burial or funeral service entry; the gravestone itself, with the monumental mason's copy; the will and associated documents; if the death was in any way unusual, a coroner's report; and perhaps memorial records – cards, newspaper entries and so on. It will not be exceptional if my death generates over a dozen different documents.

Death certificates, 1837 to the present day

Since 1 July 1837 the recording of deaths in England and Wales and the location, cost and accessibility of the certificates have been the same as those for birth certificates (pp. 18–25).

The indexes are used in exactly the same way as those for birth, with one important difference. From 1 January 1866, age at death is given in the national (not the local) indexes, so that a copy of the certificate itself need not be bought if that is the only information you require. Once the MAGPIE system is in place, these indexes will be available (on line only) showing the age at death from 1837. (See A note on presentation, p. xxiv above.) A zero in this column means death under the age of one year. From 1 April 1969 the date of birth is given instead. Some coroners, alas, still refuse to supply an approximate age when the date of birth is not known, on the grounds that approximate age is not requested in so many words!

The main problem is to know which years to search, for often you will have no clue to pinpoint when the death occurred, especially if you cannot find a will.

The copy certificate

The entry gives the following information: the date and place of death; the name, sex, age and occupation of the deceased; the cause of death; the signature (see p. 27), name and address of the informant – often a close relative and living at the same address as the deceased; and the date of registration. If the deceased had lived in an institution such as asylum, prison or workhouse, the postal address should appear on entries since 1904, not the name of the institution itself. In 1837, the Registrar General issued a direction to record the *time* of death, but that rubric does not seem to have survived for long. Since 1 April 1969 the date and place of birth of the deceased, the usual address, and the maiden name in the case of a married woman, are also given; the name of the widower is also given, an improvement added in the 1980s. Bilingual death and stillbirth entries were introduced in Wales and Monmouthshire on 1 April 1969.

Death in transit should be registered, as far as is known, in the district where the vehicle was at the time, without reference to the mode of transport. The addition of the phrase 'on the way to ...' indicates that the deceased was in motion at the time.

Name and surname are those by which the deceased was known, not necessarily those appearing on the birth entry, and the use of 'otherwise' for an alias is permitted. Monks and nuns are usually recorded in their former names rather than Brother or Sister.

No proof of age is required. The registrar will normally accept what the informant supplies, though nowadays the requested surrender of the deceased's medical card should lead to the resolution of uncertainty.

The last gainful occupation of a person should be given even when retirement is indicated, and the normal address of the deceased should be entered in the same column or space.

Normally the name of a dead woman's husband is recorded. In the case of a legitimate child under school leaving age, the name of the father (or adopted father) should be given in the occupation column. From 1 April 1982 the name of the mother and her occupation, if gainful, are also entered. 'Afterwards' before the mother's married name indicates that she was already dead.

Cause of death is notoriously inaccurate, particularly in the nineteenth century. Phrases such as 'act of God' do not inspire confidence, whether correct or not, and 'Old Age' for the over-seventies seems to be enjoying a revival in the twenty-first century! Since 1874 a doctor's certificate has been necessary before a death certificate can be issued, but even thereafter – alas, even to the present day – medical opinion is not infallible. (One doctor to my knowledge died of 'bladder cancer', having had his bladder removed ten years earlier!) At first, registrars were simply asked to request a medical statement, and were even encouraged to use popular rather than medical terminology on the entry. Until 1874 entering the cause of death was not a legal requirement, though it had partly been pressure from the medical and insurance professions that had led to civil registration of death in 1837. Between 1858 and 1874 the entry should indicate whether the cause had been 'certified' or 'not certified' by a medical practitioner, but even afterwards a few registrars were prosecuted for allowing death entries to be signed by unqualified persons. If the 'cause of death' column includes reference to a certified period of time, it possibly relates to a statutory maximum between death and burial following infectious disease – twenty-four hours in the case of cholera, for example. 'Fourteen days certified' indicates that the deceased had been under regular medical supervision.

Rules governing who should be an informant for a death entry are very clear, taken from a sequenced list in priority. If an inquest has been held, the coroner takes precedence. If not, and if the death took place in a house or public institution, descending priority is given to a relative of the deceased present at the death, a relative in attendance during the last illness, a relative in the district in which the death occurred, any person present at the death, the occupier if s/he knew of the death, any other inmate of the premises, or finally the person causing the disposal of the body – in the last case, often a representative of the local authority. If the death occurred elsewhere, it must be registered by any relative having knowledge of the data required by the registrar, any person present at the death, anyone who found the body, anyone in charge of the body, or finally anyone causing the disposal of the body.

Deaths must normally be registered within five days of the event, a rule introduced in 1875, instead of the six weeks allowed for births, though the coroner's involvement may lead to lengthy delays, especially before 1860, and where major disasters are concerned. (Jews wish to bury, let alone register, on the day of death, which can cause some bureaucratic difficulties.) The public notice of 1837 announcing the new system said that 'Though a Death *may* be registered *at any time*, it ought if possible to be registered *before Burial*, and a Certificate of Registry obtained from the Registrar, to be shewn to the Clergyman officiating at the funeral. If this is not done the Clergyman will be liable to a fine, unless within seven days he gives notice to the Registrar.'

Be careful what you do with a death certificate. A number of statutes, including section 36 of the Forgery Act 1861, are still in force, prescribing fines and imprisonment for destroying, defacing, injuring or falsifying the register or a certified copy with unlawful intent.

Since 1938 registrars collect much more information than appears on the final entry, but it is used for statistical purposes only. For a short time after 29 September 1939 some registrars were evidently in the habit of writing the deceased's identity number in the margin of the death entry. This would confirm an identification, but it would not be on a copy certificate issued by the superintendent registrar because it is not part of the official record.

Stillbirths, by the way, have an entry which combines the characteristics of birth and death entries. Compulsory registration of stillbirths and their formal registration and indexing started only on 1 July 1927, cause of death being added only in 1960; bilingual entries in Wales started on 1 April 1969. Until 1875 no certificate was needed for the burial of a stillborn child, which encouraged infanticide and under-registration of live births, especially the illegitimate (Havard, 1960; *MN* 11 Winter 90/91; even coroners rarely criticised mothers who had left their children unattended). They are still probably subject to under-registration because of the traumatic circumstances, and uncertainty about the date of conception. Stillbirths are defined as after twenty-four weeks (reduced from twenty-eight weeks in 1995) and have to be registered within three weeks of the birth. Only since 1 January 1996 have copies of the certificate been issued at the time of registration, and the registrar retains a copy permanently. Before 1983 the baby could not be named and still cannot be named after twelve months. At first, only about 10 per cent were named, until all parents were asked if they wished to do so, at which point the number rose to 60 per cent. Since 1995, there has been a space on the form for the baby's name and surname. There is no publicly available index, but registrars will now offer a certificate (long or short) at the time of registration.

There is some inservice training available for registrars – see *MN* 36 Autumn 07. Nevertheless I believe that the registration system still lags behind public opinion. For more information, see www.uk-sands.org.

Failure to find a death entry in the indexes

By now it should come as no surprise to hear that a death entry is sometimes difficult to find in the indexes, but in many cases the reasons are the same as those which create difficulties in the search for birth and marriage entries (see pp. 31–53). Again, the event is not necessarily indexed in the quarter in which the death took place, especially if the coroner is involved; only since 1993 has the month in which the event was registered appeared in the index. The national indexes have been microfilmed, and put on the Internet, in the same way as birth and marriage indexes.

Death in another district

Deaths should be registered in the district where the event took place, not necessarily in the district where the deceased lived (see p. 31), and only very rarely, in the face of a large-scale disaster, has the Registrar General allowed this rule to be broken. 528 deaths had to be registered following the sinking of the pleasure steamer *Princess Alice* in the

River Thames on 3 September 1878, and three districts were asked to share the task of registration (see *MRS* 9–10; FTM 24, 12 Sep 08).

Death not registered

A minute number of deaths continue to be registered without the individual being named. Most of these cases involve a body which cannot be identified. In 1840 over 500 unnamed corpses were registered (with many more unregistered), a figure which has fallen to about two or three a year today. Disasters often prevented identification (see *GM* 23.5). A registrar of my acquaintance was once called in by the police to register an unidentified body. They advertised for anyone to help with their enquiries and eventually contacted the wife of a local publican who had been missing for some time. She went through the traumatic experience of having to visit the mortuary and identify the body. My friend filled in the missing name on the certificate, and the body was duly cremated. Several weeks later the publican turned up, large as life, and they had to tell the police what had happened. When asked how she could have made such a mistake, his wife said that she had not been wearing her spectacles at the time! So the death entry was changed again and some poor man's death entry remains anonymous. Since then the police always photograph an unidentified customer for the crematorium, but that did not prevent a further mishap in 2007 when – in the same city – a mother failed to identify her 'dead' son and someone else's corpse was cremated.

Even in the first decade after 1837 the registration of deaths was always more complete than that of births. In the first three years of civil registration the number of deaths exceeded the number of burials recorded by about 15 per cent, though the reverse would have been expected. Contemporaries believed that no more than 2 per cent were missed – but, in the circumstances, that still seems a high figure. Research suggests that underregistration was worst in the period 1841–46, and that the majority of those missing were probably young infants. Relative completeness is encouraged by the requirement, since 1837, of a certificate from the registrar or coroner before the body can receive a normal disposal. The 1837 rubric stated that the death 'ought if possible to be registered before burial', but it was not always complied with and led to some deaths being unregistered. See Appendix 1 for some conclusions about Lancashire parishes.

The death can now be registered of a person 'missing, presumed dead' even when after seven years' disappearance legal death is pronounced by a court of law. This is a recent change, however, when in 1988 the General Register Office allowed the registration of Jessie Johnson. Her clothes were found on the banks of the river Mersey in Manchester; a coroner's inquest was held, but her body has never been recovered.

Death incorrectly indexed (see pp. 34–5)
Occasionally, there are omissions from the filmed copies of indexes, for example page 196 in the September quarter of 1970. There are mistakes especially in the early years. In September 1837, the surname Ellam is out of order, and John Thomas, Mary Ann, and Mary Ellen are squeezed in among the Mary Jacksons.

Death not in England and Wales (see also pp. 36–8, 173)
No British government has ever compulsorily recorded the emigration of individuals (except in 1773–76 – see Coldham, 1988). Although the National Health Service tries to remove emigrants from lists of doctors' patients the information is not open to the public.

Any will leaving property in England and Wales should be proved in this country. There is no rule governing whether death at sea near the coast should be registered by the local registrar or by the Registrar General of Shipping and Seamen, who also records deaths since 1972 on hovercraft and stationary oil rigs! (See *MRS* 10.) The Marine Register books in the General Register Office 1837–1965 record deaths at sea, while a series of registers covering the same subject has been divided, the more recent ones maintained by the Registrar General of Shipping and Seamen, but earlier ones (1852–90 for seamen, 1854–90 for passengers) have been transferred to the National Archives. Deaths of passengers on merchant vessels, at Kew, are part of the National Archives' digitisation programme, due for completion in 2008; see *NALD* 61. There is an index at www.nationalarchivist.com leading to a pay per view facility. RAF deaths are recorded separately from 1918.

Passenger lists can be seen at www.shipslist.com, especially those who went to Australia, Canada, or directly to the USA (see *NALO* 53; *PFH* 68 Oct 03; *FTM* 24.4 Feb 08).

Deaths of British citizens in foreign countries should be recorded in the same way as births and marriages in the returns of consuls, later High Commissioners, from 1849. If a body is returned to this country for burial or cremation, a registrar has to issue a certificate of no liability to register but is not involved at all if cremated ashes are returned. (The record of these certificates, including name, date and place of death and disposal, and related correspondence, must be kept for only five years, however.) The National Archives has death registers from about sixty different countries, listed by Bevan & Duncan (1990) and now part of the National Archives' digitisation programme, due for completion in 2008. The death of any British citizen in Spain is returned to the General Register Office under a reciprocal agreement since 1963. The GRO indexes of deaths abroad may be in some local libraries, and are available via www.findmypast.com (pay per view). If the deceased had held property in Britain, their will should be proved by the Principal Probate Registry in London.

For further information see *FTM* 14.7 May 98, 16.9 Jul 00 and 17.12 Oct 00, Saul (1995) under 'Emigration', Yeo (1995), and *MRS* 11. There is a CD-ROM with a 'Mormon Immigration Index 1840–1890', and 20 million entries to the USA, 1892 to 1924, can be seen at www.ellisisland.org. Emigrants to Australia, Canada, New Zealand and the USA, 1890–1960, can be seen from 2008 at the pay per view site www.ancestorsonboard.com. Outward bound passengers (including holidaymakers), 1890–1929, are available at www.findmypast.com, also pay per view.

Various groups have recorded the emigration of their members – for example, the Methodist Historic Roll compiled in the late nineteenth century which had an 'in memoriam' section for those who had died *or emigrated* (see *FTM* 19.10 Aug 03). A useful clue is the apparent disappearance of a whole family between one census and all subsequent ones.

Index entry missed by the searcher
See p. 38–9

Misleading clues
As indicated earlier, genealogists often have no clue about when an ancestor died, and looking for him or her in the death indexes can mean a very long and tedious search. It can also be expensive if the name is fairly common, because you must pay to have entries checked to see whether they are the ones you want.

If you have obtained information from a will or burial record it should be accurate enough, but any other source of information is distinctly fallible. Just because your ancestor no longer appears in a set of records such as an electoral register or trade directory, it does not mean that he or she had died. I've found quite often that they have gone to live with relatives or, in more modern times, into a nursing home for example, and died several years later. On the other hand, directories are notorious for including information which is out of date by a year or two. Even today, electoral registration officers usually repeat the previous year's entry if form A is not returned, rather than prosecuting the offender. Check the 'marital status' column in census returns to confirm whether a spouse is alive or dead – but even this is fallible, as occasionally widowed persons sometimes describe themselves as 'married', and those who have been deserted or divorced may prefer to describe themselves as 'widowed'. Search the death indexes for the years immediately before the name disappears from these sources, especially if the deceased was likely to have given his name to a firm which may have continued after his death. The fact that a father had died has not always been indicated on a marriage entry.

A typical problem occurred when trying to find the death of William Francis Clark in 1954. He was known to have died in Ipswich at the age of ninety-one; but he is registered as simply William Clark in the now defunct district of Samford. The name on a death certificate should be that by which the deceased was commonly known, not necessarily the name on the birth certificate, though as mentioned, monks and nuns usually revert to their original names.

The provision of information about the forenames of individuals in the death indexes is as follows:

1 July 1837 to 31 December 1865: all forenames in full.

1 January 1866 to 31 December 1866: the first forename in full, plus the initials of other forenames.

1 January 1867 to 30 June 1910: the first two forenames in full, plus the initials of other forenames.

1 July 1910 to 31 March 1969: first forename and initials.

1 April 1969 to date: first two forenames in full, and initials.

1 January 1993 to date: the month, not merely the quarter, in which the death was registered.

Finding more than one possible death

This is a very common problem, especially when the date cannot be identified from a burial or probate record. It is necessary to provide the registrar with more information than simply the name and approximate age in order to distinguish between possible certificates. The extra information required would be an address, or perhaps the name of the probable informant – the widow or widower.

Very rarely, between 1837 and 1874, a death might be registered twice, especially if the coroner was involved; it happened to William Goodess of Hulme in 1838. The introduction of medical certificates in 1874, designed to reduce infanticide, made it impossible. See pp. 218–19, and *FTM* 7.7 for an illustration of how the South Shields scandal led to double death entries. There were scandals in other areas, particularly Liverpool and St Marylebone (see *GM* 25.7). Such entries elsewhere were also the result of coroners sending information to the wrong district, causing later reregistration (see *MRS* 14).

Since 1993, the same person may be entered twice if the death was in one year and its registration in another. A death can be reregistered, following new information from, for example, a coroner.

Indexes or certificates not accessible: alternative sources

You can often get the information you want from a death certificate more cheaply from other records, but it must be said at once that there is no record automatically surviving more than five years which links the entry of death with the place of disposal. RBDs were required to send notices of death to Overseers in the relevant area, the documents being open to public inspection (Hadden, 1896). In addition to the following, see also church burial, pp. 237–40. (Since 1837, disposal without a death certificate has been illegal.)

National indexes of death have been microfilmed, and can be found in various locations, and on various websites – see Gibson (1987).

Local authority burial records, 1827 to the present day
The population explosion of the late eighteenth and early nineteenth centuries put so much pressure on the Anglican Church that its documentary seams burst, as we have seen many times already. The same pressure was being felt, especially in urban districts, by Anglican graveyards, which were expanded in area wherever possible. Even in 1675 William Wycherley could somewhat unkindly liken a maid making up her mistress for her lover's bed 'as people adorn and perfume a corpse for a stinking second-hand grave' (*The country wife*, IV, i). Graves were dug even deeper – some 30 ft deep and holding eighteen bodies – or the old earth and corpses were simply removed to make room for the new. Benjamin Shaw buried his daughter Hannah in 'a very deep grave' in 1824, 'as they some times shift them two soon, I thought she might rest undesturbed'. These were the days of cheap fertiliser for gardeners and bodysnatching.

Early private graveyards were opened in the eighteenth century. They relieved the pressure but exploited other people's misfortune. Then, in 1833, following the first private cemetery in Norwich called the Rosary (1819), London opened the first of the public graveyards (Kensal Green) to be called cemeteries, followed by other large cities. (See a detailed article in *FTM* 15.12 Oct 99.) The Metropolitan Interment Act of 1850 gave burial powers to local boards of health, which could

CERTIFIED COPY of an
Pursuant to the Births and

ENTRY OF DEATH
Deaths Registration Act 1953

HC 424781

D. Cert.
S.R.

Registration District Hulme

1838. Death in the Sub-district of Hulme in the County of Lancaster

No.	When and where died	Name and surname	Sex	Age	Occupation	Cause of death	Signature, description, and residence of informant	When registered	Signature of registrar
Columns:—	1	2	3	4	5	6	7	8	9
118	Second of September 1838 in Hulme	William GOODESS	Male	78 years	Hawker	Applexy	George Goodess in attendance 34 Brook Street Chorlton upon Medlock	Third of September 1838	John Pownall Registrar.

Certified to be a true copy of an entry in a register in my custody.

Hadyn W. Koorn Deputy Superintendent Registrar.

13. 2. 1997 .... Date.

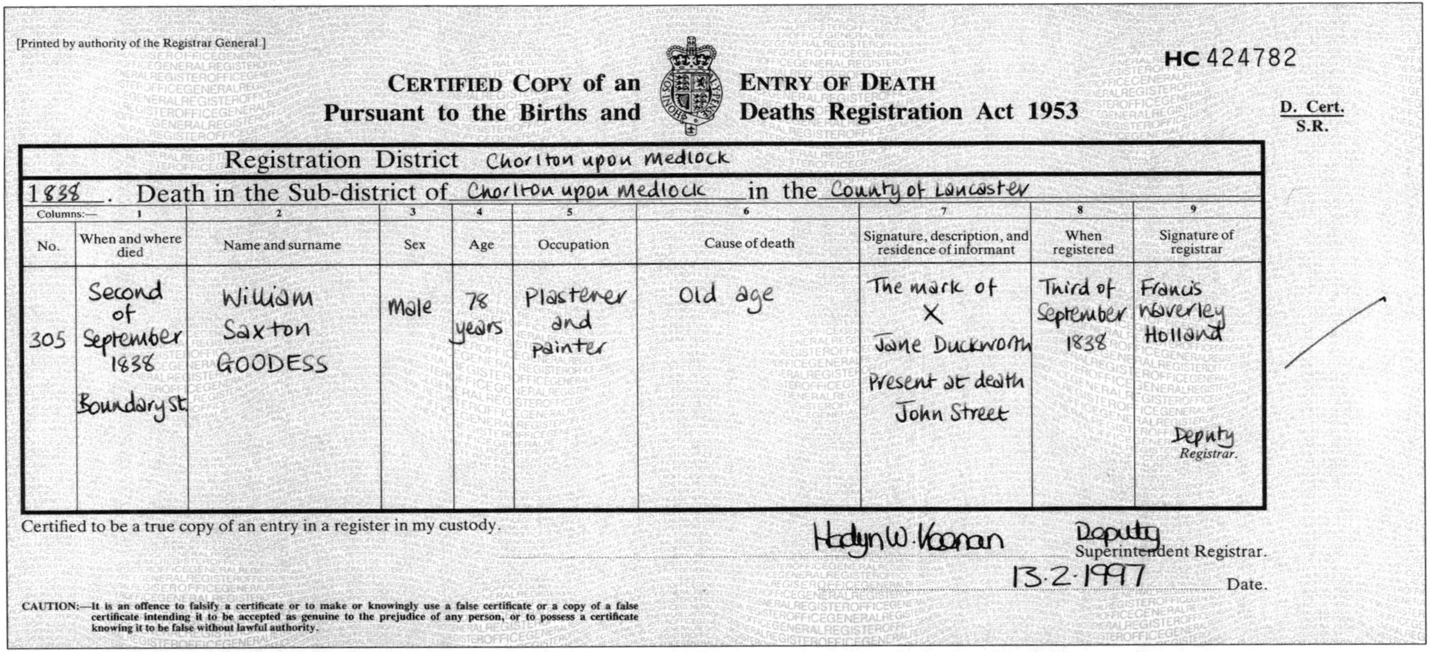

Figure 9. When registrars competed for custom. One man's death is registered in two names, with different causes, by two different registrars on the word of two different informants. Boundary Street ran between Hulme and Chorlton on Medlock!

also close down disused churchyards. Since then the public cemetery has been a local authority responsibility, usually run by a parks and cemeteries or even recreation department. Unlike places of marriage, which have had to be licensed since 1754, the place of disposal requires no formal approval so long as it is neither offensive nor dangerous to health. Burials Acts gave graves to owners in perpetuity.

The choice of burial in a church graveyard or public cemetery lies with the family of the deceased but, unfortunately, there is no formal link connecting the state's death certificate and the place of disposal of the corpse. I believe this to be a serious defect in our registration system, yet one which could so easily be rectified. It is true that a registrar of deaths issues a certificate of burial or cremation (formerly known as a disposal certificate) to the informant, and that except in the case of stillbirths it must be returned within fourteen days, showing how and where the corpse has been disposed of; but the counterfoils need be kept by the registrar for only five years. A 'certificate of no liability to register' can be issued for the disposal in this country of a person who died abroad. Unless you have information in advance, for example from an obituary or will, you will therefore have to search both church and state burial grounds in order to find the entry. To complicate matters still further, most cemeteries have sections which are used by different religious denominations, which may even be registered separately. (Styles of gravestones differ little between graveyard and cemetery.) Copies of burial entries in ground consecrated for Anglicans may sometimes be found in the diocesan archives. If you have any problems locating cemeteries, seek the advice of the local funeral directors (see p. 223).

I am sorry to report that the one register office which had decided to keep a permanent record index to the place of disposal – in my opinion an excellent example which others should follow – has now been stopped by a somewhat paranoid GRO, on the grounds that they might be sued by relatives!

One reason why a place of disposal may not come to light is if the corpse had been removed out of England and Wales beforehand. Since 1926 permission for this to happen should have been granted by a coroner, and the registrar of deaths informed accordingly. A coroner can give permission even before the death has been registered.

Cemetery records, in my experience, are excellent, and so is the service which those in authority offer to genealogists who wish to consult them. You should go first to the office attached to the cemetery, not to the graves themselves, making sure you know the hours of opening. A telephone call will clear this up, and, indeed, if you know the date of death or burial the official will sometimes search the register for a specific dated burial while you are on the telephone. This register normally contains the following information: name of the deceased; address; occupation; date of death and burial; age of the deceased; and the place of the grave in the cemetery, or a grave number. If you are lucky you may find an alphabetical order arrangement, but, usually, the entries are in chronological order of burial. This means that, unless you know at least the year of burial, you may have a long search ahead of you. There is no statutory search fee laid down, but you can find some authorities making a small charge, perhaps £1, for answering queries by post. If the index refers to a grave number rather than a place in the cemetery, there should be a grave map available showing the location of those numbers. Failing that, ask the official where the grave is – the number should be marked on the stone itself – and ask if there is a record of the name of the funeral director involved. *FTM* 19.1 Nov 02 has an article about cemetery records on the Internet.

A third document available in a cemetery office should be a grave – as opposed to a burial – register. It should tell you who owns the grave, when it was bought and who is buried in it. This is especially useful for graves without a stone, and often provides information about other family members.

If the cemetery has been closed, the records should have been transferred to the local authority's archives office. The town clerk's department or librarian will advise you. Even where it has not been closed, burial authorities are concerned about the space becoming increasingly full, and there are government proposals in the pipeline about re-use of existing graves.

Cremation records, 1884 to the present day
Public cemeteries often include crematoria, and a separate register of cremations is kept in the office concerned. This provides the same information as a burial register, except, of course, relating to the grave, but also the marital status of the deceased, the name and address of the persons who applied for the cremation and signed the certificates, the district where the death was registered, how the ashes were disposed of, and sometimes other family data. Permission to cremate has also to be granted by a medical authority attached to the crematorium itself. As a means of disposal, cremation has many advantages at a time when there is considerable pressure on our graveyards but crematoria are faced with difficulties because of high fuel costs and atmospheric pollution.

The general public has no right of access to these records. The presence in the record of individuals still alive has resulted in access being restricted to those appointed by the Home Secretary, the Secretary of State for the Environment or a chief police officer. (I know of a case in which even a tax inspector was refused access.) Information about the deceased and the disposal, however, can be provided orally by the registrar of the crematorium, who will use his discretion concerning those entries which are deemed too old to need such confidentiality.

The hazards to public health from overcrowded graveyards, plus the fact that many bodies removed from graves to make room for new ones were being burned anyway, led Dr William Price to cremate his own son, Jesus Christ Price, on Caerlan Hill in Wales in 1883. It was suddenly realised by a British public shocked by his acquittal at Cardiff assizes that cremation was not illegal, though the Cremation Society, founded by Sir Henry Thompson who had seen the system operating in Austria, had pointed this out since 1874, and an anti-orthodoxy movement had started in the USA two years later. The first crematorium opened at Woking in 1885, followed by Manchester in 1892 and Liverpool in 1896, the only ones in the nineteenth century. (The Manchester Crematorium inscriptions 1892-c.1940 have been published on CD-ROM.) There is a directory of crematoria, some of which are private; the list, with starting years, is in Davies (1976). From this small beginning the number of cremations rose very slowly. At the turn of the century there were fewer than 500 a year, rising to over 1,000 by the First World War. By 1940 the figure had risen to 25,000 but even immediately after the war only ten per cent of corpses were cremated. Since 1968 over half the people dying in England and Wales each year were no longer buried, every thousand saving a whole acre of land! You are unlikely to find a Roman Catholic cremated before 1965.

If someone is cremated, of course, there will be no grave, though there may be a burial plot with a headstone, or a plaque giving name and date of death. The ashes may be disposed of in the grounds of the crematorium, but they may be kept at home, if desired, by fond relatives. A funeral service will not necessarily be recorded, because the 1902 Cremation Act gives clergymen the right to refuse to conduct such a service before, during or after a cremation unless the ashes are subsequently buried in the consecrated ground of a churchyard, a practice first allowed by the Church of England in 1944. In that case the scattering or burial will be entered in the normal church burial register (p. 237), and the registrar of deaths will not be informed. Ashes are the property of the next of kin, and have been put in a wide variety of places – on the mantelpiece, awaiting the death of the spouse; in an egg-timer, 'so he will do more work dead than alive'; and on to the pitch at Anfield, perhaps even at the 'holy' Kop end, though Liverpool Football Club, alas, keeps no register of those whose support survives their death. (Perhaps anyone buying souvenir turf after the move to a new stadium may get more than they bargained for!) All the so-called 'burials' in Westminster Abbey since 1910 have, I am told, been cremated first.

Funeral directors' records

Although the profession of undertaking dates back to 1688, starting as a hire service for items which formerly had to be bought, I have seen no records earlier than the nineteenth century, by which time undertakers were often involved soon after a death in assembling the information required by the registrar. An act of genealogical desperation which has been known to pay off when the place of burial cannot be found is to approach the funeral director nearest to where the deceased lived to see whether his records go back as far as the burial you wish to locate. You will find undertakers in directories or the *Yellow Pages* listed under 'Funeral directors'. The National Association of Funeral Directors publishes a directory of members (see *Anc* 64 Dec 07).

Their records are normally in chronological rather than alphabetical order but can include name, address, age, occupation, relation to the person organising the disposal, place of death and disposal, and sometimes the names and addresses of people attending. However, funeral directors are under no obligation to preserve their older records. On the other hand, many preserve those of firms which they have taken over, and one or two are now beginning to place old records in public repositories.

They are the source of the death notices, as opposed to obituaries, in newspapers, and as such often insert two items, the first about the death and the intended place of disposal, the second about the funeral after the event. These records are sometimes the only surviving evidence of disposal abroad – most popularly nowadays to Ireland, Scotland, and Pakistan.

Gravestones, and failure to find them

Most of our ancestors have no gravestone. Either they could not afford one or the stone has not survived the effects of weather, church rebuilding or, in our own day, environmental improvement. Most of the earliest were made of wood, anyway. It is worth looking, however, because, if they do exist, gravestones can provide certain clues to a family's history which are unobtainable elsewhere. For example, those dating from before 1813 may provide the only evidence of age at death. Members of the same family are often buried in the same grave, with relationships stated on the stone; and it is quite common for units within an extended family to have adjoining grave plots. (Jews, however, tend to be buried one to a grave, with relatives not mentioned by name on the stone.) In every case you should copy down all the information on each stone, even about those whose relationship to your own ancestors is not clear. Look on the back, and along the footing stones, too. One day it may help. Note incidental clues inscribed on the side or the foot of the stone. Gravestone transcription can be time-consuming and prone to error, so a photograph is much better. The Federation of Family History Societies has a code of practice for proper behaviour when visiting a graveyard. (See *Anc* 40 Dec 05, and, for the history of gravestones, *GM* 22.3.)

A photograph has the added advantage of preserving the inscription in case of deterioration of the stone or environmental improvement by being laid flat – sometimes face down! There is some fear that the government's current proposal for a massive re-use of old graves will lead of loss of many old inscriptions, but some enlightened authorities are suggesting that the details of new occupants should be inscribed on the back of existing stones.

Finding a particular grave is by no means as easy as it sounds, unless the church or cemetery keeps a map or key which will connect a burial with a grave number or plot. This number is normally found on the bottom of each upright (front or back). Always ask whether such a map exists but never be surprised, in the case of a churchyard, if it does not. Tell the clergyman, verger, sexton or other official which gravestone you are seeking. They are around the graveyard quite regularly, and the position may have stuck in their minds. If the church does have a map or key, it may take the form of a grave register in which each grave is listed either in turn, possibly in the order in which the graves were started, or by its position in the graveyard, in which case the register will simply indicate the names of the people interred in each. The grave register is kept by the sexton. A comparison of a grave register with the gravestone inscriptions can indicate that there are often more people buried in a grave than appear on the stone; that many graves have no stone, including the 'public' or 'common' (or, in the twenty-first century, 'social fund') graves in which large numbers of corpses – without coffins until well into the nineteenth century – were cast; and occasionally that a corpse is not buried directly under the stone on which the name is recorded. In a rare collation of published burial and monumental inscription entries, Rivington shows some eighteenth-century grave entries which are not in the parish register.

In the nineteenth century, paupers were particularly badly treated even in death. In an effort to impress on the populace the need to avoid the workhouse, pauper corpses were subject to re-interment, denied a headstone, buried 'like sardines', and were denied a formal funeral ceremony. If unclaimed, they could be used for anatomical study, following the Anatomy Act of 1832. The north side of churchyards was historically used for the burial of society's unwanteds – executed criminals, whose bodies could be used for anatomy lessons after the 1752 Murder Act, strangers, paupers, aliens, unbaptised children, and even non-Anglicans.

I fear that you will have to search most graveyards without anybody or any document to help you find individual plots. Without wishing to be discouraging, I must warn that it can be a dirty, frustrating, time-consuming task, with no guarantee of success at the end of the search. For this reason, genealogists and family historians have, for many years now, undertaken the wholesale transcription of gravestones (hopefully remembering to look on the back as well as the front). These records are often referred to as monumental inscriptions, or MIs. One of the earliest and most famous is that of Ralph Bigland, who is said to have copied most of the inscriptions in the county of Gloucester in the late eighteenth century, and Hertfordshire is well served by a collection in the British Library. Most inscriptions are far less ambitious and usually include only one graveyard. It is the custom, and certainly an invaluable service to others, to place a copy of any monumental inscription into the local library and local record office, as well as in the church itself. The Society of Genealogists also possesses a very large collection, and the Federation of Family History Societies is encouraging family history societies to participate in the immense project of transcribing all extant monumental inscriptions (*FTM* 20.11 Sep 04). A few British graveyard transcriptions can be found at www.interment.net, an American website; try also www.epitaphs.co.uk, www.memorialinscriptions.org.uk, and *Anc* 59 Jul 07 for other MIs on the Internet. Such a transcript should certainly always be made if there is any possibility of the gravestones being moved in a modernisation project. In the case of the Church of England and local authorities at least, monumental inscriptions must be submitted before the stones can be removed. Those deposited with the Registrar General are transferred to the National Archives in section RG37, and the NLW has a large collection of MIs from Wales.

Failure to find a gravestone is common. You may be looking in the wrong graveyard anyway, and your ancestor quite possibly had no stone. Some have not survived, particularly on early graves very close to church buildings which have been extended, and in areas where only soft sandstone was available. (Stones are owned by those who erect them, but the land freehold lies with the incumbent.) At Bowdon, in north Cheshire, the church was rebuilt in 1859–60, when the parish clerk, one Eli Morgan, was also a housebuilder. Some of his houses are still standing, and have gravestones embedded in them as cellar floors or hearthstones.

Some of the more fortunate among our ancestors have been buried – or at least have a memorial – inside the church building, but even those preserved on the floor are no longer safe from shuffling feet, as denizens of the coffee shop crypt off Trafalgar Square know only too well. It is always worth looking at transcriptions of monumental inscriptions, especially old ones, as they contain inscriptions from graves which have since disappeared.

There are other reasons for failure which you may be able to overcome. One of the commonest is the sheer size of the problem, especially round an old parish church near a large town. You can, however, eliminate many areas of the graveyard by noticing the style of the gravestones. Mytum (2000, Part 3) is good for a technical description of graves. Broadly speaking, any before the early nineteenth century are likely to be fairly close to the church and flat on the ground. Those before about 1730 have more crudely carved lettering than the later ones, and those before about 1700 are likely to be entirely in capital letters. A more modern, professional inscribing was achieved only during the nineteenth century. These flat slabs, known as 'ledgers', were used until after 1850, but the older ones can contain more modern inscriptions as fresh corpses were added. Genealogists will note that directors of horror movies pay little regard to such detail and have seventeenth-century witches cavorting around Victorian gravestones.

The large, upright stones, probably blackened with pollution, will be nineteenth- or early twentieth-century; the smaller, cleaner uprights will be quite modern. It should be said, however, that the size, shape and type of stone used vary considerably, not only from one part of the country to another but also across social classes. The most disappointing are slabs which contain only the initials of the deceased. I hope, however, no one follows the example of one vicar who searched the registers for a reported eight years in an effort to find who 'H.W.P.' had been, only to be told that it stood for Hot Water Pipe! Look at *all* the surnames on each stone, even surnames used as forenames. Do not pass by if the first name on the stone is apparently of no interest to you. Occasionally you will also find inscriptions continued on the reverse side of upright stones.

Gravestones earlier than 1600 are very rare, and most from before 1700 have disappeared. The flat, ground-level stones are often overrun with weeds, which are sometimes so dense that the lettering is embossed in mirror image in the tangled roots when the stone is cleared. In contrast, some of those exposed to the weather are difficult to read and should be viewed in a slanting light if possible. (Try reflecting sunlight across the face with a small mirror, or visit when the surface is likely to be wet.) Many stones have sunk too deep to be easily recoverable. Visit your graveyard with strong gloves and suitable implements – trowel and secateurs are useful. Make sure that you search all possible hiding places for the 6 ft × 2 ft slabs. Usually, graves in churchyards lie east–west (a remnant of pagan sun-worshipping days), arranged in rows with inscriptions legible from the east. Variations from this norm can hide some interesting stories. Although the heads of most corpses are at the western end, clergymen have been buried the other way round so that, when we all rise to face the dawn on the Day of Judgement, they will be facing their congregations! One morning Francis Kilvert observed dark stones upright against a snowy landscape, 'and it seemed as if the morning of the Resurrection had come and the sleepers had risen from their graves and were standing upon their feet silent and solemn, all looking toward the East to meet the Rising of the Sun' (Diary, 3 March 1878). This is quite hard on those who, like me, wish to be buried on their side, and even worse for those spinsters who experienced cruelty beyond death by being buried face-downwards.

If a few seem to be missing from the line perhaps they are below the present surface. Others may be inside the church itself, together with memorial plaques to more prominent citizens. As early as 1689 John Evelyn complained in his diary of the 'avarice of ministers who, in some opulent parishes made almost as much from permission to bury in the chancel and the church, as of their livings'. It is still permissible to bury inside a place of public worship, except in the case of churches built in urban areas outside London since 31 August 1848.

For those who see the passion, as well as the interest, in such matters, there is an Association for Gravestone Studies in the USA, available at www.gravestonestudies.org.

Monumental masons' records

Monumental masons, like funeral directors, are not obliged to keep their records beyond the needs of HM Inspector of Taxes, but many do so. Because there are certain skills and equipment involved, firms of masons are both fewer in number and longer-lasting than those of undertakers. They will usually search their records if you can provide an approximate date, and if their records go back far enough.

Obituaries

Like notices of births and marriages, notices of death and obituaries ('obits') have appeared in newspapers for the last 250 years. (Death notices are short and factual, whereas obituaries are more discursive, not to say opinionated.) For a general introduction to the subject, see *Anc* 60 Aug 07. They often include what may be the only surviving reference to where the deceased was buried. The main difficulties are knowing which are the right newspapers for your ancestors and getting access to them. By far the oldest obits in newspapers are to be found in *The Times* and in *The Gentleman's Magazine* 1731–1907, each of which has indexes. (They are listed in the case of the former under 'Deaths' and 'Memorials' rather than 'Obituaries'.) The published *Musgrave's Obituary* has six volumes of deaths, largely pre-1800, in alphabetical order. However, only your richer ancestors are likely to be found in them. The era of mass obits and notices of death is much more modern – the late nineteenth century in most cases, by which time local newspapers were quite numerous. Not all obituaries were inserted by fond relatives – deaths associated with the demon drink were paraded for approbation by the temperance *Alliance News*. You should ask the local history librarian of the large public library nearest to where your ancestor died which of these old papers exist, and where copies are accessible. The newspaper office itself is usually the last place you should try!

Again access to London eases matters considerably, for the newspaper section of the British Library at Colindale has most regional and local papers. By 2011, this will move to Boston Spa, with those newspapers which have by then been digitised or microfilmed being available in the British Library at St Pancras in London (see *PFH* 120 Dec 07). Reference to holdings of extant local papers will be found in Gibson, Langston & Smith (2002), which also includes a note of indexes if they exist. About one in five of their holdings are currently unavailable because they are too fragile to be handled. Obituaries should also be sought in trade and professional journals and parish magazines; the fourteenth edition of *Who's who in the theatre* (1967) has a wonderful combined list of obituaries from all earlier editions. These entries are much fuller than the normal death notices in local newspapers, which are little more revealing than gravestone inscriptions.

If your ancestor was of any substance, or notoriety, or if the death was unusual, the local newspapers should be consulted anyway, in order to acquire information unobtainable from the matter-of-fact records of birth, marriage and death. Searching local newspapers will not take as long as you might imagine, because most appear weekly rather than daily, and notices of deaths and burials – which can even include paupers when they were buried at public expense – will be in the same place in each edition. However, you will probably be asked to look at old newspapers on microfilm in order to preserve the originals.

Probate since 1858

Beginners sometimes dislike the idea of using wills because of the personal association with impending death. Put one toe in the water, however, and you realise that they form an immense reservoir of information about your family tree. In many ways, a will tells you more about the living and about the deceased during their lifetime, than it does about their death, and, after all, that is the reason why you are looking for records concerning death in the first place. Indeed, probate records can also provide the first evidence of the date of death. For an introduction, see *FTM* 24.3 Jan 08, and the probate service's own website www.hmcourts-service.gov.uk (under 'wills and probate'), which includes details of all the District Probate Registries (DPRs).

11 January 1858 marks an important watershed in the history of wills. For over 300 years before, the right of proving wills had lain with the Church of England, and before that with the Roman Catholic Church. Since 1858 the state has had the right to grant probate, through a department with the Principal Probate Registry at its centre. Before 1858, as we will see later, the geographical location of probate records is complicated. Since then, there has been a uniform system, with national indexes (or, more properly, calendars because they contain much more information than a mere index). Once again, therefore, the state took over with a single administration what had been devolved for hundreds of years.

Wills have also become more jargonised and shorter, perhaps reflecting the increased influence of solicitors. Whichever period you are researching, you are strongly recommended to buy copies of any relevant probate records – they are cheap enough, and frequently come in useful later.

The act of proving a will makes it a publicly accessible document (though only after the process has been completed, and excluding the wills of the royal family). If the executors of an estate wish to have the will proved, in order to give a legal basis for the transfer of goods and property in cases where ownership has to be recorded, they arrange for it to be done in any one of two dozen or so DPRs established in the major cities and towns of England and Wales, or through a subsidiary office. Since 1926 there have been no geographical boundaries to the jurisdictions of district registries, which is convenient for distant executors. Once the process has been completed, a second copy of the registered will is sent to the Principal Registry of the Family Division, First Avenue House, 42–49 High Holborn, London WC1V 6NP, which thus houses *copies* of all wills proved in England and Wales since 1858.

Additional, registered copies of the original wills were made until 1940 in most districts, handwritten into large volumes and separately indexed. These copies and their indexes should be found in the relevant county record office or, in Wales, in the National Library. For lost wills see p. 256.

The annual calendars give the name of the deceased, the address, date of death, sometimes the place of death, the date of probate, the names of executors or administrators (with their addresses until 1892), the value of the estate and the name of the office in which the will was proved. The names of the executors have been omitted from the calendars since 1966. Do not be surprised if your ancestor's will was proved at Llandudno during the Second World War – the Principal Probate Registry was evacuated there from London. (The General Register Office went to Blackpool.)

Calendars over fifty years old are being moved from DPRs. It is said that the reason is again pressure of space, but that seems difficult to accept because, since 1973, calendars have been produced on microfiche. All cases have been entered on computer since 1996, and can be seen on screen in DPRs. Some years ago, DPRs were ordered to destroy calendars (and other papers) over fifty years old, but many did not do so, instead asking a local repository to preserve them

Since 1999, under a 25-year contract, the storage and copying of English and Welsh wills has been undertaken by Iron Mountain, a firm which is currently digitising the calendars from 1858. Public terminals required to access the calendars in this form are lodged in the DPRs and sub-registries, from which details can be obtained and copies ordered. (Original calendars or microfilm copies thereof may still be available in some areas – see Gibson & Langston, 2002.) Discussion about having the calendars available on the Internet is ongoing.

Remember to search the addenda at the end of some volumes, and ask to have copied, in addition to the will, any other document in the same file. There may be nothing; on the other hand, there could be bonds, oaths, powers of attorney, renunciations or other legal documents which cast light on the family concerned. Try to access the wills of other relatives, not only those in your direct line – particularly those who had no direct descendants.

Once you have identified a promising entry in the calendars, you can order a copy of a will or administration for £5.00 via any DPR, which will arrange to have it posted to your home address if you wish. Ask for a copy of the Grant as well as the will, as this can provide extra information, and when ordering a will tell the court official if you need a copy showing the original signature of the testator. (A further £3 is charged for each four-year search if you cannot provide the relevant detail.) They will require the name of the deceased, the date of death, the date of probate, and the office at which probate was granted. These details are given in the calendars. There may be a delay of a few weeks before you receive the copy. However, if you require a copy of an original will (showing the signature) which is no longer with the district probate registry where it was proved, you should write enclosing the £5.00 fee, explaining your requirement to the Principal Registry of the Family Division, Record Keeper's Department, Somerset House, Strand, London WC2R 1LP.

If there is a reference to a firm of solicitors, the Law Society can advise whether the firm still exists, even if it amalgamated with another. Contact with such a firm may produce extra data about the family, though you may have to pay for the privilege. Solicitors' archives, of course, contain large numbers of wills which were never proved, and there has been pressure for several years to persuade the profession to deposit its older records.

Because the calendars are national, it is easy to discover the existence of a will, no matter where it was proved in England and Wales. Even death abroad should be followed by probate in Britain if the will involved the transfer of property in this country. If your search is fruitless, it almost certainly means that no will was proved, even though a will may have existed. The survival of unproved wills normally depends on the individual family or solicitor concerned. Such a situation does not necessarily imply that the family was guilty of carelessness or worse. On the other hand, you may be looking under the wrong surname, following a change of name, or the use of a title instead.

A will can be proved after seven days following the death, so that probate may be indexed in the calendar year after the death itself. Indeed, the will could give rise to further proceedings which may extend over a number of years. Oddly enough, only between 1926 and 1938 have testators had complete freedom to dispose of their property, including real estate, how they wished. Disputes over real estate, however, should have been heard in the Court of Chancery, not the normal courts. From 1837 (and sometimes before that) a man's will was automatically revoked by his subsequent marriage, though not if he named his future bride in a will made after 1925.

If a thorough search has failed to reveal a will in the indexes, there is another avenue to explore for the period 1858–70. If the deceased died intestate, or if the will was for some reason invalid, or if all the named executors renounced their office (any single one of them could have had the will proved), the probate court can issue a Grant of Administration, which gives named individuals, normally the next of kin but sometimes the chief creditor, the right to administer the estate. Since 1870 these letters of administration have been indexed together with the wills themselves, but from 1858 to 1870, inclusive, they are indexed in a separate set of calendars. Administrations, however, are something of a disappointment. Admittedly you may learn the date, place of death and occupation of the deceased, but there is none of the detail which, in a will, can bring your ancestor to life. Before the Administration of Estates Act of 1925 not even the next of kin or relative had to be appointed as an administrator – indeed, a statute of 1357 compelled the appointment of close friends. Since 1926, if a close relative cannot be found, the estate of an intestate can be appropriated by the Crown through one of the duchies or the Treasury Solicitor. In the case of administrations over seventy-five years old it is useful to follow the cases through the Estate Duty Reports; see p. 256–7.

Wills form such an easily accessible and important source of information that genealogists have written entire books on the subject of their location (Camp, 1974; Gibson, 1974; Gibson & Langston, 2002). See also Grannum & Taylor (2004) and Scott (1997). For modern court practice, see Winegarten (c.2002) and Biggs (2003).

Hospital records
As in the case of births, deaths in these institutions are recorded in the hospitals' own archives (see p. 65). However, there is no obligation to keep the records of death longer than eight years, and in my limited experience only those held under the mental health acts are likely to

be preserved much longer. It is worth enquiring in the relevant city or county record office about extant archived hospital records.

Records of the armed forces (see pp. 56–60)
Information about the death abroad of members of the armed forces on active service in the two world wars may be supplemented by contacting the Commonwealth War Graves Commission (2 Marlow Road, Maidenhead, Berkshire SL6 7DX), which will answer postal enquiries if the relevant details are provided. Some libraries have copies of all the names in the cemeteries of France and Belgium. The Commission has recorded military resting places since 1917, and cares for 1.6 million graves, some two-thirds of which are of servicemen who died in the First World War. Its lists include data on next of kin. It has an alphabetical index of the deceased, showing number, rank, date of death and the location of the grave. Supply as much information about the soldier as possible if you are making an enquiry. (Name, date of birth, name of wife, age at death, place killed and any memorial recording the death are all helpful in identifying the person.) The data is now freely available on the Internet, at www.cwgc.org as the 'Debt of Honour' register (see *FHM* 142 Apr 07).

War memorials can lead on to very useful military records, and are listed at www.iwm.org.uk/collections/niwm; over 200,000 photos are available at www.britishwargraves.org.uk, covering 1914 to the present day. Try www.ukniwm.org.uk also for war memorials. The Imperial War Museum's ongoing National Inventory of War Memorials in the United Kingdom (see *FTM* 7.1 Nov 90) does not have a national index of names, but a search for an individual name can be undertaken given sufficient data – please send a stamped, addressed envelope or three international reply coupons. (Disasters at sea are recorded at www. nmm.ac.uk/memorials.)

The *National Roll of the Great War* gives details of the military careers, medals and addresses supposedly of all who fought in the First World War, but it was published, as a private venture, only for Bedford, Birmingham, Bradford, Leeds, London, Luton, Manchester, Northampton, Portsmouth, Salford and Southampton, and is by no means complete even for those areas. The eighty-seven-volume *War graves of the British Empire*, published in the 1920s and 1930s, lists the dead of the First World War, providing name, number, regiment, date of death, plot number, and sometimes the age and name of the parents if the relatives provided them. Unfortunately these books are arranged by country of death, then by cemetery, and only then in alphabetical order of surname. There are three further volumes covering naval cemeteries – Chatham, Plymouth and Portsmouth, arranged by year of death.

Incidentally, there is also a seven-volume published list of civilians who died in the Second World War, a copy of which may be seen on display in Westminster Abbey for that local area. The Manchester register office kept a separate list of war casualties additional to the normal death entries, but I don't know how rare this was. Holders of the Victoria Cross are listed at www.victoriacross.org.uk.

Army.   The General Register Office has a register of army deaths from 1796 to 1987, paralleled in part by the chaplains' returns of death and burial in the National Archives, 1796–1880. Some of the former contain the army number of the deceased (see *GM* 21.6). The latter series concern only events abroad, however; they are continued as Army Returns from 1881, with those of births. The General Register Office also has indexes of army war deaths 1899–1902, 1914–21 and 1939–48 giving name, regiment and date of death. Indexes to these and other GRO registers may be available on microfiche in local libraries.

Soldiers killed in the First World War are listed by the War Office publication *Soldiers died in the Great War* and *Officers died in the Great War* (1920–21), available at considerable cost on CD-ROM and searchable by name, regiment, or place of birth (see www. great-war-casualties.com). The former is also available on line via www.military-genealogy.com. It is not easy to find this work as it is available only in the largest libraries, but recently it has been reissued in microform. Using it involves a long search, unless the regiment and battalion are known in advance (see p. 58); within those categories, names are in alphabetical order.

Estates of soldiers, and unindexed Deceased Soldiers' Effects, who died 1901–60 are recorded in the National Army Museum, with name, rank, regiment, number, date and place of death, moneys owing, and who inherited the estate.

Royal Air Force.   The General Register Office has indexes of RAF deaths abroad from 1920, and a separate index of RAF war deaths 1939–48.

Royal Navy.   Deaths of naval personnel are recorded in the General Register Office from 1 July 1837; they are in the Services registers from 1955 to 1965, and thereafter in the UK High Commission papers, in the General Register Office. The General Register Office also has indexes of naval war deaths 1914–21 and 1939–48.

Pension papers in the National Archives (from 1797) have had to include certification of death, and officers' service registers from the mid-nineteenth century give date of death. Wills of ratings are in the National Archives (1786–1909), arranged alphabetically; those of officers date between 1830 and 1860. Sailors' wills can also be found in the Prerogative Court of Canterbury and other courts before 1858.

Workhouse records

Deaths in workhouses should have been recorded by the institutions (see Gibson, Rogers & Webb, 1997–2008). Occasionally they had their own graveyard, but normally the bodies were taken to the nearest Anglican church with which the Poor Law authorities had come to an arrangement, or could be sent back to the paupers' legal place of settlement as late as 1878 if not later.

Trade union and friendly society records

The records of many trade unions (see p. 68) contain details of death benefits paid to relatives of deceased members and give date, address, cause of death and sometimes a copy of the death certificate. Friendly society records (see p. 69) covering individual membership are not as numerous, but again can provide a clue to the time and circumstances of death. It should be noted that whereas early British trade unions were normally created around workers in individual trades, and in many cases were true descendants of the craft guilds (for which see *Anc* 51 Nov 06), friendly societies were usually based on a geographical area, and embraced labourers and skilled craftsmen from many occupations.

Coroners' records

A burial register and, from 1837, a death entry may indicate that the coroner's office had been involved. County directories will give you the names of contemporary coroners. See *NALL* 30, Gibson & Rogers (2000), *Local Population Studies* 78, O'Neill (2006), and Havard (1960), the last for a fascinating account of the history and importance of the office.

The office of coroner was founded in 1194 and many of the early surviving records, for Bedfordshire and Nottinghamshire, for example, have been published. A considerable amount can be gleaned from these records. One of the most famous cases was that of the dramatist Christopher Marlowe, the discovery of whose inquest report of 1593 threw a whole new light on the political aspect of his life and death.

For reasons which do the legal profession little credit, coroners' inquests fell in number between 1837 and 1860. After 1860 many coroners were salaried, and the number of inquests returned to normal. At the present day the coroner is even notified by the registrar of deaths if the deceased had not seen a doctor within fourteen days of the death, or had suffered a recent accident, violence, industrial disease or medical operation failure. The coroner will also be brought in if a complete medical certificate of death cannot be obtained for any reason. Stillbirths can be referred, if the registrar suspects that the child might have been born alive.

Coroners' records, which include the depositions of witnesses (often relatives), contain minute details of events leading up to the death, the name, age, address and cause of death of the deceased, and the verdict. They also contain some gruesome items of evidence from the hearing. Until 1926 the jury had to view the corpse; the coroner himself did so until 1980.

Apart from those which have been published, there are few indexed records before the twentieth century, so a long search may be involved for any one entry. Normally, however, you will know the approximate date of the inquest, which should be on the death entry. Indexing surviving records, including newspaper reports where the original records have not survived, would be a straightforward and worthwhile task for any family history group looking for projects to undertake, and has been done in Nottinghamshire, Warwickshire and Wiltshire. The National Archives holds many of the early records, sometimes from as far back as the thirteenth century and, for a few areas, right up to the nineteenth. They are kept in the records of the Clerk of Assize.

These records, however, present one of those annoying difficulties which serve to remind us that, as far as public archives go, we still live in a very paternalistic society. In this instance confidentiality is carried to ridiculous lengths. The coroner keeps his current records until they are fifteen years old, at which point, as the Home Office directed, only those relating to treasure trove and any deemed to be in the public interest should be transferred for permanent deposit to a specified local archive office. The remainder can be destroyed, despite the fact that inquests are held in public and interested parties can buy a copy of the case notes. All coroners' records surviving from before 1875, however, are now preserved.

Coroners had to apply to the quarter sessions for their expenses, and some detail of individual cases can be found in these records.

Unusual deaths should be followed up in newspaper reports, of course, both immediately and after a coroner's inquest In the latter case the coroner will normally appear as the informant on the death entry. For the history and present whereabouts of the surviving records see Gibson & Rogers (2000).

Professional bodies' records

Registrars of deaths are required to send copies of death entries (or form III, which provides the same information) to certain professional bodies if the deceased was a practising or retired member. Such bodies include pharmaceutical chemists, druggists, solicitors, opticians, nurses, midwives, doctors, dentists and veterinary surgeons. If you have trouble locating the death entry of a member of any such profession, it may be worth approaching the professional body concerned for information. Similar documentation is forwarded to the appropriate organisation if the deceased was in receipt of a pension from Inland Revenue, Customs and Excise, British Telecom, the Post Office, the Ministry of Defence, the Benefits Agency, the police or the civil service. There are National Archives information leaflets on a number of these bodies, and there is detail in Herber (2005, chapter 21).

Much has been written earlier in this book about the advantages of using professional records. Those relating to death are particularly useful, for at that time is gathered together the sum total of the deceased's main work, together with details of the death itself. Obituaries are often found in the relevant journals. Earlier national records have often been centralised in the National Archives or other repository, and are available for a wide range of occupations – for example, the railways (see Richards, 1989; Hawking, 1995), the Post Office, and Customs and Excise, in many of which sons followed fathers.

Church burial, 1538 to the present day

Until the Second World War burial was the most common means of disposing of corpses. It was normally preceded by a funeral ceremony, and indeed some old church registers refer to funerals rather than burials. With the rise of Nonconformity towards the end of the eighteenth century, the events in the register may be burials but not funerals. To complicate matters further, I have seen it said that 'interred' refers to a burial without Christian (or perhaps merely Anglican) rites. The funeral ceremony is always religious; a burial is not necessarily so, and since the advent of local authority cemeteries about 150 years ago the state will record the burial of a corpse without any religious ceremony having been performed. A further recent development by local authorities allows register offices to organise civil funerals. It is not statutory, and requires no approval from the GRO. For a useful history of early English burial practices and beliefs see Gittins (1984).

The history of Anglican burial registers follows closely that of baptisms (see pp. 91–101). Until 1 January 1813 the entries are normally in the same parchment books as baptisms, but since that date they have been entered on printed forms in separate books, eight to a page. During the previous three centuries the entries were subject to all the weaknesses and difficulties already described. At first, only the name of the deceased and the date of burial are entered. Further information was added in most parishes during the seventeenth century: the name of a dead child's father, and even of its mother; the township within the parish where the deceased had lived; the name of a deceased wife's husband, though very rarely that of a deceased husband's wife; and the marital status of the deceased – widow, spinster, and so on. For a short period between 1645 and 1660 you may find the date of death as well as of burial. The age of the deceased was not entered regularly before the last quarter of the eighteenth century, and it was not done in every parish even then. Between 1783 and 1794 stamp duty was imposed on entries of baptism and burial, and it is probable that among your ancestors, as among mine, there are some classified as exempt by the addition of the word 'pauper' or a letter P in the margin. Some registers include the church burial fee, or 'mortuary'.

In 1813 George Rose's Act introduced the standard form on which the following information continues to be given to the present day: name, abode, date of burial and age. You will see that in some ways a burial entry on the standard form is often less helpful than one in an earlier register. In particular it normally contains no information about the parents of dead children or the marital status of women. However, the lucky genealogist can still come across more complete registers even after 1812 (see church baptism, p. 93). The village of Witton continued to give much more detail in its auxiliary 'Dade' register until 1862. A typical entry reads, 'Elizabeth Wilcoxon, widow; died of natural decay, 20th April, 1824; buried on the north side of the churchyard on the 24th; daughter of John and Mary Shepley of Macclesfield; aged 69.'

Burial entries from 1812 to 1850 now form only the basis of a massive county-by-county indexing project by the Federation of Family History Societies, known as the National Burial Index, the currently published version of which has thirteen million entries, giving name, age, date of burial, parish, county and transcribing group. Some cremation records are also included. It is updated and reissued on CD-ROM at regular intervals by the Federation (see *GM* 28.4 and *FTM* 21.2 Dec 04). One of the intentions of the project was to complement the IGI, which has very few death entries, but like the IGI it should be remembered that it is an *index*, not a transcription. The NBI can be bought for £45 via www.genfair.com, or seen via www.findmypast. com, but like many other sources can be seen free of charge if you can use the library of a family history society.

Although you are very unlikely to be descended from anyone described in the burial register as 'son of' or 'daughter of', information about the burial of your ancestor's siblings can be useful in supplying clues to the previous marriage, as we have seen. Before the nineteenth century, child deaths accounted for almost half the number of burials in normal times, and well over half during epidemics of such diseases as measles or diphtheria. Forty-four per cent of 29,000 burials in Lancashire during the 1620s were of children (Rogers, 1974). Infant mortality – the death rate of children before their first birthday – was at least 100 times higher than in our own day, particularly in towns; it was still 15 per cent at the end of the nineteenth century and was especially high among illegitimate children. At the end of the eighteenth century half the children born in some large towns died before they were five; in London before they were three. Nicholas Blundell's diary (10 August 1712) shows no surprise at children playing at a death game with their dolls.

Searching for one particular burial entry in a parish register can be a long exercise unless the parish is small or the register has been correctly indexed. The baptism of children in a sequence will provide a general guide to the date of marriage and a good base for estimating the date of birth of the parents. There is no such clue concerning the date of death, however, unless the couple stops having children significantly before the mother reaches the age of forty. If, for example, the couple marry in their early twenties and appear to produce children for only ten years or so, you should look for the father's burial up to one year before the baptism of the last child, or for the burial of the mother up to about three months before the last baptism, as well as for the following couple of years. Of course, the couple might have simply moved parish. If, however, the mother gives birth into her forties, then you may have to cover half a century in the registers and even then not find the burial you are seeking. One of my ancestors, Thomas Blain of Norley, fathered at least eight children in the 1720s and 1730s. His wife died in 1763, but if the register had not been

indexed I would probably never have found his burial in 1791, 'aged
102', as I would not have considered searching so far forward in
time. Death at such an age was considered a rare enough event for a
memorial to be placed in the churchyard, even though he had been
'only' an agricultural labourer. On 19 May 1818 St Chad's, Rochdale,
recorded the burial of Peggy Smith 'whose husband was killed at the
battle of Culloden AD 1745'.

Failure to find an Anglican burial

Burial in Anglican graveyards has never been universal, though there
are many rural areas where it was almost so. Even in the seventeenth
century, when you should expect to find at least 90 per cent of all
burials in the Anglican registers, many were buried elsewhere. Into the
eighteenth and nineteenth centuries the percentage of Anglican burials
declined dramatically, especially in the growing industrial towns. There
are several reasons why you might fail to locate the burial of an
individual in the registers.

Burial in another parish
Any person was entitled to be buried in the parish where they lived
or in the parish in which they had died. The clergyman Ralph Josselin
complained in his diary on 24 November 1682, 'Jo. Burton buried he
had a wife and 3 sons, shee and one son rich and would not bury
him, nor accompany him to the grave, but left him to the town to
bury.' Additionally, the clergyman or churchwardens could consent
to bury anyone who had expressed a desire to be buried in 'their'
parish, though fees for burying 'strangers' were often higher than those
for parishioners. In London especially, child burials may be missing
because the child had been put out to wet nurse – see *Local Historian*
19.3. Presumably, the right of burial would also be extended to the
owners of grave plots, even if they had neither lived nor died in the
parish. From 1807, shipwrecked bodies had to be buried by the parish
where they had been washed ashore. By the nineteenth century many
churchyards were full, and the deceased sometimes had to be taken to
a neighbouring parish for burial. Finally, it has been quite common for
people to want to be buried in their parish of birth, with an irrational,
though understandable, feeling of the idea of 'dust to dust'. Parson
Woodforde wrote in his diary on 6 November 1791, 'I did not take
anything for burying the young Man, tho' he did not belong to this
Parish, his Father being poor and willing [i.e. desiring] that his Son
should lie near his Mother.' William Cobbett wrote in *Rural rides* (23
September 1823) of 'the old maxim that we all try to get as nearly as

possible in our old age to the spot whence we first sprang'. My own mother was buried in her parish of birth, having left it almost thirty years earlier, and my father followed her twenty-six years later. See R. Schofield in *Local Population Studies* 33.

Thus there could be several reasons why our ancestors may not have been buried in their own churchyard, and even after 1837, when the national death indexes begin, there is no easy way to discover where someone is buried. Searching one burial register is time-consuming enough; having to search many parishes in turn is sometimes not worth the effort. Is it not time the place of disposal was included in a permanent document such as the death certificate itself?

Some of the other documents listed earlier may indicate when the death took place, which narrows the search considerably. Until the eighteenth century it was particularly common for testators to indicate in their will where they wanted to be buried. In 1882, however, it was held in Williams *v.* Williams that such an indication is not binding on the executors. Heralds recorded place of burial in their funeral certificates (see p. 148), and so do many death notices and obituaries in newspapers.

Burial not recorded
Needless to say, parsons sometimes forgot to enter a burial, especially in the smaller benefices where they might not be resident. In the 1550s and 1640s, about a quarter of all burials seem to have gone unrecorded. It is always a good idea to consult the bishop's transcripts (pp. 140–2) if they are available. Remember, however, that most printed registers have already been collated with the transcripts anyway – the introduction to a volume should inform you. Additionally, entries such as 'a man found drowned in the river', 'a poor woman found dead in the snow' are familiar enough to most searchers to suggest that many people's burials had to be recorded anonymously.

There were, however, certain categories for whom a normal Anglican funeral service was and still is forbidden by Canon 68, confirmed by statute under Charles II. Registration and burial were both affected. Those who had not been baptised by anyone (not only the Anglican Church) could not receive Christian, i.e. Anglican burial, and evidence suggests that the number in this category increased into the eighteenth century. The minister of St James's, Manchester, apologised in his register for having buried William Hulme, a three-week-old child from Salford, on 1 November 1853 because he had not realised that the child had not been baptised. The normally humane Parson Woodforde went further, recording on 1 February 1788:

Mr Carter of Ringland sent me a Note this Morn' before breakfast, to desire my sentiments on a particular Question relating to the tolling of a Bell for a Child that died without being baptised at its decease, at any time from thence to its being interred and at the putting of it into the ground. I sent an Answer back to Mr Carter, that as the Funeral Service could not be read over it, the tolling of the Bell at any time to be inadmissable.

Until the eighteenth century the word 'Chrisome' was used to denote a very young child being buried, normally unbaptised.

Baptist children, who were not baptised until the age of fifteen, were particularly affected, though their parents disliked the idea of consecrated ground anyway. It was high Anglican feeling against the sect which led to the notorious Akenham burial case of 1878 (see Fletcher, 1974). According to the 1801 census returns, however, most Baptists did bury their dead in the parish graveyard.

It sometimes comes as a surprise to learn that the Church of England used to excommunicate – and quite frequently, at that – for what seem to us today trivial offences. But excommunicate she did, and exacted a penance or collected a fee for the excommunication to be lifted. Excommunication could also be accompanied by up to six months in jail. Although it had become obsolete by the twentieth century, the power still rests with the bishop's consistory court. Anyone who had died excommunicated for some 'grievous and notorious' crime, if no one was prepared to testify that he or she had repented before death, was deprived of a normal Anglican burial. However, from 1745, the relatives of an excommunicant could compel burial in a churchyard, and a modified form of service was available following the Burial Laws Amendment Act of 1880. Even before that date, however, any sympathetic clergyman could absolve the deceased and subsequently read the normal funeral service anyway. Canon 70 of 1603 had directed that all burials within the parish should be entered in the register, but the Anglican clergy have a reputation for independence of action in such matters.

Another category not entitled to a burial service was those who, being sane, had nevertheless killed themselves as judged by a coroner's jury (see *FTM* 20.1 Nov 03; *FHM* 136 Nov 06). Such unfortunates could be buried in an unconsecrated part of 'God's acre' only from 1823. Before that, they were buried in the public highway, often at crossroads, with a stake through the heart, or in the grounds of the prison concerned. ('That fool's body,' says Heathcliffe of the hated Hindley Earnshaw in *Wuthering Heights*, 'should be buried at the crossroads, without ceremony of any kind.') Ralph Josselin records on 11 April 1656, 'James Parnel the father of the Quakers in these parts, having undertaken to fast 40. dayes and nights, was [on the 10th] in the morning found dead, he was by the Jury found guilty of his own death, and buried in the Castle yard.' The consequences of such a verdict could be avoided by certain social classes. In a cynical intervention following Ophelia's death by drowning in *Hamlet*, one clown observes, 'If this had not been a Gentlewoman, shee should have been buried out of Christian Buriall.'

In 1961 suicide ceased to be a criminal offence, but ecclesiastical law remains unchanged. Only the goodwill of the clergy, plus the fact that the corpse has probably been buried long before the jury brings in its verdict, gives a *felo de se* a normal burial. (Inquests were often held very quickly after death until earlier last century, however.) Francis Kilvert wrote in his diary for 30 September 1871 of Mary Pugh, who had drowned herself in the river, 'It was surmised that she would be buried as a suicide without any service on the "backside of the Church", but she was buried by Mr Venables with the usual ceremony.' Good for him!

In the sixteenth century and perhaps in the early seventeenth certain other persons could also be excluded – heretics, anyone not receiving holy sacrament at least at Easter, and anyone killed in a duel, tilt or tournament. Executed criminals were also so deprived, and after 1861 murderers had to be buried within the prison walls if space was available. See Macnamara (1881, p. 65), however, for another view on this rule. Executed criminals feature in the paysite www.murderfile. net.

It is to be hoped that all such persons were few in number, but that is no consolation to the genealogist whose ancestor was a rare exception. Fortunately, except in the case of the unbaptised, the offence often gave rise to documents which can provide more interesting information about the individual concerned than those which are available for more law-abiding mortals. (In the same way, the court cases of those refusing to complete their census form nowadays will probably be more interesting than the census returns themselves!) For example, excommunications will be in the proceedings of the ecclesiastical courts, which are normally in diocesan record offices. The cases were often started in the churchwardens' papers, for the churchwardens had a duty to 'present' to the archdeacon or bishop those whom they suspected of having broken Church law. Lists of such cases sometimes appear in churchwardens' accounts; the courts themselves kept the presentments. Summonses were drawn up in citation books, and the cases were then heard. They could involve immorality, marriage, probate, church finance, unlicensed teachers, unlicensed doctors (without a medical degree) and midwives – a wide variety of mortal fallibility. The record of any subsequent punishment, whether it was excommunication, a fine or penance, will be found in the 'correction books' or Comperta and Detecta (see, e.g., Hair, 1972; Tarver, 1995; Chapman, 1992; *FTM* 15.9 Jul 99). Slowly the growth of population, urbanisation and Nonconformity reduced the powers of these Church courts (whose records have been centralised to diocesan record offices since 1962). Divorce, matrimony and probate cases were lost to the civil courts in the 1850s, bigamy in 1861 and incest in 1908, but I believe that a Church court could still try a case of adultery, if it so chose! Most readers will not be surprised to learn that Parliament made a husband's adultery a matrimonial offence only in 1857 – adultery by a wife had always been one! Adultery with a wife's sister was one of the few grounds for a woman to obtain a divorce until 1923, when the grounds were applied equally to men and women for the first time.

Burials often went unrecorded during epidemics, and indeed a diseased body could be refused admission to the church. In this context it should be remembered that institutions such as hospitals and workhouses sometimes had their own graveyard and that their burials may not be entered in the local parish register. You may find that all paupers and unidentified bodies went to one town graveyard rather than being sent at random round those available. Shipwrecked bodies were buried in the churchyard nearest to where they had been cast ashore.

It does seem natural that the normal obsequies would be cut short or cut out and, if the clergyman himself were ill, that even the burial of the healthy might go unrecorded. In Lancashire in 1623, for example, the registers of Brindle, Croston and Garstang were not written, and the clerk of Stalmine acknowledged that forty had been buried 'the tyme that I were sick'. Pepys complained that that the plague was 'making us more cruel to one another than we are to dogs' (22 August 1665). (I envy the owner of the car number plate ILL 1665, seen outside a hospital.)

There were other causes of underregistration of burials. Large numbers died abroad (see below), mostly soldiers and sailors rather than travellers. Some people gave their body for medical research, though the corpse had to be disposed of within two years. (Nowadays, there is no legal limit on the length of time a donated body can be used by the receiving institution, although in practice a body is usually kept from one to three years. The donor can restrict the time on the consent form.) Others have felt a primitive urge to be buried at sea. John Evelyn wrote on 12 April 1692 that his brother-in-law Glanville had

> died in the 84th year of his age, and will'd his body to be wrapp'e in lead and carried downe to Greenwich, put on board a-ship and buried in the sea betweene Dover and Calais, about the Goodwin Sands, which was don on the Tuesday or Wednesday after. This occasioned much discourse, he having no relation at all to the sea.

Nowadays any burial in an Anglican graveyard, even the scattering of ashes, will be recorded, whether there has been a funeral service or not, but formerly some registers seem to have been a record of funerals rather than of burials. The Abstract of Parish Register Returns, 1801, which was associated with the first census, briefly analysed the causes of deficiencies in burial registers. The list of causes includes interment without ceremony, and London, Bristol and Newcastle-upon-Tyne are singled out as particularly faulty in this respect. Writing in 1829, J. S. Burn said that more unregistered burials took place in the unconsecrated burial ground called Ballast Hills in Newcastle than in all the local churches and chapels put together, simply because the poor could not afford the burial fees. Other burials took place in non-Anglican graveyards (see pp. 249–50).

Burial not in England or Wales: evidence of emigration
It is much easier to discover evidence of the fact of emigration of named individuals in the country to which they travelled, where most documentary sources, research and publications will be found. The last, of course, may be in the larger libraries in the United Kingdom, and at the Society of Genealogists. The National Archives houses a large collection of documents relating to emigrants of all kinds, well listed by Kershaw (2002) who also has useful lists of relevant archives overseas. For the United States see Smith (1976), Hotten (1874) and Coldham (1989, 1992). On emigration generally, see *GM* 16.4, *Family History* Aug and Nov 1982, *FTM* 16.10 Aug 00 and 16.12 Oct 00, and Saul (1995).

The evidence for transported convicts has survived more completely than for the free emigrants who were about a hundred times more numerous before the end of the nineteenth century. Convicts were sent to America until 1776, and to Australia from 1787 to 1868, with some to South Africa between these periods. There is a microfiche index of 80,000 convicts transported to New South Wales (1788–1842), and a microfiche copy of the convict indents themselves, normally showing date of arrival, age, native place, marital status, occupation, offence, date of trial, sentence, and sometimes wife and children. (See *Anc* 38 Oct 05 for the transportation of children to Australia.) Transportation to the colonies was generally used as an alternative to the death penalty for 60,000 offenders from 1615 to 1776 (to America) and for 160,000 to Australia (1787–1868). For the former, see *NALD* 16, Coldham (2005), *Anc* 45 May 06 and www.immigrantservants. com for 1607–1820; for the latter, see *NALD* 17, www.ancestry.co.uk and www.slg.gld.gov.au/info/fh/convicts. Cases, with sentence, can be found in quarter sessions papers in city or county record offices or assize records in the National Archives (see Records Information Leaflet 26). Only a minority of men, but most women, so sentenced actually went abroad. Criminal registers and transportation registers are also in the National Archives (see Records Information Leaflet 94; *FTM* 2.3 Mar 86; Kershaw 2002). The latter should be consulted first if you know that the individual was transported but not the area from which he came. Over 100,000 Old Bailey trial transcripts, 1674–1834, can be seen at www.oldbaileyonline.org.

The free emigrants included those who were lured out of Britain – two-thirds departing from Liverpool – by the promise of full bellies, gold, freedom of worship or a host of other attractions. Many were encouraged to leave because the colonies were desperate for labour, and because of the belief, which filtered into government circles once Napoleon had been beaten, that the British Isles were overcrowded. Thus the state, and also local authorities, on whom the burden of the relief of unemployment and pauperism fell, began to offer assisted passages. Nearer home, even as early as the seventeenth century, people in financial difficulties were 'emigrating' to the Isle of Man, where the cost of living was lower and they could not be prosecuted for debts or misdemeanours in England and Wales (Stout's diary, p. 86). In May 1812 Ellen Weeton found that the island 'literally swarms with English vagabonds'.

For normal emigrants the evidence is thin and scattered. Indeed, for the period 1776 to 1889, most passenger lists have not survived. Passport registers, in the National Archives, show name and date of issue, and are relatively full only after 1914 when they became compulsory – see *NALD* 60. Applications can be seen at the commercial sites www.findmypast.com, and (1851–1903) www.nationalarchivist. com. There is a thirty-year access rule, and the application forms, showing address and intended destination, are destroyed after only eleven years. There is sometimes a record of a farewell service in church, and especially chapel, minute books, and a note concerning emigration in the list of church members. My favourite among these is from Tintwistle in 1858: 'Samuel Harrison, to New Zealand; Mrs Samuel Harrison, to the USA.' Men would quite frequently go some years ahead of their wives, assisted in some countries by inter-union agreements encouraging international migration.

Records of passage assisted by HM government are found in the National Archives, the earliest being 1815. Poor Law Unions were allowed to support pauper emigration from the rates after 1834, including children under sixteen from 1850. (For an account of those going to South Africa, see *FTM* 23.9 Jul 07 and 23.10 Aug 07.) Counties varied widely in the number of parishes involved in this assistance, which could be as high as half the average poor rate (see *GM* 20.11; above, p. 246). Others had a passage assisted by the lord of the manor, trade unions, or voluntary societies such as Dr Barnardo's. *FTM* 2.6 Sep 86 has an article about child emigration to Canada, indicating sources of information. For child emigration, see Richards (2004).

Published passenger lists are summarised by FitzHugh & Lumas (1998, under 'Emigration'); see also *NALD* 56. Passenger lists are rare before 1800, and most before 1890 have been destroyed. They are in the National Archives, complete from 1890 to December 1960, arranged by port and year, name, age, occupation and approximate address, and are now on line.

Finally, some records survived in this country even once the individuals had emigrated. There are many published directories, registers and military service lists which can help to trace the period when your ancestors are known to have been living abroad. The National Archives has censuses taken in Australia in the first half of the nineteenth century. Some Anglican registers of parishes abroad are in the Guildhall Library (see Harvey, 1992; Yeo, 1995). India (which included Pakistan and Bangladesh until 1947) has a particularly good set of sources which can be consulted at the India Office library in London. If an emigrant disposed of property in England or Wales, the will should have been proved in the PCC or PCY (see p. 254 and Coldham, 1989) but many are in the diocesan probate registries. See, for example, *GM* 15.11 for 'foreign' probates at Carlisle. Also, keep your eye on who provides data for fairly recent events in the International Genealogical Index. I discovered that one of my ancestors had emigrated only because his details had been entered by a descendant in Idaho Falls.

Entry missed by searcher
See pp. 38, 122.

Misleading clues (see also pp. 215–16)
Bear in mind that some people were not buried, or even married, under exactly the same name as that with which they had been baptised; a few were even buried under their nickname. My favourite is the widow Marrowbone Roeby, buried at Witton in 1769. If you cannot find the burial of a widow, check for a possible remarriage (p. 204) – you may have been searching for the wrong surname. Occasionally, remarriage of the husband did not follow widowerhood or divorce, but separation followed by bigamy, especially before 1857. Conversely, some clerks recorded the burial of 'the wife of' when it should have been 'the widow of'. Lucky discoverers of marriage allegations which state the extent of the period of widowhood of one of the parties should note that its length is frequently exaggerated (see Bonfield, 1986, chapter 5).

Perhaps the first spouse had not died before the remarriage. There was a widespread belief that a separation without contact for seven years dissolved a marriage, and that a second marriage in such circumstances was acceptable. Occasionally, when the first husband showed up, he would 'sell' the wife to her second husband in order to regularise the arrangement (see Menefee, 1981). Appearing in a will does not mean that the person was alive when the will was proved, or (before 1837) that the testator was an adult! Nor does an appearance in a land tax return. As with electoral registers, a nil return often led a clerk to repeat the previous year's entry. (Equally, the non-appearance might be because the family lived in a row of cottages only the first occupier of which is listed, with the phrase 'and others' effectively anonymising your ancestor!)

At Colyton in the late seventeenth and eighteenth centuries, the burial of widows using their maiden name was noted.

Finding more than one possible burial

Additional information will be required in order to identify the right one. Was the subsequent burial of a wife that of a widow? Did the deceased leave a will which might identify him? Is he missing from other wills in which you would expect to find him if he were still alive? In other words, information from a variety of sources should be used in order to identify the correct entry or to eliminate the wrong ones. For example, perhaps the gravestone or grave register will identify the burial you are seeking by linking it with other members of the same family, or with a known address.

Occasionally, the funeral service may have been recorded in one church (or even denomination) and the burial in another. Methodist ministers, for example, regularly conducted services in chapels other than their own.

Non-Anglican burial

If a systematic search of the Anglican burials proves fruitless, it is worth bearing in mind that other denominations have had burial grounds for centuries, the oldest probably being those of the Roman Catholics and Quakers. The law, however, gave everyone the right to be buried in their local Anglican graveyard, though some, as we have seen, had to be buried in unconsecrated ground. The Burial Laws Amendment Act of 1880 even legalised Catholic or any other Christian rites in the Anglican graveyard, conditional upon adequate notice to the incumbent before and after the event. You can find earlier examples, however; the burial of John McCarney at Salford in 1814, had the unfortunate epithet, 'N.B. Being a Catholic the Minister of the Chapel did not attend.' Such burials should be entered in the register, and the name of the person giving the incumbent notice of burial will appear in the column for the officiating minister. However, there has never been any compulsion to be buried in the parish churchyard. Welsh parishes in particular have large Nonconformist as well as 'Established' graveyards. For any one area a contemporary directory or the archivist in the city or county record office should be consulted for advice about which non-parochial burial grounds existed at particular periods, and which have registers extant. Much that has been written about non-parochial baptismal registers (pp. 135–8) also applies to burials, though not all chapels conducting baptisms had graveyards. Legislation which makes the Anglican records so useful did not normally apply to other denominations. There are no bishops' transcripts, for example, and the entries are not always on standard forms.

Non-parochial burial registers vary widely in the amount of detail they provide. The fullest are probably those of the Quakers, which give name, description, abode, date and place of death and burial, and the age of the deceased (see Milligan & Thomas, 1999). Cause of death was not always copied into the Society of Friends' transcripts. Records held by the Salvation Army (Promotion to Glory registers) are also good, though they are not kept centrally.

In my experience, the least conscientious have been the Methodists. Their burial registers are often non-existent, even when they had their own burial ground, and even after the Registration of Burials

Act of 1864, which compelled them not only to keep such registers but also to send copies to the Anglican registrars. I do not know why this should be, but one Methodist archivist I have approached on the subject suggested that many of the chapels were small, and closed down early, leading to the registers being abandoned. While this may be true of some, it by no means explains all the missing registers. Even when they do survive, Nonconformist burial registers are often incomplete. It is still common for services to be conducted by visiting ministers who, if the chapel safe is locked at the time, do not always remember to enter the interment later. There is also a suspicion that Methodist registers were considered to be the property of the minister, a phenomenon evident in the United States also. Methodists have always buried non-Methodists, if requested to do so, by the way (see FHM 103 Apr 04).

The quality of the other non-parochial burial registers lie on a spectrum between the Quakers and the Methodists. Each sect has its own peculiar, often convoluted, history, which should be examined in *The National Index of Parish Registers* (Steel, 1968, II). On the whole, Nonconformist burial grounds are rare before the end of the seventeenth century, and it has been estimated that even in Manchester in the 1770s, under 5 per cent of all burials were in Dissenters' graveyards. The proportion increased in the nineteenth century, however, especially as their burial fees were normally lower than those of the Church of England. By 1831 almost 75 per cent of all Manchester burials were in non-parochial graveyards, a figure which included many Anglicans.

Some Nonconformists have been drawn to Nonconformity in burial. The diary of Richard Kay, a doctor, of Bury, records the death of his

good and pious Uncle John Kay late of Gooseford who exchanged this world for a better October 6 1734 in the 47th year of his age; he never was married; not many years before he died he built a handsome House at Gooseford, he left it well furnished and well fited with good and useful Conveniences, and according to his Desire was buried in his Garden ten Foot deep in a square plot of Ground which it seem'd he had designed for that purpose.

Registers not accessible: alternative sources

Probate before 11 January 1858

The proving of a will before 1858 was the prerogative of the Church of England, and it is because there were so many courts (well over 300) carrying out this function that the location of earlier wills can be a complicated undertaking. Camp (1974), Gibson (1974), Gibson & Langston (2002) and Grannum & Taylor (2004) are the basic guides for finding them, and there is on line help via www.familysearch.org. Sooner or later, every genealogist should consult one or other of these books; additionally, a very full account of the law of wills prior to the nineteenth century is in Burn (1824, IV), and a study of how the courts operated is in Tarver (1995).

The tone of most of the early wills is very religious. They begin with the phrase 'In the name of God, Amen, I, A. B., of the parish of C., in the county of D ...'. The occupation is normally given, then some observations on the future of the deceased's soul and the disposal of the mortal remains. The testator claims to be sane, otherwise the will would have been invalid, but very often admits to illness (see *Local Population Studies* 40). Finally, at length, the will indicates how the worldly goods ('personalty') are to be distributed among the living. Children, grandchildren, other relatives and even servants are often named. A common technique was to divide the estate into three parts, giving one to the widow and one to the children. The final third, which the testator normally and disconcertingly gives to himself to distribute how he or she wishes, paid any debts and the funeral expenses. This tripartite division of the estate lasted in the province of York until 1693, in Wales until 1696 and in London until 1726. Any remainder would be redistributed. Wills were normally made shortly before the end – as Fielding says, 'few men think of death till they are in its jaws' (*Tom Jones*, Book V, chapter v) – whereas nowadays the average interval between writing a will and death is more like seven years. Always check the date of the will as well as the date of probate – children might have been born in the interval.

Most wills were proved by an archdeacon of the diocese in which the deceased had lived and died. This was certainly the normal court to which executors were expected to turn, though there were many areas where the bishop himself undertook probate. According to Richard Burn, chancellor of the diocese of Carlisle, 'Archdeacons as such have no power to grant probate; but they do not do it as archdeacons, but by a prescriptive right' (1824, IV, p. 231). To the genealogist the right is less important than the fact. Richmond in Yorkshire, a neighbouring archdeaconry to Burn's own diocese, enjoyed a jurisdiction extending over four counties.

The wills themselves are now normally to be found in the diocesan record office, or the National Library of Wales, and where this is combined with a city or county record office they can be consulted free of charge. All the offices with which I have had contact are prepared to send photocopies of specified wills for a relatively modest but perhaps minimum charge. When sending for photocopies, you should be as explicit as possible about what you want – for example, indicate whether you want only the will copied, or only the inventory (see p. 258), or all the associated documentation. Dioceses do not have the same geographical boundaries as counties, of course, and that is one of the reasons why the reference books quoted above are so useful – they answer the basic question about the location of wills left by testators in county areas as well as in dioceses. Wills of Anglican clerics were sometimes processed separately – for example in York.

How do you discover whether any of your ancestors left a will? The first step is to locate indexes to the wills. You will normally find that an index of testators, giving the name and date, perhaps also with the occupation, residence and date of probate, is available at the record office concerned. Many have been printed. Details of available indexes are to be found in Camp (1974) and Gibson & Langston (2002), but more have been printed since those books appeared.

The indexes are usually in alphabetical order of surname within groups of years. There is no specific starting date nationally, and many areas have wills surviving from as far back as the Middle Ages, before parish registers began (see below). Most testators were men or widows. Until 1882 married women could make a will only with the consent of their husband, sometimes following a formal agreement or settlement at the time of marriage, or a deed of separation upon the breakdown of a marriage. Subsequent marriage invalidated the will of a spinster or widow, though, if it was made since 1925, not if the future husband is named therein. It was normal, before the nineteenth century, for a testator to mention all his children, or all except the eldest son (who might have received his inheritance already) and often grandchildren. In consequence, it is possible to use wills to trace generations of a family without having to use the parish register. A study of 350 wills left between 1500 and 1800 found that an average of ten persons were mentioned in each, most of whom would be relatives.

The index may refer to specific types of document associated with probate – tuition bonds, or inventories for example (see pp. 258–9).

'Nunc.' or nuncupative wills (sometimes called 'verbal' wills) were unsigned declarations before witnesses. They were especially prone to challenge in the Church courts. In 1837 they were made invalid for all except those on active military service. John Radcliffe of Manchester shouted his will across the moat surrounding his house as he and most of his family were dying during the outbreak of plague in 1645. 'Active military service' has been interpreted liberally by the courts; in 1981 the declaration of a soldier dying in Northern Ireland was accepted as valid.

Access to the index is only the first step. Which of the many testators bearing your surname were your ancestors? There is no simple answer. Sometimes you will be looking for the will of a man whose name and date of death you already know. Sometimes you know the name but not the year he died, so that the index will be the first indication to the latter. Sometimes you will know only the surname and probable place of residence. For example, if you have not been able to find a baptism, you may be searching for possible parents, hoping to find mention of a son or daughter-in-law which may confirm another generation for you. In that case, of course, you must search all the wills left by anyone of that surname within as wide a radius as possible.

In each of the above cases you are strongly recommended to look not only at the most obvious candidate among the list of surviving wills but also at any others left by testators with the same surname in that or adjoining parishes, or even further afield in the case of a rare surname. It is possible to build up an extensive network of relationships when the genealogical information has been extracted from the wills and reconstituted into family groups. In a few enviable areas, even indexes of beneficiaries are being compiled!

If you have any difficulty with the terminology of probate records, there is a useful glossary and abbreviation list in Gardner & Smith (1956, II, pp. 28–35) and Gibson & Langston (2002).

Failure to find a probate record before 1858
There are several reasons why genealogists may fail to find a will which they are seeking. Some we have encountered already, but others arise from the peculiar nature of wills and the way in which they have been proved and indexed. More than anything else, it should be remembered that, although a surprisingly large number of people left wills, most did not do so. Gibson estimates that, on average, each household left a will which was proved in court just once every 150 years. (See Bonfield, 1986, chapter 6 for more recent studies.) The following sections suggest reasons why a will which was made may now be difficult to

trace; later sections describe other probate documents which may be available if the will cannot be found.

Wills proved by another jurisdiction. The law on the probate of wills before 1858 was somewhat complicated, and although probate by archdeacon or bishop was the norm, circumstances might dictate that another type of court was used. Furthermore, whatever the law said was often ignored in practice, especially if the executors or next of kin lived in a diocese different from that of the deceased. Executors could certainly choose to go to a higher court than necessary, and sometimes had to if for some reason the lower one was closed.

If the testator held property in more than one diocese, or even lived in one but died in another, the will should have been proved by an archbishop. If part of an overseas estate is found in England and Wales, a copy of the will should be found among the Limited Probate Books or Limited Administration Books in the Prerogative Court of Canterbury, most of which date from the nineteenth century. In most northern counties of England the archbishop would be the Archbishop of York, unless the property was partly in a diocese coming under the Archbishop of Canterbury, whose court had the superior jurisdiction. These series of wills are known by the names of the courts themselves – the Prerogative Courts of Canterbury (PCC) and York (PCY). The former, once known as 'Doctors' Commons', had the sole right of proving wills from 1653 to 1660, when there were no bishops. Some wills, which one would normally expect to have been proved by a southern court, are to be found in the PCY, for no obvious reason. PCC wills are now at Kew, and can be seen indexed (1384 to 1858) at www.documentsonline.nationalarchives.gov.uk, from which copies may be bought. The documents themselves are at PROB 10, which is microfilmed, with copies at PROB 11. See *FTM* 20.9 Jul 04 for these and the records of other London courts.

Welsh wills are indexed at www.a2a.org.uk. Click on National Library of Wales Collection Services, and Probate. They are arranged by diocese and by different periods.

For all their pride of place in the genealogical textbooks, and their clear advantage in offering to most executors a more remote, and therefore more confidential, jurisdiction, I have always been disappointed by the PCC wills, concluding in my more cynical moments that they were made largely by the rich, by south-easterners and by sailors! Be careful about asking for the printed PCC indexes in your library – they can be listed either under the Index Library or under the British Record Society, and have different volume numbers in each case.

In the diocese of Chester a will could be proved by an inferior court if the value of the property was under £40. Such wills, just as valuable genealogically, are still stored separately, and are listed separately in some of the printed indexes. Tell the archivist that the will you are applying to see is 'Infra' in that case.

If the testator lived and died in a 'peculiar' jurisdiction, the will would be proved by a small local court with powers relatively independent of the bishop. Anyone having property inside and outside the peculiar, however, had to go to the relevant archbishop's court.

According to Canon 126, those below the level of bishop who claimed to be able to prove wills should have sent copies every year to the diocesan registry, on pain of having their prerogative suspended; but it is evident that many did not do so.

Wills not proved. Until the Court of Probate Act of 1857 wills containing the disposition only of land, i.e. not goods, were not subject to ecclesiastical or to any other probate and have not normally survived, except among family papers. Before 1926 real property was supposed to pass to the rightful heir, and so did not appear in the 'will' itself. Some wills were not proved because they were invalid or because the executors renounced their duties.

Wills poorly indexed. Much of what has been written about the problems of indexing (pp. 34–5) applies to wills. Before the spelling of most surnames was standardised in the early nineteenth century these problems are acute, so it is important to check that the indexes are arranged either phonetically, collecting together all spelling variants which sound the same – the technique used by the International Genealogical Index for surnames – or alphabetically, with an efficient cross-referencing system so that all variants can be consulted. You should have little trouble with the former type, but not all cross-referencing is as good as it might be.

Wills proved late. If the indexes which you are using are arranged by groups of years, remember to search for two or three years after the date of death. Although most wills were proved within a few months (occasionally in less than the modern seven-day limit), there was sometimes a long delay, and the wills are listed by date of probate, not by the date of the death. There are also cases of second probate, caused, for example, by the death or late renunciation of an executor. Second probate in a diocesan court can follow an initial grant of probate in the PCC or PCY. The will of a man leaving a life interest to his surviving wife might have been proved decades later, when she died. Disputed cases may be followed in the consistory court papers in the relevant diocesan record office; these papers are normally indexed, and can be extremely useful to the genealogist.

Lost wills. There can be no doubt that, over the centuries, wills have been subject to the ravages of time as much as other documents, for they have not only been moved from one part of the country to another but also stored in sometimes unsuitable conditions. Wills left by anyone whose surname began with A, B, C, D, E or F in Cheshire or south Lancashire in 1670, for example, have rotted away through being stored in a damp attic. Others have been eaten by rats, destroyed by bacteria or lost in transit. Early wills from the south-west of England in the probate registry at Exeter were destroyed by enemy action in 1942, though many have been replaced by the estate duty copies for 1812–57 (see below, and *GM* 16.6.)

Up to 1858 there is some hope that you will find abstracts of the missing wills in the bishop's Probate Act books, or even copies of the wills themselves in his enrolment books, sometimes known as the Bishop's Register. (As such, of course, they will be prone to human error in copying.) The Act Book abstracts normally include the name, marital status, occupation and names of executors, and can occasionally supply information additional to that contained in the original will. You should consult the diocesan archivist for advice about the years for which the Act Books are available. Ask whether there are also registered copies of wills, made for consultation.

The current debate about the extent, and even the existence, of inheritance tax has been with us for over two hundred years! To pay for the war against Napoleon the Legacy Duty Act was introduced in 1796, changed in 1805, and abolished (like income tax) at the end of the war. However, it was immediately replaced by the Stamp Act (1815–53) and the Succession Duty Act (1853–94), and finally by the Finance Act of 1894 which introduced the novel idea that the tax was payable by *anyone who inherited*, not only relatives of the deceased.

Abstracts of all British wills subject to death duty proved between 1796 and 1903 can be found in the National Archives. Some are more abstracted than others! They are indexed by each court separately until 1812, and nationally thereafter. All files from 1903 to 1931 have been destroyed, but in any case only those registers over 125 years old can be seen by the public – yet another illogicality within our system of preserving and giving access to records. You can see an original will, and even buy a photocopy of it, but you cannot see the summary! These estate duty registers in the National Archives, often the easiest way to find a will in the nineteenth century, are described in *FTM* 17.12 Oct 01, and *GM* 15.11 and 20.8; see also *NALD* 57, 58, *NALL* 45, Herber (2005), and Grannum & Taylor (2004). As well as including the names of the legatees, the registers can provide additional information on events subsequent to probate, including disputes, and even the names of children if these have not appeared in the will itself. The Estate Duty registers are indexed on microfilm at Kew, and in the SoG's library, and are scheduled to be available on line in 2010. They are also available on the paysite www.nationalarchivist.com.

Mark Herber calculates that a quarter of all wills and admons (administration documents) from 1796 to 1805, three-quarters from 1805 to 1815, and almost all thereafter are recorded in the Estate Duty Registers. You should be able to find, at minimum, the date of the will, the date of death, the name of the executor, and the amount of duty payable.

See also *FTM* 16.7 May 00 for Bank of England will extracts, 1717–1845, summarising any interest in government stock mentioned in a will. They are available at the paysite www.origins.net.

Letters of administration (see also p. 232)

It is also possible that, even if there is no will, and occasionally even when there is one, there is a grant of administration for the estate of the deceased. Circumstances in which such a grant would be made were: intestacy; if all the named executors renounced their duty; if all the executors were under twenty-one; if the deceased had been excommunicated; and if the deceased had died in debt and his creditors were granted the administration. Oddly enough, although the grant was made by the Church of England, the bishop was in this case acting as an officer of the civil law. Death duty was payable on these estates however, so beneficiaries (sometimes with a record of their deaths) can be found in registers in the National Archives.

Sometimes you will find these 'admon bonds' indexed with the main series of wills in that jurisdiction, but not always. They can be in separate sections, and even, in the case of the PCC indexes, in separate printed volumes. In some areas there are Administration Act Books and administration bonds signed by the administrators when promising to carry out their duties faithfully.

As noted above, the bonds often provide little genealogical material, but more can sometimes be obtained by looking at the 'fiat' at the foot of the standard form, or the clerk's note on the reverse side. Unfortunately, these may be in Latin.

Miscellaneous probate records

There exist among church records a surprisingly large number of other documents associated with the processes of probate which can provide an alternative route to the information normally found in the wills themselves. Gardner & Smith (1956, II, chapter 5) and Gibson & Langston (2002) contain useful summaries.

Caveat books contain declarations from anyone with an interest in the probate of a will wishing to have their point of view heard by the court before probate was granted. In some areas, these caveats are written into the Act Books. Assignations were granted in cases of maladministration following normal probate of a will or admon. Litigation concerning wills was also heard by the Church courts until 1858; the associated documents are sometimes lodged with the wills, depositions being particularly useful to the genealogist.

Care of orphans or fatherless children was the subject of separate bonds – 'tuition' for girls under twelve and boys under fourteen, and 'curation' for the older ones up to twenty-one. Usually they are kept and indexed with the wills. Guardianship Bonds could be issued for anyone under twenty-one.

Clare Gittins (*Local Historian* 21.2) has called attention to probate accounts as a neglected source, left by executors and administrators, which can be used by a number of different kinds of historian. They survive mostly from cases of disputed wills. There are series for Berkshire, Hertfordshire, Kent, Lincolnshire, Oxfordshire, Somerset and West Sussex. For the genealogist they are particularly useful in cases of intestacy, when letters of administration normally provide little detail of family (see Spufford, 1999).

Disputes, or testamentary suits, could be heard in episcopal courts, by the Court of Arches or on appeal by the Court of Delegates, the result being called a 'sentence'. A copy of the will is normally included in the papers. Testamentary cause papers can yield considerable information not only about the disputes themselves but also about family relations which are not always evident from normal probate records. See Tarver (1995) for detail.

When a named executor or administrator decided to reject that honour, a Deed of Renunciation was taken out, which gave where appropriate the relationship between the new administrator and the deceased.

Perhaps the assessment of wealth best known to the genealogist is the inventory, which was very common in the sixteenth and seventeenth centuries but became much rarer after the middle of the eighteenth. (It has been suggested that it was because courts were running out of storage space, though it is hard to imagine how that could affect the whole country at the same time.) Few inventories survive after 1782, but an inventory and indeed an account of the administration of an estate may still be ordered nowadays by a court of probate. It was the duty of an executor to list 'all the goods, chattels, wares, merchandises, as well moveable as not moveable whatsoever, that were of the said person so deceased' (Burn, 1824, IV, p. 294a, where the appropriate form and content of the inventory are described at length). Even debts, owing to and owed by the deceased, should have been included, but not real estate. The court granting probate would do so on condition that such an inventory was made in the presence of the legatees or other competent persons. The Prerogative Court of Canterbury even required the inventory to have been drawn up before the application for probate. Each item was separately valued at the price at which at the time it might have been sold, though the valuation was not binding on the subsequent distribution of the estate. Totals, however, are sometimes incorrect, especially when they involved the addition of sums expressed in roman numerals! See *Local Historian* 14.4, 16.3–4, and *FHM* 117 May 05.

The inventories themselves had to be submitted to the ecclesiastical court and are normally stored and indexed with the relevant wills. The PCC inventories, however, are indexed separately and are at Kew.

The names of many implements and household goods from former times have now fallen out of use. A glossary of many of these archaic terms is given in West (1982) and Milward (1996). The full *Oxford dictionary* is also very helpful in identifying them and their meaning.

Records of the College of Arms (see pp. 147–9)
Death features in heraldry in three main ways. A first clue to the armigerous status of an individual may come with a reference in the probate records – a seal, for example. The death of an armigerous wife results in the husband reverting to the use of his own coat of arms (unless she was an heiress), though a widow retains the right to bear the combined coat. She reverts to her own paternal coat upon divorce.

Thirdly, the display of the coat of arms of a deceased armiger, most commonly in churches, is on a diamond-shaped 'hatchment', the colour of which denotes the sex and marital status of the deceased and even whether s/he had married more than once. A series of county hatchments is being published by Phillimore.

Miscellaneous records

Many of the records listed earlier in Chapters II and IV may be of assistance if the burial register is not available (see especially pp. 54–71, 217–37). In addition to documents concerning graves and probate, several of the alternative sources for baptismal registers (pp. 138–51) also apply to burials.

Following the Burial in Woollen Acts of 1666–80, some parishes kept copies of burials in the churchwardens' accounts, or in a separate affidavit volume. Reference to this affidavit, which had to be signed by a magistrate (or clergyman if no JP was available), often occurs in the normal parish register. Salford Sacred Trinity, for example, gives the dates issued for each burial from 1736 to 1764. For a photograph of one from Bristol, see *FTM* 23.11 Sep 07. Although the Act remained in force until 1814, it fell into disuse between 1750 and 1780, and never applied to plague victims.

These accounts can refer to burials when a fee was paid to the churchwardens, and can contain more information than the parish register entry, with the additional advantage that they may tell you whereabouts in the graveyard the body was buried. The original affidavits themselves have occasionally survived. Burial dues books, however, may be found even when the burial register is missing, as at All Saints Poplar in London, 1824–38 (*FTM* 7.4 Feb 91). Reference to the fees can also be found in earlier churchwardens' accounts, which have recently enabled the Lancashire Parish Register Society to supplement the earliest register for Prescot with burials from 1521 to 1537 and from 1549 to 1560, for example.

Any life interest in money results in documents which may be exploited by genealogists – even insurance. Tontines, introduced in England and Wales in the 1690s, were a form of annuity in which the benefits increased for the survivors among the original investors until the last enjoyed the entire revenue. The records, which include notices of marriage as well as death, are in the National Archives, and there is a Society of Genealogists' guide to them. See Leeson (1968); more have been discovered since then.

Finding a death before 1538

(See pp. 151–4)

There is no regular series recording the death or burial of individuals before 1538, and often the only clue lies in the use of the past tense about a person in written documents, or the disappearance of someone who had hitherto appeared as, for example, a regular witness or juror.

Many of the medieval sources already referred to can be used in order to detect the date of death, or at least the fact of death by a certain date. They include service books, missals and psalters, clerical annotations, heraldic records, fine rolls and Chancery records. Inquisitions *post mortem*, probate and coroners' records are indeed signalled by death itself.

V *Epilogue*

As the Federation of Family History Societies grew in influence it increasingly acted as a pressure group, securing records which are in danger of loss or damage, ensuring that the interests of genealogists in the provinces are considered when decisions are being made which affect them, and arguing for the rationalisation of the present jungle of arrangements for access to our public documents, arrangements which allow me to see my neighbour's will, but deny me a sight of my own birth entry, and charge fees in some parts of the country for access to records which are seen free of charge in others.

Some of the changes referred to in the Preface have come about largely through this sort of public pressure – these are, after all, *our* records – and we should press, individually and collectively, for the maximum amount of access consonant with the proper degree of privacy for individuals who are still alive. Some of those changes were called for in the first edition of this book, but many others await implementation, and it is perhaps appropriate to look forward to the second decade of the twenty-first century to see what other improvements might be gained. Let's see how many of the following have been put into effect by the year 2015.

> The plea for open access to birth, marriage and death entries which are more than a century old, even though it will have to be through the medium of microfilm, is of long standing, and needs to be repeated at frequent intervals.
>
> Should there not be a right of access to the adoption record of a deceased adopted parent or grandparent by a child or grandchild?
>
> An index which linked death entries with place of disposal, superseding the current forms, which are kept for only a five-year minimum, would prove an immense benefit not only to future genealogists but also to the many people who search in vain for the last resting place of relatives who died years ago.
>
> For the period before those forms survive, we should have a concerted effort to persuade funeral directors (as well as solicitors) to deposit their older records in public repositories, if only on a 'permanent loan' basis.

Prospective brides and grooms, as well as genealogists, should not have to pay dearly for the privilege of checking in the national indexes to ascertain whether a divorce has actually taken place. The divorce index should be as free and as accessible as the marriage index.

Family history societies could have a more considered approach to their voluntary indexing projects, a collective strategy to supplement the inevitable (however useful) ad-hocery of the whims of individual members. First in line should be those sources which are so voluminous that an individual researcher stands aghast at the thought of trying to find any one individual among them. Deposited records of coroners, hospitals and workhouses, for example, and anything useful in newspapers, particularly obituaries and death notices, cry out to be indexed. An immense amount can be achieved by working together, as has been well demonstrated in the case of county and national census projects.

Most genealogists, however, do not join a society. They are happy enough to discover their ancestors without the companionship of others engaged in similar activity. Whichever category you are in, I wish you as much pleasure as genealogy has given me over the years. Remember that your family tree can be as boring to others as it is fascinating to you; remember to believe nothing till it has been proved; to consult all the evidence available before deciding what to believe; to seek the advice of local historians as well as that of genealogists; and to acquire your information as soon as possible before fire, damp, bacteria, computer viruses and public servants destroy even more of our records.

Appendices

1. Underregistration in the early years of civil registration
(See pp. 32–4, 213–14)

The size of this problem has been the subject of controversy, probably resulting from the difficulty of knowing who was born, or who had died, without being registered. The two obvious sources of information are defective. The census is too blunt an instrument to provide the date of birth (let alone include those who had died since the last one), while parish registers do not normally include age at baptism. Access to the civil registers, to confirm the identities of those in the GRO indexes, is either impossible or far too costly.

A small piece of research for this book involved the location of parish registers from the old county of Lancashire (from the Lake District in the north to the industrialised areas in or near Manchester and Liverpool) which do include date of birth in the baptismal entries. They are Ashton in Makerfield*, Blackrod, Burtonwood, Heaton Norris*, Heywood, Hollinwood, Holme in Cliviger*, Kirkby*, Manchester St James George Street, Manchester St Mary, Newton in Makerfield, Rainford, Tottington, West Derby, and Winwick. Whereas most printed registers end at 31 December 1837, four (asterisked) provided detail for 1838 also.

All the above were used as a basis to compare death and burial entries, with the addition of Birch in Rusholme†, Cairo St Warrington†, Chorlton cum Hardy, Colton†, Egton cum Newland†, Finsthwaite†, Great Sankey†, Halton, Hawkshead, Hollinfare, Langho, Lowick, Newton Heath, North Meols, Rivington, Salford Holy Trinity†, St Michael's on Wyre, Tatham, and Urswick. In these, however, date of birth is not given in the baptismal registers. Those indicated by † also provided detail from 1838 in addition to those asterisked above.

Statistical results

The basic question was: how many of the baptisms and burials which should have been registered after 1 July 1837 could not be found in the GRO indexes of 1837 and 1838?

1. Of 454 baptisms in 1837, I could not find 197 (43.4%) in the GRO indexes.

2a. Of 139 baptisms in 1837 in the registers asterisked above, I could not find 66 (47.5%) in the GRO indexes.

2b. Of 339 baptisms in 1838 in the registers asterisked above, I could not find 91 (27%) in the GRO indexes.

3a. Of 668 burials in 1837, I could not find 121 (18%) in the GRO indexes.

3b. Of 421 burials in 1838, I could not find 33 (8%) in the GRO indexes.

4a. Of 403 burials in 1837 in the asterisked registers, I could not find 18 (4.5%) in the GRO indexes.

4b. Of 303 burials in 1838 in the asterisked registers, I could not find 21 (7%) in the GRO indexes.

Commentary

a. While there will always be uncertainties about exact figures, there is a marked difference in the efficiency of the new civil registration system in recording births and deaths, *even in the same parishes*. This difference was already acknowledged in the first report of the Registrar General in 1839, an assessment based on extrapolations from the 1831 *Parish Register Abstract*.

b. The figures suggest an improvement in 1838 over the two last quarters of 1837 in both birth and death registration, again already noted by 1839. Nationally, there was an increase of over 25% in the annual number of births registered in the first ten years. The Registrar General in his eighth report put this improvement down to the 'increased efficiency of the Registrars'.

c. There is a difference between areas. Hollinwood was partly in Oldham, Manchester, and Ashton under Lyne – but only those living in the latter two were registered in this period; most residents of Hollinwood were not registered at all.

d. There is a suggestion that only certain categories of people were underregistrated – illegitimate children you might expect, but near Wigan, coalminers were conspicuous by their absence. The thirty-eighth report of the Registrar General pinpointed illegitimate births in large towns as still most likely to be underregistered in the 1870s.

e. The above figures of underregistration are minima. Some of the entries might not have been correctly identified in the GRO indexes, and no account can be taken of the unknown number of children who were neither registered nor baptised.

2. The National Registration Act of 1915

The Registration Act of 1915 (5 & 6 Geo V, c.60, extended and amended in 1918 – not 1917 as in some sources – by 7 & 8 Geo V, c.60) was a consequence of the realisation that the First World War could not be continued without conscription (or even rationing) and was effectively a register of all persons between the ages of 15 and 65 on 15 August that year. What happened to this national register has been the subject of some speculation in the genealogical press.

It was compiled using the organisation of the General Register Office in order to provide both manpower statistics and a means to discriminate between those who could be called up and those whom it was better to direct into civilian jobs. 22 million individuals (identifying five million men of fighting age) had to complete the forms giving name, address, age, marital status, number of dependents (and of what kind), nationality if not British, name and address of employer, whether working for the government, previous military experience and skills. Changes of address, and new immigrants, had to be registered within 28 days. Prisoners, prisoners of war, those 'certified lunatic or defective', and inhabitants of Poor Law institutions and hospitals were exempt. The forms were then kept by local authorities, which furnished central authority with information when requested; small cards were issued to each person confirming registration, giving name, occupation and postal address.

Information was exchanged with other authorities when people moved – there was a 28-day period of grace (reduced to 14 in 1918) to inform the authorities of all changes of address. The GRO kept the list updated during the war, and issued rationing books. The data remained in local hands, however, relatively few returns going into the GRO itself, from which all surviving papers have been transferred into the National Archives under RG28/1–23.

There was a £5 fine for failing to register (plus £1 per day thereafter!), and up to three months' hard labour for anyone employed by the system divulging information from it 'acquired in the course of his employment'.

YEOVIL RURAL DISTRICT COUNCIL

THE

NATIONAL REGISTER.

INSTRUCTIONS TO THE PUBLIC.

Registration Day, Sunday, 15th August.

Under the National Registration Act, 1915, and Regulations of the Local Government Board and Registrar General, a National Register will be formed of all persons, male and female, who, on the 15th day of August, 1915, will be between the ages of 15 and 65 years, except members of the Army and Navy, and Inmates of certain excepted Institutions (Workhouse, Prison, Asylum, Hospital, Internment Camp).

THE REGISTER.

The basis of the Register will be the Registration Form. Each person liable to be registered will be supplied with a Form.

WHAT THE REGISTER WILL CONTAIN.

Every person liable to be registered will be required to state on the Registration Form:— His or her name, address, age, nationality, usual profession or occupation, any other work in which he or she is skilled, and particulars of his or her dependents, and of present employer.

DISTRIBUTION OF FORMS.

During the week from Monday, 9th August, to Saturday, 14th August, an Enumerator will distribute to every house or dwelling in the area allotted to him, a Form for every person liable to be registered, who is likely to be resident in that house or dwelling during Sunday, the 15th August. A separate Form will be provided for each person, a *Blue* Form for Males, and a *White* Form for Females.

FILLING UP THE FORM.

The Form should be filled up by midnight of Sunday, the 15th August, ready for the Enumerator when he calls, in the early part of the next week, to collect them. Great care should be taken to fill up the Form accurately, and according to the instructions on the Form. A Form may be filled up on behalf of a person who is unable to do so, but the person to whom the Form relates should sign it, or if unable to do so, affix his mark.

The Forms when filled in must be carefully preserved and handed to the Official Enumerator when he (or she) calls for them, during the week from the 16th to the 21st August. All Forms should be filled in with ink and not with a pencil. The Form when filled up may be put into an envelope if desired. Should any person be in doubt as to the proper method of filling in the Form, the Official Enumerator will give all possible assistance.

WHAT TO DO IF THE NECESSARY FORMS ARE NOT LEFT AT A HOUSE, OR IF ANY OF THE FORMS LEFT ARE SPOILT OR LOST.

If by Saturday, the 14th August, the necessary number of Forms have not been left at any house or dwelling, or if any of the Forms left have been spoilt or lost, immediate application should be made to the Offices of the Local Authority, as stated below, for the necessary forms, which should be at once filled up and returned to the Local Authority, not later than noon on Wednesday, 18th August.

PENALTY FOR NON-COMPLIANCE WITH THE ACT.

Any person over 18 who wilfully refuses or neglects to supply information, or gives false information, or who makes wilful default in the performance of any of his duties under the Act, is liable to a Fine not exceeding £5 (FIVE POUNDS).

CERTIFICATES OF REGISTRATION.

Every person whose Registration Form has been properly filled in will receive a Certificate of Registration, which should be carefully preserved.

SECRECY.

The Register will be used for Official purposes only. Any breach of secrecy or improper use renders the offender liable to a fine and 3 months' imprisonment.

Registration Forms may be obtained at the residence of the Chairman of the Parish Council or Parish Meeting of the Parish, or from the undersigned, but no Forms will be supplied in this way until Monday, the 16th August, 1915.

MERVYN V. H. RODBER,

Clerk, Union Workhouse, YEOVIL.

CHAS. KNIGHT & CO. LTD, TOOLEY STREET, S.E.

Figure 10. Poster advertising National Registration Instructions to the Public, August 1915.

NATIONAL REGISTRATION ACT, 1915. Form for MALES.

Name:
(Surname first) ...... *Backhouse James* ......

Residence:
(Permanent postal address) } ...... *39 May Street - Barrowford . Nelson ,* ......

(Present address, if away from home) } ......

Age last Birthday. (1.)	If born abroad and not British, state Nationality. (2.)	State whether Single, Married, or Widower. (3.)	How many Children are dependent on you? (4.)		How many other Persons are dependent on you, excluding employees? (5.)		Profession or Occupation (see Note below).* State fully the particular kind of work done, and the material worked or dealt in (if any). (6.)
			Under 15 years.	Over 15 years.	Wholly dependent.	Partially dependent.	
48		*Married*	2	-	*$*	*$* *none*	*Jobbing gardener* 1 *(Summer)* *Lamplighter (Winter)*

Name, Business, and Business Address of Employer. (If not working for an Employer, write " None.") (7.)	Are you employed for or under any Government Department? Say "Yes," or "No," or "Do not know." (8.)	(a.) Are you skilled in any work other than that upon which you are at present employed, and if so, what? (b.) Are you able and willing to undertake such work? (9.)	
		(a.)	(b.)
R. Hutton gardener *Oakfield gardens* *Barrowford* *Barrowford Urban District Council.*	*No*	*No*	

Signature. *James Backhouse* ......

The foregoing particulars must be supplied by all boys and men who are between the ages of 15 and 65 on Sunday, August 15th, 1915. The Form must be filled up ready for collection by **Monday, August 16th,** and may, if desired, be put in an envelope.

The penalty imposed by the Act for wilful refusal or neglect to fill up a Form, or for giving false information, is £5.

* It is of great importance that the occupation should be stated with the utmost care in all cases, but especially by persons having technical knowledge or skill, such as workers in Engineering, Shipbuilding and other metal trades, and by persons engaged in Agriculture. For example, state whether : (1) Engine Fitter, Boiler Maker, Ship Plate Riveter, Angle-Iron Smith and so on ; (2) Shepherd, Horseman, Cowman, Farm Labourer, and so on.

The contents of the Form will be used for official purposes only. It is forbidden under penalty to communicate them for any other purposes

(J 3816.) Wt. 17106—78. 3,000m. 7/15. D & S.   **BERNARD MALLET,** *Registrar-General.*

Figure 11. The National Registration Act of 1915 – an individual registration.

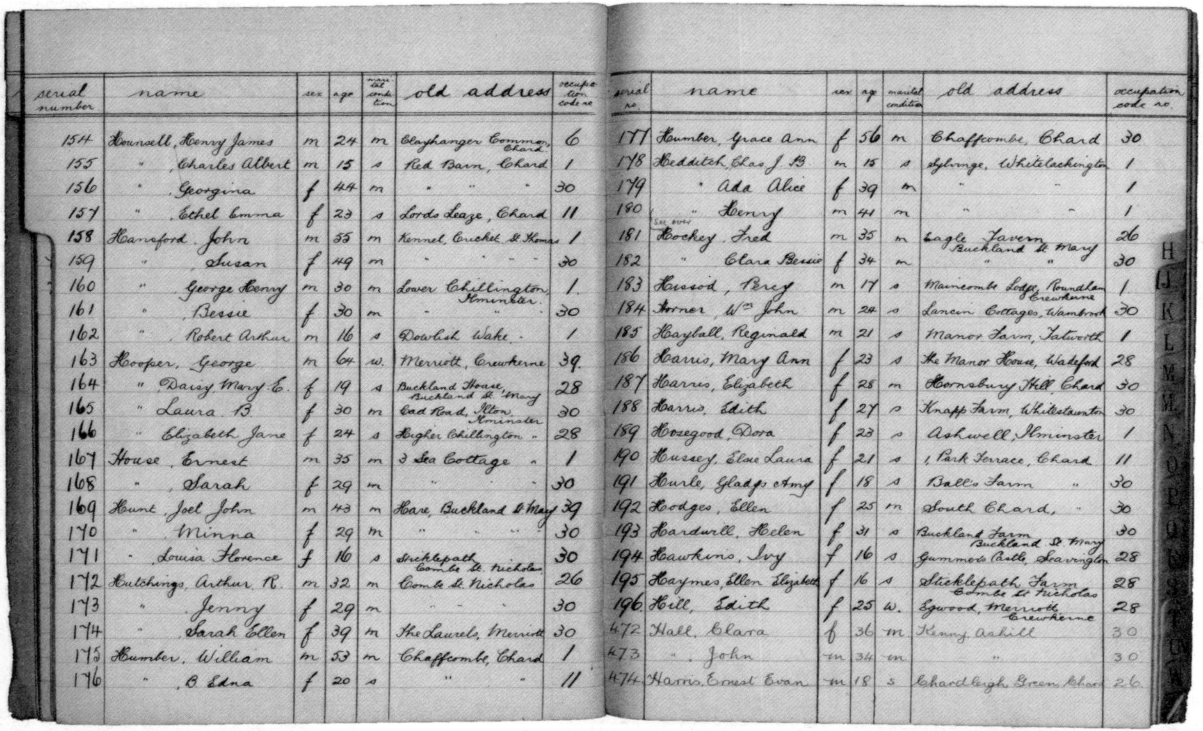

serial number	name	sex	age	marital condition	old address	occupation code no.
154	Hounsell, Henry James	m	24	m	Clayhanger Common, Chard	6
155	" , Charles Albert	m	15	s	Red Barn, Chard	1
156	" , Georgina	f	44	m	" " "	30
157	" , Ethel Emma	f	23	s	Lords Leaze, Chard	11
158	Hansford, John	m	55	m	Kennel, Cricket St. Thomas	1
159	" , Susan	f	49	m	" " "	30
160	" , George Henry	m	30	m	Lower Chillington, Ilminster	1.
161	" , Bessie	f	30	m	" "	30
162	" , Robert Arthur	m	16	s	Dowlish Wake	1
163	Hooper, George	m	64	w.	Merriott, Crewkerne	39.
164	" , Daisy Mary E.	f	19	s	Buckland House, Buckland St. Mary	28
165	" , Laura B.	f	30	m	Cad Road, Ilton, Ilminster	30
166	" , Elizabeth Jane	f	24	s	Higher Chillington "	28
167	House, Ernest	m	35	m	3 Sea Cottage "	1
168	" , Sarah	f	29	m	" "	30
169	Hunt, Joel John	m	43	m	Hare, Buckland St. Mary	39
170	" , Minna	f	29	m	" " "	30
171	" , Louisa Florence	f	16	s	Sticklepath, Combe St. Nicholas	30
172	Hutchings, Arthur R.	m	32	m	Combe St. Nicholas	26
173	" , Jenny	f	29	m	" "	30
174	" , Sarah Ellen	f	39	m	The Laurels, Merriott	30
175	Humber, William	m	53	m	Chaffcombe, Chard	1
176	" , B. Edna	f	20	s	" "	11

serial no.	name	sex	age	marital condition	old address	occupation code no.
177	Humber, Grace Ann	f	56	m	Chaffcombe, Chard	30
178	Hedditch, Chas. J. B.	m	15	s	Sylvinge, Whitelackington	1
179	" Ada Alice	f	39	m	" "	1
180	" Henry	m	41	m	" "	1
181	(See over) Hockey, Fred	m	35	m	Eagle Tavern, Buckland St. Mary	26
182	" Clara Bessie	f	34	m	" "	30
183	Hussod, Percy	m	17	s	Maincombe Lodge, Roundham, Crewkerne	1.
184	Horner, Wm. John	m	24	s	Lancin Cottages, Wambrook	30
185	Hayball, Reginald	m	21	s	Manor Farm, Tatworth	1
186	Harris, Mary Ann	f	23	s	The Manor House, Wadeford	28
187	Harris, Elizabeth	f	28	m	Hornsbury Hill, Chard	30
188	Harris, Edith	f	27	s	Knapp Farm, Whitestaunton	30
189	Hozegood, Dora	f	23	s	Ashwell, Ilminster	1
190	Hussey, Elsie Laura	f	21	s	1, Park Terrace, Chard	11
191	Hurle, Gladys Amy	f	18	s	Ball's Farm "	30
192	Hodges, Ellen	f	25	m	South Chard, "	30
193	Hardwill, Helen	f	31	s	Buckland Farm, Buckland St. Mary	30
194	Hawkins, Ivy	f	16	s	Gummer's Castle, Seavington	28
195	Haymes, Ellen Elizabeth	f	16	s	Sticklepath Farm, Combe St. Nicholas	28
196	Hill, Edith	f	25	w.	Egwood, Merriott, Crewkerne	28
472	Hall, Clara	f	36	m	Kenny, Ashill	30
473	" John	m	34	m	"	30
474	Harris, Ernest Evan	m	18	s	Chardleigh Green, Chard	26

Figure 12. A register of previous addresses in Chard, Somerset.

National Registration Act, 1915.
Form No. 14.

REGISTER OF FORMS RECEIVED FROM OTHER AUTHORITIES.

N. R. 22 (3).   Rural District of Long Ashton.

Name (surname first)	Sex.	Occupational Code No.	Address.	Local Registration Authority from whom Form was Received.	Date of Receipt.
Moore, Gladys E.K.	F.		Ladymeade, Walton	Wembley R.D.C.	9ʰ Sept. 15.
Curtis, Dorothy M.	F.		Landowne Hall, Yatton	Caine R.D.	"
James, Peter Vaughan	M.		Carline CC	Warminster R.D.C.	"
Leonard, Selina	F.		Chapel Hill Farm, Pill	Frome R.D.	"
Fisher, Joel	M.		Yew Cottage, Long Ashton	Bristol C.B.	"
Bird, Grace E.A.	F.		Abbotleare, Dundry	Frome Bridge	"
Bird, Marie M.	F.		"		"
Blackburn, Walter	M.		East Dundry	Weymouth Regis R.D.	"
Salter, George T.	M.		Burton House, Ham Green	Chichester R.D.C.	"
Hunter, George T.	M.		Riganda, Long Ashton	Bradford CK	"
Saunders, Elizabeth	F.		Oakleigh, Leigh West	Leeds A	"
Gunputh, Winifred M.	F.		The Mount, Long Ashton	Bradfield R.B.C.	"
Harper, Ellen M.	F.		Long Ashton	Teignmouth U.S.C.	"
Johnson, Sarah A.	F.		Bristol	Bristol	13./9./15.
Heydock, Mary E.V.	F.		Ingleside, Bridgewater		15./9./15.
Russell, Edith J.	F.		Laurifica Villa, Pill	Barry U.S.C.	"
Jordan, Mary A.	F.		Maple Tree, Pill	Warminster U.D.C.	"
Neale, Ada	F.		Ham Green, Pill	Bristol	"
Porter, F. Mabel	F.		The Hollow, Ham Green	Frenchay	"

Chas. Knight & Co., Ltd., Tooley Street, S.E.—(2) 1907-1915

Figure 13.
Register
of forms
received
from other
authorities:
local
authorities
had to keep
each other
informed of
changes of
address.

The National Registration (Amendment) Act of February 1918 extended this mainly for males reaching the age of 15, changing their profession, or losing their certificate of registration. Employers had to check the certificates of new employees, and the police were given powers of what we would now call 'stop and search'. The whole organisation was now headed by a 'Director-General of National Service'.

A destruction schedule for the 1915 National Register (whether held centrally *or locally*) was passed on 19 December 1919, discussions for which are in the National Archives RG 15/10 and 11, and it seems that it is another example of a valuable source being destroyed because it was apparently of no further use. Specimen forms (RG 900/1–2) were kept, but are closed for 100 years.

Luckily, the destruction of local lists was not complete, and at least two places, in Somerset and Lancashire, kept their full local registers which are open to the public! In the former, a poster with instructions for the public in Yeovil on how to register has survived, together with records of arrivals, new registrations, and a letter book for Long Ashton and Chard Rural District Councils. In the latter (now held in 40 boxes by the Lancashire Record Office at Preston under UDBA acc 3274) the 1915 list for Barrowford is in three parts, each in alphabetical order – females, males, and 'enlisted' – i.e. already in military service. Very few forms postdate 1915, but some individuals are annotated as 'over 65' or 'dead'.

With the examples of what to look for, archive and local authority offices are urged to see if any others might have survived.

In 1918, the Imperial Defence Committee began work on a better system in case the 'war to end wars' did not do so. They clearly had doubts about the effectiveness of the 1915 experiment, and eventually devised its replacement during the 1930s, put into effect by the centralised register compiled in 1939.

3. The National Registration Act of 1939

Those charged with constructing an identity system in case another world war broke out had the considerable advantage of seeing why the 1915 precedent had proved inadequate; they were also faced with the knowledge that a normal census would be expected in 1941, and they therefore laid plans to prepare for the latter which could be used if another war came earlier. They knew that such a register would have several purposes, though could hardly have predicted that the remarkable foundation they devised would still be the basis of what we are using seventy years later. The main aim was to have an identity system which covered all residents (whether British or not) and could be linked to conscription, manpower statistics and rationing; they also anticipated that the register would be able to reunite families split up in wartime. The only exceptions were those actually serving in the armed forces (i.e. not on leave on 29 September), and the mercantile marine, who were suppose to be enumerated later and separately.

65,000 enumerators were appointed during the early months of 1939, before the Act itself had been passed. This compares with only 49,000 needed for the 1931 census, the increase being partly through a rise in population, but mainly in order to reduce the size of each district in order to speed up the process as twelve million households, with some 47 million individuals, had to be issued with ID cards and rationing books very quickly on the basis of providing their name, address, sex, date of birth, marital status, their normal, detailed, occupation, and the military detail of those on leave.

The Act was signed on 5 September, with an extension to the Isle of Man three days later, and regulations under the Act passed on 21 September. Both the press and the BBC assisted the operation. There had been a press conference as early as 16 August, and the Registrar General himself broadcast on 29 September. Enumerators delivered forms to each household and institution, with the homeless being located by the police, asking for details of everyone at that address on the evening of 29 September – name, sex, date of birth, marital status, precise occupation, and any military connection, a list very similar to that collected in 1915. When forms were collected, from 30 September, identity cards were issued in exchange, and the forms were made up as the basis for ration books. ID cards did not have the date of birth included, although ration books did. Copies were sent to where the National Register was being compiled into large, white-bound volumes. The identity cards were used immediately, being taken to a local point for collection of gas masks.

Thus there were two fundamental improvements on 1915 – the central register, and the issuing of a unique identity number to every inhabitant, with provision for the newly born to be added from that date. What has fuelled the current debate is not so much the existence of an identity card (for we have all had one since 1939) but the proposed amount of data associated with each number.

Much detail about the usefulness of the ID number for patient record linkage can be seen in Farmer & Cross (1973), but its geographical basis has never been published, the Cabinet Office has several times refused to publish the report about the National Register written by the Registrar-General at the time, Sir Sylvanus Vivian (though it is now in the National Archives under CAB 102/514–515) and I have been advised that even the location of the Register itself comes under the Official Secrets Act. A brief history of the exercise was also given in the undated *Statistics of Population on 29th September 1939*, published by HMSO but obtainable 'by authorised persons only' and marked as 'Confidential'. The analysis that follows is based on several hundred volunteers and correspondents who, over many years, have willingly provided me with the relevant data about themselves and their experiences relevant to the exercise.

All those enumerated on 29 September 1939 were given a four-letter code based on a progressively small geographical area. Thus, A, B, C, D, or E as the first of the four letters denoted areas in the home counties, as far west as Hampshire and the Isle of Wight. F and G were used for Durham and Northumberland, H for Cumberland and Westmorland, J and K for Yorkshire, L and N for Cheshire and Lancashire, O for counties from Staffordshire south to Gloucestershire, Q for what is now much of Warwickshire and Worcestershire, R for the East Midlands (including Derbyshire), T for Cambridgeshire, Norfolk, Suffolk and Lincolnshire, W for the West Country from Wiltshire to Cornwall, and X and Z for Wales. WR on its own, however, stood for War Refugees, and HZ for the Isle of Man. The 'missing' letters had the following significance.

I was never used.

M was used for children born from February 1946 to 1956, the next three letters indicating a registration district.

P was used for the same purpose from 1956 to 1965 inclusive, the next three letters indicating a registration district. (A five-letter and one-to three-digit code started in 1965, indicating year, place of birth, and entry in the birth register.)

S and U were given to anyone enumerated in Scotland or Northern Ireland respectively.

V (followed by one more letter and digits) was given to the homeless ('vagrants') in 1939.

Y was issued from 1940 to the end of 1946 to anyone losing their original ID card, the next three letters reverting to the area code in which the new card was issued.

Even with seven letters missing, the system introduced in 1939 gave the designers over a third of a million sub-districts for England and Wales. Each group of letters was followed by a numeric sequence of one to three digits representing a household in that sub-district, a forward slash (or colon), and a final number of one or more digits. (Hence, one man was given the ID number AAAA1/1 – look out for his remarkable surname when the National Register is finally released to the public!) The final digit, following the slash or colon, represented the position of the individual in that household on the evening of 29 September – hence, eldest child was /2 if the father was in the armed forces at the time. Larger numbers following the slash often indicated that the person was in an institution – a boarding school, for example.

Immigrants, and those returning from military service, were given a three-letter (district) and serial number code until 1952, when the three letters became 'NHS'.

4. Employing professional help

This book was originally written for those living in Britain who desired to trace their family tree without recourse to professional help – except in dire emergencies. For readers abroad such 'emergencies' can become the norm, of course, but the techniques and sources, once understood, can be used by those unable to visit the United Kingdom in order to minimise the cost of such assistance by being as exact as possible in the instructions which you, as the client, give. (For additional advice, see *Anc* 42 Jan 06, and the SoG's leaflet *Employing a professional researcher – a practical guide.*)

Employing a genealogist or record agent (see below for the difference) can be fraught with problems, and has been the subject of some controversy in the British genealogical press over many years. It must be pointed out that anyone can establish themselves as genealogists or record agents without the necessity of training, qualifications or membership of any group or society, and you should not be fooled into thinking that normal academic qualifications, such as a degree, can in themselves be an adequate substitute. The result is that, subject to the provisos below, there can be no guarantee that the quality of research is as high as would be expected. In the absence of a controlling professional body the fees for such work can also vary, and are not necessarily linked with quality of results.

There will be no difficulty about obtaining the names of researchers. Most magazines carry advertisements, and it is quite common to find specialists – in geographical area or types of record, for example – who will be appropriate to your own particular needs. In other words, as your family tree is built up you may find it desirable to employ first an agent with access to the national birth, marriage and death indexes and subsequently a different one based in the geographical district in which your ancestors lived two centuries ago – otherwise you risk having the work subcontracted. The difficulty lies in knowing which of those advertising are competent.

As has been noted, each society produces its own journal which carries advertisements. Available to those who may or may not be society members is *FTM*, obtainable from 61 Great Whyte, Ramsey, Huntingdon, Cambridgeshire PE17 1HL, at £27.00 per annum air mail or £18.50 surface mail; six-monthly orders can be accepted for half these prices, and payment should be made by dollar cheque to the equivalent at the current exchange rates.

Record offices providing lists of researchers will make no public judgement about the quality of their work, and should not be expected to do so – they often do not have the basis for making such a judgement. Genealogists working for long-established organisations such as the Society of Genealogists (for members only) or Achievements Ltd, a subsidiary of the Institute of Genealogical and Heraldic Research in Canterbury, can be assumed to be as thorough as one might expect, and the Association of Genealogists and Researchers in Archives (AGRA, founded in 1968) exercises a degree of oversight of the work of its members in terms of experience at entry to the association and a complaints procedure by which members can be disciplined for work of unprofessional quality. In the unwelcome process of any complaint, however, take up the issue with the agent first before calling in a third party. A list of AGRA members, with their specialisms, can be obtained from the Joint Secretaries, 29 Badgers Close, Horsham, West Sussex RH12 5RU. Please enclose a cheque for £2.50 (to include post and packing), or six international reply coupons for air-mail postage. Charges vary considerably from individual to individual, but it may be of interest to indicate that the current recommendation for AGRA members is £12.00 per hour plus expenses.

It is important to distinguish between genealogists and record agents, but not simply because the former usually charge higher fees. A record agent, or record searcher, will carry out your instructions concerning specified sources – if, for example, you wish to have the 1851 census of Birmingham searched for the occupants of a specific address, a record agent should be able to do it perfectly competently. On the other hand, if your searches for an ancestor's baptism in 1788 have failed to produce an answer, for searches in sources which you had not considered you may well turn to a genealogist for advice. The genealogist is a record agent; but s/he is much more, being a problem-solver also. To reduce your costs, you should use this book to keep your employment of genealogists to a minimum, using the record agent as merely another pair of eyes. Relating your understanding of the nature of the sources to the solution to your problems will encourage a healthy respect on the part of those you are hiring, and you will have the satisfaction of really solving the problem yourself, even though you have been compelled by circumstances to use someone else to note the answer for you.

When approaching anyone for professional help, please follow some golden rules. Always send two international reply coupons with your initial request. Ask about the scale of charges before you commit yourself, and, in the initial stages of a genealogical search, do not send more than £100 even for a major search, and especially when you have no experience of using the agent before. Do not send cash. Ask for a progress report before committing yourself to further payments, including a report on which records have yielded the information you are seeking. You must, however, pay something in advance – it is not fair to expect work to be undertaken without pre-payment. Equally, it is only fair to expect a full report of progress before paying for further research, and in the case of genealogists to have an indication of future strategy for that research. It is becoming more difficult to estimate the time required to research a family tree, as there are major differences between families with many sources on line but others not.

You will receive a sympathetic response from most genealogists and record agents by being very clear and concise in your instructions, and probably a number of subsidiary questions needing to be asked. Do not fill your letters with rambling family details which will not be relevant to the search. This book should help you to judge just what may be relevant, and enable you to maximise the research already undertaken before a professional is called in – even at the simple level of obtaining 'full' GRO index references, for example. Indicate what searches have already been undertaken, and indicate whether you require the professional searcher to check any of the work already done. Without such references you are in danger of being told (and even sold) what you already know!

Write very clearly, or type the letters – otherwise, time and cost will be incurred merely for clarification. Keep copies of all the letters you send. Say what you have already done, if anything, to solve the particular problem. Give details of any deadlines you wish the agent to work to, and if you want certain documents photocopied or transcribed, ask in advance if possible. Ensure that you have exhausted all possible solutions to your problem back home. There are, as indicated above, for example, more details relating to migration from Britain which are available in the country of adoption.

When you include data about your family, be as exact as possible. Give dates rather than years, and names as well as relationships, for example, if you have them, and explain how you have obtained the information which you are providing. Give months in words, not numbers. If possible, send photocopies (never originals) of the documents concerned. Indicate the sources of your information, including which is 'firm' and which is merely the subject of family rumour or conjecture. You should not expect a professional to accept anything which cannot be verified by using primary sources.

Personal recommendation is clearly a good basis for the choice of professional help, but bear in mind that every family is different, and applying the same mind to another problem will not necessarily lead to a result either as successful or as rapid. You should remember that, though the problem may sound the same, the experience can be quite different. Searching the baptismal register of the adjoining parishes of Manchester and Prestwich for the single year 1800, for example, will take one hour or a few minutes respectively, even assuming both are equally accessible to the searcher. Searches in the National Archives in particular can consume large amounts of time merely waiting for documents to be produced so that searching can commence. Such variations make it impossible, for genealogists in particular, to quote an exact fee for a particular problem, and mean that results can come in fits and starts, whatever the competence of the professional concerned.

Always say exactly what you are requesting. Any professional will be mystified by a request to 'trace the ancestors of John Smith who lived at 35 Exeter Road, Truro in 1852'. Does it mean the previous generation, or all Smith's ancestors, or all direct ancestors, male and female, and/or their siblings? 'Discover the three previous direct male ancestors of John Smith' – with that, s/he would know what you are after.

Finally, if you feel you have had good service from your agents, do let them know. They will bear the troubles caused by other people's family trees a little more easily.

References

Listed here are the sources from which the book has been compiled, works of reference and works referred to in the text. I apologise to anyone who expected in vain to find their own works listed – I know how they feel!

Updated booklists are obtainable through the GENUKI home page on the Internet.

Periodicals

Amateur Historian
Ancestors
Family History
Family History Monthly
Family Tree Magazine
Genealogists' Magazine
International Society for British Genealogy and Family History Newsletter
Journal of Family History
Journal of Regional and Local Studies
Local Historian
Local Population Studies
Magazine of the Registration Service
Marginal Notes
Population Registration
Population Studies
Population Trends
Practical Family History

Bibliographies of genealogical works

Filby, P. W. (1983), *American and British genealogy and heraldry: a select list of books*, New England Historical Genealogical Society
Gandy, M. (1996), *Catholic family history: a bibliography*, Gandy (four volumes covering general sources, local sources, Wales and Scotland)
Gibson, J. & Raymond, S. (1991), *English genealogy: an introductory bibliography*, Federation of Family History Societies
Humphery-Smith, C. R. (1985), *A genealogist's bibliography*, Phillimore
Kaminkow, M. J. (1965), *A new bibliography of British genealogy, with notes*, Magna Carta Book Co.
Raymond, S. (1991), *British genealogical periodicals*, two volumes, Federation of Family History Societies

—— Genealogical bibliographies by county: Buckinghamshire, Cheshire, Cornwall, Cumberland, Devon, Dorset, Gloucestershire and Bristol, Hampshire, Lancashire, Lincolnshire, London and Middlesex, Norfolk, Oxfordshire, Somerset, Suffolk, Westmorland, Wiltshire published, Federation of Family History Societies. (The series was extensively reviewed by Don Steel in *Genealogists' Magazine* 23.11.)

References for genealogy in England and Wales

Reviews of new books are a regular feature of the genealogical journals, but the only indexed list of such reviews that I know of is for Americans tracing British ancestry, at www.bigwill.org. (I do wish that, when presenting a review, journals would provide the date and publisher concerned!)

Abbott, J. P. (1971), *Family patterns*, Kaye & Ward
Alcock, N. W. (2001), *Old title deeds*, Phillimore
Alder, H. (2002), *Tracking down your ancestors*, How To Books
Aldous, V. E. (1999), *My ancestors were Freemen of the City of London*, SoG
Allison, K. J. (1963), 'An Elizabethan census', *Bulletin of the Institute of Historical Research* 36
Allnutt, G. S. (1860), *The practice of wills and administrations*, John Crockford
Anderson, M. (1971), *Family structure in nineteenth-century Lancashire*, CUP
Anderson, O. (1999), 'State, civil society and separation in Victorian marriage', *Past & Present* 163
Andrews, J. & Scott-Macnab, J. (2000), *Explore your family's past*, Readers Digest
Anon. (1986), *Parish registers of Wales*, NLW
—— (1992), *Guide to the Parochial Registers and Records Measure 1978 as amended at 1st January 1993*, Church House Publishing
—— (1994), *Nonconformist registers of Wales*, NLW
—— (1999), *Tracing your family history: Royal Air Force*, Imperial War Museum
—— (2000), *Tracing your family history: Merchant Navy*, Imperial War Museum
—— (2000), *Using Navy records*, PRO
Arkell, T. et al. (2000), *When death us do part: understanding and interpreting the probate records of early modern England*, Leopards Head for Local Population Studies
Atkins, P. J. (1990), *The directories of London, 1677–1977*, Mansell
Atkinson, F. (1987), *Dictionary of literary pseudonyms*, Library Association
Baker, D. (1973), *The inhabitants of Cardington in 1782*, Bedfordshire Historical Record Society
Bardsley, A. (2004), *First-name variants and codes*, FFHS
Barrow, G. B. (1977), *The genealogist's guide*, Research Publishing
Bayley, N. (1995), *Computer-aided genealogy*, S and N
Bedell, J. (1999), 'Memory and proof of age in England, 1272–1327', *Past & Present*, 162

Bennet, J. & Storey, R. (eds) (1981), *Trade union and related records*, Modern Records Centre, University of Warwick

Benton, T. (1993), *Irregular marriage in London before 1754*, Society of Genealogists

Beresford, M. W. (1954), *The lost villages of England*, Lutterworth Press

—— (1958), 'The lay subsidies, 1290–1334', *Local History* 3.8

—— (1963), *Lay subsidies and poll taxes*, Phillimore

Bevan, A. & Duncan, A. (1990), *Tracing your ancestors in the National Archives*, HMSO

—— (2006), *Tracing your ancestors in the National Archives: the website and beyond*, NA

Biggs, A. K. (2003), *A practitioner's guide to probate*, Tolley

Blake, P. & Loughran, M. (2006), *Discover your roots*, Infinite Ideas

Bloore, J. (1989–) , *Computer programs for the family historian on IBM-compatible PCs*, nine volumes, Birmingham and Midland Society for Genealogy and Heraldry

Bonfield, L. (ed.) (1986), *The world we have gained*, Blackwell

Bourne, S. & Chicken, A. H. (1994), *Records of the Church of England*, published by the authors

—— (1994), *Records of the medical profession*, S. Bourne

Bradley, A. (1996), *Family history on your PC: a book for beginners*, Sigma

Breed, G. R. (1995), *My ancestors were Baptists: how can I find out more about them?*, SoG

Brook-Little, J. P. (1975), *An heraldic alphabet*, Macdonald & Jane's

Brooks, B. & Herber, M. (2006), *My ancestor was a lawyer*, SoG Enterprises

Brown, J. (1996), 'Recording war memorials in Northumberland', *Local History* 26.4

Brown, M. (1976), 'Clandestine marriages in Wales', *Journal of the Historical Society of the Church in Wales* 25

Burn, J. S. (1833), *The Fleet registers*, Rivington

—— (1862), *The history of parish registers in England*, Suter, 2nd edition

Burn, R. (1824), *The ecclesiastical law*, Strachan

Burns, N. (1962), *Family tree*, Faber

Caley, I. (annual), *National genealogical directory*, National Genealogical Directory

Camp, A. J. (1974), *Wills and their whereabouts*, Camp

—— (1978), *Everyone has roots*, Star Books

—— (1987), *My ancestor was a migrant* (republished as *My ancestors moved in England and Wales: how can I trace where they came from?*), SoG

—— (1988), *My ancestors came with the Conqueror: those who did and some who probably did not*, Society of Genealogists

Camp, A. J. & Spufford, P. (1969), *Genealogist's handbook*, SoG

Carlton, C. (1974), *The Court of Orphans*, Leicester University Press

Catlett, E. (1990), *Track down your ancestors and draw up your family tree*, Isis

Census reports of Great Britain, 1801–1931 (1951), HMSO

Chambers, P. (2005), *Medieval genealogy: how to find your medieval ancestors*, Sutton

—— (2006), *Early modern genealogy*, Sutton

Chapman, C. R. (1990), *Pre-1841 census and population listings*, Lochin
—— (1991), *The growth of British education and its records*, Lochin
—— (1992), *Ecclesiastical courts: their officials and their records*, Lochin
—— (1996), *Tracing your British ancestors*, Lochin
—— (1999), *Using educational records*, FFHS
Chapman, C. R. & Litton, P. M. (1996), *Marriage laws, rites, records and customs*, Lochin
Chater, K. (2006), *Tracing your family tree in England, Ireland, Scotland and Wales*, Southwater
Cheney, C. R. & Jones, M. (2004) *Handbook of dates for students of British history*, CUP
Christian, P. (2003), *The genealogist's Internet*, NA
Clarke, J. F. (1977), *Pseudonyms*, Elm Tree Books
Clifford, D. J. H. (1997), *My ancestors were Congregationalists in England and Wales: with a list of registers*, SoG
Cock, R. & Rodger, N. A. M. (2006), *A guide to the naval records in the National Archives of the UK*, Institute of Historical Research
Coldham, P. W. (1988), *Emigrants from England to the American colonies*, Genealogical Publishing
—— (1989), *American wills and administrations in the Prerogative Court of Canterbury*, Genealogical Publishing
—— (1992), *American wills proved in London, 1611–1775*, Genealogical Publishing
—— (2005), *British emigrants in bondage, 1614–1775*, Genealogical Publishing
Cole, A. (2000), *An introduction to Poor Law documents before 1834*, FFHS
Cole, J. A. (1988), *Tracing your family history*, Family Tree Magazine
Cole, J. A. & Titford, J. (2003), *Tracing your family tree*, Equation
Collins, A. (2001), *Basic facts about using Colindale and other newspaper repositories*, FFHS
Collins, R. P. (1984), *A journey in ancestry*, Alan Sutton
Colwell, S. (1984), *Tracing your family tree*, Faber
—— (1989), *The family history book*, Phaidon Press
—— (1991), *Family roots: discovering the past in the PRO*, Weidenfeld & Nicolson
—— (1992), *Dictionary of genealogical sources in the PRO*, Weidenfeld & Nicolson
—— (1996), *Teach yourself tracing your family history*, Hodder & Stoughton
—— (2006), *The National Archives*, NA
Cornwall, J. (1964/1993), *How to read old title deeds, 16th–19th centuries*, FFHS
Cox, J. (1993a), *Hatred pursued beyond the grave*, HMSO
—— (1993b), *Never been here before?* National Archives
Cox, J. C. (1910), *The parish registers of England*, reprinted by EP Publishing, 1974
Craig, F. W. S. (1972), *Boundaries of parliamentary constituencies 1885–1972*, Political Reference Publications
Cullen, M. J. (1975), *The statistical movement in early modern Britain*, Harvester Press

Currer-Briggs, N. (1979), *A handbook of British family history*, Family History Services

Currer-Briggs, N. & Gambier, R. (1981), *Debrett's family historian*, Debrett (reissued as *Debrett's guide to tracing your ancestry*, Headline Press, 1992)

—— (1985), *Huguenot ancestry*, Phillimore

Dale, J. M. (1859), *The clergyman's legal handbook*, Seeley Jackson & Halliday

Darlington, I. (1962), 'Rate books', *History* 47.159

Davey, S. (1922), *Maintenance and desertion*, Poor-Law Publications

Davies, M. R. R. (1976), *The law of burial, cremation and exhumation*, ed. David A. Smail, Shaw and Sons, 1993

Dixon, B. (1999), *Birth and death certificates: England and Wales, 1837 to 1969*, published by the author

Dowell, S. (1965), *History of taxation in England and Wales*, Cass

Drake, K. (1996), *Computer programs for the family historian on Amstrad PCW computers*, Birmingham and Midland Society for Genealogy and Heraldry

Drake, M. (1982), *Population studies from parish registers*, Local Population Studies

Drake, M. & Finnegan, R. (1994), *Sources and methods: a handbook*, Vol. 4 of Open University DA 301, 'Studying family and community history', Cambridge University Press with the Open University

Eaton, J. & Gill, C. (1981), *Trade union directory*, Pluto Press

Edwards, W. J. (1976), 'National parish register data: an evaluation of the comprehensiveness of areal cover', *Local Population Studies* 17

Efficiency scrutiny report (1985), *Registration of births, marriages and deaths*, Office of Population Censuses and Surveys

Ellis, M. (1997), *Using manorial records*, PRO

Evans, E. J. (1993), *Tithes: maps, apportionments and the 1836 Act*, British Association for Local History

Eversley, D. E. C. (1966), *An introduction to English historical demography*, Weidenfeld & Nicolson

Faithfull, P. (2002), *Lunacy in England and Wales for family historians*, FFHS

Fenwick, C. (1998, 2001, 2005), *The poll taxes of 1377, 1379 and 1381*, OUP for the British Academy

Field, D. M. (1982), *Step-by-step guide to tracing your ancestors*, Hamlin

Fiennes, C. (1949), *The journeys of Celia Fiennes*, Cresset Press

Fisk, A. & Logan, R. (1994), *Grandfather was in the Foresters*, Ancient Order of Foresters' Trust

FitzHugh, T. V. H. & Lumas, S. (1998), *A dictionary of genealogy*, Black

Fletcher, R. (1974), *The Akenham burial case*, Wildwood House

Floate, S. S. (1999), *My ancestors were gypsies*, SoG

Foster, J. (1891–) , *Alumni Oxonienses*, Parker

Foster, J. & Sheppard, J. (1995), *British archives: a guide to archive resources in the United Kingdom*, Macmillan

Foster, M. W. (1998), *A comedy of errors, or the marriage records of England and Wales, 1837–1899*, privately published in New Zealand

—— (2002) *A comedy of errors, Act 2, the registration records of England and Wales, 1837–1899*, privately published in New Zealand

Fowler, S. (2001), *Using Poor Law records*, PRO

—— (2003), *Tracing your First World War ancestors*, Countryside Books

—— (2006a), *Tracing your Second World War ancestors*, Countryside Books

—— (2006b), *Tracing your army ancestors*, Pen & Sword Military

—— (2007), *Workhouse: the people, the places, the life behind doors*, NA

Fowler, S., Elliott, P., Conyers Nesbit, R. & Goulter, C. (1994), *RAF records in the Public Record Office*, PRO

Fowler, S. & Spencer, W. (1998), *Army records for family historians*, PRO

Fowler, S., Spencer, W. & Tamblin, S. (1996), *First World War army service records in the PRO*, HMSO

—— (1997), *Army service records of the First World War*, PRO

—— (1998), *Army service records for the family historian*, PRO

Foxworthy, A. (1996), *Genealogy on the Internet*, Macbeth/Coherent

Franklin, P. (1994), *Some medieval records*, FFHS

Friar, S. (1987), *A new dictionary of heraldry*, Alpha Books

—— (1992), *Heraldry for the local historian and genealogist*, Alan Sutton

Gandy, M. (1993), *Catholic missions and registers, 1700–1880*, six volumes, published by the author

—— (1994 edition), *Short cuts in family history*, Countryside Books

—— (1995), *My ancestor was Jewish: how can I find out more about him?*, SoG

—— (2001), *Tracing Catholic ancestors*, PRO

—— (2002), *Tracing your Catholic ancestry in England*, FFHS

Gardner, D. E. & Smith, F. (1956–64), 3 vols, *Genealogical research in England and Wales*, Bookcraft

Gatfield, G. (1897), 'The history and preservation of parish registers', *Essex Review* 6.21

Gibson, J. S. W. (1974), *Wills and where to find them*, Phillimore

—— (1987), *General Register Office and International Genealogical Indexes: where to find them*, Federation of Family History Societies

—— (1988), *Unpublished personal name indexes in record offices and libraries*, Federation of Family History Societies

—— (1996), *The hearth tax, other later Stuart tax lists and the association oath rolls*, Federation of Family History Societies

—— (2001), *Bishops' transcripts and marriage licences, bonds and allegations: a guide to their location and indexes*, Federation of Family History Societies

—— (2007), *Quarter sessions records for family historians*, Family History Partnership

—— (2008), *Electoral registers 1832–1948, and burgess rolls*, Family History Partnership

Gibson, J. S. W. & Churchill, E. (2008/9), *Probate jurisdictions: where to look for wills*, Family History Partnership

Gibson, J. S. W. & Dell, A. (1991), *Tudor and Stuart muster rolls: a directory of holdings in the British Isles*, Federation of Family History Societies

—— (2004), *The protestation returns, 1641–42, and other contemporary listings*, Federation of Family History Societies

Gibson, J. S. W. & Hampson, E. (2001), *Census returns 1841–1891 in microform: a directory to local holdings in Great Britain, Channel Islands and Isle of Man*, Federation of Family History Societies

—— (2008/9), *Specialist indexes for family historians*, Family History Partnership

Gibson, J. S. W., Hampson, E. & Raymond, S. (2007), *Marriage indexes for family historians*, Family History Partnership

Gibson, J. S. W. & Hunter, J. (2008), *Victuallers' licences: records for family and local historians*, Family History Partnership

Gibson, J. S. W. & Langston, B. (2002), *Probate jurisdictions: where to look for wills*, Federation of Family History Societies

Gibson, J. S. W., Langston, B. & Smith, B. W. (2001), *Local census listings, 1522–1930*, Federation of Family History Societies

—— (2002), *Local newspapers, 1750–1920, a select location list*, Federation of Family History Societies

—— (2004), *Militia lists and musters: a directory of holdings in the British Isles*, Federation of Family History Societies

Gibson, J. S. W., Medlycott, M. T. & Mills, D. (2004), *Land and window tax assessments, 1690–1950*, Federation of Family History Societies

Gibson, J. S. W. & Peskett, P. (2002), *Record Offices: how to find them*, Federation of Family History Societies

Gibson, J. S. W. & Rogers, C. D. (1990), *Electoral registers since 1832, and burgess rolls*, Federation of Family History Societies

—— (2000), *Coroners' records in England and Wales*, Federation of Family History Societies

—— (2008), *Poll books c. 1696–1872: a directory to holdings in Great Britain*, Family History Partnership

Gibson, J. S. W., Rogers, C. D. & Webb, C. (1997–2008), *Poor Law Union records*, four volumes, Federation of Family History Societies/Family History Partnership

Gillis, J. R. (1985), *For better, for worse: British marriage, 1600 to the present*, CUP

Gittins, C. (1984), *Death, burial and the individual in early modern England*, Croom Helm

Glass, D. V. (1951), 'A note on the underregistration of births in Britain in the nineteenth century', *Population Studies* 5.1

—— (1973), *Numbering the people*, D. C. Heath

Goss, C. W. F. (1932), *The London directories, 1677–1855*, Archer

Grannum, K. & Taylor, N. (2004), *Wills and other probate records*, NA

Gwynne, R. (2001), *Huguenot heritage*, Sussex Academic Press

Hadden's Overseers' Handbook (1896) Hadden Best & Co.

Hair, P. E. H. (1970), 'Bridal pregnancy in earlier rural England further reexamined', *Population Studies* 24

—— (ed.) (1972), *Before the Bawdy Court: selections from Church court records, 1300–1800*, Elek

Hanks, P. & Hodges, F. (1990), *A dictionary of first names*, Guild Publishing

Hanson, J. (2007), 'How to use Free BMD', *Practical Family History* 113

Harley, J. B. (1961), 'The hundred rolls of 1279', *Amateur Historian* 5.1

Harvey, P. D. A. (2000), *Manorial records*, British Records Society

Harvey, R. (1992), *Genealogy for librarians*, Library Association

Hatcher, J. (2003), 'Understanding the population history of England, 1450–1750', *Past & Present* 180

Havard, J. D. J. (1960), *The detection of secret homicide*, Macmillan

Hawgood, D. (1994a), *Computers for family history: an introduction*, Hawgood

—— (1994b), *Genealogy computer packages*, Hawgood

—— (1996), *Internet for genealogy*, Hawgood

Hawking, D. T. (1992), *A guide to historical criminal records in England and Wales*, Alan Sutton

—— (1995), *Railway ancestors: a guide to the staff records of the railway companies of England and Wales, 1822–1947*, Alan Sutton

—— (2003), *Fire insurance records for family and local historians, 1696 to 1920*, Francis Boutle

Hector, L. C. (1980), *The handwriting of English documents*, Kohler and Coombes

Herber, M. (2005), *Ancestral trails – the complete guide to British genealogy and family history*, Sutton

Hey, D. (1993), *The Oxford guide to family history*, Oxford University Press

—— (1998), *The Oxford companion to local and family history*, Oxford University Press

—— (2000), *Family names and family history*, Hambledon & London

—— (2004), *Journeys in family history*, NA

Higgs, E. (1989), *Making sense of the census*, HMSO

—— (1996), *A clearer sense of the census*, HMSO

—— (2004a), *The information state in England*, Palgrave

—— (2004b), *Life, death, and statistics: civil registration, censuses, and the work of the General Register Office, 1836–1952*, Local Population Studies

—— (2005), *Making sense of the census revisited*, U. London/NA

Hobson, C. (1995), *Airmen died in the Great War, 1914–18*, Hayward

Holding, N. (1991a), *World War I army ancestry*, Federation of Family History Societies

—— (1991b), *Locating British records of the army in World War I*, Federation of Family History Societies

—— (1991c), *More sources of World War I army ancestry*, Federation of Family History Societies

—— (1991d), *The location of British army records: a national directory of World War I sources*, Federation of Family History Societies

Hollowell, S. (2000), *Enclosure records for historians*, Phillimore

Hotten, J. C. (1874), *Original lists of persons emigrating to America 1600–1700*, Chatto & Windus

Hoyle, R. W. (1994), *Tudor taxation records: a guide for users*, PRO

Hugman, B. J. (1998), *The PFA Premier and Football League players records 1946–98*, Queen Anne Press

Humphery-Smith, C. R. (1985), *The Phillimore atlas and index of parish registers*, Phillimore

—— (2003), *Armigerous ancestors*, Institute for Heraldic and Genealogical Studies

Ifans, D. (1994), *Nonconformist registers of Wales*, NLW

Iredale, D. & Barrett, J. (1985), *Your family tree*, Shire Publications

Irvine, S. (1993), *Your English ancestry: a guide for North Americans*, Ancestry

Istance, J. & Cann, E. E. (1996), *Researching family history in Wales*, Federation of Family History Societies

Jacobs, P. M. (1964), *Registers of the universities, colleges and schools of Great Britain*, Institute of Historical Research

Johnson, K. A. & Sainty, M. R. (annual), *Genealogical research directory*, published by the editors

Josling, J. F. (1985), *Change of name*, Oyez

Joyce. M. (2004), *Football league players' records 1888–1939*, Tony Brown

Jurkowski, M., Smith, C. I. & Crook, D. (1998), *Lay taxes in England and Wales*, PRO

Kain, R. J. P., Chapman, J. & Oliver, R. R. (2004), *The enclosure maps of England and Wales 1595–1918*, CUP

Kain, R. J. P. & Oliver, R. R. (1995), *The tithe maps of England and Wales: a cartographic analysis and county-by-county catalogue*, CUP

Kain, R. J. P. & Prince, H. C. (1985), *The tithe surveys of England and Wales*, CUP

Kershaw, R. (2002), *Emigrants and expats: a guide to sources in UK emigration and residents overseas*, PRO

Kershaw, R. & Pearsall, M. (2004), *Immigrants and aliens: a guide to sources on UK immigration and citizenship*, NA

—— (2006), *Family history on the move*, NA

Kitzmiller, J. M. (1988), *In search of the 'Forlorn Hope': a comprehensive guide to locating British regiments and their records, 1640–WW1*, Manuscript Publishing Foundation

Kuper, A. (2002), 'Incest, cousin marriages, and the origin of the human sciences in nineteenth century England', *Past & Present* 174

Lambert, D. (2000), *The Data Protection Act 1998: guidance notes for family history societies and their members*, FFHS

Laslett, T. P. R. (1977), *Family life and illicit love in earlier generations*, CUP

—— (1980), *Bastardy and its comparative history*, Edward Arnold

—— (1983), *The world we have lost further explored*, Methuen

Latey, W. (1970), *The tide of divorce*, Longman

Lawton, G. (1994), *Spreadsheet family trees*, Hawgood

Lawton, R. (1978), *The census and social structure*, Cass

Laxton, P. (1981), 'Liverpool in 1801: a manuscript return for the first national population census', *Transactions of the Historic Society of Lancashire and Cheshire* 130

Leary, W. (1993), *My ancestor was a Methodist: how can I find out more about him?*, SoG

Leeson, F. L. (1968), *Guide to the records of the British state tontines and life annuities of the seventeenth and eighteenth centuries*, SoG

Levine, A. *et al.* (2006), 'Illegitimacy in Britain, 1700–1920', *Local Population Studies* 79

Lewis, B. R. (Aug 2003), 'Tracing Huguenot ancestry', *Practical Family History* 68

Lewis, P. (1999), *My ancestor was a Freemason*, SoG

Linkman, A. (2000), *The expert guide to dating Victorian family photographs*, Greater Manchester Record Office

Litton, J. (1991), *The English way of death: the common funeral since 1450*, Hale

Logan, R. (2000), *An introduction to Friendly Society records*, FFHS

Lumas, S. (2002), *Making use of the census*, NA

Lynskey, M. (1996), *Family trees: a manual for their design, layout and display*, Phillimore

Macfarlane, A. (1977), *Reconstructing historical communities*, Cambridge University Press

Macnamara, W. H. (ed.) (1881), *Steer's parish law*, Stevens

Mander, M. (1984), *How to trace your ancestors*, Panther

Marshall, G. W. (1903), *The genealogist's guide*, reprinted by *Heraldry Today*, 1967

Matthews, C. M. (1982), *Your family history*, Lutterworth Press

McGregor, O. R. (1957), *Divorce in England*, Heinemann

McKinley, R. A. (1990), *A history of British surnames*, Longman

McLaughlin, E. (1989), *First steps in family history* and (1995) *Further steps in family history*, Countryside Books, based on her series of guides which are reissued regularly

Menefee, S. P. (1981), *Wives for sale*, Blackwell

Miege, G. (1701/1750), *The new state of England*, R. Baldwin

Milligan, E. H. & Thomas, M. J. (1999), *My ancestors were Quakers*, SoG

Milward, R. (1996), *A glossary of household, farming and trade terms from probate inventories*, Derbyshire Record Society

Mitford, J. (1963), *The American way of death*, Hutchinson

Moore, T. S. (2004), *Family feuds: an introduction to Chancery proceedings*, FFHS

Mordy, I. (1995), *My ancestors were Jewish*, Society of Genealogists

Morris, J. (1989), *A Latin glossary for family and local historians*, FFHS

Mosley, C. (ed.) (2003), *Burke's peerage*, 3 vols, Boydell

Moulton, J. W. (1988), *Genealogical resources in English repositories*, Hampton House, Columbus, Ohio (new edition by the Genealogical Publishing Co., 1997)

Mullett, M. (1991), *Sources for the history of English nonconformity, 1660–1830*, British Records Association

Mullins, E. L. C. (1958), *Texts and calendars* I, Royal Historical Society
—— (1983), *Texts and calendars* II, Royal Historical Society

Munby, L. M. (2002), *Reading Tudor and Stuart handwriting*, British Association for Local History

National Library of Wales (1986), *Parish registers of Wales*, National Library of Wales

Nichols, E. L. (1993), *Genealogy in the computer age: understanding Family Search*, Family History Educators
—— (1995), *The International Genealogical Index, 1992 edition*, Society of Genealogists

Nissell, M. (1987), *People count: a history of the General Register Office*, HMSO

Norton, J. E. (1950), *Guide to the national and provincial directories of England and Wales, excluding London, published before 1856*, Royal Historical Society

Oates, P. J. (2003), *My ancestors were Inghamites*, SoG

O'Neill, J. (2006), 'An untimely end', *Family History Monthly* 128

Outhwaite, R. B. (1973), 'Age at marriage in England from the late seventeenth century to the nineteenth', *Transactions of the Royal Historical Society* 23

—— (1981), *Marriage and society*, Europa

Paley, R. (2004), *My ancestor was a bastard*, SoG

Palgrave-Moore, P. (1979), *How to record your family tree*, Elvery-Dowers

—— (1985), *How to locate and use manorial records*, Elvery-Dowers

—— (1987), *Understanding the history and records of Nonconformity*, Elvery-Dowers

Palmer, J. (May 2007), 'Tracing militiamen', *Practical Family History* 113

Pappalardo, B. (2003), *Tracing your naval ancestors*, NA

Park, K. & T. (1992–93), *Family history knowledge*, Family History Club

Park, P. B. (2002), *My ancestors were manorial tenants: how can I find out more about them?*, Society of Genealogists

Pelling, G. & Litton, P. (1991), *Beginning your family history*, FFHS

Phillimore, W. P. W. & Fry, E. A. (1905), *An index of changes of name ... 1760 to 1901*, Phillimore

Pine, L. G. (1969), *Genealogist's encyclopaedia*, David & Charles

—— (1984), *Trace your family history*, Hodder & Stoughton

Pomery, C. (2004), *DNA and family history: how genetic testing can advance your genealogical research*, NA

Poole, R. (1995), '"Give us our eleven days": calendar reform in eighteenth century England', *Past & Present* 149

Price, V. A. (1989), *Tracing your family tree: a genealogical guide*, Brewin

Ratcliffe, R. (2007), *Basic facts about quarter sessions records*, FFHS

Raymond, S. (1997), *Occupational sources for genealogists: a bibliography*, FFHS

—— (2004), *Words from wills and other probate records*, FFHS

—— (2006), *Family history on the web*, ABM publishing

—— (2007), *Netting your ancestors: tracing family history on the Internet*, Family History Partnership

Razzell, P. E. (1972), 'The evaluation of baptism as a form of birth registration through cross-matching census and parish register data', *Population Studies* 26

Read, A. & White, S. (1999), *Central Register. Southport: the early years* (Office for National Statistics)

Redmonds, G. (1987), *Surnames and genealogy: a new approach*, New England Heraldic Genealogical Society

—— (2004), *Christian names in local and family history*, NA

Registrar General (1937), *The story of the General Register Office and its origins from 1538 to 1937*, HMSO

Richards, E. (2004), *Britannia's children*, Hambledon

Richards, T. (1989), *Was your grandfather a railwayman? A directory of railway archive sources for family historians*, FFHS

Riden, P. (1987), *Record sources for local history*, Batsford

Rodger, N. A. M. (1998), *Naval records for genealogists*, PRO

Rogers, C. D. (1966–67), 'The Bowdon marriage licences, 1606–1700', *Lancashire and Cheshire Historian* 1.10, 2.1

—— (1970), 'The case against the school boards of Cheshire, 1870–1902', *Journal of the Chester Archaeological Society* 57

—— (1974), *The Lancashire population crisis of 1623*, Department of Extramural Studies, University of Manchester

—— (1986), *Tracing missing persons*, MUP

—— (1995), *The surname detective: investigating surname distribution in England, 1086 to the present day*, MUP

Rogers, C. D. & Smith, J. H. (1991), *Local family history in England, 1538–1914*, MUP

Room, A. (1981), *Naming names: a book of pseudonyms and name changes, with a 'Who's who?'*, Routledge

Rose, L. (1986), *The massacre of the innocents*, Routledge

Rowlands, J. *et al.* (1993), *Welsh family history: a guide to research*, Association of Family History Societies of Wales

Rowlands, J. & S. (1996), *The surnames of Wales*, Federation of Family History Societies

—— (1999), *Second stages in researching Welsh ancestry*, FFHS

Rudinger, E. (ed.) (1978), *What to do when someone dies*, Consumers' Association

Rushton, A. (1993), *My ancestors were English Presbyterians/Unitarians*, SoG

—— (2005) *My ancestor worked in the theatre*, SoG

Sandison, A. (1972), *Tracing ancestors in Shetland*, Manson

Saul, P. (1995), *The family historian's 'Enquire within'*, Federation of Family History Societies, previously published with F. C. Markwell as *Tracing your ancestors: the A–Z guide*

Schofield, R. (1984), 'Traffic in corpses: some evidence from Barming, Kent, 1788–1812', *Local Population Studies* 33

Schurer, K. & Arkell, T. (1992), *Surveying the people: the interpretation and use of document sources for the study of population in the later seventeenth century*, Leopard's Head

Scott, M. (1997), *Wills and other probate records*, PRO

Seymour, C. (1915), *Electoral reform in England and Wales*, reprinted 1970 by David & Charles

Shaw, G. & Tipper, A. (1988), *British directories: a bibliography and guide to directories published in England and Wales, 1850–1950, and Scotland, 1773–1950*, Leicester University Press

Shearman, A. (2000), *My ancestor was a policeman*, SoG

Sims, J. (1984), *A handlist of British parliamentary poll books*, Department of History, University of Leicester

Sims, R. (1856), *A manual for the genealogist, topographer, antiquary and legal professor*, John Russell Smith

—— (1856), *Index to the pedigrees and arms contained in the heralds' visitations and other genealogical manuscripts in the British Museum*, reprinted by Genealogical Publishing, 1970

Smail, D. A., see Davies (1976)

Smith, F. (1976), *Immigrants to America appearing in English records*, Everton

Smith, K. & Watts, C. & M. (1998) *Records of Merchant Seamen*, PRO.

Smolenyak, M. & Turner, A. (2005) *Trace your roots with DNA*, Rodale Press

Spencer, W. (1997), *Records of the militia and volunteer forces, 1757–1945*, PRO

—— (2001), *Army service records of the First World War*, NA

—— (2003), *Air Force records for family historians*, NA

Spufford, P. (1973–74), 'Population mobility in pre-industrial England', *Genealogists' Magazine*, 17.8–10 (December 1973–June 1974)

—— (ed.) (1999), *Index to the probate accounts of England and Wales*, 2 vols, British Record Society

Squibb, G. D. (1978), *Visitation pedigrees and the genealogist*, Pinhorn

Stafford, G. (1993), *Where to find adoption records*, British Agencies for Adoption and Fostering

Steel, D. J., and subsequent editors (1968–) , *National index of parish registers*, Society of Genealogists

—— (1986), *Discovering your family history*, BBC Publications

Steel, D. J. & Taylor, L. (1984), *Family history in focus*, Lutterworth Press

Stewart, A. (2005), 'Finding Welsh forebears', *Practical Family History* 91, 92

Stone, L. (1977), *The family, sex and marriage*, Weidenfeld & Nicolson

Stuart, D. (1992), *Manorial records*, Phillimore

—— (2000), *Latin for local and family historians*, Phillimore

Swart, E. R. (1989), 'A computer simulation of the ineradicable uncertainty in genealogical research', *Family History*, 14.118

Swinfield, G. (2006), *Smart family history*, NA

Swinnerton, I. (2000), *Identifying your World War One soldier from badges and photographs*, FFHS

Swinson, A. (1972), *A register of the regiments and corps of the British army*, Archive Press

Tarver, A. (1995), *Church court records*, Phillimore

Tate, W. E. (1983), *The parish chest*, Phillimore

Taylor, L. (1984), *Oral evidence and the family historian*, FFHS

Thomas, G. (1993), *Records of the militia since 1757*, National Archives

—— (1994), *Records of the Royal Marines*, National Archives

Thomson, R. R. (1976), *A catalogue of British family histories*, Research Publishing

Tibbutt, H. G. (1964), 'Sources for Congregational Church history', *Transactions of the Congregational Historical Society* 19

Times, The (1920), *Handlist of English and Welsh newspapers, 1820–1920*, Times Publishing

Tippey, D. (1996), *Genealogy on the Macintosh*, Hawgood

Titford, J. (1996), *Writing and publishing your family history*, Countryside Books

—— (2000), *Succeeding in family history: helpful hints and time saving tips*, Countryside Books

—— (2002), *Searching for surnames: a practical guide to their meanings and origins*, Countryside Books

Todd, A. (1987), *Basic sources for family history* I, *Back to the early 1800s*, Allen & Todd

Todd, J. E. & Dodd, P. A. (1982), *The electoral registration system in the United Kingdom*, Office of Population Censuses and Surveys

Tonks, D. (2003), *My ancestor was a coalminer*, SoG Enterprises

Towey, P. (2006), *My ancestor was an Anglican clergyman*, SoG Enterprises

Trough, A. (1990), 'Trade unions and their records', *Archives*, 19.83

Turner, E. S. (1962), *What the butler saw*, Michael Joseph

Turner, J. H. (ed.) (1881–85), *The Rev. Oliver Heywood, B. A., 1630–1702: autobiography, diaries, etc.*, Brighouse

Twinch, C. A. (2001), *The tithe war, 1918–39: the countryside revolt*, Media Associates

Unett, J. & Tanner, A. (1997), *Making a pedigree*, David & Charles

Venn, J. & J. A. (1922–) , *Alumni Cantabrigienses*, Cambridge University Press

Vincent, J. R. (1967), *Poll books: how Victorians voted*, Cambridge University Press

Vital registration in England and Wales (1979), Office of Population Censuses and Surveys

Wagner, A. R. (1961), *English ancestry*, Oxford University Press

Wallis, P. J. (1965), 'Histories of old schools: a preliminary list for England and Wales' I, *British Journal of Educational Studies* XIV

—— (1966), 'Histories of old schools: a preliminary list for England and Wales' II, *British Journal of Educational Studies* XIV

War Office (1919), *Officers died in the Great War*, J. B. Hayward (republished 1995)

—— (1920–21), *Soldiers died in the Great War*, J. B. Hayward (republished 1988–)

Waters, L. (1987), *Notes for family historians*, Police History Society

Waters, R. E. C. (1883/2000), *Parish registers in England*, Waters

Watts, C. (2004), *Tracing births, marriages and deaths at sea* SoG

Watts, C. T. & M. J. (1995), *My ancestor was in the British army: how can I find out more about him?*, Society of Genealogists

—— (2004), *My ancestor was a merchant seaman: how can I find out more about him?* Society of Genealogists

Webb, C. (1996), *My ancestors were Londoners*, Society of Genealogists

Webster, W. F. (1988), *Nottinghamshire hearth tax, 1664–74*, Thoroton Record Society 37

Wenzerul, R. (2000) *A guide to Jewish genealogy in the United Kingdom*, Jewish Genealogical Society of Great Britain

—— (2002), *Genealogical resources in the Jewish home and family*, FFHS

West, J. (1982), *Village records*, Phillimore (first edition 1962)

—— (1983), *Town records*, Phillimore

White, J. L. (1987), *Monuments and their inscriptions*, Society of Genealogists

Whitehead, B. (1987), *Dig up your family tree: a beginner's guide to records since 1837*, Sphere Books

Whitmore, J. B. (1953), *Genealogical guide*, SoG

Willard, J. F. (1934), *Parliamentary taxes on personal property, 1290–1334*, Mediaeval Academy of America

Williams, C. J. & Watts-Williams, J. (1986), *Parish registers of Wales*, NLW

Willis, A. J. & Proudfoot, K. (2003), *Genealogy for beginners*, Phillimore

Wilson, E. (1991), *Records of the Royal Air Force*, Federation of Family History Societies

Winegarten, J. I. (*c*.2002) *Tristram and Coote's probate practice*, Butterworth

Withycombe, E. G. (1988), *The concise dictionary of English Christian names*, Omega

Wolfram, S. (1987), *In-laws and outlaws: kinship and marriage in England*, Croom Helm

Woodcock, T. & Robinson, J. M. (2001), *The Oxford guide to heraldry*, OUP

Woods, R. (2006), *Children remembered: responses to untimely death in the past*, Liverpool University Press

Wrigley, E. A. (ed.) (1972), *Nineteenth-century society*, CUP

—— (1973), *Identifying people in the past*, Edward Arnold

Wrigley, E. A. *et al.* (1997), *English population history from family reconstitution, 1580–1837*, CUP

Wrigley, E. A. & Schofield, R. S. (1981), *The population history of England, 1541–1871*, Edward Arnold

Yeo, G. (1995), *The British overseas: a guide to records of their births, baptisms, marriages, & deaths and burials available in the United Kingdom*, Guildhall Library

Young, S. D. (2002), *The I. G. I. De-mystified!*, St. Catherine's Ontario: Family Historian

References, by country, for genealogy overseas

The following works in English are guides for those researching the origins of immigrants to England and Wales and for Britons who spent part of their lives abroad. The International Genealogical Index is available in the United Kingdom for many of these countries, and others. Advice and information concerning many individual countries can be found on the Internet. (There are in addition many references relating to research in individual regions.) I am very grateful to the Society of Genealogists, and to many Internet correspondents around the world, for their help in providing bibliographical details for some of these references.

Immigration and naturalisation
Horton-Smith, L. G. H. & Wulcko, L. M. (1949–50), 'Naturalisation and where to look', *Genealogists' Magazine* 10.12 (December 1949), 10.13 (March 1950)

Index to names: certificates of naturalisation, 1844–1900 (1908), HMSO

Monger, R. F. (1970), 'Immigrants in the public records', *Genealogists' Magazine* 16.5 (March)

Page, W. (1893), 'Letters of denization and Acts of Naturalization for aliens in England 1509–1603', Huguenot Society of London, vol. 8

Shaw, W. A. (1923/1932), *Letters of denization and Acts of naturalisation for aliens in England and Ireland, 1603–1800*, with a supplement by W. and S. Minet, Huguenot Society of London, Quarto Series vols 18, 27, 35

Works covering several countries

Baxter, A. (1985/1995), *In search of your European roots: a complete guide to tracing your ancestors in every country in Europe*, Genealogical Publishing
Baxter, I. A. (1990), *A brief guide to biographical sources*, India Office Library and Records [for Asia]
Currer-Briggs, N. (1982), *Worldwide family history*, Routledge
Konrad, J. (1987) *Mexican and Spanish family research*, Ye Olde Genealogie Shoppe
—— (1993), *French and French Canadian family research*, Ye Olde Genealogie Shoppe
Law, H. T. (1987), *How to trace your ancestors to Europe*, Cottonwood Books
Pedersen, S. (1989), *Searching overseas: a guide to family history sources for Australians and New Zealanders*, second edition, Kangaroo Press NSW
Platt, L. de (1978), *Genealogical and historical guide to Latin America*, Gale
Poulsen, E. M. & Kowallis, G. P. (1969–71), *Scandinavian genealogical helper*, Everton
Rogers, T. (1992), *Archives New Zealand 4 – a directory of archives in New Zealand and the Cook Islands, Fiji, Niue, Tokelan, Tonga and Western Samoa*, Archives Press
Thomson, F. W. (1980), *Scandinavian genealogical research manual*, Thomson's Genealogical Center

For titles of works on genealogy in a large number of countries, see www. cyndislist.com.

Australia (with thanks to Sue Macbeth)

Gray, N. (1993), *Compiling your family history*, Society of Australian Genealogists
Joseph, A. (1981), 'Anglo-Australian genealogy', *Genealogists' Magazine* 20.5 (March), 20.6 (June)
Joseph, A. P. (1964), 'On tracing Australian Jewish genealogy', *Genealogists' Magazine* 14.12 (December)
Num, C. (1999), *A to Z Australian genealogy helper*, published by the author
Vine Hall, N. (2002), *Tracing your family history in Australia: a guide to sources*, Scriptorium
Young, F. & Harris, D. (1993), *Birth, death and marriage certificates in Australia*, Australian Institute of Genealogical Studies
See also Peake, A. G. (1988) *Bibliography of Australian family history*, Tudor Australian Press
FTM 23.2 Dec 06 and 23.3 Jan 07 have articles about Australian genealogy on the Internet

Austria

Senekovic, D. (1979), *Handy guide to Austrian genealogical records*, Everton

Bahamas

Whittleton, E. H. (1975), 'Family history in the Bahamas', *Genealogists' Magazine* 18.4 (December)

Barbados

Lane, G. (2006), *Tracing ancestors in Barbados: a practical guide*, Genealogical Publishing Co., Inc.

Stanford, C. J. (1974), 'Genealogical sources in Barbados', *Genealogists' Magazine* 17.9 (March)

See also www.barbadosancestors.com

Belgium

Jaques, J. (1988), 'Family history in Belgium', *E. Surrey Family History Society* 11.1 (April)

Van Hille, P. (1968), 'Genealogy in Belgium', *Genealogists' Magazine* 15.5 (September)

Bermuda

Willing, J. A. (1984), 'Genealogical research in Bermuda', *Glasgow and West of Scotland Family History Society* 17 (November)

Canada

Anon. (1995), Reference sources for Canadian genealogy, National Library of Canada.

Baxter, A. (1990/1994), *In search of your Canadian roots*, Macmillan of Canada/ Genealogical Publishing

Bourrie, D. (2003), *Finding your Canadian ancestors*, Heritage Productions

Douglas, A. (1990), 'Genealogical research in Canada', *Genealogists' Magazine* 23.6 (June)

Dryden, J. (2002), *Genealogy and Canadian law: an introduction to access, privacy & copyright legislation*, Heritage Productions

Irvine, S. (2007), *Canadian connections*, Ancestors, April

Mennie-de Varennes, Kathleen (1986), *Annotated bibliography of genealogical works in Canada*, Fitzhenry & Whiteside with National Library of Canada

Murphy, S. L. (2001), Researching Canadian land records, Heritage Productions

—— (2003), *Researching Canadian vital statistics records: births, marriages and deaths*, Heritage Productions

National Archives of Canada (2005), *Tracing your ancestors in Canada*, National Archives of Canada

Roy, J. (1993), *Tracing your ancestors in Canada*, National Archives of Canada

St. Denis, Louise (1998), *A Canadian directory for genealogists*, Heritage Productions

Taylor, R. (2001), *Researching Canadian archival centres: an introduction to using archives in genealogical research and to examine the kinds of records which you will encounter*, Heritage Productions

—— (2001), *The Canadian genealogical sourcebook*, Canadian Library Association

Waxman, K. (1977), 'How to dig for your Canadian roots', *Relatively Speaking* 5.4
See also FTM 24.12 Sep 08

Channel Islands
Backhurst, M. L. (1978), *Family history in Jersey*, Channel Islands Family History Society
Burness, G. R. (1978), 'Genealogical research in the Channel Islands', *Genealogists' Magazine* 19.5 (March)
Le Poidevin, D. W. (1978), *How to trace your ancestors in Guernsey*, Quality Service

Cuba
Carr, P. E. (1992), *Guide to Cuban genealogical research: records and sources*, Adams Press

Czech Republic
Hudick, J. A. (2002), *Slovak roots: getting started: a guide for researching your roots in the Slovak and Czech Republics*, available at www.slavicroots.com/SlovakRusynRoots.html (accessed 6 June 2008)
Schlyter, D. M. (1990), *Handbook of Czechoslavak genealogical research*, Genun
Wellauer, M. W. (1980), *Tracing your Czech and Slovak roots*, Wellaur
For Czech archives online, see www.ceresearch.cz/adresar.htm

Denmark
Carlberg, N. E. (1992), *Beginning Danish research*, Carlberg Press
Kowallis, G. P. & Poulsen, E. M. (1979), *The Danish genealogical helper*, Everton Publishers
Smith, F. & Thonsen, F. A. (1969), *Genealogical guidebook and atlas of Denmark*, Bookcraft
Thomsen, F. A. (1984), *The beginner's guide to genealogical research*, Thomsen's Genealogical Center

Fiji (see also New Zealand)
Burness, L. R. (1993), 'Genealogical research in Fiji', *Genealogists' Magazine* 24.6 (June)

Finland
Choquette, M. *et al.* (1985), *The beginner's guide to Finnish genealogical research*, Thomsen's Genealogical Centre
Vincent, T. (1994), *Finnish genealogical research*, Finnish Americana

France
Audin, M. (1980), *Barking up that French tree*, Cook-McDowell Publishing
—— (1981), 'Tracing ancestors in France', *Genealogists' Magazine* 20.8 (December)

Bird, J. (1960), 'Some sources for French genealogy and heraldry', *Genealogists' Magazine* 13.8 (December)

Durye, P. (1977), *Genealogy: an introduction to continental concepts*, Polyanthus

Pontet, P. (1993), *Researches in France: a basic guide for family historians*, Anglo-French Family History Society

—— (1996), *Genealogical sources in France*, Anglo-French Family History Society

—— (1998) *Ancestral research in France: the simple guide to tracing your family through French records*, published by the author

Rabino di Borgomale, H. L. (1946), 'Genealogical research in France', *Genealogists' Magazine* 9.15 (September)

Wileman, R. (1986), 'Family research in France', *Leicestershire Family History Society* 44

Germany

Baxter, A. (1992/1996), *In search of your German roots: a complete guide to tracing your ancestors in the Germanic areas of Europe*, Genealogical Publishing

Bernard, R. (1992), *Tracing your German ancestors*, Anglo-German Family History Society

Bird, J. (1960), 'Some sources for German genealogy and heraldry', *Genealogists' Magazine* 13.5 (March)

Friedrichs, H. F. (1951), 'Genealogical research in Germany', *Genealogists' Magazine* 11.4 (December)

—— (1969), *How to find my German ancestors*, Degener

Jensen, L. O. (1978), *A genealogical handbook on German research*, two volumes, Jensen

Konrad, J. (1992), *German family research made simple*, Ye Olde Genealogie Shoppe

Lind, M. (1992), *Researching and finding your German heritage*, Linden Tree

Minert, R. P. & Riemer, S. J. (2001), *Researching in Germany*, Lorelei Press

Pearl, S. (1989), 'Basic German sources', *FTM* 5.5 (March), 5.6 (April)

—— 'Were your ancestors German?' *North Middlesex Family History Society* 11.4 (Summer)

Smelser, D. (1991), *Finding your German ancestors*, Ancestry Inc.

Thode, E. (1992), *German–English genealogical dictionary*, Genealogical Publishing

Towey, P. (1999), *Tracing German speaking ancestors*, Research Guide 2, Anglo-German Family History Society

—— (2002), *An introduction to tracing your German ancestors*, FFHS

Tunstill, L. (1990), 'Were your ancestors German?', *Oxfordshire Family Historian* 5.6 (Autumn)

Wellauer, M. A. (1978) *Tracing your german roots*, Wellauer

Gibraltar

Burness, L. R. (1983), 'Genealogical research in Gibraltar', *Genealogists' Magazine* 21.1 (March)

Bryden, J. A. (1993), 'Genealogical research in Gibraltar', *Genealogists' Magazine* 24.7 (September)

Hungary

Glendenning, A. M. (1994), 'Family history in Hungary', *Genealogists' Magazine* 24.11 (September)

Suess, J. H. (1980), *Handy guide to Hungarian genealogical records*, Everton

India

Hardy, F. (1987), 'A young lady named Susan Halford: tracing "Rank and File" civilians in nineteenth-century India', *Genealogists' Magazine* 22.5 (March)

Taylor, N. C. (1990), *Sources for Anglo-Indian genealogy in the library of the Society of Genealogists*, Society of Genealogists

Wilkinson, T. (1981), 'Searching for ancestors in India', *North Middlesex Family History Society* 4.1

Wood, T. (1990), 'The British in India', *FTM* 6.4 (February)

See also www.ozemail.com.au/~clday and *Ancestors* 57 May 07

Ireland

Adolph, A. (2007), *Tracing your Irish family history*, Collins London

Begley, D. F. (1980/1984), *A handbook on Irish genealogy*, Heraldic Artists

—— (1981), *Irish genealogy: a record finder*, Heraldic Artists (a sequel to the previous work)

—— (1985), *The ancestor trail in Ireland*, Heraldic Artists

Black, J. A. (1974), *Your Irish ancestors*, Paddington Press

Camp, A. J. (1990), *Sources for Irish genealogy in the library of the Society of Genealogists*, Society of Genealogists

Caragher-Manning, D. (1985), *Catalogue of genealogical research sources, Ireland*, Caragher Family History Society

Catalogue of sources for genealogical research: Ireland (1985), Caraher Family History Society

Davis, B. (1992), *An introduction to Irish research*, Federation of Family History Societies

Durning, W. & M. (1986), *A guide to Irish roots*, Irish Family Names Society

Falley, M. D. (1962/1988), *Irish and Scotch-Irish ancestral research*, two volumes, Genealogical Publishing

ffolliott, R. (1967), *A simple guide to Irish genealogy*, Irish Genealogical Research Society

Grenham, J. (1999), *Tracing your Irish ancestors: the complete guide*, Gill & Macmillan

Maxwell, I. (1997), *Tracing your ancestors in Northern Ireland*, The Stationery Office

McCarthy, T. (1995), *The Irish roots guide*, Lilliput

Moynihan, A. (1990), 'Tracing Irish ancestors', *E. Surrey Family History Society* 13.3. (September)

Quinn, S. E. (1996), *Trace your Irish ancestors*, Irish Genealogy Press

Sources for research in Irish genealogy, with particular reference to Ulster (n. d.), J. P. Reid

Stanley, N. P. (1986), 'Hints for genealogists visiting Dublin', *Genealogists' Magazine* 22.2 (June)

Yurdan, M. (1990), *Irish family history*, Batsford

See also www.nationalarchives.ie/

Isle of Man

Bellerby, R. (2005), 'Isle of Man investigations', *Family History Magazine* 113 (January)

Crowe, N. (1994), 'Genealogy in the Isle of Man', *Isle of Man Family History Society* 16.2, 16.3

'Manx ancestry' (1990), *Woolich and District Family History Society* 39 (September)

Narashinham, J. (1994), *Manx family tree: a beginner's guide to records in the Isle of Man*, Isle of Man Family History Society

You may have Manx ancestry: hints on how to trace your links with the Isle of Man (1979), Manx Tourist Board Pamphlet

Italy

Cole, T. R. (1955), *Italian genealogical records*, Genealogical Publishing

Collette, J. P. (1995), *Finding Italian roots: the complete guide for Americans*, Genealogical Publishing

Glynn, J. M., junior (1981), *Manual for Italian genealogy*, Italian Family History Society, Maine

Konrad, J. (1990), *Italian family research*, Ye Olde Genealogie Shoppe

Lener, D. J. (n.d.), *Tracing your Italian heritage in Italy*, Preservation Emporium, Texas

—— (n.d.) *The most comprehensive guide to Italian genealogical research*, Lener

Lewis, B. R. (2005), 'Tracing Italian ancestors', *Practical Family History* 88 (April)

McCleod, C. (1982), 'Research in Italy', *Relatively Speaking* 10.1

Preece, P. P. & Preece, F. S. (1978), *Handy guide to Italian genealogical records*, Everton

See also www.italgen.com

Jamaica

Mitchell, M. E. (1998), *Jamaican ancestry: how to find out more*, Heritage Books

Wright, P. (1966), 'Materials for family history in Jamaica', *Genealogists' Magazine* 15.7 (September)

Lithuania

Miller, J. (2004), 'Were your ancestors Lithuanian?' *FTM* 20.8 (June)

Malta

Lewis, B. R. (2005), 'Tracing Maltese ancestors', *Practical Family History* 86 (February)

Stephens, P. J. (1988), 'The Malta connection', *Oxfordshire Family History Society* 4.7

Netherlands

Fahy, T. G. (1961), 'Genealogical research in the Netherlands', *Genealogists' Magazine* 13.12 (December)

Franklin, C. M. (1982), *Dutch genealogical research*, Ye Olde Genealogie Shoppe

Hofstee, J. (1983), 'Researching ancestors from the Netherlands', *Families* 22.3

Kirk, R. (1988), 'Research in Holland', *FTM* 4.12 (October)

'Some sources for Dutch genealogy' (1962), *Genealogists' Magazine* 14.1 (March)

Van Resandt, W. W. (1972), *Searching for your ancestors in the Netherlands*, Central Bureau Voor Genealogie

—— (1974), 'Genealogy in the Netherlands', *Genealogists' Magazine* 17.10 (June)

Witte, A. J. (1988), 'Genealogical research in the Netherlands', *Genealogical Research Directory*

New Zealand

Bromell, A. (1984), *Family history research in New Zealand: a beginner's guide*, New Zealand Society of Genealogists

—— (1988/1991), *Tracing family history in New Zealand*, G. P. Publishing

Ivory, A. (1976), 'Genealogy in New Zealand', *Bristol and Avon Family History* 6

Joyce, B. (2004), 'Kiwi family history', *Family History Magazine* 111 (December)

Marshall, L. & Mossong, V. (1980), 'Genealogical research in New Zealand', *Genealogists' Magazine* 20.2 (June) (reprinted as Society of Genealogists Leaflet No. 11)

Mossong, V. (1993), 'Beginning research in New Zealand', *International Society for British Genealogy and Heraldry Newsletter* (April–June)

FTM 23.2 Dec 06 and 23.3 Jan 07 have articles about New Zealand genealogy on the Internet

Norway

How to trace your ancestors in Norway (1996 but many editions), Royal Norwegian Ministry of Foreign Affairs free leaflet, ref. UDA316ENG (based on work by Y. Nedreboe, G. Bøe and J. H. Oldtad). It is available from Norwegian missions abroad or via www.regjeringen.no/

Larsen, M. R. (1979), 'How to trace Norwegian ancestors', *The New Zealand Genealogist* 10

[Marshall, L.?] (1979), 'Research in Norway', *The New Zealand Genealogist* 15

Smith, F. & Thomsen, F. A. (1979), *Genealogical guidebook and atlas of Norway*, Everton

Thomsen, F. A. (1984), *The beginner's guide to Norwegian genealogical research*, Thomsen's Genealogical Center

Wellauer, M. A. (1979), *Tracing your Norwegian roots*, Wellauer

Poland

Chorzempa, R. A. (1995), *Polish roots*, Genealogical Publishing
Hoskins, J. W. (1987), *Polish genealogy and heraldry: an introduction to research*, Hippocrene Books
Klec-Pilewski, B. (1969), 'Some sources for Polish genealogy', *Genealogists' Magazine* 16.4 (December)
Konrad, J. (1992), *Polish family research*, Ye Olde Genealogie Shoppe
Lewis, B. R. (2005), 'Tracing Polish ancestors', *Practical Family History* 87 (March)
Szczepanski, J. (1989), 'Look for your Polish forefathers', *North West Kent Family History Society Journal* 5.1 (March)
Wellauer, M. A. (1991), *Tracing your Polish roots*, Wellauer

Russia

Bird, A. (2001), 'Tracing your ancestors in Russia', *FTM* 17.4 (February)

Scotland (there is an Anglo-Scottish Family History Society)

Beginner's guide to Scottish genealogy (1992 edition), Tay Valley Family History Society
Bigwood, R. (2006), *The Scottish family tree detective*, MUP
Cory, K. B. (1996), *Tracing your Scottish ancestry*, Polygon
Hamilton-Edwards, G. (1986), *In search of Scottish ancestry*, Phillimore
James, A. (1985 edition), *Scottish roots: a step-by-step guide for ancestor hunters in Scotland and overseas*, MacDonald
Sandison, A. (1985 edition), *Tracing ancestors in Shetland*, privately published
Sinclair, C. (1997), *Tracing your Scottish ancestors: a guide to ancestry research in the Scottish Record Office*, HMSO
Steel, D. J. (1970), *Sources of Scottish genealogy and family history*, National Index of Parish Registers, Vol. 12, Phillimore
Whyte, D. (1979/1982), *Introducing Scottish genealogical research*, Scottish Genealogy Society
—— (1984), *Scottish ancestry research: a brief guide*, Scotpress

Singapore

Barnard, S. M. (2002), 'Singapore – a hard nut to crack', *FTM* 19.1 (November)

Slovakia (see Czech Republic)

South Africa

Frykberg, P. (1991), 'South African records', *The New Zealand Genealogist* 22.210
Harrison, E. (1996), *Family history: a South African beginner's guide*, Harrison
Lombard, R. T. J. (1978), 'Genealogical research in South Africa', *Genealogists' Magazine* 19.8 (December)
—— (1984), *Handbook for genealogical research in South Africa*, Institute of Historical Research
Tapping, M. (1992), 'Beginning research in South Africa', *International Society for British Genealogy and Heraldry Newsletter* 14.3

Spain
Ryskamp, A. (1997), *Finding your Hispanic roots*, G. P. C.

Sweden
Brenner, S. O. (1967), *Family history sources for Skane, Halland and Blekinge*, Skane Genealogical Society
Johansson, C.-E. (1967/1981/1996), *Cradled in Sweden*, Everton
Olsson, N. W. (1977), *Tracing your Swedish ancestry*, Royal Ministry for Foreign Affairs (also in *Relatively Speaking* 5.1, 1977)
Peterson, J. G. (1990), *Leafing out your Swedish family tree*, Vantage Press Inc.
Routledge, C. (1982), 'Tracing your Swedish ancestry', *Relatively Speaking* 10.1
Thomsen, F. A. (1981), *Genealogical guidebook and atlas of Sweden*, Thomsen's Genealogical Center
—— (1984), *The beginner's guide to Swedish genealogical research*, Thomsen's Genealogical Center

Switzerland
Nielson, P. A. (1979), *Swiss genealogical research*, Downing
Suess, J. H. (1978), *Handy guide to Swiss genealogical records*, Everton
Wellauer, M. A. (1988), *Tracing your Swiss roots*, Wellauer

Ukraine
Komarnyckyj, S. (2008), 'The king of the castle', *Family Tree Magazine* 24.5 (February)
Mazur, D. (1990), 'Ukrainian research sources', *Fam Footsteps (Kamloops)* 6.1

United States
American Society of Genealogists (1960, 1971), *Genealogical research*, two volumes, published by the society
Boam, T. L. (1977), 'Modern sources for genealogical research in the United States', *Genealogists' Magazine* 19.1 (March)
Drake, P. (1992), *In search of family history, a starting place*, Heritage Books
Eakle, A. & Cerni, J. (1996), *The source: a guide book of American genealogy*, Ancestry Publishing Co.
Greenwood, V. D. (1990/1996), *The researcher's guide to American genealogy*, Genealogical Publishing
Helmbold, F. W. (1978), *Tracing your ancestry: a step by step guide to researching your family history*, Oxmoor House
Linder, B. R. (1978), *How to trace your family history*, Everest House
MacSorley, M. E. (1995), *Genealogical sources in the United States of America*, MacSorley
McCracken, G. E. (1977), 'State and federal sources for American genealogy', *Genealogists' Magazine* 19.4 (December)
Neagles, J. C. & Neagles, L. L. (1974), *Locating your immigrant ancestor: a guide to naturalization records*, Everton
Schaefer, C. K. (1997), *Guide to naturalization records in the United States*, Genealogical Publishing

Stryker-Rodda, H. (1977/1995), *How to climb your family tree*, Genealogical Publishing

The handy book for genealogists (many editions), Everton

Turner, F. H. (1980), 'Using America's national archives', *Genealogists' Magazine* 20.3 (September)

Wright, N. E. (1974), *Building an American pedigree*, Brigham Young University Press

—— (1981), *Preserving your American heritage: a guide to family and local history research*, Brigham Young University Press

West Indies (see also under individual countries)

Camp, A. J. (1987), 'Some West Indian sources in England', *FTM* 4.1 (November)

Grannum, G. (2002), *Tracing your West Indian ancestors*, PRO

—— (2006) 'Caribbean connections', *Family History Magazine* 127 (February)

—— (2006) 'Tracing your British West Indian ancestors', *Family History Magazine* 129 (April)

Index

abortion 203
'abroad' 200
addresses 28, 53, 61, 69, 78, 83, 85,
    89, 169, 208–10, 216, 223,
    230, 236, 246–7
adoption 44, 46, 66, 165, 169, 181,
    210, 262
    Adopted Children Register 46
    Adoption Contact Register 47
    index of 45
    societies 47
adultery 244
affidavits 195, 260
affiliation 27, 68
'afterwards' 26, 210
Akenham burial case 242
'alias' 26, 96–7, 141, 173, 210
apprenticeship 98, 151, 174
archbishop's special licence 171
archdeacons 139
Arches, Court of 183, 258
armed forces 56–60, 182, 233–5
    Deceased Soldiers' Effects 234
    medal search 57
    marriages 173
    Victoria Cross 234
    see also Royal Air Force; Royal
        Navy
Artificial Insemination by Donor 2
Association for Gravestone Studies
    227
Association Oath 110
asylum 209
'attornies-at-law' 116

ballot, secret 113
Bank of England will extracts 257
banns see marriage
baptism 91–138, 155
    certificates 59, 116
    Christening 134

collective 130
'conditional' 134
'Dade' registers 95, 192, 238
'the gap' 119, 142
'half-baptism' 120
'hypothetical' 134
late 130–1, 134
private 120, 134
'supposed' 96
Baptists 138, 242
bibles 14
bigamy 172, 180, 193, 248
bilingual certificates 18, 168, 210,
    212
birth 18–54
    at sea 37
    cost of certificates 24
    'female' 39, 53
    index detail 42
    late registration 18, 33, 44
    'male' 38, 53
    Miscellaneous Registers 37
    multiple 25
    reregistration 29, 30, 52, 54, 175,
        217
    short birth certificate 29
    surrogate 30
Bishop's Register 256
Bishop's Transcripts 104, 129, 140–1,
    143, 175, 198
    'register bills' 140
body snatchers 217
Boyd, Percival 198
breast feeding 101
British Library catalogue 71
brothels 89
Buckingham Palace 54
'bundling' 97
burial 131, 223–7, 237–50
    of children 240
    in church 237–245

at crossroads 243
dues books 260
'interred' 137, 237
National Burial Index 238
pauper corpses 225
at sea 245
shipwrecked bodies 240
in woollen 260
see also cemeteries, graves

Catholic Record Society 65
caveat books 258
cemeteries 84, 217, 220
censuses 71–91, 108, 111, 126, 174,
    199, 202, 247
    abbreviations 75
    disability in 75
    National Strays Index 88
    'scholars' in 62
    ships in 87
Chancery, Court of 12, 189, 232,
    261
change of name 52, 129, 158
    deeds 49
Chaplains' Returns 37, 173, 234
Charter Rolls 159
Chelsea Pensioners 182
Child Support Agency 2, 30
child minding 45
children's uniforms 130
'chrisome' 242
'churched' 134
Church of Jesus Christ of Latter Day
    Saints *see* Mormons
churchwardens 83, 243
citation books 244
Civil Partnerships 180–1, 185
Civil Service Evidence of Age index
    36
Civil War 119
clergy 82
Close Rolls 158
coastguards 60
coats of arms 207
cohabitation 170
Collection for Distressed Protestants
    108
College of Arms 147, 154, 259

Commonwealth War Graves
    Commission 233
confirmation 52, 130
Congregationalists 138
Consistory Court 101–2
constables 83
consular returns 37, 173, 182, 214
Coram, (Captain) Thomas 99
coroners 209, 211–12, 214, 216, 220,
    235–7, 242, 261, 263
corpses, disposal of 211, 213–14,
    217, 220, 223, 241, 262
    for medical research 244–5
    unidentified 213, 244
'correction books' 244
Court Baron 145
Court Leet 145
'cousin' 127
cradle roll 71
cremation 221–3
    ashes 245
cricketers 82
criminals 5, 11, 70, 147, 246
    infanticide 212, 216
Curia Regis rolls 159
Customs and Excise 82

data protection xx
day books 143
death duty 257
deaths 208–61
    cause of 209–10, 236
    certificates 43, 56, 89, 209–17
    certificates of no liability to
        register 214, 220
    'certified' 210
    of children 239
    disposal abroad 223
    index details of 216
    infant mortality 239
    'missing presumed dead' 213
    notices 223, 241, 263
    'old age' 210
    place of disposal 223, 240–1,
        262
    presumed 169
    registered twice 216
    at sea 37, 214

stillbirths 28, 142, 212, 220
suicide 137, 242–3
    in transit 210
'Debt of Honour' register 233
Declaration of Parentage 30
Deed Poll *see* Change of Name Deeds
deeds 159
Delegates, Court of 258
Dictionary of National Biography
    xix
Diocesan Record Offices 99, 143,
    244, 252
    private 139
Diocesan Registry 255
directories 79–82, 114, 137
Dissenters *see* Nonconformists
divorce 167, 169, 170, 182–5, 248,
    259, 263
    decrees absolute 183–5
DNA xxiii, 2, 30
doctors 82
'Doctors' Commons' 254
dog (licences) 84, 91
'Domesday book' 84
DoVE xxiv
dowry 207
Dr Barnardo's 30, 247
Dr Williams' library 192
drivers and vehicles 84

EAGLE xxiv, 23
Easter books 113
education 60–65, 158
Efficiency Scrutiny Report 19
electoral registers 71, 90, 175, 215,
    248
    abbreviations 78–9
    absent voters 58
elopement 207
emigration 214, 245–6
    of children 247
    of paupers 247
    transportation 245–6
epidemics 239, 244
episcopal visitation 142
essoins 145
Estate Duty Registers 257
excommunication 137, 242

fairgrounds 89
    National Fairground Archives 82
Family History Partnership 7
Family Records Centre 22
Federation of Family History Societies
    6, 7, 73, 88, 224–5, 238, 262
'feet of fines' 157
felo de se *see* suicide
'fiat' 257
Final Concords 157
Fine Rolls 159
fishermen 60
footballers 82
forenames 4, 39, 201
    change of 29, 49–53, 129–30,
        135, 175
    double 42, 174
    sequence of 134
    surnames as 201
forgeries 119
'formerly' 26, 97
'formerly known as ...' 53
foundlings 30, 99
    Foundling Hospital 130
    Register of Abandoned Children 30
    see also Coram, (Captain) Thomas
Free and Voluntary Present 108
Free BMD 23
freemasons 82
freemen 149, 161
friendly societies 68–70, 235
funerals 148, 237
    certificates 241
    civil 238
funeral directors 220, 223, 262
    National Association 223

GEDCOM 10
Gender Recognition 26
genealogical programs 10
General Register of Shipping and
    Seamen 37
General Register Office xix, xxi, xxiii,
    19–26, 28–33, 35, 37–8, 42–3,
    47, 52, 54, 56–9, 67, 72, 89,
    99, 101, 137, 164–8, 170–1,
    173, 180, 182–3, 209, 213–15,
    220, 230, 234, 238, 264

indexes 22–3, 34, 36, 38, 42, 46, 53–4, 67, 108, 166–7, 173, 184, 217
inspectorate 55
general searches 21
'genetic attraction' 191
GENUKI 20, 92
George Rose 95, 117, 131, 142–3, 188, 238
godparents 94, 127, 134, 136, 157
graves 43, 123, 223–5
    grave map 221
    'public' graves 224
    register 221, 224
    style 226
Greenwich Hospital 59
Gregorian calendar 93
Gretna Green 186
Guardianship Bonds 258
guardians 45, 54, 68, 84, 171
guilds 161
Guild of One Name Studies 16
gypsies 89, 117

Hardwicke 186
'hatchments' 259
health records 65
'heaping' 126
hearth tax 109
heraldry 147, 207, 241, 259
heretics 243
'heriots' 145
High Commissions 36, 59, 214
histogram 118
Historical Manuscripts Commission 37
hospital records 66, 232–3, 244, 263
    Hospital Records Project 66
house tax 109
hovercraft 214
Hundred Rolls 163
Hustings, Court of 161

Identity and Passport Service xxi, 22
illegitimacy 11, 12, 26–9, 33, 35, 37, 39, 42, 44, 47, 54, 68, 96–9, 115, 117, 126, 128, 130, 135, 169, 175, 192, 198, 201, 212, 239

bastardy files 68
within marriage 96
immigration 36, 121, 172
    aliens 36
    British citizenship 36
    certificates of arrival 121
    'denization' 121
    naturalisation 75, 121, 158
    societies 121
'imputed' 96
income tax 112, 256
infant life protection 45
informants 27, 28, 211, 216
inquisitions *post mortem* 149, 156–7, 261
insanity 11
    lunatic asylums 25, 70
Institute of Heraldic and Genealogical Studies 20, 32
insurance records 67, 210
International Genealogical Index 103–7, 138, 143–4, 153, 197, 200, 239, 247, 255
internet xix, 6, 8, 16, 20, 38, 57, 70–1, 73, 144, 152, 167, 231
inventory 252, 258–9
Iron Mountain 230

Jews 5, 36, 121, 134, 136–7, 164–5, 172, 183, 187, 205–6, 211, 224
    Board of Deputies 172
jurors' lists 84, 145, 157
Justices of the Peace 185

King's Bounty 54

Lady Huntingdon's chapels 136
Land Registry xxiii, 159
land tax 111, 248
'late Smith' 26
Latin 93, 128, 145
Law Society 231
lawyers 82
lay subsidies 108, 161–2
'ledgers' 226
Legacy Duty 256
Lent 194

'Lic' 196
'livery of seisin' 157

MAGPIE xxiv, 23, 167
maiden name 3, 23, 26, 164, 167,
   174, 201, 210, 248
maintenance 68
manorial records 144, 156, 207
   Manorial Documents Register 144
marginal notes 28
Marine Register Book 37, 59, 182,
   214
Marriage Duty Act 110
marriage 164–207
   abroad 173
   Act Books 196
   age at 43, 168–9, 202, 207
   allegations 195–6, 248
   'approved premises' 166
   'askings' 193
   'authorised person' 165, 171, 180
   'authority for marriage' 171
   banns 89, 123, 129, 169–71, 173,
      185–6, 188–9, 192–200, 202
   bonds 196
   'by certificate' 188
   'by publication' 193
   certificates 56
   of children 207
   civil 166
   'clandestine' 186, 198
   'common-law' 172
   during Commonwealth 205
   'condition' 169
   with consent 188, 195
   contracts 207
   of cousins 191
   in daylight hours 187
   to deceased brother's widow 165
   to deceased wife's sister 165
   'dispensations' 194
   double 180, 205
   Fleet 186
   forced 98
   'full' age 168
   index detail 174
   iPhillimore transcripts 198
   'irregular' 186

licences 116, 123, 126, 129,
   185–8, 192–200, 202, 205–6
   military personnel 173
   non-Anglican 206
   Notice Books 89, 171, 173
   'of this parish' 123, 205
   Pallot Index 198
   prohibited degrees 165, 181,
      189–90
   proclamations 171, 193
   registrar's certificate 171
   settlements 207
   of widow(er)s 174–5, 180, 204–5,
      248
medical card 210
mercantile marine 60
Methodists 138, 206, 249
   Historic Roll 215
Middlesex deeds 145
militia 111
minors 168, 188, 202
missals 155
mobility 102
monks 210
monumental inscriptions 224–5
monumental masons 228
Mormons 3, 73–4, 103, 113, 137,
   191, 215
   Ancestral File™ 104
   Pedigree Resource File 104
   see also International Genealogical
      Index
'mortuaries' 145, 238
mosques 165
'Mrs' 127, 203, 205
Muster Rolls 110
'my now wife' 204

National Archives 8, 12, 36–7, 56–60,
   65, 72–4, 82, 84, 86, 108–10,
   112–13, 121, 135, 138, 146,
   149, 151, 152, 156–9, 162,
   173, 182, 184, 186, 192,
   214–15, 225, 234–7, 245–7,
   256–7, 260
National Health Service 19, 43, 66,
   214
   Central Register 66

Information Centre for Health and Social Care 67
number 29, 46, 66, 78, 211
National Inventory of War Memorials 233
National Register of Archives 144, 156
National Registration Act (1915) 72, 266–71
National Registration Act (1939) 67, 271–4
National Roll of the Great War 83, 233
Navy List 59
New Poor Law 98
'new style' 93, 134
newspapers xix, 6, 17, 52, 71, 99, 135–6, 181, 207, 223, 228–9, 241, 263
nicknames 90, 97
Nonconformists 96, 135–7, 185, 195, 237, 244, 249–50
registers 92, 135–6, 138, 249–50
'not certified' 210
nuns 210
nurse children 44, 114
nurses 82

obituaries 71, 228–9, 237, 241, 263
Officers died in the Great War 234
'old style' 93, 134
'On the authority of the Registrar General' 29, 44
'on the way to' 210
oral history 16
orphans 98, 129, 150
'otherwise' 26, 168, 210
outlaws 12
overseers 217

parish registers *see* baptism, marriage, burial
Parochial Registers and Records Measure 119, 122, 138–9
passenger lists 214
passport registers 246
Patent Rolls 158

patronymics 201
paupers 98, 238, 244, 246, 247
'peculiar' parishes 141, 194, 255
pensions 67, 182
'per lic' 196
pew rents 111
photographs 14, 36
police 82
poll books 113–14
poll tax 110, 146, 163
Poor Law Unions 31, 70, 247
Prerogative Court of Canterbury 235, 247, 254–5, 257, 259
Prerogative Court of York 247, 254–5
presentments 99, 243
primers 155
Principal Registry of the Family Division 231
prisons 25, 70, 209
'Priv' 120
probate 84, 128, 160, 204–5, 229–32, 251–9
accounts 258
Act Books 256
Administration Act Books 257
administration bonds 257
'curation' 258
glossary 253
Grant of Administration 232
Letters of Administration 257
Limited Administration Books 254
Limited Probate Books 254
married women 252
'Nunc' will 253
Principal Probate Registry xxiii, 215, 229–30
seamen's wills 60
'tuition' bonds 258
professional bodies 237
'proofs of age' 157
Protestation 108
psalters 155
Public Record Office 8, 37
'publications' 171

Quakers 136, 164, 187, 191, 206, 249

Quarter Sessions 99
questionnaire 13

railwaymen 82, 237
rate books 83, 110
Recusant Rolls 136
Registrars of Birth and Death 18, 20, 29
Registrar General 12, 18, 19, 23–6, 28–9, 32–3, 37, 39, 44–6, 49, 55–6, 72, 77, 137, 164, 171–3, 195, 209, 212, 225
Registrar General of Shipping and Seamen 60, 214
'relict' *see* widows 127
'relief' 156
Renunciation, Deed of 258
reputed 96
reregistration 29, 30, 52, 54, 175, 217
Royal Institute of British Architects 82
Roehampton Project 109
Roman Catholics 56, 65, 94, 97, 111, 135–8, 147, 171, 185, 201, 206, 222, 249
Registration Online (RON) 19, 55, 166
Royal Air Force 59, 182, 214, 234
royal bounty 182
Royal Chelsea Hospital 182
Royal Navy 59, 182, 234
royalist composition papers 151

Salvation Army 249
samplers 71
school registers 84
secretary script 92
separation 183, 248
Services Register 59
settlement 114–15
    certificates 115
    examination papers 115–16
    removal orders 115–16
shepherds 89
ships' musters 59
signatures 53, 170, 180, 200, 209, 231

Society of Genealogists 6, 36, 148, 151, 225, 245, 257, 260
Soldiers died in the Great War 58
solicitors 116, 262
Somerset House 22, 184
Spain 38, 215
Society for the Propagation of Christian Knowledge 193
'son-in-law' 127
spelling 35, 93, 173, 174
St Catherine's House 22
stamp duty 95, 238, 256
step-father 169
stillbirths 28, 142, 212, 220
suffragettes 76
suicide 137, 242–3
Sunday schools 62
Superintendent Registrars 19–25, 28, 31, 46, 53–5, 65, 164–6, 168, 170–1, 194, 211
Superintendent Registrar's licence 171
surnames 7, 36, 195
    atlas 74, 114
    change of 29, 49–53, 175
    distribution 102–17
    hyphenation 96, 130
    variants 16, 255

Test Oath 111
theatre 82
Thomas Coram Register 99
tithe 112–13
tontines 260
trade directories 92, 215
trade unions 68–9, 84, 235
transportation 245–6
treasure trove 236
tuition bonds 252
twins 25

UKBMD 21
unbaptised 225
underregistration 212, 244, 264–6
unidentified bodies 213, 244

vaccination 53, 70, 89, 95
Vatican 155
Victoria County History 154

'view of frankpledge' 144
visitation pedigrees 154
visitations 148

Wakefield deeds 145
Wales 15, 75, 112, 138, 141, 158,
    166, 168, 185, 196, 201, 210,
    212, 225, 230, 249, 251, 252,
    254
War Graves of the British Empire 233
war memorials 233

wardship 202
widow(er)s 127, 175
wife selling 183, 248
wills *see* probate
window tax 109–10
witnesses 170, 181, 187–8, 206, 236,
    253
workhouses 25, 70, 98, 209, 225,
    235, 244, 263

'yellow peril' 18